Innovating with Integrity

Innovating with Integrity

How Local Heroes Are
Transforming American Government

SANDFORD BORINS

GEORGETOWN UNIVERSITY PRESS / WASHINGTON, D.C.

Georgetown University Press, Washington, D.C.
© 1998 by Georgetown University Press. All rights reserved.
Printed in the United States of America

10   9   8   7   6   5   4   3   2   1   1998

THIS VOLUME IS PRINTED ON ACID-FREE OFFSET BOOK PAPER

Library of Congress Cataloging-in-Publication Data

Borins, Sandford F., 1949–
    Innovating with integrity : how local heroes are transforming
American government / Sandford Borins.
        p.   cm.
    Includes index.
    1. Total quality management in government—United States.
    2. Benchmarking (Management)—United States. 3. Administrative
    agencies—Technological innovations—United States.
    4. Organizational change—United States.   I. Title.
    JK468.T67B67   1998
    352.3'57'0973—dc21
    ISBN 0-87840-687-5 (cloth)
    ISBN 0-87840-688-3 (paper)   98-12628

To Irene and Michael Borins

Contents

List of Tables

Foreword

Throughout most of the twentieth century public management reformers have been preoccupied with the challenge of restraining discretion, whether exercised by career officials, political appointees, or even elected chief executives. Their primary objectives have been reduced waste, patronage, corruption, and other forms of abuse. They have sought the adoption of precise rules covering every conceivable circumstance (including the appointment, promotion, and supervision of career bureaucrats themselves), the extension of judicial and investigatory oversight, and a wide variety of other techniques designed to make government more honest, impersonal, and rule-bound. The leading specific reforms of each generation have varied widely, but their common premise has been that when executive branch personnel exercise initiative, the citizenry had better watch out.

These longstanding concerns remain very much with us. But there has been as well a constant undercurrent of reform, since at least the New Deal era, focused on how to make government more effective in addressing substantive problems. And there has been dawning recognition, particularly since the 1960s, that the aim of greater effectiveness is often sharply at odds with that of routinization. When citizens complain about government, they more often speak of bureaucrats who are wedded to established routines, and seemingly indifferent to the impacts of their activities on real clients, than about problems of fraud or illegality.

It is also the case that public management reform almost always follows patterns first charted in business. And the corporate world has become preoccupied in recent years with the centrality of innovation as a competitive factor. This preoccupation has not rendered mass production (based on routinization) obsolete, but it has redirected attention to the issues of how to combine flexibility, creativity, and speed of adaptation with cost control.

The pressures of competition are far less in the public sector, but those flowing from citizen service demands, tax resistance, and expressions of dissatisfaction with government are intense. During the 1980s, moreover, there was a sense of despair among supporters of positive government as politicians, including the most hoary incumbents, competed to establish their credentials as inexperienced outsiders. It often seemed that no one had anything good to say about government, or interest in improving it.

It was in this context that the Ford Foundation, in 1985, established the Program on Innovations in American Government, with the aims of identifying exemplars of creative problem-solving in the public sector, celebrating their accomplishments, helping to diffuse their innovations, and furthering thought about how to encourage democratically accountable innovation in American government. Harvard's John F. Kennedy School of Government has administered the program from its outset. From over 10,000 applications, the Program has to date made awards totaling more than $12 million dollars to 180 government programs. Additionally, the Program has encouraged research on the sources and dynamics of innovation in American government.

In the course of its activities, the Innovations Program has assembled a considerable database, which is available to researchers. There are serious questions, however, about the value of this database for research purposes. It is not in any sense based on random sampling. Candidates for innovations awards must apply, so the sample is self-selected (though programs nominated by third parties receive specific invitations to apply). Those who submit applications all think that they have done something exemplary (rather than average). Screening for those that actually have, the Program collects increasingly detailed information on programs that survive to later rounds. It even sends expert site visitors to investigate the 25 finalist programs on the ground, meeting with critics as well as advocates of the candidate programs. The site visitor reports are, not surprisingly, among the richest sources of information in the database, but they are about 25 highly unusual, often remarkable, programs each year.

This is, in short, a database for "best" rather than "standard" practices research. Most researchers have treated it as a source of candidates for in-depth case study investigation, and indeed the Innovations Program has underwritten more than 45 case studies over the past decade. Cases can only take one so far, though. Each case is, in the end, just an anecdote, suitable perhaps as inspiration for hypothesis-formulation, but not for hypothesis-testing.

The great challenge is how to go beyond hypothesis-formulation in this field. Government programs and institutional arrangements are not very amenable to the techniques of survey research or (in most cases) experimentation. They are more like social systems than, for example, opinions or common psychological patterns. So hypotheses have a tendency in the field of public management to gain widespread credence without ever going through a serious testing stage. And this tendency has been as typical in the field of innovations research as in other areas of public management scholarship.

It was this situation that Sandford Borins confronted as he embarked on the present study during a yearlong sabbatical visit to the Kennedy School in 1993–1994. And he was determined to do better, that is, to engage in some serious hypothesis-testing rather than just more hypothesis-generation. How, you may ask, could that be possible, given the non-random character of the Innovations database?

My first response is to cite Nelson Polsby's well-known quip about political science that "the plural of anecdote is data." My "mature" response is to reflect on what Borins in fact did. He took advantage of the fact that, in some circumstances and for some limited purposes, nonrandom cases can be assembled into valid hypothesis-testing databases.

Borins's purpose was to discern common patterns among innovative public programs, as exemplified by programs reaching the semifinal round (roughly, the top five percent of applicants) during the then most recent five years of the Innovations competition (1990 to 1994). He argued that the Innovation Program's strenuous efforts to solicit applications means that those received provide a reasonably representative sample of the innovations that are occurring "out there" and that the Program's extensive evaluation process ensures that the semifinalists embody best practice. Thus Borins believed, quite reasonably in my view, that we should be able to learn quite a bit from this sample about the circumstances and strategies conducive to effective innovation in American government. Not enough, perhaps, to provide a definitive test of any hypothesis. But enough to go well beyond the level of confidence justified by most of the existing literature, based as it is on quite personal interpretations of just one or a few case studies. It is also reassuring that the patterns and trends observed in this volume have been reinforced by the applications that the program has received since 1995.

Borins divided the universe of semifinalist innovations into six broad groups: programs based on applications of information technology; programs involving major organizational change; programs in the domains of energy and environmental policy; programs oriented toward assisting communal institutions, particularly in the areas of policing, housing, and economic development; social programs oriented toward assisting individuals directly; and programs in education. As the basis for his characterizations of these innovations (and the factors that gave rise to them), Borins developed sophisticated taxonomies including a precise statement of the boundaries of each category, and employed independent coders to determine which program fit where. In the end, he was able to develop comprehensive characterizations of 217 applications in this way, a far larger sample of public sector innovations than anyone had previously examined rigorously before.

What has emerged is a fascinating analysis, not only more solid empirically than any of its predecessors in the field of public innovations research but directly in their line of development as well, subjecting the generalizations they have spawned to serious testing. Nor, as the title of this volume indicates, has Borins lost sight of the human dimension of innovation. This book is, finally, a book about "local heroes" as well as about statistical generalizations.

Among the characteristics that Borins finds with striking frequency in the group of agencies he examined are the following: an orientation toward collaboration with other entities, business and nonprofit as well as public; openness to the insights of front-line workers; a focus on measurable goals; and a disposition toward utilizing market incentives in the production of public services. Regulatory agencies, particularly in the environmental domain, have been pioneering methods of negotiated (rather than purely adversarial) compliance. Information technology innovators have been concentrating on how computers and telecommunications can be deployed to provide more convenient and tailored, yet also more consistent and reliable, service to citizens.

A few of Borins's observations will surprise even experienced public management scholars. Based on studies by Robert Behn, Olivia Golden, and coauthors Martin Levin and Bryna Sanger, it has become conventional wisdom in recent years that innovations tend to emerge ad hoc, as mission-driven officials "grope along," rather than from more systematic planning processes. Borins finds, by contrast, that most of the innovations in his sample emerged in significant part from planning exercises. Additionally, he identifies the circumstances in which planning was most likely to play an important role.

The value of this volume, finally, lies in much more than its identification and frequency estimation of specific patterns of innovation.

Innovating with Integrity is chock full of insights and observations that should be of interest to anyone who cares about how to make American government more adaptive and effective. And it is packed as well with compelling portrayals of real-life public officials facing extraordinary challenges. Hopefully it will inspire and inform many other public servants to successful feats of creative problem-solving, even as it significantly advances academic thought about innovation as a dimension of excellence in American public management.

ALAN D. ALTSHULER
Stanton Professor of Urban Policy and Planning, Harvard University
Director, Kennedy School of Government's Taubman Center for
State and Local Government and
Program on Innovations in American Government

Preface

I began this book seven years ago, when Joe Galimberti, executive director of the Institute of Public Administration of Canada (IPAC), invited me to be on the panel of judges for IPAC's first innovative management award. Applicants came from departments and agencies at all levels of government in Canada. Evaluating them would be, I thought, a familiar task, akin to grading student exams. However, all the applicants were superb and of nearly equal merit. The appropriate analogy for the judges' task was not grading examinations but judging an Olympic event, such as diving or figure skating, in which all the competitors are excellent and some are exceptional. It was extremely difficult to differentiate between the performances.

After the competition, I continued to be interested in the applicants from another viewpoint, namely, as a potential database in which to study public sector innovation. I began with a paper about the characteristics of the innovations and the innovative process (Borins, 1991), and in the years that followed, I continued to study public management innovation.

In 1992, Osborne and Gaebler's *Reinventing Government* and Barzelay's (1992) *Breaking Through Bureaucracy* appeared in print, and both influenced my thinking. I spent the 1993-1994 academic year as a Fellow at the Taubman Center for State and Local Government at the Kennedy School of Government. The Kennedy School, through the Taubman Center, was responsible for administering the Ford Foundation's State and Local Government Innovation Awards program. By the time of my visit to Harvard, this program had been in operation for six years, and had received hundreds of semifinalist applications.

The idea for this book emerged from my reading of the applications that these semifinalists had prepared. The year after my return to the University of Toronto, this competition was extended (in 1995) to the federal government and renamed the Innovations in American

Government Awards Program. By then, however, the parameters of my research had already been drawn.

The State and Local Government Innovations Awards program supported this research generously for four years and enabled me in 1996–1997 to reduce my teaching load to focus on the project. The Division of Management and Economics at the University of Toronto at Scarborough also supported the project, particularly with travel money to various conferences where the research could be discussed as it progressed. In addition, the administrative duties I faced as chair of the division gave me opportunities to reflect on the meaning of academic entrepreneurship and to empathize with the local heroes of whom I write. Finally, Georgetown University Press, represented by its Director John Samples, helped me stay the course through an appropriate mix of interest in the product and patience with the process.

The research involved (1) coding the applicants' (innovators') responses to a complex open-ended questionnaire, and subsequently, (2) analyzing the vast amount of quantitative data contained in these responses. In both activities, I had the good fortune of substantial assistance. Members of the "coding team," Scott Evans and Collin May, then graduate students at Harvard in Eastern European studies and divinity, respectively, and Don Redl and Sarah Dryden, then Harvard undergraduates in economics and social studies, respectively, worked energetically and with good judgment.

As the de facto leader of the team, Don Redl played a unique role. He designed the database and began the statistical analysis. When he graduated from Harvard in 1994 and moved to Princeton to begin graduate work in economics, the project passed to David Wolf, a Torontonian then doing undergraduate study, also in economics, at Princeton. David did an excellent job of completing the statistical analysis. He also spent the summer of 1995 analyzing the applications on a thematic basis, and his insights into different types of innovations considerably strengthened the analysis contained in part 2. Sylvia Kocovski, then an undergraduate at the University of Toronto; Ilya Shapiro, a Princeton undergraduate; and Sandra Wong, a University of Toronto undergraduate, all helped me with the final stages of the book. Rachel Reeder's copyediting added clarity and grace to the manuscript. I am grateful also to Camiliakumari Wankaner, at the Kennedy School, and Judith Smith, at the University of Toronto at Scarborough, for their superb secretarial support.

Numerous formal and informal interactions with colleagues have also shaped this book. I presented seminars at Quincy House and the

Taubman Center at Harvard, the Public Policy Institute at Georgetown University, and the World Bank. I also presented papers at the annual conferences and workshops of the Association for Public Policy and Management; the International Association for Schools and Institutes of Administration; and the Research Institute for Public Administration in Speyer, Germany.

The list of colleagues with whom I discussed this project is as long as their patience was deep. My thanks to each of them, especially, Graham Allison, Alan Altshuler, Peter Aucoin, Michael Barzelay, Michael Beer, Samuel Beer, Bob Behn, Otto Brodtrick, Rory Browne, Colin Campbell, Jane Fountain, Joe Galimberti, Gernod Gruening, Arie Halachmi, Ron Heifetz, Ralph Heintzman, Malcolm Holmes, Arn Howitt, Bill Hsiao, Howard Husock, Steve Kelman, Ken Kernaghan, Alex Kouzmin, Martin Levin, Meryl Libby, Michael Lipsky, Elke Loffler, David Luberoff, Larry Lynn, Nick Manning, Caroline Marple, Brian Marson, Jerry Mechling, Ellen Messer, John R. Meyer, Henry Mintzberg, Mark Moore, Richard Neustadt, Bill Parent, Roger Porter, Heinrich Reinermann, Jerry Rothenberg, Bryna Sanger, Donald Savoie, Ellen Schall, Jim Sebenius, Leslie Seidle, Malcolm Sparrow, Norman Spector, Andy Stark, Art Stevenson, Fred Thompson, Sidney Verba, Sanford Weiner, Richard Zeckhauser, and Marc Zegans.

PART 1

Innovating with Integrity

This book is a study of recent public sector innovations and the local heroes who made them. It undertakes a rigorous analysis of a large sample of new ideas and their champions—and describes the characteristics of both in some detail. Thus, it goes beyond speculation about innovation to knowledge of its dynamics and its ability to renew government in a number of policy areas. The result is a data-based picture of public management innovation that satisfies our need to know how innovation happens and our need to encourage it as widely and as often as possible.

AN ANECDOTAL BEGINNING

Former Secretary of Labor Robert Reich (1997) recounts a quintessential "local hero" story. Two months after coming to Washington in 1993, Reich convened a town meeting of the entire department to ask for ideas from the trenches—having first indicated his willingness to listen. After the initial incredulity and hesitation, people responded. At one point, a "thin and balding . . . tall, hollow-eyed career public servant," one Steve Wandner from the Employment and Training Administration, suggested that a determination be made at the time people register for unemployment insurance whether their layoffs were likely to be temporary or permanent. The permanently unemployed could then be given retraining and job-placement services immediately, rather than in six months when their benefits ran out. Reich promised to examine the idea, but initially nothing happened.

However, the economic recovery was more fragile than expected in 1993, and the job market did not rebound quickly. The

Secretary soon found himself being pressured by members of Congress to extend the maximum unemployment insurance benefit beyond six months. Simultaneously constrained by the Clinton Administration's fiscal policy to spend no new money, Reich had to end the benefits at six months or find savings to fund their extension. At that point, his chief of staff remembered Wandner's proposal, found him, and learned that a pilot project had shown that early retraining shortens the average length of unemployment two to four weeks. Using this pilot as evidence, Reich convinced the Congressional Budget Office that future savings on unemployment claims would cover the extension of benefits. Quickly the two proposals (extending benefits for those temporarily laid off and immediate retraining and job placement for those permanently laid off) were packaged together, and Congress passed the legislation two months later.

Reich invited Wandner to the signing ceremony, and despite his reluctance, brought him forward to meet President Clinton. Clinton said little, but he shook Wandner's hand and gave him what Reich calls his "you-are-the-only-person-in-the-world-who-matters gaze." Reich noticed that Wandner was glowing and speculated that this moment of recognition would inspire him for years.

Wandner's experience has many of the characteristics of a local hero story. First, he had a chance to put his ideas forward because Reich held a meeting designed to seek new ideas. Second, it may be doubted whether Wandner was as diffident as Reich portrays him; after all, he did speak up before several thousand of his colleagues. Third, it appears unlikely that Reich and his staff would have acted on the idea if the economic and political pressures to extend unemployment had not collided with budgetary pressures to fund the extension internally. Fourth, and finally, Wandner's idea passed scrutiny only because a pilot program had documented results.

Such displays of problem-solving local heroism are extremely valuable. Indeed, one of government's roles is to provide the structure and incentives to encourage its citizens, and especially government workers, to display such heroism. But are all government workers local heroes? What can we say, generally, about people who, like Steve Wandner, initiate new programs—innovations—in the public sector? Do they come from certain organizational levels, or share certain personality traits? And, more important, are there common conditions that must be met before their ideas become pilot programs and the pilot programs become policy? The process of identifying local heroes may give us the key to encouraging others to follow their lead.

SETTING THE QUESTION

When we think of heroes abstractly we think of them as people of integrity and principle. So when we seek for heroes in the public sector, we should perhaps look for traits and behaviors that consti-tute integrity. For example, do we expect public innovators to be dedicated and intellectually disciplined individuals? Is it a deep and understanding knowledge of policy that enables them to innovate? Is it their ability to plan? We surely would not expect them to be inflexible or dogmatic, or unable to adapt their plans to changing circumstances.

Suppose further that we find people with these sterling quali-ties, will we also expect their innovations to be evaluated (as Wand-ner's was) through pilot projects? But if so, are we not saying that a program is an innovation and its founder a local hero only if the program in fact has certain outcomes? Does it always have to be judged by neutral outsiders? If the first response to an innovation is indifference or worse—criticism and outright opposition—how are innovators able to persuade the critics to act on their ideas?

In retrospect Reich's anecdote has told us little about innovators and less about the process they go through to get their program or ideas accepted by others. We do not know, for example, what role Wandner had, if any, in the pilot project, or what he was doing in the months before Reich's aide remembered his suggestion and called him forward. An analysis in more depth is needed before we can know with confidence whether local heroes have the same or similar traits as we have here described. Lacking this, we cannot aptly characterize either the heroes or the situations that impel their actions.

This volume looks at innovators and the innovative process through an analysis of questionnaires completed by 217 semifinal-ists for the Ford Foundation's state and local Government Innovation Awards program between 1990 and 1994. By comparing and contrasting actual programs, it goes significantly beyond the anecdotal to make the study of public management innovation a practical tool for the continuing reinvention of government.

As a study of public sector innovations and the local heroes who have introduced them, this book began as a rigorous analysis of a large sample of public sector innovations and local heroes. By presenting the characteristics of innovations and innovators in some detail, this analysis goes beyond speculation about the meaning of innovation to a description of innovative behaviors. It develops a picture of public management innovation based on actual data in several policy areas. It is for anyone who wants to know about and encourage public sector contributions to innovative and fulfilling government service.

1

Objectives and Methodology

In the last ten years, an increasing number of innovations have occurred in the public sector to enhance its efficiency and service—many of them have been the work of local heroes like Steve Wandner. At first sporadic, such innovations now seem to be part of a trend defining a range of best practices available to managers. Public management innovation competitions were among the first institutions to recognize the links among these innovations. As initially conceived, these competitions were a defensive response to the bureaucrat-bashing that became popular among both politicians and the public in the 1980s, particularly in the Reagan Administration. They have, however, evolved to recognize today's innovators and to provide incentives for the innovators of tomorrow.

A NEW PARADIGM

The largest and best known public management innovation competition is without doubt the Ford Foundation-Kennedy School of Government's State and Local Government (Ford-KSG) innovation awards. Ford-KSG has been in operation since 1986 and receives an average of 1,500 applications a year. The sample examined in this book is drawn from this competition.

As these competitions gather and disseminate information about public sector innovation, they also inspire replication of the best innovations. Analysts and scholars who write about them foster and extend the community of interest that they build.

A seminal work in this regard is David Osborne and Ted Gaebler's *Reinventing Government* (1992). Osborne and Gaebler looked at fifty-one innovative programs—some derived from their own experience as consultant and city manager, respectively; some they discovered while networking, and some had been reported in the literature.[1] From these cases, they derived ten principles which, they claim, constitutes a new paradigm in public management in the United States. So great was the public's interest in this usually arcane subject that for the first time in living memory, a book on public management became a best-seller. Osborne and Gaebler were criticized by academics on a number of grounds:

- their treatment of case material was anecdotal rather than rigorous;
- the cases they selected may not be representative of the universe of public management innovation;
- the public sector entrepreneurship they advocate may conflict with traditional values, such as accountability to the electorate and equitable treatment of all citizens;
- their embrace of market mechanisms as a means of service delivery ignores market failures, such as collusion when there are few bidders; and
- the innovations they cite will not survive or if they do, will not be replicated (Goodsell, 1993; Lynch and Markusen, 1994; Winnick, 1993).

Nevertheless, their work made public management reform a subject of national discussion.

The Clinton Administration created the National Performance Review (Gore, 1993) to implement the principles of *Reinventing Government*. Its efforts are described in two major interim reports (Gore, 1995 and 1996b), and the program has been subjected to extensive analytic and academic attention, as authors attempt to interpret and evaluate the reform process (Kettl and DiIulio, 1995; Moe, 1994; Peters and Savoie, 1994).

The United States is not alone in its efforts to reform government. In fact, an international movement often referred to as the New Public Management, is in full swing. In this context, two countries are noted for early and thorough-going innovative programs, namely, the United Kingdom and New Zealand. In both countries, inescapable external forces united with strong ideologies to drive comprehensive public management reforms. In New Zealand, the impetus was the country's 1984 foreign exchange crisis and subsequent recognition that the world's markets were no longer willing to finance the debt its public sector deficits were generating. Economists, noted above all for their keen appreciation of the virtues of competition and their resolve to replace public sector monopolies with competition, promulgated this idea from the commanding heights of the Treasury (Boston et al. 1996; Osborne and Plastrik, 1997; Schwartz, 1994).

The United Kingdom's crisis had a similar impetus: the International Monetary Fund's warning to its debt-ridden public sector in the late 1970s. Prime Minister Thatcher called for new programs and initiatives from the even more commanding heights of Number 10 Downing Street (Osborne and Plastrik, 1997; Thatcher, 1993).

Scholars who have examined these public management reforms individually and in global perspective see in them the major components of a new paradigm in public management. This new paradigm is not reducible to a few sentences, let alone a slogan. However, its key ideas can be articulated. The following list is based on the experience of countries in the British Commonwealth (Borins, 1995c):

- Government should provide high-quality services that citizens value.
- The autonomy of public managers, particularly from central agency controls, should be increased.
- Organizations and individuals should be evaluated and rewarded on the basis of how well they meet demanding performance targets.
- Managers must be assured that the human and technological resources they need to perform well will be available to them; and
- Public sector managers must appreciate the value of competition and maintain an open-minded attitude about which services belong in the private, rather than public, sector.[2]

This paradigm is similar to the paradigm current among public sector innovators in the United States.

Besides expanding the data that Osborne and Gaebler and others have used to elucidate new public management paradigms, this book will examine some important questions about successful public sector innovation. What is really innovative about public sector innovation? What kind of people come up with innovative ideas? Do they encounter resistance, and if so, how do they overcome it? What have their innovations achieved, and are they being replicated? Are innovations in policing, for example, similar to those in social services, environmental management, or other policy fields?

This book is written for practitioners—front-line workers, middle managers, union leaders, agency heads, or politicians—who want to improve a program or launch an innovation within their realm of public service. Each chapter contains ideas and suggestions based on actual case histories, and most of them conclude with practical suggestions. No one should think, however, that this or any other book will provide a complete and detailed map to innovative behavior. Readers must apply the principles and examples given here to their own experience.

The book is also for those in the United States and other countries who study the new public management. It is my intention to inform not only the practice but also the theory of public management. I have endeavored throughout this project to bring new data to bear on the questions such as those posed in the previous paragraphs—questions that matter to my colleagues. Sometimes my views are consistent with others, but sometimes they differ. The data, I believe, though they can be variously interpreted, can unite us in a collective, dispassionate, evidence-based search for truth.

PLAN OF THE BOOK

The book examines data derived from a large sample of successful public sector innovations: the 217 semifinalists for the Ford-KSG innovation awards. Other literature in this field often relies on small and sometimes idiosyncratic samples and is justly criticized for that reason. For example, Lynn (1996) has accused some writers of "culling whatever [they] seek to celebrate from the countless instances of things happening in the world."

This book surveys its larger sample in two ways. The first part of the book provides a broad analysis of the innovations. It uses quantitative evidence such as statistical distributions, correlations, and regressions to discuss (1) the various types of innovations; (2) the characteristics of the local heroes who originate these innovations; (3) the characteristics of the innovative process (that is, the reasons for each innovation, and whether it was preceded by comprehensive planning or by evolutionary groping); (4) the organizational change process, including the obstacles that the innovators overcame and those they were unable to overcome, the innovation's external critics, and its self-identified shortcomings; (4) the financial resources supporting public sector innovations, in particular the roles of the private sector and user fees; (5) the organizational structures that characterize these innovations; and (6) the evaluation of their outcomes (i.e., the results they achieved, their formal evaluation, and replication).

Following this look at the entire sample, the second part of the book deals with innovations in a number of policy areas, focusing on their unique characteristics, and their relationship to theory and practice in that area. Here the analysis is more qualitative, often drawing on the accounts provided in the questionnaires. Ultimately, I divided the sample into six areas:

- information technology,
- organizational change,
- energy and environment,
- building community (policing, housing, economic development, and transportation programs),
- social services, and
- education.

Information technology and organizational change are generic areas as observations for these fields can also be found in other areas.[3] Roughly 40 percent of the innovations in information technology and organizational change are also classified in one of the other areas. Cases in these areas also account for almost all instances in which a case is classified in two areas.

Energy and environment are treated together because innovations in both these areas follow similar approaches. Policing, housing, economic development, and transportation can also be aggregated. Here, too, a common thread unites the areas; in this case, the idea of building community or the use of community action to solve problems.

The social services category includes programs responding to a variety of issues affecting individuals, such as health, violence, and poverty. Each chapter discussing a particular policy area concludes with practical recommendations.

ADVICE TO THE READER

Different readers may tackle this book in different ways. Some will be most interested in their own policy area; nevertheless, the general discussion of innovation and innovators in the first part of the book should not be neglected. A second priority may be information technology and organizational change, given their relevance to all policy areas.

Because analyzing a large sample of innovations is intrinsic to the book's argument, I have chosen not to subordinate discussions of research methodology or statistical analysis by relegating them to appendixes. Nevertheless, some readers may choose to skip the methodological section that concludes this chapter and the discussion of future research at the end of the book. If so, I recommend that they pay closer attention to the conclusions reached than to the statistics, particularly the regression analyses in chapters 3 and 6.

Other readers who are more interested in methodology and ongoing research will find the statistical analysis helpful, although they, too, may decide to enter Part 2 through the policy areas in which they are most interested. Finally, some readers may be interested in learning more about the particular innovations that I have cited. To facilitate this interest, I have included information about how to contact each program in the reference list.

RESEARCH METHODOLOGY

Between 1990 and 1994, the Ford-KSG Awards produced 350 semifinalists, and a sample of these applications were used in this study. On becoming semifinalists, each applicant or innovator was asked to respond to a questionnaire. I have used these questionnaires (hereafter: applications) in two ways. First, the responses were coded to reduce open-ended questions to statistical categories. That is, a small number of the applications were coded to include all possible answers to the questions. This sample became the code book, which was tested and refined as additional applications were coded—each by several investigators. The level of inter-coder reliability between each research assistant and me was about 80 percent, an acceptable level for this type of research (Yin, 1984).[4] Second, I used these applications to begin a narrative description of innovation. They are included in the references and often quoted in the analysis to illustrate key points.

Using the semifinalists to the Ford-KSG innovation awards as my sample raised two preliminary methodological questions. First, does this sample truly represent public management innovation in the United States? Second, does this opportunistic research design—that is, my use of an instrument intended to identify winners of the Ford-KSG award for the purpose of research—lead to any biases?

Securing a Representative Sample

The first question—the representativeness of semifinalist applications to the Ford-KSG awards—has three sequential parts: first, whether the preliminary applications to the Ford-KSG awards program are a representative sample of all public management innovations; second, whether the semifinalist applications are a representative sample of the preliminary applications; and third, whether the sample this study uses is representative of all semifinalist applications.

Whether the preliminary applications are representative of all innovations. The Ford-KSG awards program is designed to produce as many preliminary applications as possible from state and local government officials who identify themselves as having established innovative programs. Each year 50,000 entry forms are sent out to state, county, and local agencies. The program has a substantial marketing budget; for example, it searches for newspaper articles about innovative programs and contacts the subjects to encourage their application. It also works through professional networks, particularly in the different policy areas, to identify promising innovations. The initial application process is easy, requiring only the completion of a short questionnaire asking for a description of the program and how it is innovative; its clients, budget, and achievements; and how it has been replicated. Finally, the Ford-KSG program does not limit the number of applications by choosing an annual theme, and it is open to all programs that have been in operation for at least one year.[5] The benefits of applying for the Ford-KSG awards include the opportunity to learn about other innovative organizations, publicity, and cash awards—the latter to cover the costs of disseminating information about themselves.

A first concern about representativeness arises in the two types of innovative state and local government programs that the Ford-KSG awards program does *not* hear from: successful innovations whose managers are too busy to complete an application and failed innovations. The awards program courts the busy manager by keeping the expected benefits of applying high and the costs low, but it does not even look for failed innovations. It would, of course, be a valuable exercise to study failed innovations to see what differentiates them from successful ones, thus isolating the critical factors leading to success. But public servants, like most people, are unlikely to confess their failures in public. To some extent, the literature on implementation deals with failed innovation by looking at problems that arise in attempting to implement particular programs or policies; in it, the standard case study has required a book (Pressman and Wildavsky, 1973; Neustadt and Fineberg, 1983).

A second concern about the representativeness of the sample is that it contains only state and local government innovation, and excludes federal government innovations. The 1980s and early 1990s were, however, the era of local heroes acting independently. While there were instances of innovative federal government agencies, programs, or experiments, such as the Air Force's Tactical Air Command (Creech, 1994) and Model Installations experiment (Osborne and Gaebler, 1992); the Navy's China Lake Demonstration Project (Wilson, 1989); and efforts to improve customer service by the Internal Revenue Service, Postal Service, and Social Security Administration (Gore, 1993), a student of federal government innovation would probably want to focus on the years after 1993, when the National Performance Review was launched. One approach would be to study the National Performance Review directly. A second approach would be to study innovations going on in the different departments, a sample of which became available in 1995 when the Ford-KSG awards were extended to include the federal government.

A third issue concerning the representativeness of the preliminary applications arises from the Ford-KSG program's practice of considering applications eligible only if 50 percent of their funding comes from state or local government sources, a stipulation that was explicitly stated on the application in 1994 for the first time. Innovations financed by user fees are eligible because user fees are treated as comparable to taxes paid to the public sector. Nevertheless, this restriction may have discouraged some applicants whose programs involved substantial federal or direct private sector financial input. But this restriction against applications with majority federal financing seems reasonable if the award is only open to state and local innovations. Permitting intergovernmental partnerships in which the federal government plays the dominant role would obviously be inappropriate if activities entirely within the federal domain are ineligible.

On the other hand, the restriction against programs where the majority of financing comes from the private sector is unfortunate and may exclude innovations in which the private sector plays a significant role. It would, for example, exclude privatizations in which the privatized entity is by definition ineligible to apply for the Ford-KSG, and partnerships of the type that interested Osborne and Gaebler, namely, those that use a small amount of public sector resources to leverage many private sector resources. However, there are reasons to believe that this bias may not be too severe. It is clear from reading the applications that many involving private sector input were funded through nonprofit corporations, which were not excluded from consideration. Applicants could also have segregated the public and private sector funding components of an innovation, thus remaining eligible for consideration. Several eligible semifinalists had their program administration costs paid for by the public sector though their program implementation costs, which were much greater, were assumed mainly by the private sector.

Whether the semifinalist applications are representative of the preliminary applications. The 1,500 preliminary applications covered sixteen policy areas: administration and management; arts and cultural policy; communications and information policy; community economic development; criminal justice and courts; education; environment; health; housing; job training and placement; open space and recreation; public finance; public safety; public works and infrastructure; social services; and substance abuse treatment and prevention. Judges—including public sector managers, academics, and members of the award's professional staff— are assigned to policy areas on the basis of their expertise. They choose the seventy-five semifinalists, attempting as they do, to balance their choices among the sixteen policy areas so that each area is represented in the semifinals in direct proportion to its representation in the preliminary applications. This strategy helps ensure that the semifinalist sample accurately reflects the diversity of the original applicant pool.

The judges use four criteria to select the semifinalists: the novelty of the innovation, its significance in addressing an important problem of both local and national concern, the value it brings to its clients and other citizens, and its transferability, that is, the degree to which it shows promise of inspiring successful replication. In looking for novelty, the judges ask whether an innovation displays a leap of creativity, for example, by combining a number of elements of other programs in an unexpected way. As experts, the judges are expected to know whether something is new or simply a local replication of something already begun elsewhere. The significance and value of the service can be demonstrated through various impact measures. For example, a program deemed to be relevant only to a unique local situation is considered less significant.

Finally, transferability can best be demonstrated if an innovation has actually been replicated; however, some innovations may be so recent that the transferability test is more likely to be an expert assessment of its potential replication (Altshuler and Zegans, 1990). Another tension in the judging process is between programs that have been in operation long enough to demonstrate results and become less novel; and programs that are on the cutting edge, but have only begun to demonstrate results. Ford-KSG deals with the latter by urging them to reapply in future years when their results become available.

The seventy-five semifinalists are then asked to submit another application, which is more detailed than the preliminary application. Besides expanding on information provided in the preliminary round (i.e., on the nature of their innovation and its clients, budget, results, and prospects for replication), they must also describe the organizational structure and implementation process to which their innovation had been subjected. They may and should describe any obstacles that were overcome, who their supporters and opponents were, and how formally their program was evaluated. Finally, they should also assess their program's future and list any previous awards it has received. Based on analyses of these semifinalist applications, experts and the Ford-KSG awards program staff choose twenty-five finalists to participate in the final competition.

Whether this sample is representative of all semifinalist applications. Between 1990 and 1994, approximately 350 semifinalists competed in the Ford-KSG program (i.e., slightly fewer than five times seventy-five semifinalists per year because in some years a few semifinalists were also previous contestants). This study coded 217 semifinalists, fully 62 percent of the total.

This sample of semifinalist applications was a stratified sample, derived in the following way. Initially, all 1993 and 1994 applications were coded and assigned to one of five groups (a simplification of the sixteen policy areas used in the Ford-KSG program). Thus, each program represented an innovation dealing with information technology; organizational change or restructuring; energy or environmental policy; community building; or social programs to help individuals. The last group was by far the largest in 1993 and 1994, incorporating close to half of all semifinalists in those years. Consequently, no earlier applications for social services to individuals were coded. Community building programs were the next largest group, and programs from 1992 were also coded. Innovations in the other three areas (information technology, organizational change, energy and the environment) occurred less frequently in 1993 and 1994; therefore our investigation reached all the way back to 1990 to complete these strata.

This process yielded a total of 217 coded applications with subsamples of a reasonable size for all different types of innovations. The subsamples can be used to highlight differences among the types of innovations; the full sample can be used when differences in type are not relevant. When, however, the full sample is used and differences do exist among the subsamples, the weight of the study falls more heavily on the less frequently occurring subsamples than would be the case if all semifinalist applications from 1990 to 1994 had been used.

Using an Opportunistic Research Design

Using the semifinalist questionnaire is opportunistic because it employs an instrument designed to identify winners of the Ford-KSG award to study public management innovation. This tactic has two advantages: it saves time and money, since it eliminates the need for data collection; and it generates a response rate that is higher than we could expect an academic survey to be, since the latter would have lacked a comparable incentive for its return.[6]

Still, a methodological concern arises from this opportunistic design. Can we be certain that the semifinalist questionnaire is an unbiased research instrument? This question may be asked of the questionnaire in general or it may pertain to one or other of its various questions.

In general, the experts' evaluation of the applications makes it reasonable to believe that the semifinalists truly represent the most innovative public sector programs in the original field of preliminary applications. The semifinalist application form asks applicants whether their innovation has been independently audited or examined by policy analysts; and, if it has, who its auditors or analysts were; and reserves the right to contact them. In addition, the twenty-five finalists are each visited by an expert in the field, who submits a detailed site visit report to the innovations program. Questions about independent auditors and the prospect of a site visit should deter semifinalists from making dishonest or unsubstantiated claims about their results. In addition, many of the questions in the semifinalist application do not appear relevant to the judges' evaluation; thus, applicants cannot know exactly what the judges are looking for, and cannot slant their answers accordingly.

Though the semifinalist questionnaire is, in general, an unbiased research instrument, it contains two particular questions that might introduce bias. These questions ask what other individuals or organizations, in addition to the originator, have played the most significant roles in the innovation's development and ongoing operation, and what individuals or organizations are the strongest supporters of the program (Appendix, qq. 11–12). The preliminary applications require the signature of the head of the agency involved in the innovation, and semifinalist applications also require the signature of the organization's chief elected or presiding official. Some applicants included the names of these senior officials among those who played major roles in the program, even though they did not figure in the rest of the application. This circumstance may indicate a tendency to exaggerate the role of senior officials to obtain their signatures.

The second problem observed in the applications was a tendency to give credit to a wide variety of people, some of whom also did not figure in the rest of the application (success has a thousand parents but failure is an orphan). To avoid even the suspicion of bias these questions were omitted from the coding process. All other questions were used.

*   *   *

These methodological formalities were undertaken—and are here explained—to avoid the criticisms that have been made of earlier studies of public management innovation, including Osborne and Gaebler's. In the present case, every effort has been made to avoid using too small a sample and to rule out idiosyncratic and unrepresentative cases in the sample set. How successful the effort has been, the reader may now determine.

2
Characteristics of
Public Sector Innovations

The Ford-KSG program defines innovation as "novelty in action." An innovation has two components: a fresh idea and its practical expression in a course of action (Altshuler and Zegans, 1990). The judges attempt to ensure that the *idea* is new by excluding programs that have already been done elsewhere. They also look for *working* programs rather than untried good ideas. This definition, though valuable, is incomplete. A more specific definition can be derived from the innovators themselves. Applicants for the Ford-KSG award describe their programs in their own words, which can be linked by further analysis to reveal a range of characteristics pertaining to state and local government innovations.

The characteristics of innovations deduced from the analysis can be used to test the principles for reinventing government that Osborne and Gaebler (1992) deduced from their less formal sample of public sector innovations. Critics, like Goodsell (1993), argue that Osborne and Gaebler's sample may not have been representative. Osborne and Gaebler insist, however, that they based their principles on observations of successful public sector innovations across the country. I will consider in the second part of this chapter how their principles compare to our findings.

SELF-IDENTIFIED CHARACTERISTICS

Questions 1 to 4 of the semifinalist application ask the applicants to describe the purposes and activities of their programs and to specify exactly what makes them innovative. Tables 2-1 and 2-2 were generated from their responses. Table 2-1 encapsulates the applicants' own ideas. It uses only their descriptions, not the judges' or the researchers' ideas about what they said. Table 2-2 examines the material based on their responses to other questions and using a scheme that I developed during previous research on public sector innovations in Canada (Borins, 1991,

19

TABLE 2-1 CHARACTERISTICS OF INNOVATIONS IDENTIFIED
BY APPLICANTS
(Table entries are percentages)

Characteristic	All	IT	OC	EE	P	H	EC	Soc Serv	Educ
					GROUP				
Systems approach	26	11	54	41	31	29	8	15	29
Coordinates organizations	29	26	32	32	25	36	50	31	24
Multiple services	28	25	24	13	18	21	17	46	24
TOTAL HOLISTIC	61	47	76	60	44	57	67	66	71
New technology	28	98	14	30	0	7	17	14	19
Simplified technology	2	4	0	5	0	0	0	0	0
TOTAL TECHNOLOGY	29	100	14	35	0	7	17	14	19
Faster process	31	64	32	16	19	29	17	29	14
Simpler process	7	2	3	8	6	7	8	9	5
TOTAL PROCESS IMPROVEMENT	34	64	32	22	19	29	17	29	19
Empowerment	34	13	14	11	75	64	33	46	57
Prevention	16	4	16	22	19	7	0	25	19
Uses incentives, not regulation	8	2	14	24	0	7	8	5	5
Use of private sector	17	13	16	22	19	36	8	20	10
Use of volunteers	7	2	5	8	13	7	8	12	10
New management philosophy	15	4	41	11	13	14	25	6	19
Attitude change	13	0	3	16	25	7	33	17	14
Groundwork for others	6	2	14	5	6	0	8	5	19
Spillover benefits	8	2	5	22	16	7	0	7	10
Pilot program	1	0	3	3	0	0	8	0	5
Total (%)	249	253	253	261	249	242	232	252	277
N	217	47	37	37	16	14	12	65	21

N = number of observations.

IT (information technology), OC (organizational change), EE (environment, energy),

P (policing), H (housing, neighborhoods), EC (economic development, transportation),

Soc Serv (social services), Educ (education).

TOTAL HOLISTIC = one or more of systems approach, coordinates organizations, multiple services

TOTAL TECHNOLOGY = new technology, simplified technology, or both

TOTAL PROCESS IMPROVEMENT = faster process, simpler process, or both
Systems approach (takes a systems approach to a problem), coordinates (activities of various) organizations, multiple services (makes available a wide range of services to target population), new technology (introduces or increases use of a new or existing technology), faster process (makes a process faster, more accessible, friendlier, etc.), simpler process (for dealing with problems), empowerment (of citizens and/or communities), prevention (rather than remediation), uses incentives, not regulation (program voluntary, uses incentives in addition to or in place of regulation), use of private sector (to achieve public purposes).

and 1995a). It provides a comparison between patterns of public sector innovation in the United States and Canada.

Both tables depict results for the entire sample (characteristics that apply to all innovations) and for each policy area. The total number of cases reviewed in the policy areas adds to 249, which is slightly more than the number sampled (217) since 32 innovations involved more than one policy area. Innovations in information technology and organizational change were more likely than other areas to involve a second policy area.

Although community building programs—policing, housing, and economic development and transportation—are discussed as a group in chapter 10, they appear separately in these tables. Percentages of the total sample and the subsamples for all characteristics in Table 2-1 exceed 100 percent. In fact, they sum to 250 percent because most applicants used multiple characteristics to describe their innovation. That is, the applicants used an average of 2.5 characteristics to describe their programs.[1]

Innovations were most frequently characterized as holistic, technological, or process improvements. Further characteristics suggest that they offer empowerment, seek to prevent rather than treat problems, rely on incentives rather than regulation, work in some partnership with the private sector, use volunteers, implement new management philosophies, encourage attitude changes, lay the groundwork for other programs, and/ or have spillover benefits. They may also begin with a pilot project.

Holism

Among the Ford-KSG semifinalists, innovations were most frequently described as "holistic," a term applicants used to indicate that they or their programs (1) took a systems approach to problem solving; or (2) coordinated the activities of several organizations to deal with a problem; or (3) provided multiple services to program clients. Holism, in one or more of these guises appeared in 61 percent of the applications.

The City of Chicago Parking Enforcement Program, for example, adopted a systems approach to problem solving. It uses information technology and enhanced enforcement to increase the payment of parking ticket fines and deter parking violations, thereby improving the flow of traffic. The program considered its enforcement activities and the role of parking in the economic life of the city to create an integrated system:

> The entire system is designed to work like a well-oiled machine. It's a matter of working smarter, making sure that there are no wasted

motions or pieces that don't fit. For example, all desired management
information was built into the design of tickets. . . . Too often in the
past decisions about parking have been made very reactively, in
response to particular requests from businessmen or aldermen. Decisions were rarely evaluated in the context of the whole transportation
system. . . . [Now] any given decision must be evaluated in terms
of its ripple effects throughout the system and whether the net effect
is a plus for the city considering economic effects and traffic flow
(City of Chicago, Illinois, 1991).

The Orange County, California, Child Sexual Abuse Service Team
coordinated the activities of several organizations to reduce the number
of examinations that abused children are subject to following a complaint
(Orange County, California District Attorney, 1993). In the past, abused
children were subjected to examinations conducted by different government agencies; the innovative program created a team and recruited representatives from each agency to serve on it. Now only one examination is
needed, and the child's trauma is greatly reduced.

Pennsylvania's Job Centers (Pennsylvania Department of Labor and
Industry, 1992) run a holistic program that delivers multiple services to
program clients. The innovation empowers these centers to provide a
variety of skill development and job search services to the unemployed
in a "one stop shopping" context.

Holistic innovations occur in every policy area (Table 2-1, reading
across the rows). Further, even where it least occurs (e.g., in policing,
only 44% of the applicants have this characteristic and in information
technology, only 47%), it is not too far from the mean (61% overall).
Holistic descriptions of innovations are also evident in the literature on
private sector innovation. For example, in a review article, Kanter (1988)
notes the following "distinctive characteristic":

The innovation process crosses boundaries. An innovation process
is rarely if ever contained solely within one unit. First, there is
evidence that many of the best ideas are interdisciplinary or inter-
functional in origin—as connoted by the root meaning of entrepreneurship as the development of "new combinations"—or they
benefit from broader perspective and information from outside the
area primarily responsible for the innovation. Second, regardless
of the origin of innovations, they inevitably send out ripples and
reverberations to other organization units, whose behavior may be

required to change in the light of the needs of innovations, or whose cooperation is necessary if an innovation is to be fully developed or exploited (p. 171).

Technology, Process Improvements, and Empowerment

Three characteristics appear in about a third of the applications: the use of technology, process improvement, and empowerment. Defining innovation as a new technology includes programs that introduce a new or existing technology to the public sector; or (less frequently) programs that simplify a technology already in use. This characteristic occurs in all applications in the information technology group, in 35 percent of the applications for energy and environment, and occasionally among the other areas.

Information technology innovations are discussed in detail in chapter 7 and new technologies in the energy and environment area in chapter 9. The latter reports the highest frequency of innovations that simplify technology. For example, the New York State Self-Help Support System (New York Department of State, 1994), whose goal is to help small towns handle pollution problems, has reintroduced slow-sand filtration systems, a nearly forgotten approach to purifying drinking water. This simplified technological solution is much less expensive than building standard purification plants.

Applicants described their innovation as a process improvement in 34 percent of all cases. Either a process was made faster, more accessible, or friendlier ("faster process" in Table 2-1) or procedures for dealing with problems were simplified ("simpler process" in Table 2-1). By far, the highest incidence of process improvements (64%) occurred in the information technology group. However, process improvements are characteristic of innovations in other policy areas and do not necessarily involve the application of information technology. Some process improvements, for example, allocate more resources to speed a process or redesign a process to make it simpler. An example of process improvement in social services is the Quincy, Massachusetts, Model Domestic Abuse Program, which is a court-based program intended to help the victims of domestic abuse by making the court process faster and more supportive (Quincy, Massachusetts District Court, 1992).

Fully a third of the applicants (34%) also claimed that empowering citizens, individually or as communities, is a characteristic of their programs. Such programs help individuals or groups increase their ability to overcome problems through their own initiative. For example, Safe Streets Now! (1993), an Oakland, California, program empowers citizens' groups to fight drug use by helping them launch multiple suits in small claims court against the owners and occupants of drug houses. Empowerment appears frequently in policing (75%), housing (64%), education (57%), social services (46%), and economic development (33%); less frequently in other areas.

Other Characteristics Appearing in the Sample

Another eight characteristics, namely, prevention rather than problem-solving; the use of incentives rather than regulation, partnership arrangements, the use of volunteers, the adoption of new management philosophies, efforts to encourage attitude changes, laying the groundwork for other programs, and having benefits that spill over into other areas complete the list of characteristics. Each of these characteristics appears, however, in fewer than 20 percent of the programs.

About 16 percent of the applicants said that their programs were preventive; that is, they focused on preventing problems, rather than waiting until problems had occurred to deal with their consequences. This characteristic was most evident among environmental programs (22%), social service programs (25%), policing (19%) and educational programs (19%). An example is the Massachusetts' Student Conflict Resolution Experts (Massachusetts Attorney General's Office, 1994), which trains high school students in conflict resolution to prevent disagreements from escalating into violence. Another example is the Washington State Workers' Compensation System (1992), which has begun to work with industry to develop education programs to reduce accident rates.

Another 17 percent of the applicants identify their innovations as "using the private sector to achieve policy objectives." Such partnership-type programs were most frequent in housing (36%), environment (22%), and social services (20%). Maryland's Project Home AIDS (Maryland Department of Human Resources, 1994), for example, used the private sector to carry out a program providing housing and social services to a client population. This program places single people with AIDS in certified private homes with public funding; it is an alternative to government-run institutional residences.

In 15 percent of the applications, the innovations were characterized as using a new management philosophy or a new approach to the organization's internal management. This description appeared most frequently in the organizational change area (41%) but also in all other areas. The New York City Bureau of Motor Equipment's In-house Research and Development Network is a good example of a new management philosophy (New York Bureau of Motor Equipment, 1992). As the party responsible for repair and maintenance of the city's sanitation and snow removal fleet, the bureau greatly improved its operations by breaking down the traditional distinction between engineers (white collar thinkers) and mechanics (blue collar workers). It achieved parity of status and improved its maintenance performance by getting the mechanics involved in research and development.

Attitudinal changes were characteristic of innovations in 13 percent of the applicants' programs. References to this characteristic were most frequent in transportation and economic development (33%) and policing (25%). For example, the Go Boulder Program (City of Boulder, Colorado, Public Works and Transportation, 1993) attempts to persuade people to take public transit to work, instead of driving.

Another 8 percent of the applicants characterized their innovations as being voluntary or as using incentives along with, or as substitutes for, regulation to bring about socially desired behavior. This characteristic was particularly evident among environmental programs (24%). For example, the Texas Water Commission's (1992) Ground Water Protection Program will, but only at the request of local water systems, analyze the local geology and provide system-specific advice about how to prevent groundwater contamination.

In 8 percent of the applications, the innovations were characterized as having created benefits with spill-overs that benefited additional clients. The Los Angeles County Telecommuting Program (Los Angeles County, California, 1993), for example, increases convenience for workers and benefits the general public by reducing urban traffic congestion and pollution.

The use of volunteers to gain program objectives characterizes another 7 percent of the applications. Arizona's Volunteer Abandoned Mines Program (Arizona State Mine Inspector, 1991) operates by recruiting volunteers (e.g., retirees and members of naturalist groups). The volunteers search for and seal abandoned mineshafts, thus eliminating a safety hazard.

Finally, 6 percent of applicants said that their programs were innovative because they laid the groundwork for the success of other programs. New Hampshire's Thayer High School is one of the most successful and innovative high schools in the United States. "Here, Thayer, and

Everywhere" is its attempt to help other high schools throughout the country emulate its success (Thayer, New Hampshire, High School, 1994).

AUTHOR-IDENTIFIED CHARACTERISTICS

The second approach to identifying the key characteristics of innovations is shown in Table 2-2. Here, I coded the Ford-KSG applicants using categories derived from previous research about public sector innovation in Canada.

Using these categories, the most common characteristic, appearing 46 percent of the time, is that an innovation is a new program or initiative

TABLE 2-2   CHARACTERISTICS OF INNOVATIONS IDENTIFIED BY AUTHOR
(Table entries are percentages)

Characteristic	All	Canada	IT	OC	EE	P	H	EC	Soc Serv	Educ
New program	46	15	17	32	57	56	36	50	52	62
Within public partnership	21	22	11	21	27	13	21	25	23	38
Public private partnership	28	24	15	19	24	38	50	50	29	33
TOTAL PARTNERSHIPS	39	n.a.	25	35	43	44	43	75	42	43
Use improved technology	27	15	100	16	30	6	7	8	12	24
Empowerment of clients	26	0	11	5	5	69	50	17	40	38
Better marketing	24	8	17	0	24	38	14	33	28	48
ORGANIZATIONAL CHANGE										
Turnaround	3	4	2	16	0	0	0	0	0	0
Geographic decentralization	2	6	2	3	0	0	0	0	3	10
Participatory management	5	12	0	19	0	1	7	0	3	10
Continuous improvement	5	4	0	16	3	13	0	0	2	10
Restructuring, flattening	1	3	0	8	0	0	0	0	0	0
Client orientation	2	3	0	5	0	13	0	0	2	0
Education of staff	8	13	2	16	3	6	0	0	11	19
Employment equity	1	3	0	0	0	0	0	8	2	0
Better systems, procedures	33	17	43	46	22	19	36	17	32	24
TOTAL ORGANIZATIONAL CHANGE	43	n.a.	47	76	24	31	43	25	42	48
Privatization, competition	2	1	2	5	0	0	0	0	3	0
Total (%)	207	149	219	169	318	244	319	208	219	263
N	217	339	47	37	37	16	14	12	65	21

Note: N = number of observations.
TOTAL PARTNERSHIPS = within public partnership, public private partnership, or both

in the public sector, something the jurisdiction had not been doing before as opposed to the improved delivery of an existing service. Notice that this characteristic is less frequently used to describe information technology applications, which generally involve faster and cheaper ways to deliver existing programs.

Total partnerships, observed in 39 percent of the total sample, were cases of partnerships within the public sector or between the public sector and the private sector (the latter including partnerships with nonprofit organizations). To arrive at this percentage, a program was deemed a partnership only if the agreement appeared to be permanent and formalized. Since short-term informal cooperation was not included, partnership does not appear as frequently in this analysis as its holistic counterpart in Table 2-1.

The use of improved technology appears in 27 percent of all applications, with a similar distribution in both tables: it characterizes all programs in the information technology group and 30 percent of the environment and energy group (accounting for new environment and energy technologies). Its appearance in other policy areas were innovations to apply information technology to a new field.

Empowerment (26% of all cases) refers to the empowerment of individuals or communities; it, too, is unevenly distributed, but in complete contrast to improved technology, it occurs most frequently among the policing, housing, social services, and education areas. Better marketing (24% of all cases) refers to improved marketing of public services and client education; it includes innovations in which informing the public is meant to encourage their participation, and innovations in which informing the public is the main goal.

The category of organizational change (43% of all cases) is the union of all organizational changes, including

- organizational turnarounds or dramatic improvements in performance;
- geographic decentralization of operations, that is, increasing the authority of staff in local offices;
- participatory management or the increased delegation of authority to staff;
- continuous improvement, quality, or total quality management (TQM) initiatives;
- restructuring organizations;
- staff education programs;

- employment equity initiatives; and
- programs to improve systems, procedures, and policies so as to improve customer service.

The latter category dominates the organizational change group. It is only in the organizational change category that characteristics other than improved systems are observed with any frequency.

The final category includes privatization and other initiatives to introduce competition within the public sector or between the public and private sectors (e.g., requiring public sector organizations to bid against the private sector for contracts to perform public services).[2] First, instances of privatization were not expected in the Ford-KSG sample, since a privatized entity no longer qualifies as a public sector innovation—though the organization that mandated the privatization would be eligible for the award. This expectation was upheld; the sample contained no privatizations and only three cases of competition within the public sector or between the public and private sector.[3] A case in point: Minnesota's Consolidated Chemical Dependency Treatment Fund (Minnesota Department of Human Services, 1993) pools all state and federal funding for substance abuse treatments, allocates this money to counties and tribal governments, and authorizes these jurisdictions to negotiate with, and purchase, treatments from state-licensed public or private vendors.

To test the similarity between the applicants' classification of their innovations and the classifications that I developed, I calculated the correlation coefficients among characteristics for the two classification schemes (Table 2-3). The correlation coefficient was derived using a four-cell table for two dichotomous characteristics. It is positive when the sampled applications display both or neither characteristics, and zero when the applications are relatively evenly divided among all four cells.

Table 2-3 presents the variables with the strongest positive correlations under the two classification schemes, those that are significant at .05 or better. In both analyses, technological characteristics ($r = .88$) and empowerment characteristics ($r = .73$) identify the same cases. The holistic characteristic identified by the applicants is similar to total partnerships under my scheme ($r = .26$), but the correlation is stronger between innovations that "coordinate multiple organizations" and "partnerships within the public sector" ($r = .49$). The applicants' process improvement is also closely related to my characteristic of an innovation as involving better systems and procedures ($r = .39$). Finally, instances of the applicants' new management philosophy were correlated with various types of organiza-

TABLE 2-3   CORRELATIONS BETWEEN CHARACTERISTICS OF INNOVATIONS
IDENTIFIED BY APPLICANTS AND BY AUTHOR

Applicants' Characteristics	Author's Characteristics	Correlation Coefficient	Significance
Total holistic	Total partnerships	.26	p<.0001
Coordinates organizations	Within public partnerships	.49	p<.0001
Total technology	Use improved technology	.88	p<.0001
Empowerment	Empowerment	.73	p<.0001
Total process improvement	Better systems, procedures	.39	p<.0001
New management philosophy	Turnaround	.16	p<.02
New management philosophy	Participatory management	.25	p<.0002
New management philosophy	Restructuring, flattening	.28	p<.0001
New management philosophy	Client orientation	.13	p<.05
New management philosophy	Education of staff	.20	p<.003

tional change (turnarounds, r = .16; participatory management, r = .25; restructuring, r = .28; client orientation, r = .13; and staff education, r = .20). Among the main characteristics, the consistency is obvious; though our terminology is slightly different, the applicants and I speak the same language. It remains to be seen, however, whether others, for example, in Canada or elsewhere, also speak this language.

COMPARING THESE CHARACTERISTICS TO OTHER DESCRIPTIONS

Canada's Innovative Management Award

Look again at Table 2-2. The second column in this table shows how the Ford-KSG sample stands in relation to my earlier classification of characteristics based on a sample of 339 applicants for IPAC's innovative management award (Borins, 1995a). The Institute of Public Administration of Canada is a professional organization of public servants and academics, similar to the American Society for Public Administration. The figures shown in column two of Table 2-2 include all applicants for the IPAC award between 1990–1993. The award is open to all levels of government and has annual themes: service to the public in 1990, empowerment in 1991, partnerships in 1992, and better with less in 1993. The themes had the effect of focusing the applications and reducing their number. Thus, the Ford-KSG and IPAC competitions are not identical; on the other hand, the two societies that generate the applications have great economic and cultural similarities.

The Canadian applications, like their American counterparts, were coded in multiple categories and sum to 149 percent. Thus, they contain fewer multicategory applications than the American sample, which sums to 207 percent. The Canadian competition also contained a smaller percentage of new programs, proportionately fewer cases involving improved marketing and technology, and no instances of empowerment of clients. The latter result seems paradoxical, given that the theme of the 1991 IPAC competition was empowerment. However, a reading the IPAC applications clearly shows that empowerment was universally interpreted as empowerment of staff, rather than clients. Thus, all IPAC empowerment innovations were categorized as instances of organizational change. As a result, the Canadian competition contains a higher incidence of geographic decentralization, participatory management, and staff education programs than the U.S. competition.

There are also quite a few similarities between the two samples: comparable proportions of partnerships both within the public sector and between the public and private sectors, turnarounds, continuous improvement initiatives, and privatizations. Despite the differences in the two competitions, the patterns of innovation are relatively similar, rather than greatly disparate. Innovative public managers in both the United States and Canada are innovative in similar ways.

Osborne and Gaebler's Reinvention Principles

Osborne and Gaebler's principles for reinventing government can also be understood as an effort to identify the characteristics of public sector innovation.[4] Applicants to the Ford-KSG awards were not asked whether their innovations were consistent with Osborne and Gaebler's principles. We can, however, examine their answers in terms of their correspondence with these principles using the applicants' characteristics (Table 2-1) and the author's subsequent analysis (Table 2-2).

Since there are substantial differences in the frequencies with which the characteristics appear in different policy areas, we should not expect to find all of Osborne and Gaebler's principles in each of the applications. Instead, we should look for, and note the frequency of times that analogues of their principles can be found in the characteristics. Do they appear in certain areas only, or in the entire sample—and with what frequency?

Departing from the order in which the principles were discussed in *Reinventing Government*, the following paragraphs briefly describe five principles that appear frequently in the Ford-KSG sample, two that appear infrequently, and three market-oriented principles that have created a good deal of controversy within the academic community (Goodsell, 1993; Lynch and Markusen, 1994).

Frequently Appearing Principles

Customer-driven government. Osborne and Gaebler described public sector organizations that get close to their customers, that adopt total quality methods, that give customers a choice of public sector providers, and that integrate services as "customer-driven government." Among the Ford-KSG applicants, however, there were few explicit attempts to change from functional to client-based organizations (1% of all cases in Table 2-2) and to institute continuous improvement or Total Quality Management (TQM) methods (5% of all cases in Table 2-2). On the other hand, holistic innovations that provided multiple services to target populations (28% of all applications in Table 2-1) and efforts to improve systems, procedures, and policies with a goal of providing better service (33% of the applications in Table 2-2) were found much more often, and in all areas. (Programs that give customers a choice of public service providers are discussed under competitive government.)

Mission-driven government. Under the rubric of mission-driven government, Osborne and Gaebler described innovations that decentralize the control of budgeting and personnel systems, and others that enunciate and use mission statements. Very few of the applicants described their innovation as the creation of mission statements, but in some of the turnarounds (3% of all cases in Table 2-2), new mission statements were part of the process. However, process improvements (a total of 34% of all cases in Table 2-1) were applications of this principle. Despite the absence of formal mission statements, the applicants claimed to have achieved the results that mission-driven government strives to attain: making processes simpler, faster, more accessible, or friendlier.

Community-owned government: empowering rather than serving. In their discussion of this principle, Osborne and Gaebler described numerous examples of empowerment—of community organizations doing the public sector's work: resident management of public housing, community development corporations, community volunteers working as part of community-based policing programs, and black churches being used to place black children for adoption. Their example of the latter, One Church,

One Child, won a Ford-KSG award in 1986. And this theme appears frequently in the Ford-KSG applications. Empowerment was used by 34 percent of the applicants to describe their innovation (Table 2-1), most of them in policing, housing, educational, and social service initiatives. When the 65 applications in the social service area were reexamined, 18, or 28 percent, had some community component, in the sense that community organizations were involved in program delivery.

Many of the innovations in the policing area involved community initiatives, some originating within police departments and others coming from community groups involved in fighting problems like crack houses (Safe Streets Now!, 1993). At least 7 percent of the applicants referred to the use of volunteers as a key element in their program, with the highest frequency being in police, social service, and educational innovations.

Anticipatory government: prevention rather than cure. Here Osborne and Gaebler presented examples of fire prevention, health care, and environmental programs designed to prevent problems from occurring, rather than deal with their consequences. They also used the word "anticipatory" to look toward the future and gave examples of governments engaged in long-term planning and budgeting. Table 2-1 indicates that 16 percent of the applicants described their innovation as one of preventing rather than remedying problems. The groups most likely to include this element were environmental programs, social service programs (for example, those working with at-risk pregnant women to improve life chances for their children), policing programs, and educational programs (for example, Student Conflict Resolution Experts). On the other hand, no applicant described an innovation as essentially involving long-term planning and budgeting systems.

Enterprising government: earning rather than spending. Under the rubric of earning rather than spending, Osborne and Gaebler cited a number of innovative practices by government: using public assets to generate income, selling services to other governments, or granting franchises to the private sector; imposing user fees; gainsharing for managers and frontline workers who reduce costs; and establishing internal innovation funds. User fees contributed to the operating budget of 24 percent of the applicants' programs; the size and extent of the contribution, particularly in the different policy areas, is discussed in chapter 5.

There were a handful of applications involving enterprising practices other than user fees. For example, the City of Pittsburg, California, established a gainsharing program for public sector workers who reduced costs or improved productivity (City of Pittsburg, California, Public Services Department, 1993); and the City of San Carlos, California, created an internal productivity enhancement fund to support projects and acquire equipment intended to reduce ongoing operating costs (City of San Carlos, California, City Manager's Office, 1994).

Principles Appearing Infrequently

Results-oriented government: funding outcomes, not inputs. Osborne and Gaebler's primary example of a results-oriented program was Sunnyvale, California's, performance-based budgeting system. Only one Ford-KSG applicant explicitly described an innovation as the establishment of a performance-based management system. However, that applicant was Oregon Benchmarks, the State of Oregon's program to use 272 social and economic indicators to measure the performance of the state government (Oregon Progress Board, 1994). Oregon Benchmarks was one of ten winners in the 1994 competition, and has since received a great deal of publicity as the precursor of similar benchmarking programs now being implemented in other state and local governments. For example, of 900 jurisdictions responding to a 1997 Government Accounting Standards Board survey, 400 said they are using performance measures and another 300 said they were planning to use them in the near future (Walters, 1994 and 1997).[5]

Decentralized government: from hierarchy to participation and teamwork. Osborne and Gaebler's examples of decentralized government give more authority to front-line workers, flattening organizations, and encouraging labor-management cooperation and other forms of teamwork. A relatively small percentage of applicants described programs in this area, including turnarounds (3%, Table 2-2), geographic decentralization (2%, Table 2-2), participatory management (5%, Table 2-2), and organizational restructuring or flattening (1% of cases in Table 2-2). In addition, two of the cases cited by Osborne and Gaebler—for example, the New York City Bureau of Motor Equipment's (1992) In-house Research and Development Network and Minnesota's Strive Toward Excellence in Performance, or STEP, Program (Barzelay, 1992)—were Ford-KSG award winners.

Market-Oriented Principles

Catalytic government: steering rather than rowing. Osborne and Gaebler provided several descriptions of government acting as a catalyst. They cited, for example, public sector investments that leverage private sector investment, programs that create partnerships between government and business or nonprofit organizations in which government steers and either business or nonprofit organizations row, and programs that contract out some services.

Market-oriented government: leveraging change through the market. Under market-oriented government, Osborne and Gaebler included a wide range of practices, such as the creation of tradeable emissions permits, measures to improve information in the market, subsidies to augment the demand or supply of certain goods, and forms of risk-sharing, such as loan guarantees. There is, then, a conceptual similarity between market-oriented and catalytic government. For example, implementing policy through markets of private sector producers could also be seen as government steering and the private sector rowing. As a consequence, evidence for these two principles will be considered together. Table 2-2 shows that a substantial proportion—28 percent of all applications—described partnerships between the public and private or nonprofit sectors. The highest incidence occurred in policing, housing, and economic development. These partnerships indicate some type of private sector involvement, though it may not be an exact dichotomy between public sector steering and private sector rowing.

In Table 2-1, 17 percent of the applicants described their innovation as using the private sector to achieve policy objectives, which gets closer to the steering-rowing dichotomy. For example, in the information technology area, programs like Chicago's Parking Enforcement Program outsourced the operation and maintenance of the technology. In addition, 8 percent of the applicants described their innovations as establishing a voluntary program, or using incentives in addition to or in place of regulations. This definition comes closer to the use of markets than to use of the public sector programs.

Most frequently, this principle is found in the energy and environment area, with some initiatives involving the creation of markets for recycled goods, for example the Pennsylvania Governor's Recycled Material Market Development Task Force (Pennsylvania Department of Administration and Public Affairs, 1991). Others provided better information to businesses and the public about how environmental impacts can be mitigated (California Air Resources Board, 1994); and still others created voluntary cleanup programs to avoid the complications of the Superfund (Minnesota Pollution Control Agency, 1994).

Another perspective for viewing private sector participation in these innovations is in terms of financial contributions to their budgets; the private sector contributed to the operating budget of 32 percent of the applications, as will be discussed in chapter 5.

Competitive government: injecting competition into service delivery. Here Osborne and Gaebler discussed examples of competition between the public and private sectors. They saw competition as having three uses: competition between the private and public sectors can increase the efficiency of the latter; competition within the public sector can increase the efficiency of public institutions; and outright privatization can establish competition among bidders. Few Ford-KSG semifinalists are likely to be involved in privatization; as a consequence, the award does not identify whether much or little privatization is occurring in state and local government. However, programs involving competition between the public and private sectors and competition within the public sector are eligible for these awards. Still, Table 2-2 shows that only 2 percent of the applicants in our sample—a total of three innovations—involved such competition.

Governing magazine recently published a guide to privatization, which estimates that the total value of outsourcing, competitive bidding, or privatization by state and local government is $800 million to $1 billion a year, and this figure is likely to grow 10 to 30 percent per year in the near future (Kittower, 1997). Still, this is only a minuscule percentage of state and local government assets or transactions.

CONCLUSION

This chapter has identified the major characteristics of public sector innovation. They include systematic thinking, the delivery of multiple services, partnerships among organizations, the application of new technology, process improvement, organizational redesign, empowerment, incentives in place of regulation, prevention in place of remediation, the use of the private sector to achieve public purposes, voluntarism, and internal competition. Each of four different efforts to identify these characteristics—namely, the applicants' self-evaluation, my classification of their innovations, my analysis of public sector innovations in Canada, and

Osborne and Gaebler's sample of public sector innovations—produced similar characteristics and, somewhat more surprising, relatively consistent estimates of their frequency or popularity.

Of Osborne and Gaebler's principles for reinventing government, customer-driven, community-owned, enterprising, and anticipatory government appeared most frequently in the Ford-KSG sample. Expanding the private sector's role in the delivery of public services appeared less frequently but was still evident in partnerships between public and private sector organizations. In such cases, the private sector was sometimes the instrument of governance; in others, voluntarism replaced regulation. If one accepts Osborne and Gaebler's description of their principles as a preliminary map and not the final word about reinventing government, then the Ford-KSG sample and our analysis of it supports their description as reasonably accurate. The principles without doubt captured the essence of what was going on in the reinvention of state and local government, both at the time they were writing and immediately afterward. Their work has since gone forward with the publication of *Banishing Bureaucracy* (Osborne and Plastrik, 1997). We will discuss this book in chapter 8.

The characteristics of public management innovations outlined in this chapter can be thought of as a tool kit for innovators who, like artisans, must learn what each tool is about, when to use it, and when a number of tools should be employed. The Ford-KSG applicants whose innovations we have examined used different tools in various policy areas—and sometimes different combinations of tools. The second part of the book will focus on these different combinations.

The poet Yeats asked how can we know the dancer from the dance. I suppose he meant that we cannot imagine dance without seeing dancers perform it. Still, choreographers have clear ideas about what sort of person would make a good dancer. An innovation is more abstract than a dance, and we are more likely to picture innovations without seeing the innovator. But innovations cannot happen without innovators; the next chapter shifts focus from innovations to innovators and in it I begin to describe them.

3
The Who, Why, and How of Innovation

This chapter answers three questions about this sample of public management innovations: who initiated these innovations; what factors led them to innovate; and how the innovations came about. Did they evolve, or were they conceived and implemented in accord with a more comprehensive planning process? Answers to these questions are important to academics, who have been pondering them for years, and to practitioners, who can use the information to stimulate and manage innovation. The answers also reveal the role of integrity in innovation by showing us how these innovators responded to the challenges they faced.

WHO INNOVATES—EXAMPLES OF LOCAL HEROES

Two questions in the Ford-KSG semifinalist application concerned how the innovation was conceived and who initiated it. The responses were expected to provide a historical narrative of how the innovation had evolved (Appendix, qq. 8–9). In the subsequent analysis, we sought to locate whether the impetus for these innovations was internal to government, or external. The distribution was surprising. By a wide margin, the most frequent initiators were not politicians (18% of the entire sample), nor agency heads (23% of the entire sample); but in 48 percent of the sample, they were career public servants below the agency head level, that is, middle managers and front-line workers, people like Steve Wandner in the Department of Labor. Innovations spurred by interest groups or nonprofits (13%), individual citizens (6%), and program clients (2%) fall far behind. Multiple answers were possible, but relatively infrequent; each application averaged only 1.14 responses.

This result seems to contradict a basic tenet of democratic, especially United States, government. Voters elect politicians to enact policies. The upper levels of the bureaucracy are political appointments expected to make their particular agency responsive to politicians. In addition, the standard model of public bureaucracy in the United States emphasizes the existence of stringent central agency controls on entrepreneurship and innovation in the name of minimizing corruption and ensuring due process (Altshuler and Zegans, 1990; Barzelay, 1992; Gore, 1993 and 1995). Career public servants, it is assumed, will not be rewarded for successful innovation and may well be punished for unsuccessful innovation. Despite these assumptions, career public servants in the lower levels of the organization initiate more innovations than any other group. I consider this result so unexpected—and significant—that I incorporated it in the title of the book. The term "local heroes" goes beyond a mere reference to state and local government; it denotes people who do not command large organizations, but who act and lead from within the organization.

The literature on private sector innovation supports this finding. Peters and Waterman (1982) argue that innovation comes about through the efforts of mavericks at "skunkworks" far from central offices, operating without a clear mandate from above and using bootlegged resources—a view that has now become conventional wisdom in the private sector (Altshuler and Zegans, 1990). Our analysis shows that this maverick identification is also true in the public sector.

How robust this finding is, is shown in Table 3-1. The result holds, though to varying degrees, for all policy areas. The area with the highest incidence of initiators of innovation among middle managers and front-line staff is information technology. As politicians and agency heads of the early 1990s were not often trained to understand the technology or realize its potential, the innovators are computer wonks in the middle levels of the organization.

The area with the lowest frequency of innovation by other public servants is policing. The immediate hypothesis is that traditionally, police officers are taught to obey orders, not to be innovative. This table has two other interesting outliers. First, when agency heads do appear as the initiators of innovation, they do so usually in the organizational change area; presumably politicians are not particularly interested in undertaking comprehensive organizational change, and middle managers and front-line workers lack the authority to initiate it. Second, by far the highest incidence of interest groups and nonprofit institutions initiating innovations is in the educational sector. Again, a long tradition supports the notion that nonprofit institutions and parents—as vicarious consumers—

TABLE 3-1 INITIATORS OF INNOVATIONS
(Entries are in percentages)

Initiator	All	IT	OC	EE	P	H	EC	Soc Serv	Educ
								GROUP	
Politician	18	15	19	30	19	29	42	14	10
Agency head	23	19	43	11	25	21	33	19	29
Other public servant	48	70	32	41	19	43	42	54	43
Interest group, non-profit org'n	13	9	5	14	13	14	8	11	43
Individual citizen	6	2	5	11	13	7	8	3	10
Clients of program	2	0	3	0	6	0	17	0	0
Other	4	2	3	5	6	0	0	6	0
TOTAL INITIATORS	114	117	110	112	101	114	150	107	135
N	217	47	37	37	16	14	12	65	21

N = number of observations
IT (information technology), OC (organizational change), EE (environment, energy), P (policing),
H (housing, neighborhoods), EC (economic development, transportation), Soc Serv (social
services), Educ (education).

are the parties most interested in improving the performance of the educational system.

FRONT-LINE AND MIDDLE MANAGEMENT PUBLIC SERVANTS

- Rich Feldman and Patricia Barry were two staff members at the Seattle Worker Center, a small, relatively new community action agency whose original mission was to find jobs for displaced workers. Feldman and Barry's mission was to develop programs that would win the respect of the larger, better-funded state and federal employment and training agencies. During a late-night discussion about the agency's strategy, they were interrupted by a homeless man, living in a nearby shelter, whom they had been trying to locate for days to tell him about several job leads. From this encounter, they developed the idea of providing voice mail boxes for homeless people. They were able to convince the State Department of Community Development to fund a pilot project, involving 50 mailboxes for one year (Husock, 1992a; Seattle Workers' Center, 1993).
- Ed Rowe, originally a mid-level manager in the Los Angeles Department of Transportation, championed the Automated Traffic

Surveillance and Control Program, in which traffic management was assisted by video cameras, road-bed traffic monitoring, and computer-controlled signals. Rowe is now General Manager and the program he initiated has grown from a pilot project to one that encompasses the metropolitan area (City of Los Angeles, California Department of Transportation, 1992).

CITIZENS ACTING FROM OUTSIDE THE PUBLIC SECTOR

- In Portland, Oregon, a Landlord Training Program was conceptualized by John Campbell, a self-employed consultant working at home, who decided to do something about the drug-dealing he saw going on outside his front door. After he convinced the city to try landlord training as a way to reduce the drug activity, the city applied for and received a grant from the U.S. Department of Justice to develop and pilot a program. Campbell was hired as designer and trainer (City of Portland, Oregon Police Bureau, 1992).

POLITICIANS

- Jerry Abramson, described in a Kennedy School teaching case study as being "possessed of apparently boundless energy," developed many ideas in his first campaign for mayor of Louisville, Kentucky (Kennedy, 1992). Abramson recounted afterward that he "was asked over and over again by citizens whom he met to clean up the city." In his desire to respond rapidly, he had his staff look for models, and in two months he launched a neighborhood cleanup and beautification program called Operation Brightside (City of Louisville, Kentucky, Department of Community Services, 1993).

INTEREST GROUPS

- An advocacy organization for the disabled approached the police department in Syracuse, New York (Onondaga County, New York Sheriff's Department, 1994), with a plan to prevent illegal parking in spaces reserved for the handicapped. They convinced the department that having disabled people working as parking enforcement officers would solve the problem. Their idea gave rise to the Sheriff's Handicapped Ambulatory Parking Enforcement program.

WHY INNOVATE?

In their narratives, innovators described the different conditions or challenges that led to their innovations. In the coding process, the conditions fell into five groups: various internal problems, new opportunities, crises, political factors, and new leadership.[1] Each of the five groups had multiple components, which could be found singly or together. Thus, for each group of conditions, the total number of occurrences is the number of times any of its components occurred. For example, the total number of cases that involved political conditions refers to all innovations that had one or more of three political factors. The frequency of both individual conditions and groups is shown in Table 3-2.

TABLE 3-2   CONDITIONS LEADING TO INNOVATIONS
(Entries are in percentages)

| | GROUP | | | | | | | | |
Condition	All	IT	OC	EE	P	H	EC	Soc Serv	Educ
Election	2	2	0	3	0	7	0	2	5
Legislation	11	9	30	19	0	7	17	11	10
Pressure, lobbying	6	0	5	8	13	7	0	8	0
TOTAL POLITICAL	19	11	32	30	13	21	17	20	15
New leader (outside)	6	11	11	3	0	0	17	2	0
New leader (inside)	4	2	11	0	13	0	0	2	14
TOTAL NEW LEADER	9	13	19	3	13	0	17	3	14
Crisis	30	36	24	27	25	21	25	29	48
Environment changing	8	0	19	14	6	14	8	6	5
Unable to reach market	27	19	11	8	50	50	8	45	33
Unable to meet demand	11	9	11	3	25	7	8	15	5
Resource constraint	10	9	16	0	6	21	0	9	10
No policy coord'n	4	4	14	5	0	0	0	0	0
TOTAL INTERNAL	49	38	57	27	69	71	25	62	48
Technology opp'y	18	68	5	16	0	7	0	9	10
Other new opp'y	16	2	16	27	13	14	58	12	19
TOTAL OPPORTUNITIES	33	70	22	38	13	21	58	22	29
TOTAL CONDITIONS	154	171	172	133	151	155	142	150	149
Number of observations	217	47	37	37	16	14	12	65	21

Conditions Leading to Innovation

Internal problems. The most frequently occurring set of conditions leading to innovations are internal problems, at least one of which occurred in 49 percent of all applications in the sample. Internal problems encompassed the following organizational challenges:

- failure to reach its market or target population (27%);
- being unable to meet the demand for services (11%);
- increasing financial or other resource constraints (10%),
- falling behind changes in the environment (8%), and
- failure to coordinate their policies (4%).

Programs with the greatest difficulty in reaching their target populations were those in housing, social services, education, and policing. Although the intent of such programs is to help people, some people are suspicious of help, or lack the means to accept it. Programs attempting to overcome this difficulty had a significant outreach component. Thus, for example,

- The Baltimore Project trains residents of Sandtown-Winchester, a low-income housing district, to be community health workers, particularly among pregnant women (City of Baltimore, Maryland Health Department, 1993).
- The Arizona QuickCourt System set up electronic kiosks to give people who could not afford lawyers access to the justice system. At the kiosks they could prepare court documents for small claims, landlord/tenant disputes, marriage dissolutions, and child support; and for additional outreach, the kiosks operate in both English and Spanish (Arizona Supreme Court, 1994).

Programs unable to meet the demand for their services have the opposite problem: they have successfully reached their target populations, but do not have the resources or other capabilities to provide service.

- Kentucky's Financial Institutions Expert Examination System, for example, an innovation set up to prepare clients to handle bank examinations was established because the state had so much difficulty in retaining bank examiners (Kentucky Department of Financial Institutions, 1994).

An example of an innovation that was sparked by a financial con-straint—the unpleasant prospect of lost revenue—was Indiana's Commu-nity Corrections Grants Program. It was established because the state had been incarcerating young offenders in adult jails, in violation of the federal Justice and Delinquency Prevention Act. Had the practice continued, it would have led to the withdrawal of federal grants (Indiana Department of Corrections, 1994). Similarly, the City of San Carlos, California, estab-lished its internal productivity enhancement fund because the state had unexpectedly diverted local property taxes to cover its own deficit (City of San Carlos, California, City Manager's Office, 1994).

Revenue constraints appeared in only 10 percent of all cases, less frequently than my study of public sector innovation at the federal level in both the United States and Canada had led me to expect. In the United States, the federal government's National Performance Review has always put a great deal of emphasis on reducing costs (its subtitle is "government that works better and costs less") (Gore, 1993, 1995). Similarly, in Canada both the federal and provincial governments have been taking drastic action to reduce large budget deficits and the ensuing debt loads; the purpose of innovation is thus to find ways to maintain, or even expand, existing activities with fewer resources.

In the survey of Canadian public management innovation, 23 percent of all applications to the Institute of Public Administration of Canada's innovation award cited resource constraints as a causal factor, with the frequency increasing over time (i.e., between 1990 and 1993) as federal deficits worsened (Borins, 1995a). Perhaps this factor does not appear as frequently in the Ford-KSG sample because it contains only state and local government innovations and not all states and municipalities have experienced the inexorable budgetary pressures facing the two countries' federal governments.

- An example of an innovation that originated because an organiza-tion was unable to keep up with a changing environment appears in the Manchester, New Hampshire, program that issues housing code certificates of compliance (City of Manchester Housing Code Department, 1992). During the real estate boom of the mid-1980s, people were flipping substandard properties; the department made it illegal to sell or transfer a property unless it had a certificate of compliance with the city's housing code.
- The Orange County Child Abuse Service Team initiated a single comprehensive examination of abused children when it became

clear that the failure of organizations to coordinate their activities had adverse consequences for the children (Orange County, California District Attorney 1993).

Opportunities. Opportunity is the second most frequent condition leading to innovations. Opportunities, including technological and other opportunities, appeared as a driver in 33 percent of all applications in the sample. Thus, a technological opportunity led to an innovation at Info/California. In this case, Russell Bohart, manager of the California Health and Welfare Data Center, saw a demonstration of the Hawaii Health and Welfare Department's electronic kiosks, which use a touch-screen monitor to provide program information to the public. Bohart decided that he would convince the California state government to build a system of kiosks for as many departments as possible. In addition, the public would be able to use the kiosks to perform transactions, such as getting birth certificates (California Health and Welfare Data Center, 1993; Simon, 1994). In another instance, the Coles Levee Ecosystem Preserve was established after officers at the California Department of Fish and Game observed an oil company drilling a well without the necessary permits. What might have been simply an enforcement matter became a dialogue between the company and the department, resulting in a new way of doing environmental mitigation (California Department of Fish and Game, 1994).

Crisis or failure. The third most frequent condition leading to innovations can be defined as a "crisis or publicly visible failure, whether current or anticipated." This definition sets crises apart from internal problems by adding the element of external visibility. People within a public sector organization may know that its performance is not up to par but this problem becomes a crisis only when it is manifestly visible to the public. Crises occurred in 30 percent of all cases, and were relatively constant in all policy areas.

Crisis-driven innovations found in the Ford-KSG data include

- the Florida Department of Environmental Protection's establishment of a geographic information system for the state's coastal waters following its visible difficulty in responding to an oil spill off Jacksonville in 1987 (Florida Department of Environmental Protection, 1994);
- Arizona's implementation of a volunteer abandoned mines program after a young man fell to his death in an abandoned mine shaft (Arizona State Mine Inspector, 1991); and

- the City of Seattle's establishment of a comprehensive recycling program after environmental conditions at its landfills led to two landfill closings, the use of county facilities at double the price, and the eventual designation of the closed landfills as Superfund sites (City of Seattle Engineering Department, 1990; Husock, 1991).

Political factors. The last two conditions leading to innovation are political factors and new leadership. To an extent, these conditions may be responses to internal and external problems or to technological and other new opportunities previously discussed. However, they may also be sui generis in the sense that a political innovation may be initiated by a state legislator or city councilor who sees a problem or opportunity that people in the organization do not see. General political factors can include legislative mandates, electoral mandates, and other political pressure or lobbying.

Political factors occur relatively infrequently, in only 19 percent of the innovations. The least frequent political factor is an electoral mandate, evident in only 2 percent of all cases; these innovations do not often come about in response to the high-profile issues over which elections are fought. However, election campaigns do provide opportunities for politicians to take the public pulse, as Jerry Abramson did in Louisville.

The most frequent political factor is legislation, appearing in 11 percent of all cases in the sample. An example is the San Francisco Bay Area Metropolitan Transportation Commission's JUMP Start Program, which initiated many interjurisdictional transportation projects by taking advantage of new federal funding made available under the Intermodal Surface Transportation Efficiency Act (Metropolitan Transportation Commission, 1993).

Finally, 6 percent of innovations were in some measure the result of pressure or lobbying by individual legislators, such as the Los Angeles County Telecommuting Program, which was championed by Michael Antonovich, one of the members of the County Board of Supervisors (County of Los Angeles, California, 1993). This program also illustrates an autonomous political initiative.

New leadership. New leadership, either from within or outside the organization, occurs even less frequently than political conditions as a reason to innovate. It occurs, in fact, in only 9 percent of the applications. Cases in point include the New York City Bureau of Motor Equipment, whose innovative In-house Research and Development Network was launched by a new director and senior management team, and the restructuring of the Hampton, Virginia, public service, which was initiated by a new city manager (City of Hampton, Virginia, Department of Human Resources, 1990; New York City Bureau of Motor Equipment, 1992; Osborne and Plastrik, 1997).

These results challenge two items of conventional wisdom. The first is the notion that innovation in the public sector occurs primarily in response to a major crisis. The argument underlying this view is that many public sector agencies, because they are monopolies and because they have no clear performance measures, will continue to perform below their potential until they encounter a publicly visible crisis. In their book on public management innovation, Levin and Sanger (1994) wrote:

> Agencies likely to innovate often begin in crisis. Opportunity is a great engine of innovation here, as it is in science. Constraints loosen in a crisis because there tends to be more acceptance of the need for radical change, and this provides considerable freedom to innovate. Rather like the impetus provided by natural selection when old biological solutions and structures cease to meet the needs of a changing environment, crises in public organizations provide the fuel for change. Crisis often quiets natural opposition and provides the political and organizational support for innovation (p. 132).

The Ford-KSG data do not, however, support the attribution of such an important role to publicly visible crises: they are the third most frequent cause of innovation, after internal problems and new opportunities, neither of which were visible to the public (see Table 3-3).

A second tenet of conventional wisdom is that problems and opportunities are two sides of the same coin, two aspects of the same reality. It is possible to test this idea by exploring the relationships among the five conditions leading to innovations. Our coding system permitted multiple responses for the conditions leading to innovations. Table 3-3 shows that the innovations averaged 1.4 responses. Had we not been able to identify multiple responses—that is, had the conditions been mutually exclusive— the correlation coefficients between any pair of conditions would have been negative. However, since there were multiple responses, there is no reason for correlation coefficients to be negative. Nevertheless, there are negative and significant correlations between internal problems and all other conditions and between opportunities and all other conditions, as shown in Table 3-3. The negative correlation coefficient between opportu-

TABLE 3-3   CORRELATION MATRIX, FACTORS LEADING TO INNOVATIONS
Table entries are Correlation Coefficients
(Significance Levels Below)

	Total Political	Total New Leader	Crisis	Total Internal	Total Opportunities
Total political	1	−.07	.02	−.15 (.03)	−.19 (.006)
Total new leader		1	.07	−.25 (.0002)	−.12 (.08)
Crisis			1	−.26 (.0001)	−.16 (.02)
Total internal				1	−.35 (.0001)
Total opportunities					1

Note: Correlation coefficients less than .1 are not significant at 10%. Significance levels are indicated for correlation coefficients greater than .1.

nities and crises (r = −.16) indicates that they do not generally occur together. Similarly, the negative correlation coefficient between opportunities and internal problems (r = −.35) indicate that they are usually distinct from one another. Third, the negative correlation coefficient between internal problems and both political factors (r = −.15) and new leadership (r = −.25) indicate that they are not often responses to internal problems. Therefore, in this sample of public sector innovations, crises, internal problems, and new opportunities are often unique phenomena. Each is able to motivate innovation on its own, and it is not necessary that all, or even two of the three, appear concurrently.

These findings bring us back to the idea of integrity in innovation. If public management innovations were solely the result of crises, we would likely conclude that public sector organizations are characterized by uncaring people who do not act until problems become crises, or they are gridlocked systems that do not permit action until problems become crises. In fact, we have seen that, in the majority of these cases, public servants were able to act to resolve problems before they become crises, or to take advantage of opportunities to deliver new services or to deliver existing services more efficiently. Thus, one aspect of integrity in innovation involves the ability to recognize problems or opportunities in a proactive manner.

Correlations Among These Conditions and the Initiators Who Respond

Table 3-4 shows a number of relationships among these conditions and those who initiated responses to them. One would expect a correlation between political factors as a condition leading to an innovation and politician as initiators, but the correlation coefficient ($r = .26$) shows that one of these conditions does not always imply the other. For example, an innovation may come about because a new piece of legislation makes it possible, but the idea for the innovation may have come from a public servant, as was the case when the Intermodal Surface Transportation Efficiency Act facilitated the Bay area JUMP Start Program. Politician initiators respond to publicly visible crises ($r = .22$), but do not come up with ideas to solve internal agency problems ($r = -.10$), nor do they seize new opportunities ($r = -.12$).

Agency heads tend to be the initiators when they take over an agency ($r = .17$ with new leadership) but they, too, are not the ones to grasp new opportunities ($r = -.10$). Conversely, middle and front-line public servants

TABLE 3-4   CORRELATIONS OF CONDITIONS LEADING TO INNOVATION,
INITIATORS OF INNOVATION
Table Entries are Correlation Coefficients
(Significance Levels Below)

| | Initiator of Innovation | | | | | |
Conditions Leading to Innovation	Politician	Agency Head	Other Public Servant	Public Interest Group	Citizen	Client
Political	.26 (.0001)	−.04	−.15 (.02)	−.01	−.02	−.06
New leader	.09	.17 (.01)	−.18 (.01)	.07	.12 (.08)	−.04
Crisis	.22 (.001)	.04	−.02	.05	.09	−.01
Internal problems	−.10	.03	.13 (.05)	−.02	−.25 (.0002)	.07
Technological opportunities	−.09	−.11 (.11)	.14 (.03)	−.07	.04	−.06
Other opportunities	−.07	−.03	−.02	.06	.10	.03
All new opportunities	−.12 (.07)	−.10 (.14)	.10 (.13)	−.03	.11 (.09)	−.02

Note: Correlation coefficients less than .1 are not significant at 10%. Significance levels are indicated for correlation coefficients greater than .1.

are less likely to be the initiators when the impetus for an innovation comes from the political system ($r = -.15$) and when there is a new leader ($r = -.18$). They are associated with innovations that are responses to internal problems ($r = .13$) and technological opportunities ($r = .14$).

These results provide a neat trichotomy: politicians tend to be the initiators of innovations in times of crisis; agency heads when they take over the reins or in an organizational change context; and middle-level and front-line public servants innovate in response to internal problems and take advantage of technological opportunities. I use words like "tend to" and "often" to indicate that these results are not mathematical theorems or even perfect correlations. The fact that the correlation coefficients are not $+ 1$ or -1 indicates that there are exceptions to this trichotomy.

Notwithstanding this caveat, the Ford-KSG data include some clear examples of this trichotomy. In Seattle, the mayor and city council directed the solid waste utility to respond to the crisis of landfill closings and cost escalation by carefully studying the options. They were particularly interested in understanding the tradeoffs among incineration, distant landfill, and recycling (Husock, 1991).

Two examples of new agency heads initiating innovations are Ernest Curtsinger, the new police chief of St. Petersburg, leading his department to implement community policing (City of St. Petersburg, Florida, Police Department, 1994); and Dr. Katherine Lobach taking over New York City's 55 child health clinics, and changing their mission from infant care to comprehensive care from birth to adolescence (New York City Bureau of Child Health, 1994). Neither Curtsinger nor Lobach took over in a crisis situation; however, each one had a vision for how performance could be improved in their areas. Finally, examples of middle managers and front-line staff taking advantage of opportunities include Russell Bohart developing the Info/California kiosks and Rich Feldman and Patricia Barry inventing Seattle's Community Voice Mail program.

THE HOW OF INNOVATION

Two alternative hypotheses for describing how innovations occur are (1) that they are the result of careful planning based on a preconceived vision, or (2) that they are reached rather spontaneously by a groping process.[2] In a recent and seminal article on public management, Behn (1988) describes "groping along"; and argues on the basis of the small number of cases with which he was very familiar that innovative public managers have improved their organizations through an experimental process of groping toward goals that are initially loosely defined. He advocates that would-be innovators follow this process.[3]

Planning or Groping?

Behn's original work was amplified by Golden (1990) and Levin and Sanger (1992, 1994). Both used relatively small samples—Golden analyzed seventeen cases, Levin and Sanger, twenty-nine of the successful applications to the Ford-KSG Awards in its initial years (1986 to 1990). Behn also illustrated the groping hypothesis in a book-length study of Massachusetts's Employment and Training Choices program (Behn 1991).

We used the narrative responses (qq. 8–9) about the initiation and evolution of the innovations to determine how frequently they displayed Behn's "groping," as opposed to comprehensive planning. The coding of these different approaches is displayed in Table 3-5. Clearly, there were two types of comprehensive planning: first a strategic plan for the organization behind the innovation; and second, a comprehensive plan for the innovation itself.

TABLE 3-5   MODE OF ANALYSIS FOR INNOVATIONS
(Entries are in percentages)

Mode	All	IT	OC	EE	P	H	EC	Soc Serv	Educ
Comprehensive Plan or Analysis	59	54	65	68	31	64	75	59	43
"Groping Along"	30	28	22	22	56	29	25	31	38
Pilot Study	35	40	27	30	25	36	33	43	29
Replicate Public Sector Practice	12	19	5	5	19	7	8	11	24
Public Consultation	11	4	11	8	31	14	8	9	19
Consultant	7	21	5	8	6	0	8	6	5
Legislative Process	8	0	19	19	0	7	8	9	0
Strategic Plan for Organization	7	6	19	3	0	7	17	2	14
Client survey	4	4	3	0	19	7	0	3	5
Replicate nonprofit organ'n practice	4	2	0	5	0	14	0	3	5
TOTAL MODES	177	178	176	168	187	185	182	176	176
N	217	47	37	37	16	14	12	65	21

N = number of observations

Following our analysis of the Ford-KSG data, Behn's "groping" process was also coded—along with the use of pilot studies, consultants, public consultation, the replication of the program by other public sector and nonprofit organizations, policy or legislative analyses, and client surveys.

The first issue to consider is the contrast between groping and comprehensive planning. Here attention was paid to whether the applicant said that a comprehensive plan was followed, or that the innovation began with a broad idea that was implemented in an evolutionary manner. Milestones were also used to help determine how long it takes innovation to take hold, and how the original conception was modified. The data provided a very strong negative correlation ($r = -.66$) between groping and comprehensive planning. This correlation is not -1 because some applications involved neither groping nor planning, and a few involved both. In these cases, a long process of evolution was interrupted at some point by the formulation of a comprehensive plan.

The Wishard Patient Record System is a prototype of the groping method. It is a state-of-the-art computer record system and common database that 10 major hospitals in Indianapolis use to avoid duplication and improve the quality of care for their Medicaid recipients. Its description in the Ford-KSG application provides a classic description of groping:

> The core system has been under continuous development by Dr. Clem McDonald of the Regenstrief Institute at Wishard Hospital for almost 20 years. It started in a 35-patient diabetes clinic in 1972. It was gradually extended to the general medicine clinic through the late seventies and then to all Wishard clinics by 1984. During this time ancillary service systems—laboratory, pharmacy radiology—were brought on line. The system grew on an evolutionary basis through the present. The community extensions were conceived in 1989 and initiated in 1990 through the Campaign for Healthy Babies, in response to the city's high infant mortality rate. . . . The stimulus and imagination for this project came from many people: [4 doctors] . . . and a host of state and local political and civic leaders.

The project's milestones stretched over 22 years and show the evolution of the project through the types of medical services provided and the increasing number of hospitals and clinics that adopted the system (Wishard Memorial Hospital, 1993).

In contrast to the process of groping that led eventually to the Wishard Patient Record System, Chicago's Parking Enforcement Program provides an equally unambiguous story of comprehensive planning:

Over the past 10 years, several civic groups had recommended de-criminalizing parking tickets, and substituting an administrative process that would remove these cases from traffic court, making room for more serious violations. Several mayors announced plans to clean up parking tickets. In 1987, the Legislature passed a statute, effective November 7, 1987, that permitted municipalities to adopt 'administrative adjudication' for parking tickets ... Nothing happened.

On April 24, 1989, Richard M. Daley took office as Mayor, and announced that administrative adjudication would indeed be implemented. The position of City Parking Administrator was cre-ated, and Inge Fryklund was hired November 1, 1989, to implement the new system. With the Mayor's public commitment to a new program, it moved ahead, rapidly and without a hitch.

The system as implemented—especially the use of imaging technology to permit neighborhood adjudication centers and adjudi-cation by mail—has been implemented almost exactly as is was conceived. The most notable difference from the public's point of view is that the neighborhood centers opened one year ahead of schedule—in October 1990 rather than Summer 1991. On the other hand, the system has certainly evolved at an operational level, and continual adjustment and fine tuning has been necessary. . . .

The milestones for this innovation started with the state legislation in 1987 and the election of Mayor Daley in April, 1989; the rest are sand-wiched between November 1, 1989, the appointment of the new adminis-trator, and fall 1990, as the system became operational (City of Chicago, Illinois, 1991).

These examples are polar opposites; however, the data in Table 3-5 indicate that 59 percent of all innovations were closer to the comprehen-sive planning pole, while 30 percent of all applications were closer to the groping pole. Table 3-5 also shows a high incidence of comprehensive planning among all groups of innovations, with the exceptions of policing and education. In addition, in only 7 percent of the cases, was the innova-tion derived from a strategic planning process for the entire organization. This finding is consistent with Mintzberg's (1994) work on strategic planning in the private sector which finds that few organizations had overall strategic plans.

Pilot projects appear slightly more frequently than groping (35% of all cases) and fairly frequently among all policy areas. Pilot programs exemplify Karl Weick's (1984) argument that an effective means of attacking social problems is through a series of small wins. He wrote:

Small wins provide information that facilitates learning and adaptation. Small wins are like miniature experiments that test implicit theories about resistance and opportunities and uncover both resources and barriers that were invisible before the situation was stirred up (p. 44).

Pilot projects, understood as an implementation process, are a compromise between groping and planning because they involve implementing a program design incrementally, so as to learn from early experience. In some instances, pilot projects were coded together with comprehensive planning; in others, with groping. They could be a part of either process. Seattle's recycling program, for example, developed a comprehensive plan for dealing with the solid waste crisis, but it also used pilot projects to test and adjust some components of the plan, such as curbside pickup of recycables and composting at transfer stations (City of Seattle, Washington, Engineering Department, 1990).

The Automated Traffic Surveillance and Control program in Los Angeles started as a pilot program in 1980, incorporating traffic signals in three parts of the city. The program has evolved incrementally since then, and passed a major milestone in the 1984 Olympics, successfully controlling traffic flows around the Coliseum, the major Olympic venue (City of Los Angeles, California, Department of Transportation, 1992).

Robert Behn (1996b) makes an ingenious argument for launching full-scale programs from the beginning, rather than pilot projects. Programs are implemented throughout an organization's local offices, so putting them in full play from the beginning means that instead of learning from one pilot, all local offices will be learning from one another. Nevertheless, pilot programs do appear frequently in the sample; the reason may have less to do with maximizing learning than with minimizing opposition. Pilot projects are a way to overcome opposition gradually.

Other models for how programs can be implemented occur much less frequently, at 12 percent or less for the entire sample. Some interesting outliers are the high frequency of public consultation (31%) and client surveys (19%) among policing initiatives; the frequent use of consultants (21%) in the information technology area, and the frequency of overall strategic planning (19%) in the organizational change area. These outliers will be discussed in the second part of this book.

The Determinants of Planning and Groping

The next step, after illustrating the difference between innovations involving planning and those involving groping, was to find the systematic factors associated with each of these methods. If those elements could be discovered, it might be possible to determine when an organization is more likely to choose one of the methods over another. We might expect to find two sets of factors, those associated with the process of initiating an innovation and those associated with the innovation itself.

This section deals with the components of innovations and the implementation process as simple correlation coefficients with groping and planning and then combines them in a multiple regression analysis. Readers unfamiliar with multiple regression analysis may focus on the conclusions, rather than the methodology.

To determine whether and how factors in the process of initiating an innovation are associated with groping, planning, and some other modes of analysis, we used correlation coefficients between the modes of analysis, the initiators, and the conditions leading to the innovation. This is shown in Table 3-6. Not all modes of analysis are shown: those without any significant correlations, either positive or negative, have been excluded.

Comprehensive analysis is negatively correlated with initiation by public servants (r = −.11) and with new leadership for the organization (r = −.19); on the other hand, it is positively correlated with the three political factors leading to innovation (r = .14). Given the high negative correlation coefficient between groping and planning, it is no surprise that the opposite appears to be the case for groping: a positive correlation with initiation by public servants (r = .14) and new leadership (r = .10) and a negative correlation with the three political factors (r = −.21).

This result appears consistent with the trichotomy presented previously. When an innovation emerges from the political process, either in response to a priority or a crisis, politicians want the bureaucracy to develop implementation plans. The Chicago Parking Enforcement Program and the Seattle Recycling Program are cases in point.

TABLE 3-6   CORRELATIONS OF MODE OF ANALYSIS AND INITIATORS
LEADING TO INNOVATION, CONDITIONS LEADING TO INNOVATION
Table entries are Correlation Coefficients
(Significance levels below)

| | MODE OF ANALYSIS | | | | | |
	Compre-hensive Analysis	Groping Along	Replicate Public Sector	Replicate Non-Profits	Consultant	Legislative Process
INITIATOR						
Politician	−.02	−.07	−.10	.04	.01	.27 (.0001)
Agency head	.08	−.02	.09	−.05	.02	−.08
Other public servant	−.11 (.11)	.14 (.03)	−.02	−.04	.07	−.11 (.12)
Public interest group	−.10	−.01	.02	.14 (.04)	0	−.01
Citizen	.09	−.08	−.04	.16 (.02)	.01	−.07
CONDITIONS LEADING TO INNOVATION						
Political	.14 (.04)	−.21 (.002)	−.04	.03	−.04	.25 (.0002)
New leader	−.19 (.0006)	.10 (.12)	−.02	.02	.23 (.0007)	−.09
Crisis	.03	−.03	−.09	−.02	.06	.03
Internal problems	−.02	.04	0	−.05	−.12 (.08)	.09
Technological opportunities	.01	−.06	.19 (.004)	−.03	.26 (.0001)	−.13 (.05)
Other opportunities	−.04	.04	−.01	.05	−.12 (.08)	−.03

Note: Correlation coefficients less than .1 are not significant at 10%
Significance levels are indicated for correlation coefficients greater than .1

On the other hand, when the initiators are agency heads or public servants at lower levels, there is a tendency for them to experiment by groping, refining their ideas and gradually obtaining support within the organization. Dr. Clem McDonald at the Wishard Memorial Hospital used this method to develop his patient record system. Still, it should be remembered that these correlations, while significantly different from zero, are not perfect. We may very well find examples of politicians groping or public servants planning.

The literature on groping often cites examples of newly appointed agency heads taking over an organization—particularly one that is performing poorly—and experimenting with a variety of initiatives to improve its performance. One of the cases that Behn (1988) and then Levin and Sanger (1994) discuss is Ira Jackson's takeover of the Massachusetts Department of Revenue:

> When Ira Jackson became head of the Massachusetts Department of Revenue in 1983, the agency was so demoralized that it was barely functioning. Error correction and adaptation were essential to his evolutionary, iterative process of innovation. . . . But then he moved fast and tried to compensate for a historical error of too little tax enforcement by pursuing a "ready, aim, fire" approach. Without much pause or prior analysis, he picked up on one of the most obvious and familiar things lying around for a revenue department—enforcement of tax collection—and initiated a series of decisive actions. His dramatic enforcement activities—closing popular restaurants and seizing the yachts of wealthy tax evaders—were pursued repeatedly, with a lot of learning by doing. There was more firing than aiming.

The Jackson case, and many similar ones in the literature, have the characteristics that I think of as "organizational turnarounds." As these turnarounds occur infrequently in the United States and Canada, the question arises whether it is appropriate to build a theory of public management innovation on such exceptional cases. Chapter 8 goes into this question in greater detail.

In addition to the light it sheds on the determinants of planning and groping, Table 3-6 delineates the circumstances in which other modes of analysis are likely to come into play. There is a tendency for innovations to replicate public sector practice when there are technological opportunities to innovate ($r = .19$). Given that the private sector was ahead of the public sector in the 1980s in implementing information technology, one would expect a significant positive correlation between technological opportunities and the replication of private sector practices; however, that correlation coefficient (not shown in Table 3-6) is $-.03$. We conclude, therefore, that public sector innovators, like most of us, search locally for suggestions, rather than globally (Cyert and March, 1963). Public sector innovators, that is, look closer to home than far afield for models to emulate.

This finding seems to be confirmed by the next variable, the replication of the practice of nonprofit organizations. When this occurs, the initiators tend to be public interest groups (r = .14) or individual citizens (r = .16), both of whom are likely to be familiar with nonprofit organizations and practices and to recommend those practices to the public sector.

Consultants are used in two situations, primarily: first, when there is a new leader for the organization (r = .23); and second, when technological opportunities are present (r = .26). Thus, it is quite common for new leaders, especially if they are unfamiliar with the organization and nature of the business, to call in consultants to help them draw their conceptual maps. In addition, if the new leaders know that they will need to take radical action, they may hire a consultant to help legitimate it.

The use of consultants to deal with technological opportunities expands on the notion of searching locally. If public servants replicate another's practice, it is more likely to be public sector practice with which they are directly familiar than private sector practice, which they do not know. However, if they have some awareness of what is happening in the private sector, but lack detailed knowledge, they are likely to hire a consultant to provide that detailed knowledge. The best example of consultants playing a major role in an organizational change process involving information technology was in the Chicago Parking Enforcement Program. In this case, a consulting firm (Ernst and Young) was hired to design the requests for proposals for both hardware and software, and another firm, Electronic Data Systems (EDS), was chosen to build the system.

When politicians initiate an innovation, they often follow the familiar route of introducing it through legislation. The correlation coefficients between the analysis of an innovation as part of the legislative process (e.g., a legislative committee report) and the politician as initiator is .27 and between legislative analysis and the three political factors leading to innovation, the correlation is .25. Conversely, legislative analysis is less likely to be involved when public servants initiate innovations (r = .–11) and when the innovation involves a technological opportunity (r = −.13). This finding is consistent with the previous finding that political and bureaucratic routes to innovation tend to be distinct from each other.

In considering how the intrinsic characteristics of the innovations can explain the choice between groping and planning, Golden (1990) made some interesting, and apparently overlooked, comments in her article about groping in human service programs—and about extending her conclusions to other policy fields. She suggests that capital-intensive fields such as information technology or transportation infrastructure might require more planning based because of the size of the initial investments. This hypothesis is consistent with the findings of the private sector literature (Mintzberg, 1994). Golden suggests that when chains of cause and effect are well understood, there may be less need for groping; and finally, that if a program is part of a complex intergovernmental system (such as conditional grants from the federal government), then program requirements may limit the use of groping.

It is possible to test each of these hypotheses with data from the semifinalist questionnaires, as is shown in Table 3-7. The first hypothesis was tested by correlating planning and groping with capital budgets of $500,000 and $ 1,000,000, respectively. Both measures yielded positive and significant correlation coefficients for planning ($r = .16$ and $r = .14$, respectively) and negative and nearly significant coefficients for groping ($r = -.07$ and $r = -.10$, respectively).

Golden's second hypothesis was tested in the following way. The Ford-KSG semifinalists were asked to provide three measures to evaluate their program and then to specify their most important achievement. The answers to the latter question sometimes dealt with a program's impact on its clients (thus repeating the previous one), but also with the impact of an innovation on the individuals and organizations involved. One response to this question, given in 16 percent of the entire sample, was that the program provided an opportunity to make a theoretical model

---

TABLE 3-7   TESTS OF GOLDEN'S HYPOTHESES
Table entries are Correlation Coefficients
(Significance levels below)

	Comprehensive Plan	Groping Along
FACTOR		
Large capital budget (> $500,000)	.16 (.02)	−.07 (.31)
Large capital budget (> $1,000,000)	.14 (.04)	−.10 (.16)
Operationalized theory	.18 (.01)	−.03 (.63)
Innovation used in unforeseen ways	−.16 (.02)	.13 (.05)
All holistic (Table 2-1)	.16 (.02)	−.11 (.09)
All partnerships (Table 2-2)	.18 (.01)	−.09 (.20)

operational; if applicants are working from a theoretical model it is likely that they would plan their program carefully. The correlation coefficient between the opportunity to operationalize a theory and the existence of a comprehensive plan was positive and significant ($r = .18$); the correlation coefficient between the opportunity to operationalize a theory and groping was insignificant ($r = -.03$).

Other applicants responded that the innovation's most important achievement was that it had unforeseen uses. One would expect this response to be positively correlated with groping and negatively correlated with planning, and indeed it was ($r = .13$ and $r = -.16$, respectively).

Golden's third hypothesis, that programs that are part of complex intergovernmental systems are more likely to require planning than groping is supported by Behn (1995). In *Governing*, he writes about the need for planning in programs involving partnerships between the public and private sectors:

> To obtain resources from the private sector, public managers have to make their case differently [than to a legislature or city council] . . . [the private sector] will need something that looks more like a traditional business plan. [Public managers] will have to explain exactly what they want to accomplish, how they will accomplish it, and how they will measure performance. The private sector wants to know what results its resources will buy (p. 103).

Jerry Mechling (1995a), a commentator known for his views on public sector reengineering through information technology, makes the same point more generally about cross-organizational initiatives in the same issue of *Governing*:

> Reduce the confusion of cross-organizational initiatives through explicit analysis. . . . The key point for public leaders is that cross-organizational initiatives are unlikely to emerge on their own, absent the analytic activities needed to make them understandable and credible to the participants.

Golden's complex intergovernmental systems and Mechling's cross-organizational initiatives were evident in the Ford-KSG sample in two ways, namely, as holistic innovations or as partnerships, either within the public sector or between the public and private sectors. In both cases, there were positive correlations with planning ($r = .16$ and $r = .18$, respectively) and negative correlations with groping ($r = -.11$ and $r = -.09$, respectively). Thus, all three of Golden's hypotheses are supported by the Ford-KSG semifinalist questionnaires.

Not only can Golden's hypotheses be tested individually; they can also be tested together with the influences of the process of initiating an innovation using multiple regression analysis.[4] In addition to these variables, however, I was still interested in whether the characteristics of an innovation have any influence on planning or groping. Simple correlation coefficients show that apart from the holism variables (in the applicants' responses) and the partnership variable (in my analysis), the only other variable with a significant effect was the "new program" variable, which had a positive correlation with groping ($r = .16$). This finding makes sense intuitively; designing a new program may require more trial and error than attempting to improve the operation of an existing program.

In the multiple regressions explaining groping and planning, the dependent and as well as independent variables are categorical (i.e., zero, meaning that a characteristic is absent; or 1, meaning that it is present). The predicted values of the dependent variable are probabilities that a characteristic will be either present or absent, which means that they should fall between 0 and 1.

We have two ways to estimate such a regression: the easy way, known as a linear probability model; and the statistical purist's way, known as a logit. Using a linear probability model for categorical data is problematic since some predicted values of the dependent variable can be greater than 1 or less than zero, which, as probabilities, would be meaningless.[5]

This problem can be avoided by using a logistic transformation of the dependent variable. Instead of using a probability (p) as a dependent variable, the odds—$(p/(1-p))$—are used as a dependent variable. The odds range from 0 to positive infinity, and the natural logarithm of the odds ranges from negative to positive infinity. Thus, a variable between zero and one can be transformed into a variable between negative and positive infinity. The linear probability model is estimated by ordinary least squares, a procedure that has been available on statistical software for almost 40 years. The logistic model is estimated by a nonlinear search procedure intended to determine the best overall fit, known technically as maximizing a log likelihood function (Pindyck and Rubinfeld, 1991, especially 248–281).[6]

This approach involves a more difficult computation and only became available recently as the capacity of computers expanded. I estimated both a linear regression model and a log likelihood model, with similar results from both methods, with all independent variables having the same signs and similar significance levels.[7]

Table 3-8 shows the regression results for planning and groping and for both the linear probability and logit specifications. The signs and significance of the coefficients of the independent variables are more interesting, I think, than the goodness-of-fit results in the regression equations; the goodness-of-fit measure, R^2 for the linear probability specifications, is fairly low, which is generally the case with cross-sectional data. The test statistic for the independent variables is the t-statistic for the linear probability model and Wald's Chi-square (which is the square of

TABLE 3-8   REGRESSION ANALYSIS OF COMPREHENSIVE PLANNING
AND GROPING
Table Entries are Coefficients
(Chi square, significance levels for logit below)
(t value, significance levels for linear model below)

| | Dependent Variable and Specification | | | |
| | Comprehensive Planning | | Groping Along | |
Independent Variable	Linear Probability	Logit	Linear Probability	Logit
Intercept	.53 (8.4, .0001)	.13 (.18, .67)	.26 (3.9, .0001)	−1.2 (10.8, .001)
Large capital budget	.40 (2.6, .009)	2.43 (4.8, .03)	−.19 (1.3, .19)	−1.45 (1.7, .19)
Operationalize theory	.28 (3.2, .002)	1.53 (9.0, .003)	−.09 (1.1, .27)	−.51 (1.2, .28)
Unforeseen use	−.38 (1.5, .13)	−5.9 (.8, .38)	.28 (1.2, .23)	1.34 (1, .31)
All holistic	.14 (2.1, .04)	.63 (4.1, .04)	−.08 (1.4, .18)	−.46 (2, .15)
New program	−	−	.16 (2.6, .01)	.88 (6.9, 009)
Political influence	.09 (1.1, .26)	.51 (1.5, .23)	−.21 (2.0, .05)	−1.56 (7.0, .008)
New leadership	−.33 (2.8, .006)	−1.58 (7.0, .008)	.17 (1.5, .13)	.92 (2.5, .11)
Initiated by public servant	−.14 (2.2, .03)	−.67 (4.5, .03)	.13 (2.0, .05)	.71 (4.4, .04)
R^2	.16	−	.13	−

a t-statistic) for the logit model. The test statistics and their corresponding confidence levels are shown in Table 3-8 below the coefficients. An independent variable with a positive sign can be thought of as increasing the probability of a dependent variable occurring and, conversely, an independent variable with a negative sign can be thought of as decreasing the probability of the dependent variable occurring. Thus:

- A large capital budget (e.g., over $1,000,000) will significantly increase the probability of planning and negatively and nearly significantly (confidence level of .19) decrease the probability of groping.
- Making a theory operational will increase the probability of planning (at a confidence level of .002 or .003, depending on the specification) and decrease the probability of groping (at a not-quite-significant confidence level of .27 or .28). Making unforeseen use of an innovation has the expected signs (negative for planning, positive for groping) but neither is significant.
- Holistic innovations will increase the probability of comprehensive planning (at a confidence level of .04) and decrease the probability of groping (at a nearly significant confidence levels of .15 or .18). Because holistic innovations and partnerships are closely correlated with one another, it is better to use one or the other in a regression but not both, since using both introduces multicollinearity, which would make the coefficients unstable. Indeed, regressions using both had lower significance levels for both variables.

When the variables in Golden's analysis are combined in a multiple regression, the results are consistent in sign with her hypotheses, and usually statistically significant. The new program variable was used only in the equations for groping, since its simple correlation with planning was insignificant. Newness increases the probability that the innovation will involve groping and is significant at a high confidence level of .009 or .01. New leadership increases the probability of groping, at a nearly significant confidence level of .11 or .13 and decreases the probability of planning, at a very significant confidence level of .006 or .008. Political factors (that is, electoral mandates, legislation, or other political pressures) have a positive but not significant effect on the probability of planning (confidence level of .23 or .26); they have a negative effect on the probability of groping, and are strongly significant (confidence level of .05 or .008). When an innovation is initiated by public servants the probability of planning is decreased, the probability of groping increased, both with significant confidence levels (.03 and .04 or .05, respectively). For any given application, the predicted probability that an innovation would be characterized by either planning or groping would depend on all these different influences together.

CONCLUSION

This chapter provides a number of strong messages for public sector innovators.

- First, agency heads or politicians are not the only ones to initiate innovations. Many innovations were initiated by middle managers and front-line workers, and still others, by interest groups and individual citizens. Thus, I would urge middle-managers and front-line workers not to hesitate but to put their ideas forward.

  The implication of this finding for agency heads and politicians is that they should not see the bureaucracy as an undifferentiated impediment to change; instead, they should see public servants as people having lots of innovative ideas. The challenge for those at senior levels in the hierarchy is to find the career workers who have innovative ideas and to erect the structures that will encourage innovation, not stifle it.
- Second, public management innovations are not solely crisis-driven. Many innovations came about because managers spotted internal problems before they became publicly visible; others came about because managers spotted opportunities. The negative correlations among externally visible crises, internal problems, and opportunities show that each is a factor that can lead to innovation. This finding is optimistic because it shows that public servants can act without waiting to be authorized.
- Third, there are three reasonably popular paths to innovation: politicians responding to crises; newly appointed agency heads restructuring organizations; and middle-level and front-line workers responding to internal problems and taking advantage of opportunities. While this trichotomy is based on stochastic correlations rather than the certainty of mathematical theorems, it does suggest that all paths are not equally likely. Awareness of this trichotomy should help public servants understand the

innovative processes going on around them, thereby giving them more opportunity to participate effectively.

- Fourth, despite the popularity of the groping model in the literature on public sector innovations, many of the innovations in this sample were the result of a comprehensive planning process. In fact, both comprehensive planning and pilot projects occurred more frequently than groping.

Levin and Sanger (1994) criticize some of the more renowned graduate schools of public policy for their emphasis on policy analysis, particularly derived from microeconomics as a core discipline. They fear that these curricula place too much weight on planning and insufficient weight on groping. They advise schools to spend more time teaching students the skills of leaders who succeed by groping, likely through the case method. Though I support their call for more emphasis on leadership skills, planning skills, such as policy analysis and program evaluation, should not be removed from the curriculum. They are essential for encouraging the wide variety of innovative programs that involve planning.

In addition, the statistical analysis in this chapter also suggests that theory-driven programs are more likely to be characterized by planning; it is in the course of formal education that a public manager is most likely to encounter these theories. Further, planning often involves a great deal of work such as statistical analysis and modeling, and it is students emerging from the universities with the most up-to-date knowledge of analytical techniques who will have a competitive advantage in this work.[8] Of course, the challenge that professors face is how to design a curriculum that fits everything a student should know into a finite number of sessions, courses, and years of study.[9]

- Fifth, planning and groping are both important ways to make innovations, but public servants should know when to plan and when to grope. Integrity in innovation demands that one plan when it is desirable and possible to plan, but when it is not possible to plan, one experiments and learns from one's experiments. Judgment is necessary to determine which of the two procedures is appropriate in a particular set of circumstances. The statistical analysis in this chapter should help us make informed judgments: large capital investments, programs that involve the coordination of a large number of organizations, and theory-driven programs are more likely to require planning. Planning is more likely to be required when the impetus for an innovation comes from the political system.

The converse of these hypotheses is also true: groping is more likely to be acceptable in the absence of large capital investments, when it is not necessary to coordinate several organizations, and when we lack well-articulated theories or a political impetus. Groping is also more appropriate for new programs, for organizations that have new leadership, and for innovations initiated by public servants.

The value of such contextual awareness is that a public servant can anticipate the process by which an innovation is likely to unfold, and then involve himself or herself most productively in that process, as opposed to resisting it.

But whether a person becomes engaged with an innovation or resists it, is, appropriately, the subject of chapter 4.

4

Obstacles Overcome,
Problems Persisting

This chapter is about obstacles to innovation—those that the Ford-KSG applicants faced and defeated, those that they faced but did not overcome, and those that they expected to face in the future. Based on their descriptions, that is, on the experience of actual innovators, the obstacles presented here will, it is hoped, help would-be local heroes know what difficulties to expect when they begin an innovation and how to overcome them.

The discussion incorporates the variety of emotional expressions that accompany innovation and the color or quality of the innovators' responses: they were defiant toward obstacles, reflective and critical of their own strengths and weaknesses, and optimistic about the future. As chapter 3 discussed integrity in the context of originating and defining innovations, chapter 4 discusses integrity in the context of establishing and maintaining them.

OVERCOMING THE OBSTACLES

Ford-KSG applicants were asked to describe the most significant obstacle they had encountered and how they had dealt with it. They were also asked to describe any remaining obstacles (Appendix, q. 10). Among the 217 applications, 512 obstacles were identified—approximately 2.5 per application. The distribution of the obstacles, as shown in Table 4-1, was also revealing: fully 54 percent were internal to the bureaucracy; another 26 percent involved the political system in some way, and 21 percent originated outside government. The question that emerges is why. Why is there more internal opposition than external? Before answering this question, however, we must understand the different types of obstacles included under each of these heads.

Identifying Obstacles

Internal difficulties. Internal obstacles are difficulties within the innovating organization or in another part of the public sector. On forty-eight occasions, long-standing attitudes within the bureaucracy constituted an internal obstacle or barrier to change. Professional groups often held these attitudes and resisted innovations they thought would require them to do their jobs in different ways. Thus, for example, police officers were skeptical about community policing, and teachers were unenthusiastic about team teaching. Part 2 deals with such obstacles at greater length and shows how innovations can challenge established professional practice.

TABLE 4-1   OBSTACLES TO INNOVATION

Obstacles	Occurrences	Percent of Total	Frequency Obstacle Overcome (in percent)
INTERNAL OBSTACLES			
Bureaucratic attitudes	48	9%	65%
Turf fights	9	2	89
Other bureaucratic resistance	35	7	74
Total bureaucratic	92	18	71
Difficulty coordinating	52	10	65
Logistics	51	10	55
Maintaining enthusiasm, burnout	33	6	45
Implementing technology	30	6	70
Union opposition	7	1	71
Middle-management opposition	7	1	71
Opposition to entrepreneurs	4	1	0
TOTAL INTERNAL	276	54	63%
POLITICAL SYSTEM			
Inadequate resources	89	17	19
Legislative, regulatory constraints	34	7	53
Political opposition	8	2	63
TOTAL POLITICAL	131	26	31%
EXTERNAL OBSTACLES			
External doubts	48	9	90
Reaching target group	30	6	60
Affected private sector interests	14	3	64
Public opposition	7	1	72
Private sector competitors	6	1	50
TOTAL EXTERNAL	105	21	74%
TOTAL	512	100	58%

On nine occasions, the obstacles involved bureaucratic turf fights, for example, the contention among Pennsylvania's departments concerning who was really responsible for recycling (Pennsylvania Department of Administration and Public Affairs, 1991). On thirty-five occasions, the innovators met other types of bureaucratic resistance. For example, Seattle's politicians were eager to establish an intensive recycling program, but city staff were hesitant, unsure about the program's reception (i.e., its popularity). In another case, the Massachusetts Department of Environmental Protection established the Blackstone Project to test a new way of doing environmental inspections. Because it was a pilot project, this program received increased funding at a time when other program budgets were being severely cut—creating an obvious source of controversy (Massachusetts Department of Environmental Protection, 1991).

In fifty-two instances, the applicants reported that coordination among participating organizations presented challenges. For example, the Wishard Patient Record System had difficulty encouraging different hospitals to take the necessary steps to make their patient records compatible. In fifty-one cases, the problems were logistical, often involving scheduling. For example, Kentucky Educational Television established an interactive distance education program, only to find that participating schools schedule their courses at different times of day (Kentucky Educational Television, 1991).[1]

On thirty-three occasions, applicants reported that the greatest obstacle was motivating participants or maintaining their enthusiasm. Burnout or dropout often troubled programs using volunteers, such as Arizona's Volunteer Abandoned Mines Program, which needed motivated volunteers to search for and seal abandoned mines, and Louisville's Operation Brightside, which needed motivated volunteers to work on cleanup programs. Another thirty applicants reported difficulties in implementing a technology. Kentucky's Department of Financial Institutions, for example, had to help bank examiners become comfortable with the expert system it had developed.

The sample contained seven cases of opposition by public sector unions, and seven cases of opposition coming specifically from middle managers (as opposed to the more general category of bureaucratic opposition). The Los Angeles County Telecommuting Program encountered both of these obstacles; the union wanted the county to pay for the computers employees would use at home, and also wanted participation in the program assigned on the basis of seniority. Middle managers, on the other hand, were concerned about not having the employees under their direct supervision.

Lastly, in four instances, the innovators had difficulty being entrepreneurial because of constraints endemic to the public sector. For example, Dr. Lobach found her efforts to redirect the organization of New York's Child Health Clinics frustrated by (1) "a rigid civil service system, which made staff changes a long, painful process," [and 2] "labyrinthine contracting requirements, which made the clinic renovation process extend over a period of years." Yet Dr. Lobach innovated: she responded to these obstacles with a judicious application of the maxim that it is better to ask forgiveness than permission (New York City Bureau of Child Health, 1994).

Political obstacles. The second major category of obstacles identified in this sample involved the political environment. In eighty-nine cases (17% of the sample), innovators complained of inadequate resources, usually, money. This obstacle is deemed political because the budgetary process ultimately involves legislative appropriation. Though many resource constraints come from within the bureaucracy, there may be political input as well.

On thirty-four occasions, the innovators found themselves hampered by existing legislation or regulations. For example, when Wichita, Kansas, attempted to clean up a major source of groundwater contamination without recourse to Superfund, it was prepared to use local organization and funding—to make, in fact, a long-term commitment of tax dollars. However, a Kansas law requiring cities to operate on a cash basis made such a commitment impossible (City of Wichita, Kansas, 1991).

In eight cases, the innovators faced actual political opposition, at either the level of government where the program was initiated or at another level. Oregon Benchmarks was opposed by some state legislators who did not want to participate in a nonpartisan program and who disagreed with its priorities (Oregon Progress Board, 1994).

External obstacles. The third set of obstacles were external to the public sector and included forty-eight cases in which doubt or skepticism threatened to impede a program. When Portland, Oregon, began its Landlord Training Program, for example, landlords were skeptical; they felt that they were being asked to do police work. Tenants groups were also skeptical; they felt that the program would restrict tenant rights (City of

Portland, Oregon, Police Bureau, 1992). On thirty occasions, the problem was how to reach the target group. Seattle's Community Voice Mail, Arizona's QuickCourt system, and Info/California experienced this problem, which is common among programs that serve populations with Spanish-speaking minorities or other groups with special needs.

On fourteen occasions, private sector interests opposed an innovation that they thought would adversely affect them. Equipment manufacturers who used a "low price, but poor quality and late delivery" strategy to sell garbage trucks to New York City opposed the Bureau of Motor Equipment's effort to establish more exacting standards (New York City Bureau of Motor Equipment, 1992).

In seven instances, according to our sample, the public's opposition went beyond skepticism or doubt. For example, Pittsburg, California, discovered that its Shared Savings Program was opposed by people in the local community and in the broader academic and professional communities who felt that public servants should not receive a portion of the savings they identified (City of Pittsburg, California, Public Services Department, 1993).

Finally, the applicants reported six cases in which private organizations perceived an initiative as being in competition with them. Engineering firms opposed New York State's Self-Help Support System because they thought that introducing simplified wastewater technology into rural areas, especially a technology that local groups could install with volunteer labor, would take their business (New York State Department of State, 1994).

Interpreting the Data

Looking at these obstacles as a whole, I find it surprising that such a large proportion of the opposition was internal to the bureaucracy (at a minimum, 276 of 512 cases or 54%) or internal to the bureaucracy and political system (407 of 512 cases or 80%). Much of the political opposition concerned resources, which may in fact have had a bureaucratic component, and most of the rest was a result of legislation passed before these initiatives occurred. Similarly, external doubts (forty-eight cases) were much more frequent than actual public opposition (seven cases).

The preponderance of internal opposition might have happened for a number of reasons. In some areas—possibly organizational change and information technology—the innovations were internal to the bureaucracy, so politicians and the public were not really aware of them. It might also have been the case that strong political or public opposition was sufficient to kill public sector innovations, so that the innovations in this sample are those that were sufficiently acceptable to politicians and the public that they did not draw that opposition (Zegans, 1992).

Returning, then, to the distinction between successful and failed innovations: it may be argued that a necessary, but not sufficient, reason for an innovation's success (and therefore its inclusion in our sample) is that its program is acceptable to politicians and public opinion, while many innovations that fail are not. It can be argued, however, that political opposition was not insurmountable; when it did occur in this sample, it was frequently overcome (in five of eight cases or 63% of the time), as was public opposition (in five of seven cases or 72% of the time). Further, as will be shown in the second part of this book, the public sector innovations included in this sample are not limited to publicly invisible improvements, but also include high-profile initiatives in many policy areas.

My interpretation of this evidence, therefore, is that Americans are quite aware that performance in the public sector can be enhanced, and that policy outcomes in many areas can be improved. And since they are not committed to existing policies or procedures, they are receptive to public sector innovation and entrepreneurship. The rarity of external opposition in the sample supports this conclusion and should be good news to Osborne and Gaebler and other advocates of the New Public Management.

Dealing with Obstacles

Table 4-1's third column shows the frequency with which each obstacle to innovation was overcome.[2] If an obstacle was not overcome, the program did not necessarily fail, but continued to operate as best it could. About 60 to 70 percent of the time, however, the applicants claim to have overcome their obstacles. They were most successful at overcoming external doubts (in forty-eight instances or 90% of the time). This success can be seen as confirmation of the public's receptivity to public sector innovation.

Inadequate resources is the problem that was least frequently overcome (only 19% of the time). Applicants often described the need for additional resources in terms of where they tried to get them and how, even after trying, they usually received less than they wanted. Still, they managed to run their programs—at least in the short run.

Tactics Used for Overcoming Obstacles

Table 4-2 describes the tactics that innovators used to overcome the obstacles they had identified. The surprising outcome here is that the most frequently used tactics fall under the rubrics of persuasion and accommodation, while the least frequently used can be described as "bureaucratic hardball." Before we discuss this outcome, however, it is necessary to understand these tactics and how they are linked to the obstacles they helped overcome. Table 4-3 lists the tactics most frequently used to respond to each obstacle.[3]

Demonstrating program benefits. The tactic most frequently used to overcome obstacles (fifty-six times) was to demonstrate how a program could benefit its opponents. It was employed in response to internal problems, political problems, private sector opposition, and public doubts. There are numerous examples: the initiators of the Los Angeles County Telecommuting Program convinced union leaders not to stand in the way of workers who wanted to telecommute; the City of Wichita persuaded the Kansas legislature that it was in everyone's interest to clean up a pollution

---

**TABLE 4-2   TACTICS TO OVERCOME OBSTACLES TO INNOVATION,
TOTAL FREQUENCY USED**

Tactic	Times Cited
Demonstrate to opponents that program really advances their interests, provides benefits to them	56
Finding additional resources of any kind consultation	55
Training	51
Consultation	50
Persistence, effort	49
Logistical problems were resolved	41
Cooptation/buy-in (opponents or sceptics become participants)	40
Marketing	29
Demonstration project	28
Other	28
Gaining political support, building alliances	25
Focus on most important aspects of innovation, develop a clear vision	21
Technology was modified	20
Program design made linguistically, culturally sensitive	14
Legislation or regulations were changed	10
Provide recognition for program participants or supporters	7
Compensation for losers, design so that losers won't be worse off	5
Changing managers responsible for program implementation	4

TABLE 4-3 TACTICS MOST FREQUENTLY USED TO OVERCOME EACH OBSTACLE TO INNOVATION
Five Most Frequent Tactics (% of N)

Obstacle	N						Percent Success
INTERNAL							
Bureaucracy	92	training (24)	show benefits (23)	consultation (20)	effort (20)	demo.project (14)	71%
Coordination	52	consultation (31)	cooptation (27)	clear vision (19)	effort (15)	training (12)	65
Logistics	51	solve problems (86)	training (7)	effort (7)			55
Burnout	33	show benefits (41)	effort (26)	marketing (11)	consultation (11)	cooptation (11)	45
Implementing tech.	30	modify tech (52)	training (31)	marketing (7)	find resources (7)		70
Unions	7	consultation (43)	compensation (29)	show benefits (29)	cooptation (14)	effort (14)	71
Middle management	7	show benefits (29)	training (29)	compensation (14)	cooptation (14)		71
POLITICAL							
Resources	89	find resources (71)	effort (8)	political support (3)			19%
Leg'n., reg'n.	34	leg. change (27)	political support (23)	effort (20)	show benefits (9)	consultation (6)	53
Political opposition	8	political support (25)	show benefits (25)	effort (25)	training (13)	cooptation (13)	63
EXTERNAL							
Doubts	48	show benefits (31)	consultation (23)	demo. project (21)	cooptation (19)	marketing (17)	90%
Reaching target group	30	marketing (32)	cultural sensitivity (20)	effort (20)	training (12)	cooptation (8)	60
Affected private sector	14	show benefits (62)	training (15)	marketing (8)	consultation (8)	cooptation (8)	64
Public opposition	6	consultation (43)	political support (29)	demo. project (29)	cooptation (14)	marketing (14)	72
Competitors	6	political support (17)	show benefits (17)	marketing (17)	cooptation (14)	marketing (14)	50

problem that would have devastated downtown Wichita's business community; and the initiators of the Pittsburg, California, Shared Savings Program convinced the council and the public that it was in everyone's interest to reduce the cost of government services.

Attempts to find funding. The most common response to the lack of resources was simply to try finding resources (fifty-five citations)—and resources were often found. However, such resources were usually more short-term than permanent. Examples include the following programs:

- The Arizona QuickCourt System received a grant from the State Justice Institute to fund three pilot kiosks.
- Russell Bohart persuaded IBM to cover half the cost of developing the Info/California kiosks, and the
- Los Angeles Department of Transportation found 10 different funding sources for its Automated Traffic Surveillance and Control Project, including federal gasoline taxes, funding by the California Department of Transportation, and fees to private developers.

These examples point to the ongoing resource problems that innovators usually faced: how to turn pilot projects into full-fledged programs, or how to continue cobbling together funding from diverse sources.

Training and consultation. Training was used on fifty-one occasions to respond to internal obstacles, particularly to overcome resistance to new information technologies or programs that change the way people work. For example, the Los Angeles County Telecommuting Program provided training for telecommuters and their managers that included a refresher course on management by objectives. The training clarified expectations on both sides and gave suggestions about how to manage the employer-employee relationship.

Consultation was another frequently used tactic (fifty times), both to respond to internal obstacles, such as problems coordinating organizations; and external obstacles, such as doubts or skepticism. Consultation is somewhat different from demonstrating the benefits of a program, in that it involves more listening. In consultation, the innovator asks other people about their interests, then modifies the program to take these interests into account. For example, the Portland, Oregon, Landlord Training Program, cognizant of the conflicting views of landlords and tenants organizations wrote that "we addressed the concerns of both tenant advocates and skeptical landlords by listening carefully and integrating their concerns into the very fabric of the training" (City of Portland, Oregon, Police Bureau 1992).

Co-opting the opposition is an extension of consultation in that a program's actual or potential critics are given an ongoing role in designing the program. This tactic was used on forty occasions in response to internal problems, particularly the lack of coordination, and sometimes in response to political or external problems. Info/California established an advisory group of departmental Public Information Officers to help design its kiosks and, ultimately, to encourage other departments to participate.

Developing a vision. Another tactic used on twenty occasions, primarily in response to the problem of coordinating multiagency programs, was to focus on the most important aspects of an innovation, that is, to develop a clear vision of the program. Participating agencies were asked to put aside other agendas and focus on the objectives of their common program. Put differently, the applicants did not dilute the program to bring participants on board; rather, they invited participants to help clarify the essential elements of the program. Vision derives from being honest about what an innovative program should and should not do, and is another example of the role of integrity in innovation. For example, the Pennsylvania Job Centers not only cross-train participating staff, but also seek their agreement on taking a "whole concept approach to providing services," rather than count the number of services provided by each agency (Pennsylvania Department of Labor and Industry, 1992).

Innovators often (forty-nine times) said that they responded to obstacles simply by being persistent. That is, they did not change their tactics, but repeated their efforts until the environment was supportive or until the cumulative effect of their messages got through. Dr. McDonald, for example, spent twenty years building the Wishard Patient Record System.

Levin and Sanger (1994) suggest another way to make the point about persistence. They quote Hirschman's hiding hand principle to the effect that because successful innovators tend to underestimate the obstacles facing them, they can boldly attack the obstacles, rather than being daunted by them. This determination to bring an innovation to life, especially when success is not instantaneous, is yet another aspect of integrity in innovation.

Logistical problems, when they arose, simply had to be resolved (forty-one citations). For example, the Pennsylvania Job Centers found it hard to locate new operations in their current offices because additional space was seldom available. The program often had to rent space in new buildings. In many other programs, such as the Volunteer Abandoned Mines Program and the New-York State Self-Help Support Program, the logistical issue involved scheduling problems—of volunteers in the former case and program staff, who were on loan from their home departments, in the latter.

Marketing. Marketing is a tactic similar to the first tactic of demonstrating the benefits of a program. The difference is that demonstrating benefits involves one-on-one communications and meetings, while marketing involves broadcasting a message using techniques developed in the private sector. Marketing was used on twenty-nine occasions to reach a program's target group, to respond to public skepticism or opposition, or to reach potential users of a technology. The Seattle Recycling Program used a marketing campaign, including billboards, radio spots, and a door-to-door distribution of literature, to inform the public of recycling options and to convince them to recycle (Innovations in State and Local Government, 1992).

Demonstration projects. Demonstration projects were used twenty-eight times to overcome external skepticism and opposition or to respond to internal opposition. The Multistate Procurement of Recycled Xerographic Paper, which now involves ten midwestern states, began as a demonstration project by Wisconsin and Minnesota to show skeptics in industry and in other states that such an initiative could work. Its success led to the expansion of the recycled paper initiative to eight other states and to subsequent initiatives for the purchasing of other recycled products (Wisconsin Department of Administration, 1993). Demonstration projects, like the pilot projects discussed in the previous chapter, are an example of Weick's (1984) "small wins" approach to attacking social problems.

Political appeals. On twenty-five occasions, innovators appealed to politicians for support, generally to get approval for a legislative or regulatory change needed to implement their programs, or to respond to political or public opposition. Significantly, this tactic was not used in response to internal problems. An example of a program that needed and received political support is Oregon Benchmarks, for which successive Oregon governors have sought bipartisan support.

Making program modifications. Innovations involving information technology were modified on twenty occasions to make a program more user friendly. Early versions of the Kentucky Financial Institutions Expert Examination System, for example, were field-tested by bank examiners, then modified; and the Wishard Patient Record System modified its data collection procedures to suit doctors' practices. In addition to modifying technology, innovative programs provided training for those using it.

Programs were made linguistically or culturally sensitive on fourteen occasions, particularly in response to the problem of reaching target groups. As previously mentioned, when the obstacle was a preference for languages other than English, the response was to extend the service through bilingual or multilingual capabilities, as exemplified by Community Voice Mail, Info/California kiosks, and Arizona QuickCourts—all of which provide services in English, Spanish, and other languages as necessary.

Seeking political support and legislative change. The response to obstacles posed by existing legislation or regulations was, quite naturally, to build enough political support to change the legislation or regulations. This tactic was used in ten instances. For example, the Kansas law requiring municipal governments to operate on a cash basis was amended to permit Wichita to make a multiyear commitment of tax dollars to pay for its downtown groundwater cleanup. In such cases, local heroes were not able to solve problems on their own; they had to enter the political arena.

Recognition. On seven occasions, programs recognized participants to keep them motivated. While this tactic does not appear in Table 4-3—since it is not one of the most frequently used tactics—it was used for programs in which volunteers played an important role, such as Arizona's Volunteer Abandoned Mines Program and Louisville's Operation Brightside.

Compensation. On five occasions, compensation was provided for public workers whose lives were made worse as a result of an innovative program. Front-line workers made redundant by the advance of information technology or outsourcing arrangements and middle managers made redundant as a result of organizational delayering or power sharing received such compensation. When, for example, the Chicago Parking Enforcement Program outsourced its data processing components, forty-two data entry clerks were no longer needed; the city compensated them by reassigning them to other positions.

Management changes. Finally, on four occasions, innovative programs required a change in management. For example, staff who did not like the New York City Child Health Clinics' shift in focus (to a comprehensive health care model) were encouraged to leave.

The tactics that these innovators used to overcome obstacles can be compared to the repertoire of tactics that Kanter outlined in 1988:

> My research identified a number of tactics that innovators used to disarm opponents: waiting it out (when the entrepreneur has no tools with which to directly counter the opposition); wearing them down (continuing to repeat the same arguments and not giving ground); appealing to larger principles (tying the innovation to an unassailable value or person); inviting them in (finding a way that opponents could share the "spoils" of the innovation); sending emissaries to smooth the way and plead the case (picking diplomats on the project team to periodically visit critics and present them with information); displaying support (asking sponsors for a visible demonstration of backing); reducing the stakes (deescalating the number of losses or changes implied by the innovation); and warning the critics (letting them know they would be challenged at an important meeting—with top management, for example) (p. 193).

Tactics found in the Ford-KSG sample are similar: effort and persistence are similar to waiting it out and wearing them down; demonstrating that an innovation will benefit opponents is similar to appealing to larger principles and sending emissaries; logistical changes, modifying the technology, and compensation for the losers are similar to reducing the stakes; co-optation is similar to inviting them in; and gaining political support is similar to displaying support and warning the critics.

However, a fundamental difference in tone separates this sample from Kanter's presentation. When our applicants sent emissaries it was to listen as well as speak, and on the basis of what they heard, programs were redesigned. When these applicants invited other organizations in, it was less to "share the spoils," than to seek their support for the program by having them participate in its design.

Now consider the relative frequencies with which these different tactics were used. By far, the most common tactics can be broadly described as persuasion (e.g., demonstrating benefits, demonstration projects, and marketing) or accommodation (e.g., training, consultation, co-optation, modifying a technology, making a program culturally or linguistically sensitive, and compensating losers). These local heroes resorted to the *force majeure* of upper level political support only when the challenge was political, not when it was internal to the agency or department.

In the Ford-KSG sample, the tactic that was least frequently used to solve problems was changing the manager responsible for program implementation. In other discussions of organizational change, including Kanter's, "hardball" tactics usually include an appeal to higher authorities to crush opposition and remove opponents.[4] The nature of responses in Table 4-2 makes it clear that local heroes act with more integrity. They usually attempt to persuade or accommodate their opponents, rather than trying to overcome them. This result may simply indicate that the innovators themselves are often front-line workers or middle managers, not holders of great power. But it is also true that the use of power is intrinsically antithetical to the spirit of innovation. One of the ways we judge the value of an innovation is by its replications; by definition, those who replicate an innovation are in another jurisdiction than the one where the innovation was introduced and are therefore free to choose it or reject it. We conclude that an innovation is good if many people or organizations *choose* to adopt it. If this logic applies to replication, it should apply to introduction as well.

RESPONDING TO CRITICS

Following their identification of obstacles to an innovation, the Ford-KSG applicants were asked to identify its strongest critics and the nature of their criticism (Appendix, q. 13). Responses to this query amplify the discussion on obstacles, since those who present obstacles to an innovation are among those who continue to criticize it.[5] It is, however, the distribution of responses to this question that is most surprising. Criticisms often concern an innovation's philosophy and its priority relative to other government programs, and not its impact on the critic (e.g., job or business losses and other negative effects at home or work). Innovators often had clearly articulated—but controversial—ideas about how to improve practice in a policy area, and critics disagreed with their ideas. If innovation were not controversial, or novel, would it be innovation? Or to put it differently: to innovate with integrity seems to require that the innovator be capable of engaging in discussion about why a new alternative is more likely than current practice to enhance the public good.

Table 4-4 reveals a matrix of critics and various types of criticism. The first column lists the number of times each group (e.g., professionals)

TABLE 4-4   CRITICS OF INNOVATIONS AND THEIR CRITICISMS
(Table Entries are Percentages of Numbers in First Column)

					TYPE OF CRITICISM				
Critic	N	Philosophical	Job or Business Loss	Negative Effects	Conditions of Work	Inappropriate Use	Spend Differently	Expand Program	Other
Professionals	35	74	3	3	9	11	3	9	0
Unidentified	35	69	0	0	0	0	17	14	7
Affected businesses	27	7	30	59	7	0	0	0	0
Participants	22	55	0	0	23	0	5	18	14
Politicians	21	43	5	0	5	33	5	5	19
Unions	20	50	20	10	30	0	0	0	10
Public interest groups	17	53	0	0	0	6	6	18	12
Clients of program	16	56	0	0	6	13	0	25	19
Affected individuals	8	63	0	0	0	38	0	0	0
Business competitors	9	0	89	22	0	0	0	0	0
TOTAL CRITICS	210								
NONE	54								
TOTAL CRITICISMS	234	106	24	21	17	17	13	19	17

N = number of instances of criticism by each group in first column. Table entries are percentages of instances of criticism by each group, i.e. percentage of numbers in first column. Bottom row is total number of times each type of criticism was made.

80

appeared as a critic. The row entries indicate what portion of the group's criticisms fit a certain type. For example, 74 percent of the professionals made philosophical criticisms and 3 percent criticized a program because it was likely to cost them a job. The percentages in the rows sum to more than 100 because each group made multiple criticisms. The table shows the total number of critics (210) and the total number of criticisms (234). Finally, the table indicates that 54 applicants (or 25 percent of the sample), said they had no critics. Conversely, 75 percent of the sample said that they did.

The most frequently identified critics were professionals, sometimes within the organization initiating the innovation, sometimes from outside; and the criticism was most frequently philosophical (74% of the time). Many innovations were attempts to institutionalize new management ideas or theories concerning particular policy areas, both of which created controversy between their proponents and the followers of older theories. In education, the policy area that had the highest incidence of criticism by professionals (38%), a number of programs that evaluate students based on projects were criticized by the proponents of traditional examination-based evaluations.

Businesses adversely affected by innovations were critics. For example, when Minnesota established its Consolidated Chemical Dependency Treatment Fund to open competition between private and public hospitals, hospitals in both sectors criticized the new regime. Similarly, businesses that perceived themselves to be in competition with a government program were critical because they feared a loss of business. Consulting engineers made this criticism about the New York State Self-Help Support Program; however, the program blunted the criticism by reaching a gentlemen's agreement with the engineers whereby it would operate only in jurisdictions with populations of less than 10,000 (Husock, 1994).

Staff participants in innovative programs had a variety of criticisms. Sometimes, like professionals, their differences were philosophical. On other occasions, they felt the innovations would adversely affect the conditions of their work. For example, some staff participating in the Orange County Child Abuse Service Team were frustrated by long delays in lining up the team to do the interview. On other occasions, staff supported the innovation and wanted to see it expanded.

Politicians usually voiced philosophical differences with innovations, concern that innovations were not being used properly, or concerns that money should have been spent differently. For example, some politicians in Santa Monica felt that the City's Public Electronic Network, a

precursor of the Internet's electronic discussion groups, was being inappropriately used to allow a small group to make strident criticisms of
politicians (City of Santa Monica, California, 1993). Politicians criticized
Oregon Benchmarks because they did not like the priorities it established
and their implications for program funding.

Public sector unions often made criticisms similar to those made by
professionals and program participants. Half the time, the criticisms were
philosophical; the rest of the time, they dealt with shop-floor issues, such
as terms and conditions of employment and the impact of technology on
job tenure. For example, the union representing workers in Los Angeles
County criticized the county for not buying the computers and modems
that workers would need if they chose to telecommute; and the union
representing hospital workers in Minnesota (American Federation of State
County and Municipal Employees) was critical of the Consolidated Chemical Dependency Treatment Fund because it feared that its members in
state-operated clinics could lose their jobs.

Public interest groups generally presented philosophical criticisms.
For example, many of the innovations sought to reduce the complexity
of environmental regulations affecting business and replace regulation
with negotiated compliance. Some environmental groups are critical of
this approach and prefer the traditional emphasis on regulation and
litigation.

THE CRITIC WITHIN

In addition to presenting the criticism of others, Ford-KSG applicants
were also asked to be their own critics, that is, to identify their programs'
most significant remaining shortcoming (Appendix, q. 16). Table 4-5
shows that the applicants provided many answers to this question and
related their shortcomings to the obstacles and criticisms they had cited.
Integrity demands being honest about the shortcomings of one's own
program.

The most common shortcoming, mentioned in 39 percent of the
applications, was the lack of resources, a finding consistent with the notion
that the obstacle least likely to be overcome is the lack of resources. The
simple correlation coefficient between lack of resources as a remaining
obstacle and as a shortcoming was .28, significant at .0001. There were,
however, substantial variations in the frequency of this shortcoming
among policy areas. Only 20 percent of the housing, economic development, and information technology initiatives reported this shortcoming,

TABLE 4-5 MAJOR SELF-IDENTIFIED SHORTCOMING
(Table Entries are Percentages)

Shortcoming	GROUP								
	All	IT	OC	EE	P	H	EC	Soc Serv	Educ
Lacks resources	39	23	38	32	50	14	17	51	43
Needs fine-tuning	29	43	27	30	31	43	17	25	19
Other	15	8	19	25	25	29	17	11	14
Program hasn't spread	12	17	11	14	0	0	25	12	5
Related programs must improve	7	9	3	3	6	7	8	13	10
Difficulty maintaining partnership	5	0	8	3	0	7	33	5	5
Coping with growth	4	9	8	0	0	0	8	3	10
Total (%)	111	109	114	107	112	100	125	120	106
N	217	47	37	37	16	14	12	65	21

N = number of observations
IT (information technology), OC (organizational change), EE (environment, energy), P (policing),
H (housing, neighborhoods), EC (economic development, transportation), Soc Serv (social services), Educ (education).

while approximately half of the social service, policing, and educational initiatives reported it. In some cases, it was the instability of funding that was criticized. For example, the Los Angeles Department of Transportation worried that the funding for its Automated Traffic Surveillance and Control Project could be summarily cut, since it was coming from the city's general fund, rather than from ear-marked gasoline taxes. In other cases, such as Seattle's Community Voice Mail and the Massachusetts Office of the Attorney General's Student Conflict Resolution Program, demand for the program was growing, and managers were unsure whether they would receive sufficient funding to meet the demand.

The shortcoming identified in 29 percent of the sample was that an innovation needed fine tuning. This criticism was highly correlated with unsolved logistic problems (r = .18, significant at .001). For example, the Seattle Recycling Program worked well for street-level houses, but its managers wanted to begin recycling in apartment buildings. An amusing problem that needed fine-tuning was reported by the Chicago Parking Enforcement Program:

[This] shortcoming stems from police handwriting. A keypuncher misreading "U" as "V" will key in an erroneous plate number. If that number happens to match a live plate on the Illinois Secretary of State's database, a notice will be sent to the owner of the plate even if (as we are frequently told) he "never set foot in the City of Chicago." Citizens (especially those downstate) do not believe in the reality of data entry errors, and attribute all such billing errors to fraud and extortion on the part of Chicago. Instead of following instructions on the notice and contesting by mail, many people call the nearest radio station or State Representative! (City of Chicago, Illinois 1991).

About 12 percent of the applicants said that a program fell short of becoming as widespread as had been expected. Managers of the Los Angeles County Telecommuting Program, for example, wanted more supervisors to allow their staff to telecommute. Similarly, Dr. McDonald wanted the Wishard Patient Record System to expand to more hospitals, serve more patients, and incorporate more types of medical records.

Some 7 percent of the applicants said that their program's improved performance put pressure on other geographically or functionally related programs to improve as well. For example, one aspect of the Chicago Parking Enforcement was creating an on-line database of parking meters; the benefits of this database led the Parking Administrator to recommend the creation of similar computerized inventories for other infrastructure items, such as signs and hydrants. The district court in Quincy, Massachusetts, found that its Model Domestic Abuse Program, was attracting many women from other cities to initiate domestic abuse actions; therefore, the court wanted neighboring cities to adopt similar programs to alleviate the strain on its resources. These examples show that innovations challenge the organizations around them. In some instances, they may be threatened because they are out of character with the organizational environment; in other instances, the innovation may serve as the end of the wedge, forcing change and improving performance in related organizations.

In 5 percent of all cases, and in a third of cases in the economic development area, keeping a partnership together was hard—in fact, a shortcoming. It was also highly correlated with ongoing problems involving coordination (r = .16, significant at .02). For example, the San Francisco Bay Area Metropolitan Transportation Commission's JUMP Start Program, a partnership of 36 different transportation agencies whose goal is to implement collaborative projects, reported this shortcoming. The program does effectively stimulate collective action; nevertheless, the applicants at the Metropolitan Transportation Commission believe that it could be even more effective. The shortcoming they cite is that the program puts an unduly heavy staffing burden on them, while other agencies occasionally do not contribute their fair share.

The last shortcoming, cited by 4 percent of the applicants, is coping with program growth. For example, in an attempt to encourage other schools throughout the country to follow their example, the faculty at Thayer High School ran the Here, Thayer, and Everywhere program on their own time, especially during the summer, but the popularity of the program has made the faculty increasingly unable to meet its demands.

The discussion of shortcomings provides an interesting picture, in which we can see that local heroes may not rest triumphantly following their initial effort. Instead, they must continue the struggle. In some cases, this struggle is to maintain the success of a program against the centrifugal forces that threaten any partnership; in others, it is a struggle against the uncertainty of financial support. In yet other cases, the programs are victims of their own success, and the applicants must constantly seek new ways to serve the growing demand for their program. For some, the challenge is how to take the logical next step in the evolution of their program.

FACING THE FUTURE

In question 18 of the semifinalist questionnaire, Ford-KSG applicants were asked to discuss the future of their programs, first by describing how the problem addressed by their programs would evolve over the next five years, and then by indicating how they expected to respond to this evolution.

Table 4-6 presents their expectations. The most common response, given by 65 percent of the applicants, was that demand for their programs would increase each year because the problems or needs that the programs address will continue. This expectation was found in all policy areas, though it was highest in areas responding to the needs of the disadvantaged (i.e., social services, housing, education). The Child Abuse Service Team, for example, has witnessed an increase in reported child abuse cases and expects the trend to continue; Seattle's Community Voice Mail program expects homelessness to continue; and Portland's Landlord Training Program expects people to continue to use and traffic in illegal drugs.

Other applicants believe that the demand for the program will grow simply because the population is growing or because the economy is

TABLE 4-6   EXPECTATIONS REGARDING EVOLUTION OF PROBLEM
IN FIVE YEARS
(Table Entries are Percentages)

| | GROUP | | | | | | | | |
Expectation	All	IT	OC	EE	P	H	EC	Soc Serv	Educ
Problem won't disappear	65	62	49	62	69	79	33	77	76
Economic population growth will increase demand	14	9	19	19	6	7	33	12	14
Technology will change	12	40	14	11	0	7	0	5	0
Government finances will constrain program	10	2	14	8	6	14	8	6	19
Significant progress has been made	9	13	11	8	13	7	0	9	10
Other	7	4	5	5	19	0	25	3	5
Major policy change will affect program	6	4	11	0	0	0	8	11	10
Total (%)	123	134	123	113	113	114	107	123	134
N	217	47	37	37	16	14	12	65	21

N = number of observations

growing. This response, given by 14 percent of the applicants, was encountered most frequently—one-third of the time—in the economic development and transportation program areas, which are most closely tied to economic growth. Both the JUMP Start Program in the Bay Area and the Automated Traffic Surveillance and Control Program in Los Angeles expect population growth to exacerbate traffic problems.

Another 12 percent expect the program's technology to change or develop. This response was most frequent (40% of the time) in information technology programs. Thus, Santa Monica's Public Electronic Network anticipated improvements in on-line service and the Los Angeles County Telecommuting Program expected improvements in the transmission of voice, data, and images.

Some 10 percent of the applicants said that constrained government finances would continue to affect their programs. An observer may wonder if this expectation is not a ploy calculated to get more resources. It was, however, cited only when the applicants perceived clear evidence of financial constraint. For example, the Oregon Benchmarks Program expects the priorities it has established to help policymakers determine how to allocate limited, and possibly decreasing, tax dollars. The expected decline in the state's budget was linked to Oregon voters approval of a 50 percent property tax reduction in 1990.

About 9 percent of the applicants, rather than describe how the problem was changing, said that they had made significant progress in overcoming it, and that they expected to make further progress. Thus, the Chicago Parking Enforcement Program felt it had made progress in the ticketing and adjudication components of parking and was looking forward to improving other aspects of the system. It is interesting to note that in answering this question, few of the applicants simply pointed to progress to date. The infrequency of the claim to have made significant progress was consistent with the applicants' extensive and frank discussions of their programs' shortcomings. The applicants seemed to be looking to future challenges rather than back to those they had already overcome.

Finally, 6 percent of the applicants felt that major policy changes would affect their program. This response was most frequent among programs in the health care area, such as the Wishard Patient Record System, New York City's Child Health Clinics, and the Minnesota Consolidated Chemical Dependency Treatment Fund. Many of these programs were intended to improve health care for the poor and the uninsured.[6] These programs assumed that if a comprehensive national health insurance plan were enacted—which still seemed a possibility in 1993—the demand for their services would increase dramatically.

Having identified these problems, how were the applicants going to respond? Table 4-7 shows that the most common answer, as might be expected given the frequency with which resources appeared as an ongoing problem, was to find more resources for the program or expand the program. This answer, given by 57 percent of the applicants, was strongly correlated ($r = .27$, significant at .0001) with the most common forecast for the future, namely, that the problems they were responding to would continue unchanged or deteriorate further. For example, Arizona Quick-Court hoped that sufficient resources would be made available to support a statewide expansion. One measure of its acceptance was that administrators had started to book appointments to use the kiosks, and soon the bookings had to be made three weeks in advance.

The second most frequent response to the evolution of the problem came from 38 percent of the applicants who expected to customize their services, or provide a different set of services. For example, the managers of the Baltimore Project, concerned by a growing incidence of maternal

TABLE 4-7   RESPONSE TO EVOLUTION OF PROBLEM
(Table Entries are Percentages)

Response	All	IT	OC	EE	P	H	EC	Soc Serv	Educ
								GROUP	
Provide more resources	57	43	49	62	56	43	50	66	76
Customize service, provide different services	38	55	41	43	31	50	25	31	33
Fold into a more comprehensive program/policy	22	13	19	8	38	21	17	31	33
Use improved technology	16	49	19	8	0	7	8	8	10
Other	4	0	8	2	6	14	8	3	0
Total (%)	137	160	136	123	131	135	108	139	152
N	217	47	37	37	16	14	12	65	21

N = number of observations

substance abuse, planned to include more interventions. Oregon Benchmarks, feeling that its program was well-established at the state level, was attempting to persuade local government, community, and nonprofit organizations to develop benchmarks.

Fully 22 percent of the applicants thought that their program should be part of a more comprehensive initiative, or integrated more closely with overall policy (indicated in the table as "fold into a more comprehensive program/policy"). Thus, the Chicago Parking Enforcement Program argued that the Chicago should create a broader transportation management organization, in which parking enforcement would be one activity. Recycling programs, such as those in Seattle and Pennsylvania, wanted to recycle additional materials such as tires, batteries, motor oil, and used appliances, and to go beyond household recycling to establish commercial and industrial recycling programs. The desire to be part of a more comprehensive program or policy is positively correlated with the applicants' belief that their programs had already made significant progress ($r = .22$, significant at .001) and suggests that even applicants who feel that they have made significant progress plan to continue building on this progress to respond to other problems and become part of a larger initiative.

The last response, to use improved technology to meet the future, was given most frequently by applicants in the information technology area, and correlates strongly ($r = .59$, significant at .0001) with the applicant's expectations that technology will continue to change. Since information technology is changing very rapidly, it is not surprising that the applicants had fascinating ideas in this policy area, including how to take advantage of new developments. The Florida Marine Spills Analysis Program wanted to use satellite pictures to create real-time GIS maps of the spills. Thayer High School wanted to incorporate multimedia digital portfolios of student work into the Here, Thayer, and Everywhere program that could be shared with other schools over the Internet.

CONCLUSION

The message for public sector innovators is clear:

- First, potential innovators can expect that *most* obstacles to innovation will be internal. These obstacles will include the ingrained attitudes of professional groups, turf fights, coordinating difficulties, logistics and scheduling concerns, difficulty installing a new technology, opposition from unions and middle management, difficulty maintaining the enthusiasm of participants, and resource constraints. Other obstacles may lurk in the intersection of the bureaucratic and political arenas (e.g., resource constraints), or in the political arena (e.g., legislative or regulatory constraints).

  In my judgment, the obstacles to innovation tend to be predominantly internal because the public (the external audience) has become receptive to public sector innovation and entrepreneurship or because the local heroes in this study had the good sense to know not to propose "innovations" that would be publicly or politically unacceptable. Nevertheless, external obstacles will *sometimes* emerge, such as public or political skepticism or opposition, difficulty reaching target groups, or opposition from the private sector.

- Second, in attempting to overcome these obstacles, an innovator's first two quivers should be labeled "persuasion" and "accommodation." In the first, the arrows (or tactics) would include demonstrating that an innovation is in the public interest, marketing to large groups, clarifying the program's vision, and using demonstration projects. In the second, the arrows would be consultation, co-optation, training, making the technology user-friendly, and linguistic or cultural sensitivity. These tactics were by far the most frequently used; they are also relevant to all obstacles, whether internal or external. Integrity in innovation demands knowing which arrows to shoot, in which order, and when to shoot several arrows together.

When obstacles come from the legislative or public arenas, it is appropriate to enter those arenas. Thus, we have seen local heroes pressing for legislation that would facilitate innovations. We have also seen the applicants work with politicians to respond to political or public opposition. However, we have seen few instances of hardball tactics, such as using political support to quash bureaucratic opposition. On occasion such tactics may be necessary, but only when all the arrows in persuasion and accommodation have been let fly. If political or other high level support is required it should be exercised subtly. Surely it is best for all concerned, including the politicians, to embrace an innovation because it is good policy or in the public interest. There are instances, generally cases of dramatic change in organizational direction, in which managers closely associated with the old direction should resign or be released.[7] But this tactic is only a last resort.

- Third, innovations have many critics, though most criticisms will involve philosophical issues, rather than self-interest. By philosophy, I mean concerns about whether an innovation represents good public management or good public policy in a particular area. Part 2 of this book contains a sample of doctrinal disputes about public management, educational and environmental policy, and the nature of policing, among other lively topics. The significance of the disputes underscore, again, the importance of tactics.

  In cases of conflicting doctrines, the most appropriate tactics to overcome opposition involve persuasion. When criticism is motivated by self-interest, accommodation may also be an appropriate response. For example, legitimate objections, such as the front-line workers' mistrust of labor-saving technology and outsourcing, or the middle-managers initial rejection of empowerment initiatives, must be accommodated. When self-interested critics are not seen as legitimate, such as the owners of crack houses objecting to rigorous housing code enforcement, the public interest will preclude accommodation.

- Fourth, innovators must recognize that even when a program has made great progress, there is more to do. Integrity in innovation demands honesty about what one has already and has not yet accomplished. The innovators in this sample continue to live with over 40 percent of the obstacles they have identified—and with ongoing criticism. Finally, the innovators themselves identify the

shortcomings within their innovations: unstable funding, constrained resources, centrifugal forces threatening partnerships,
dissonance between innovative programs and the traditional bureaucracies that surround them, and even the necessity of fine-
tuning.

- Fifth, innovators will also want to scan the environment and plan
  for the future. The Ford-KSG innovators were aware of environmental trends, such as population growth, changes in the incidence
  of social problems, major policy shifts, technological change, the
  overall fiscal posture of their governments, and how these trends
  might affect their programs. They had plans about how to extend
  their services if additional resources became available, how to use
  new technologies, how to respond to new policy initiatives, and
  even how to subsume their programs into broader initiatives. The
  future visions that they paint have integrity, that is, flexibility
  and a salutary lack of organizational boundaries or limits. The
  important thing is to continue working creatively on the problems
  that led to the innovations.

5
Financing and Organizing Innovations

Discussion in this chapter concerns the bread and butter issues of financing and organizing public sector innovations. In it, we look at the size of these programs measured in terms of their budgets, the diversity of their funding base, their preferred organizational structures, and their accountability relationships. The observations, though brief, will, it is hoped, yield much practical advice.

FINANCING INNOVATIONS

The Ford-KSG semifinalists were asked about their budgets and financial resources in q. 6 (Appendix). Programs that did not have a majority of state or local government funding were eventually eliminated from the competition. As a result, the sample may underestimate the amount of private sector involvement in state and local government innovation, and therefore also the extent to which Osborne and Gaebler's market-oriented principles apply.

Operating and Capital Budgets

The distribution of answers to the budget question is shown in Table 5-1. Note, however, that in some cases the applicant's description of the program's operating budget is unavailable or unclear. At times, the organization's entire operating budget was given, but not the portion directly applicable to the innovation. Similarly, not all applicants supplied a capital budget. The average capital budget is based on the forty-one applications whose capital budgets could be identified. Some items that would normally be treated as capital in an accrual accounting system, for example, start-up costs or capital equipment, were attributed to the capital budget even if the applicant had included them in the operating budget.

TABLE 5-1 INNOVATIONS' BUDGETS AND SOURCES OF FUNDS
(Entries are in $ × 10⁶; number of cases in parentheses)

	All	IT	OC	EE	P	H	EC	Soc Serv	Educ
					GROUP				
Average operating budget	$5.9 (185)	$4.0 (36)	$25.3 (32)	$1.0 (30)	$3.4 (14)	$1.8 (11)	$.6 (11)	$3.5 (60)	$1.5 (20)
Average capital budget	$5.9 (41)	$6.2 (22)	$.7 (1)	$1.4 (1)	$.2 (2)	$41 (1)	$25.7 (2)	$.4 (7)	$.8 (1)
% of group with public financing of operating budget	85%	79%	84%	76%	94%	93%	83%	97%	91%
% of group with user fees toward operating budget	24%	30%	32%	41%	6%	36%	33%	8%	19%
Average user fee revenue	$4.7 (38)	$1.7 (7)	$16.6 (9)	$.9 (10)	$.02 (1)	$.4 (5)	$.09 (3)	$1.3 (4)	$2.9 (3)
Average % of operating budget from user fees	58% (38)	90% (7)	46% (9)	68% (10)	9% (1)	42% (4)	47% (3)	52% (4)	38% (3)
% of group with donations to operating budget	32%	9%	24%	24%	31%	43%	50%	40%	62%
Average donation revenue	$.2 (46)	$.3 (2)	$.4 (7)	$.2 (7)	$.5 (2)	$.1 (2)	$.1 (5)	$.1 (21)	$.3 (8)
Average % of operating budget from donations	24% (46)	44% (2)	31% (7)	30% (7)	30% (2)	85% (1)	22% (5)	16% (21)	23% (8)

IT (information technology), OC (organizational change), EE (environment, energy), P (policing), H (housing, neighborhoods), EC (economic development, transportation), Soc Serv (social services), Educ (education).

The average operating budget for the 185 cases that reported specific operating budgets totaled $5.9 million; the average capital budget (forty-one cases) was also $5.9 million. These are not large operating or capital budgets. The only outlier for average operating budgets was in the organizational change area. There, the average operating budget was $25 million because these innovations often affect entire organizations, and thus the budgets are for entire organizations. Organizations involved in information technology, the one area with a large number of capital projects (twenty-two of forty-seven cases), had relatively small capital budgets. The average capital budget in this area was $6.2 million, which is much less than the cost of a large information system. Such programs are, therefore, relatively small-scale projects, which is consistent with our previous finding that innovation is usually initiated by career civil servants at the middle management and front-line levels.

Government Appropriations and Alternatives

Regular government appropriations were by far the most popular form of financing innovations; 85 percent of the applications preferred this source, and in the policing, housing, social services, and education areas, the preference rose to over 90 percent. Regular appropriations were most frequent in programs providing a pure public good, such as policing; or in programs intended to help low income individuals, such as social services.

Alternatives to regular appropriations were user fees and private sector donations or grants. User fees were observed in 24 percent of all applications—far less common than public sector financing, but still reasonably frequent. When the beneficiaries of programs could be identified or when businesses or the general population were the beneficiaries, user fees were used more frequently. When there were user fees, revenue totaled on average $4.7 million, or about 58 percent of the operating budget. In short, if an innovation was supported by user fees, the user fees paid for a large share, or even most, of the total costs. The data demonstrate that Osborne and Gaebler's theme of enterprising government, at least as operationalized through user fees, is evident in our sample.

The second alternative to public sector appropriations is private sector donations (cash, grants, in-kind, or volunteers) for both operating and capital budgets. Private sector donations were incorporated into operating budgets by 32 percent of all applications, ranging from a low of 9 percent of the budgets in information technology; to over 40 percent in housing, economic development, and social services; and over 60 percent in education. Still, the total private sector contributions were, on average, relatively small, about $200,000.

The last line of table 5-1 shows how much of the total operating budget came, on average, from private sector donations. This datum was calculated by averaging over all applications with private sector donations the percentage of the operating budget accounted for by such donations. The result (24%) is much larger than it would have been had we simply divided the average donation ($200,000) by the average operating budget ($5.9 million) because donations often account for small percentages of large operating budgets and large percentages of small operating budgets. When private sector donations—often corporate or foundation philanthropy—are a small part of a large operating budget, they help the program but are not crucial to its existence. When donations are a large part of small operating budgets, they may be crucial to the program's survival, especially if they are provided as seed money.

I did not include private sector contributions to capital budgets in Table 5-1 because the number of programs with identifiable capital budgets is very small. Capital budgets do illustrate, however, on a case-by-case basis, a variety of private sector contributions. The Baltimore Community Development Finance Corporation's operating budget of $1 million was almost entirely funded by the city. It made $41 million in subsidized loans for low and moderate income housing, with $10 million provided by the city and $31 million by financial institutions. It is therefore a classic case of what Osborne and Gaebler call "leveraging the market."

Programs in the information technology area received hardware or software donations from manufacturers. For example, Hewlett-Packard provided the hardware for Santa Monica's (1993) Public Electronic Network, an early e-mail discussion group, and IBM paid half of the $1 million development cost of Info/California's electronic kiosks (California Health and Welfare Agency Data Center, 1993). In these cases, the manufacturers were using donations to establish a *competitive advantage* in marketing the technology. Other programs received *charitable donations*. The Indianapolis Campaign for Healthy Babies funded a component of the Wishard Patient Record System by raising $560,000 for a system that would track Medicaid-eligible mothers being treated in Indianapolis hospitals (Wishard Memorial Hospital, 1993). A foundation grant provided startup funding of $46,000 for the first year of the Child Witness to Violence Project, a Boston program that provides counselling for young children who witness domestic violence. In subsequent years, the program has received its funding entirely from state and federal sources, at an annual level of about $75,000 (Boston City Hospital, 1994).

Budgetary data supplied by the Ford-KSG applicants support Osborne and Gaebler's principles of catalytic and market-oriented government. Public sector innovators have convinced the private sector to participate substantially in their innovative programs. More discussion and examples of private sector contributions will be provided in the second part of the book.

THE CHOICE OF ORGANIZATIONAL STRUCTURES

Table 5-2 and Table 5-3 describe the organizational structure and accountability relationships that occur in innovations (Appendix, q. 7). The key structural distinction that emerges is between those innovative programs set up with and those without formal coordinating procedures. Programs without formal coordination usually involve one organization; for example, they are simple line operations or nonprofit corporations. Or they may involve line operations in several organizations. The latter illustrate

TABLE 5-2   ORGANIZATIONAL STRUCTURE OF INNOVATIONS
(Table entries are percentages)

Structure	All	IT	OC	EE	P	H	EC	Soc Serv	Educ
Line operation, one organization	43	43	43	49	44	50	25	43	29
Several line operations	5	9	3	0	0	7	0	11	0
Nonprofit corporation	12	9	14	16	13	7	17	11	24
TOTAL WITHOUT FORMAL COORDINATION	61	60	60	65	56	64	42	65	52
Program coordination in line organization	25	28	11	19	25	14	33	29	38
Program coordination in central agency	7	9	14	8	0	0	8	5	5
Interdepartmental committee	7	6	11	5	6	21	17	6	5
TOTAL WITH FORMAL COORDINATION	39	43	35	32	31	36	58	40	48
Other	4	2	8	3	12	0	0	5	5
N	217	47	37	37	16	14	12	65	21

N = number of observations

TABLE 5-3   ACCOUNTABILITY RELATIONSHIP OF INNOVATIONS
(Table entries are percentages)

	GROUP								
Relationship	All	IT	OC	EE	P	H	EC	Soc Serv	Educ
Normal channels	71	79	73	68	69	57	58	75	57
Directly to supreme political authority	6	2	11	8	13	7	0	6	5
Board of directors	13	4	14	11	13	36	25	6	29
Advisory committee	27	21	27	19	13	21	58	32	29
Funding source	7	9	3	11	6	0	0	12	0
Other	1	0	3	0	0	0	0	0	0
N	217	47	37	37	16	14	12	65	21

N = number of observations

Lindblom's (1965) model of partisan mutual adjustment, by which organizations are coordinated through negotiation and manipulation, rather than a central authority.

Coordinating Arrangements

Programs having central coordination work through mechanisms such as a program coordinator located in a line organization, a program coordinator located in a central agency (such as the mayor's or governor's office or a budget bureau), or interdepartmental committees. Organizational structure varies little from one policy area to another. Roughly 60 percent of the Ford-KSG innovations were structured without formal coordination (usually these programs are a line operation in a single organization). The remaining 40 percent had a coordinating structure (usually a program coordinator in a line organization).

Accountability

Table 5-3 describes five types of accountability relationships within the innovative programs—and not a great deal of variation in accountability structures among the policy areas. The most frequent form of accountability relationship was the hierarchical reporting relationship through normal channels, which was observed in more than 70 percent of the programs. The next most frequent accountability relationship (27%) was to an advisory committee. Occasionally reports were made to a board of directors (13%), to a funding source (7%), or directly to the supreme political authority, the mayor or governor (6%). Multiple accountability relationships were occasionally observed; for example, a program might report hierarchically and also report to an advisory committee.

The relationships between organization structures and channels of accountability are explored in Table 5-4. Programs structured as line operations in one organization or as line operations in several organizations without formal coordination were treated together and are positively correlated with an accountability relationship through normal channels (r = .36); they are negatively correlated with the other accountability relationships. Nonprofit corporations usually report to a board of directors (r = .63) or a funding source (r = .28); the former is the expected legal structure for nonprofits, and the latter occurs because the public sector often works with nonprofits who receive government contracts.

Programs having formal coordinating structures also have preferred accountability channels. When a program consists of activities in several organizations coordinated by a line organization, it reports to an advisory committee, usually structured to represent the different participating or-

TABLE 5-4   CORRELATIONS BETWEEN ORGANIZATIONAL STRUCTURES AND
ACCOUNTABILITY RELATIONSHIPS
Table Entries are Correlation Coefficients
(Significance Levels Below)

	Accountability Relationship				
	Normal Channels	Direct to Political	Board of Directors	Advisory Committee	Funding Source
ORGANIZATIONAL STRUCTURE					
Line operations	.36 (.0001)	−.15 (.02)	−.22 (.001)	−.08	−.12 (.08)
Nonprofit corporation	−.53 (.0001)	.03	.63 (.0001)	.02	.28 (.0001)
Coordination in line organization	.05	−.09	−.07	.17 (.01)	−.03
Coordination in central agency	.09	.17 (.01)	−.11 (.12)	−.08	−.07
Interdepartmental committee	−.13 (.06)	.16 (.02)	−.11 (.10)	−.01	−.07

Notes: Correlation coefficients less than .1 are not significant at 10%. Significance levels are indicated for correlation coefficients greater than .1.
Line operations includes both line operations in one organization and line operations in several organizations without formal coordination.

ganizations (r = .17). Two types of coordinating structures are correlated with an accountability channel direct to the political level. In the first one, a program that encompasses several organizations is coordinated by a central agency. Such programs are likely to involve issues that the mayor or governor is actively interested in (r = .17). The Wichita groundwater cleanup project is a clear example: the Ford-KSG applicant called this project a "priority of city government and consequently, Chris Cherches, the Wichita City Manager, [had] direct oversight of the project." Two project managers reported directly to Cherches: one, an attorney, dealt with policy; the other, a public information officer, dealt with technical issues. In addition, Cherches's special assistant was a member of a public advisory committee for the project (City of Wichita, Kansas, 1992).

The second type of coordinating structure correlated with an accountability channel direct to the political level is the interdepartmental committee (r = .16). In this case accountability may flow to the political level because of strong political interest or because the political level is required to mediate conflicting departmental interests. The governor of Pennsylvania's Recycled Material Market Development Task Force (Pennsylvania Department of Administration and Public Affairs, 1991) provides an example. The task force, which has representatives from eight departments, is responsible for developing markets to encourage recycling. Its Ford-KSG applicant wrote that the governor had overcome interagency turf battles by appointing agency heads to the task force and the lieutenant governor to its chair. The task force itself then assigned activities to each agency.

One of the main findings in the literature dealing with business policy in the private sector is the linkage between strategy and structure, the notion that organizational strategies influence the choice of organizational structure (Chandler, 1962). Given that the most prevalent characteristic of Ford-KSG innovations was their holistic approach—and their key organizational characteristic, the presence or absence of coordinating mechanisms—I investigated the linkage between strategy and structure by correlating holism with organizational structure. This is shown in Table 5-5.

Holistic innovations that involve the activities of several organizations or provide multiple services to target populations are coordinated by line agencies (r = .16 and r = .15, respectively) or, to a lesser extent, by interdepartmental committees (r= .17 and r = .02, respectively). Similarly, partnerships, either within the public sector or between the public and private sectors, are correlated with coordinating structures—by a line

TABLE 5-5 CORRELATIONS BETWEEN CHARACTERISTICS OF INNOVATIONS AND ORGANIZATIONAL STRUCTURE

Table Entries are Correlation Coefficients
(Significance levels below)

Characteristic of Innovation	Organizational Structure				
	Line Operations	Non-Profit Corporation	Line Agency Coordination	Central Agency Coordination	Interdepartmental Committee
IDENTIFIED BY APPLICANTS					
Holistic—coordinates several organizations	-.19 (.04)	.01	.16 (.02)	-.05	.17 (.01)
Holistic—provides multiple services	-.09	.04	.15 (.02)	-.01	.02
Total holistic	-.19 (.006)	.05	.16 (.02)	.03	.08
Use of private sector	-.17 (.01)	.02	.16 (.02)	-.03	.06
IDENTIFIED BY AUTHOR					
Within public partnership	-.29 (.0001)	.03	.20 (.003)	.03	.15 (.03)
Public private partnership	-.32 (.0001)	.20 (.003)	.18 (.008)	-.01	.14 (.04)
Total partnerships	-.39 (.0001)	.10	.26 (.0001)	-.01	.19 (.005)

Notes: Correlation coefficients less than .1 are not significant at 10%. Significance levels are indicated for correlation coefficients greater than .1.
Line operations includes both line operations in one organization and line operations in several organizations without formal coordination.

agency (r = .20 and r = .18, respectively) or by an interdepartmental committee (r = .15 and r = .14 respectively). Public-private partnerships are also likely to involve nonprofit corporations (r = .20). Innovations using the private sector to achieve public purposes have the same pattern. Though they prefer coordination by line agencies (r = .16); they also accept coordination by interdepartmental committees (r = .06).

The converse of these findings is also true, namely, holistic programs (r = −.19) and partnerships (r = −.39) are not carried out as line operations in one organization or as line operations in several organizations without formal coordination. These statements are not tautological. We could hypothesize that partnerships or holistic programs can exist as line operations in several organizations without formal coordination; indeed, Lindblom (1965) argued that partisan mutual adjustment would often make formal coordination unnecessary. The data reject this hypothesis—and Lindblom's model—in favor of the alternative hypothesis that partnerships or holistic programs do require formal coordinating mechanisms.

Kanter (1988) observed that "indeed, it is the general characteristics of integrative structures that make a difference in terms of encouraging innovation: looser boundaries, crosscutting access, flexible assignments, open communication, and the use of multidisciplinary project teams (p. 178)." Her example of integrative structures was the matrix organization. The Ford-KSG sample was also coded for matrix organizations, but they were hardly ever observed. In addition, the data reveal that much public sector innovation occurs in simple line operations without structural integration. However, when the innovation involved a holistic strategy, integrating mechanisms were used. In other words, our sample supports Kanter's correlation, but reverses her causality.

CONCLUSION

This chapter provides practical advice for managing innovative programs.

- First, user fees can be used to fund programs, especially if the beneficiaries of the programs can be identified and are able to pay.
- Second, the private sector may also be counted on to provide support of various types. Private interests can provide seed grants for demonstration projects and investment funds that are leveraged by the public sector. They may also provide goods in kind, either as a marketing venture (particularly for new technologies) or as donations to a worthy cause. Donations are unlikely to

provide a large proportion of funding, but they can provide discretionary resources whereby a program can improve its service or undertake ongoing innovation.

- Third, accountability relationships should be appropriate to the program's vision. For example, if a number of organizations are involved in delivering a service, the lead agency, that is, the agency responsible for coordination, should establish an advisory committee on which all participant organizations are represented. Or, if there is a very clear political interest in the program, coordination should be handled by a central agency, such as the governor's or mayor's office.

- Fourth, if the innovation is a partnership, or if it calls on various organizations to provide multiple services to clients, a formal coordinating structure would be appropriate. Examples of such structures would be a designated lead agency or an interdepartmental committee. Collaboration across organizational boundaries does not happen naturally; it must be made to happen.

6
Results, Verification, and Replication

The gurus of various management philosophies often say that the model or methodology that they advocate is a journey, not a destination. Nevertheless, the journey will be worthwhile only if the stops en route indicate that the traveler is going in the right direction. This chapter addresses that concern in relation to the Ford-KSG sample of state and local government innovations. First, what measurable outcomes, if any, do Ford-KSG applicants claim they have achieved? Second, how are these outcomes verified? Third, and finally, are there consistent factors underlying the decisions to give awards to some programs and not others; and, if so, are they the same reasons for replicating some programs but not others?

Put differently, is recognition related to performance? If such a relationship or some consistent underlying factors can be found, they can become the necessary guidelines, the touchstone, that sets managers going in the right direction.

ACHIEVING RESULTS

The Ford-KSG semifinalist questionnaire asked applicants to provide at least two years of outcomes based on the three most important measures that they had used to evaluate their success (Appendix, q. 14). Results are shown in Table 6-1: Among other accomplishments, successful innovations provide improved client services, attain goals, boost morale, and reduce costs. Obviously a substantial diversity can be expected when the measures of success are self-selected.

Note that some of the methodologies used to establish these results, namely, formal surveys, experimental designs, and informal expressions of support, have also been coded. In some ways, they appear to add special cogency to the various claims.

TABLE 6-1   RESULTS OF INNOVATIONS
(Table Entries are Percentages)

Result	All	IT	OC	EE	P	H	EC	Soc Serv	Edu
				GROUP					
Goals for program met	70	47	68	81	69	79	75	74	81
Clients using program, demand growing	52	57	49	51	50	50	58	51	48
Improved service or operations	32	57	54	14	38	21	17	34	19
Formal client survey	22	19	16	16	44	21	8	23	33
Reduced cost of providing service	19	25	35	22	0	14	0	20	0
Informal expressions of stake-holder support	19	15	16	27	25	21	17	11	19
Improved morale	8	2	16	0	13	21	0	8	10
Increased revenue	6	8	3	5	0	7	25	2	5
Experimental design	6	6	0	3	6	0	8	11	5
Other	5	6	0	8	0	0	8	5	0
Improved productivity	5	13	8	3	0	0	0	2	5
Too early to tell	2	2	0	0	0	7	0	5	0
Total (%)	246	257	265	230	245	241	216	246	225
N	217	47	37	37	16	14	12	65	21

N = number of observations
IT (information technology), OC (organizational change), EE (environment, energy), P (policing), H (housing, neighborhoods), EC (economic development, transportation), Soc Serv (social services), Educ (education).

Selected Outcomes

Goals fulfillment. The most widely reported outcome—occurring in 70 percent of the applications (and across all policy areas)—was that the program's goals were being met. The only real outlier in this category was information technology; only 47 percent of its programs used this measure.

Program goals were generally set by the program managers; to code them, we (my research assistants and I) looked for a statement of the program's goals, a way of measuring progress toward the goals, and an indication that they had been met or were in the process of being met. We did not consider or judge the appropriateness of the goals or whether they were too demanding or too easy.[1]

Some programs made it their goal to reach a certain percentage of their target population and persuade them to join the program or at least to behave in a certain way. Thus, the Seattle Recycling Program reported that as 78 percent of eligible households in the city were participating in curbside recycling in 1988, the program was on target to meet its next goal: 85 percent participation by 1991. On a much smaller scale, the Baltimore Project's goal was to have 85 percent of all pregnant women in the Sandtown-Winchester district participate in the program, and affirmed that it had met that goal during the program's first year.

Other goals concerned the behavior of people in the program: the goal of the Quincy Model Domestic Abuse Program was to increase the number of batterers who completed a year-long intensive treatment program; the New York City Child Health Clinics was determined to provide comprehensive health care on a "family doctor" model, and measured progress toward that goal by reporting the frequency with which children saw the same physician and the percentage of appointments that were kept. Some programs' goals were measured in terms of discrete events: the San Francisco Bay area Joint Urban Mobility Program measured progress in terms of the completion of multiagency projects, such as developing transferable bus-rail transit tickets. The Florida Marine Spills Analysis System evaluated its performance in terms of the usefulness of the information it provided during an actual oil spill in Tampa Bay in 1993.

Of all the innovative programs in this sample, the one most obviously involved in goal-setting is Oregon Benchmarks, which was specifically designed to articulate a set of goals and ways of measuring progress for the entire state government. Though no other explicitly goal-setting programs appear in the sample, the fact that so many of these innovations established goals and measured their progress toward such goals is consistent with the exhortations of Osborne and Gaebler (1992), Behn (1994), and other writers who urge government to become more results oriented.

Client services. The second most commonly claimed outcome is that clients are using a program or demand for its services is growing. This result was observed in 52 percent of the sample, again with little variance among the policy areas. Thus, the Quincy Model Domestic Abuse Program reported that an increasing number of women, including many nonresidents of Quincy, were initiating court actions; Oregon Benchmarks noted that an increasing number of state agencies had incorporated Benchmarks into their planning and budgeting process between 1991 and 1995; and the Orange County Child Abuse Service Team said that it had planned to conduct 200 examinations in its first year, but it had actually conducted 700 during that time.

Improved service or operation. Almost 32 percent of all applications said that their programs had improved a service or operation. Responses for information technology and organizational change (57% and 54%, respectively) were far higher than the mean. Generally, improvements in physical measures of services were coded under this category. For example, the New York City Bureau of Motor Equipment reported, that its In-House Research and Development Network successfully reduced the number of city garbage collection trucks that were out of service on any given day. In 1979, 46 percent of all trucks were out of service; by 1991 that percentage had dropped to 17 percent. Info/California indicated as its measure of improved service that 56 percent of the use of its kiosks occurred outside normal business hours, representing an increase in convenience, hence better service. The Wishard Hospital observed that Medicaid recipients got better preventive care, including more flu shots, after its patient record system was installed. And even more impressive: their winter hospitalizations for flu decreased by a third.

Reduced costs. The cost of providing services, which decreased in 19 percent of the Ford-KSG sample, can be distinguished from improved service because it refers to lower costs for existing services only. An innovation that improves service and lowers cost would be coded under both headings. The cost of providing service was reduced most frequently in the information technology and organizational change areas: for example, the Chicago Parking Enforcement Program decreased its running costs by $5 million; the Wishard Hospital reported that having patient data readily available resulted in fewer emergency room medical tests being ordered and shorter hospital stays; and the Seattle Recycling Program reported that it had achieved sufficient scale to make recycling less expensive than sending garbage to a landfill.

Morale. Improved morale was observed in 8 percent of the sample. For example, the Los Angeles County Telecommuting Program reported that a staff survey indicated that 87 percent of supervisors thought that morale had improved.

Productivity. Productivity was defined by applicants as labor productivity, as opposed to more sophisticated measures of total factor productivity. In the Ford-KSG sample, productivity increases were a notable outcome for 5 percent of the sample. The Los Angeles Telecommuting Program, in a case study of the County Assessor's Office, found that telecommuters were processing work 64 percent faster than office workers, with the result that productivity for the unit increased by 34 percent. Further, its survey of supervisors found that 95 percent felt that telecommuters had either increased or maintained their level of productivity.

Increased revenue. In 6 percent of all cases, the innovations resulted in improved revenue or—for those innovations operating on a commercial basis—profitability. For example, the Chicago Parking Enforcement Program reported that stronger enforcement led to increased revenue.

Client surveys. Fully 22 percent of the applications incorporated a formal client survey in their evaluation process. A distinction can be made between an improved service and a survey. The former is a physical measure; the latter a sign that this improvement was indeed felt by the clients. Client surveys were performed most frequently (44%) as an element in community policing and other policing initiatives, and in education (33%). Examples include the following: the St. Petersburg, Florida, Police Department survey of citizen attitudes about the police; the Massachusetts Office of the Attorney General's statistics on the nature and results of conflicts mediated by the Student Conflict Resolution Experts Program and the students' evaluations of the program's training efforts; the Info/California and Arizona QuickCourt programs' surveys of kiosk users; and the Portland Landlord Training Program survey of landlords (six months after their training program) to determine what changes they had made in their property management activity as a result of the training.

Informal expressions of support. In contrast to formal client surveys, informal expressions of stakeholder support were reported by 19 percent of the applications. At first glance this method may appear too subjective to be included as a measure of achievement, particularly if it were the sole outcome measure. However, of the forty-one cases where this support was observed, in forty it was observed together with at least one other more objective outcome measure. For example, the Student Conflict Resolution Experts Program, in addition to the statistical measures previously noted, collected anecdotal reports from student mediators about how they had used their conflict resolution skills to extricate themselves from difficult situations. Similarly, the Arizona QuickCourt System, in addition to presenting the results of user surveys, reported that the judicial and legal communities were "vocal in their support" for the kiosks.

Experimental design. Another 6 percent of the Ford-KSG sample used an experimental design method to measure results. Some programs, particularly those in the social services area, compared the performance of program participants with that of a control group. These tests were usually done as quasi-experimental designs; the programs did not seek the nearly unattainable ideal of a scientific experimental design in which participants do not know whether they are in the treatment or the control group.[2]

In other instances ("Other," Table 6-1), the applicants conducted before and after comparisons. The Wishard Hospital surveyed the quality of medical care received by its target group before and after various components of its record system were extended into the community and, in some cases, measured impacts by means of randomized controlled trials. Similarly, the Los Angeles Department of Transportation compared traffic delay before and after implementing its Automatic Transportation Surveillance and Control System and also measured speed and delays for a sample of drivers who did not know whether or not the system was in operation.

Finally, in 2 percent of the sample, the applicants admitted that it was too early to determine the outcomes of the innovation. Given that outcomes are one of the four criteria used to determine the Ford-KSG finalists, such admissions were likely to prevent these applicants from receiving further consideration. Presumably, the small number of applicants for whom it was too early to have results who had nevertheless advanced to the semifinals had done so because they were truly on the leading edge, with high scores on the novelty factor.

The question about results again focuses our attention on the role of integrity in innovation. The vast majority of innovators developed quantitative measures of their results. Very few provided only qualitative measures or reported that it was too early to provide results. Programs in all areas used formal client surveys, and many are beginning to use sound evaluation methodologies in an effort to compare states of the world with and without their programs.

The Most Important Achievement

Ford-KSG applicants were next asked to identify their program's single most important achievement (Appendix, q. 15). The answer to this question was often a repetition of one of the outcome measures identified in the previous question. However, outcome measures deal with the impact of an innovation on its target population. On the other hand, *achievement* is a much broader term than *outcome*; it encompasses the programs' effects on client populations and on the organizations or individuals involved in running the program. More than 50 percent of the applicants felt that the most important achievement of their innovations concerned the latter. This question enabled these local heroes to make their personal agendas explicit. Results are shown in Table 6-2.

As previously noted, many applicants (44% of the sample) repeated one of their program's outcomes as its most important achievement. The most frequently cited achievement that was not a restatement was that the innovation had permitted individuals or groups to work together or combine their efforts. This answer appeared in 17 percent of the sample. Not surprisingly, it was cited most frequently by programs involving partnerships among public sector organizations or between the public and private sectors.[3] For example, the Pennsylvania Job Centers counted placements and referrals as outcomes but listed its achievement as the "coordination between community-based organizations and governmental agencies to provide employment and training services" (Pennsylvania Department of Labor and Industry, 1992). Similarly, the Bay area JUMP Start program cited the implementation of transportation projects as its

TABLE 6-2   MOST IMPORTANT ACHIEVEMENT OF INNOVATION
(Table Entries are Percentages)

	GROUP								
Achievement	All	IT	OC	EE	P	H	EC	Soc Serv	Edu
Repeated results	44	57	38	41	38	50	17	40	43
Enabled individuals or groups to work together	17	15	19	22	0	29	25	14	24
Operationalized a theoretical model	16	4	14	11	13	7	25	25	29
People educated about a problem	11	2	5	14	25	14	25	11	19
Implemented innovation well	8	8	14	11	13	0	0	11	0
Other	6	6	5	3	6	0	0	6	5
Initiated a dialogue	3	2	5	3	6	0	17	3	0
Innovation used in unforeseen ways	2	0	5	3	0	0	0	2	5
Getting technology to work	1	4	0	3	0	0	0	2	0
Total (%)	108	98	105	111	101	100	109	114	125
N	217	47	37	37	16	14	12	65	21

N = number of observations

outcome but referred to "the proliferation of new interagency alliances" as its achievement.

The next most frequently reported achievement—in 16 percent of the applications—was that an innovation had operationalized a theoretical model. This achievement was discussed in chapter 3 as one of the determinants of comprehensive planning. The Baltimore Project, for example, described a reduction in infant mortality and high enrolment and retention levels as its results, but identified its achievement as having operationalized a model whereby neighborhood residents—without prerequisites in terms of work history or educational attainments—could be trained to carry out outreach and case management for pregnant women. Minnesota's Consolidated Chemical Dependency Treatment Fund's most important achievement was operationalizing a "dollar to follow the client" model entailing competition among treatment programs. Both of these programs (as the regression analysis in chapter 3 would have predicted) were established as the result of comprehensive planning, rather than a groping process.

Other applicants (11% of the sample) claimed that their most important achievement was educating people about, or sensitizing them to, a problem or a way of responding to a problem. Maine's Video Display Terminal Safety in the Workplace Program, a course designed to reduce work-related illnesses among office workers, measured its results in terms of operators and supervisors trained and workstations evaluated and improved. Its most important achievement, however, was heightening overall awareness throughout state government of workplace health and safety issues in an office setting (Maine Department of Risk Management, 1991).

Another 8 percent of the sample claimed that their most important achievement was implementing the innovation well. For example, the Chicago Parking Enforcement Program measured its results in terms of lower costs and increased revenues. Its most important achievement, given Chicago's history of machine politics, in general, and indifferent enforcement of parking regulations, in particular, was something else:

> We did exactly what we said we were going to do. The new, technically innovative, program was implemented on schedule and within budget. It has worked smoothly from the citizen's point of view, and [the] press has been very positive (City of Chicago, Illinois, 1991).

Another 3 percent of the sample reported that their innovations had "initiated a dialogue." For example, Santa Monica's Public Electronic

Network wrote that its electronic dialogue about homelessness had given rise to a program to provide showers, lockers, and washing machines to homeless people. Similarly, the Bay Area JUMP Start program thought that an important reason for bringing transportation agencies together is that it gives community and environmental groups a focal point for a public dialogue about transportation issues.

In 2 percent of the sample, the achievement was that an innovation could be used in unforeseen ways. This achievement is no doubt associated with programs in which the innovation process was characterized as being driven by groping along rather than planning (see chapter 3). For example, after the New York City Bureau of Motor Equipment began to improve the quality of its own work, it realized that it could also improve performance by working with manufacturers to improve equipment design. Once the New York City Child Health Clinics began to treat large numbers of children on an ongoing basis, they developed a program to deal with asthma, the most frequent chronic medical problem of childhood. As predicted by the regression analysis in chapter 3, both these programs were established as the result of groping, rather than comprehensive plans.

Finally, only 1 percent of the sample listed getting a technology to work as an achievement. Even in the information technology area, this outcome was infrequently noted (4%). This finding suggests that local heroes who introduce new technologies are generally confident that the processes or equipment will work, and are not surprised, therefore, when they do. Chapter 7 looks more closely at these local heroes and their attitudes.

VERIFYING THE INNOVATIONS

The Ford-KSG awards program set out four different ways to test whether the innovations were achieving the results that the applicants claimed they were. First, they asked the semifinalists if their programs had ever been formally evaluated or audited by an independent organization, and if so, to provide information so that the evaluator or auditor could be contacted (Appendix q. 17). The results are shown in Table 6-3.

The most interesting and, it would appear, troubling answer to this question is that almost 40 percent of the sample had not been formally evaluated. Here, however, there was substantial variation among the policy areas: housing programs were not often formally evaluated (71% of its programs lacked formal evaluations); by contrast, programs in the social services and education areas often had formal evaluations, and in

TABLE 6-3   FORMAL INDEPENDENT EVALUATION OR AUDIT
(Table Entries are Percentages)

Type of Evaluation	All	IT	OC	EE	P	H	EC	Soc Serv	Edu
				GROUP					
None	38	47	46	43	44	71	33	28	14
Policy analysis/evaluation by consultants	25	34	27	19	31	7	33	20	29
Financial audit	20	11	24	22	6	21	17	22	38
Central agency evaluation	14	11	11	19	6	7	8	17	14
Academic research	12	6	8	5	13	0	8	22	19
Total (%)	109	109	116	108	106	106	99	109	114
N	217	47	37	37	16	14	12	65	21

N = number of observations

fact, only 28 and 14 percent, respectively, of these programs were not formally evaluated. In some instances, organizations did their own customer surveys and cost analyses to determine the results of their programs; nevertheless, there is always added value in engaging an outsider to ensure that the methodology of such studies is rigorous and unbiased.

When evaluations were done, the most popular form was a policy analysis or program evaluation undertaken by consultants. This route was taken by 25 percent of the entire sample and at a similar frequency in most policy areas. About 20 percent of the sample had financial audits. However, a financial audit is more likely to ask whether money is being spent for the purposes for which it was allocated, rather than more important evaluative questions such as whether the money achieved its goals. Finally, in 14 percent of all cases, an evaluation had been conducted by a central agency, such as a central budget office, and in 12 percent of all cases, the innovation was the subject of academic research.

Do certain types of outcomes lend themselves more readily to certain types of formal independent evaluations? We can explore this question by correlating the responses to this question with the applicants' own measures of outcomes and achievements. And here, we find some significant results. There is a simple correlation coefficient of .18 between doing a formal client survey and engaging a consultant to do a policy evaluation. As noted previously, while some programs conducted their own surveys, programs were more likely to conduct such surveys by using a consultant.

When the innovators indicate that their achievement involved providing an opportunity to test a theory, their answer is strongly correlated with evaluation conducted by academic researchers (.32), significantly correlated with central agency evaluation (.11), and significantly but *negatively* correlated with no formal evaluation (-.16). These results indicate that the applicants' claims about the importance of applying theory must be taken seriously, given that their theories are actually being tested by outside evaluators.

The Ford-KSG's second way of verifying the applicants' claims was to determine whether their innovations had received any awards or media attention (Appendix, qq. 20 and 21). Table 6-4 shows the answers to both questions. Almost two-thirds of the applicants have won an award, a finding that was consistent across all policy areas. I was, in fact, quite astonished to discover the existence of so many different innovation or quality awards. Some were defined geographically, some by agency, some by function (for example, an award for human resources programs), and some for personal achievement. Almost half the innovations had also received some media attention, with the highest percentage being among social service innovations (65 percent of applications) and the lowest among information technology innovations (only 26 percent of applications). The latter is consistent with the tendency, first noted in the discussion of local heroes in chapter 3, for information technology innovations to be low-profile. Finally, "none" refers to those innovations (21 percent of the entire sample) that had received neither awards nor media attention.

The third verification method used by the Ford-KSG examiners was to determine whether the applicants' innovations had been replicated or if they were potentially replicable (Appendix, q. 19). During the analysis, we coded this statement, not on the basis of the applicants' own estimates of potential replicability but on expressions of interest or actual replication

TABLE 6-4   AWARDS, MEDIA ATTENTION RECEIVED BY INNOVATIONS
(Table Entries are Percentages)

				GROUP					
Awards or Attention	All	IT	OC	EE	P	H	EC	Soc Serv	Educ
Any award	63	64	57	68	69	43	33	66	71
Media attention	46	26	41	35	44	43	33	65	52
None	21	26	24	19	15	36	42	15	14
N	217	47	37	37	16	14	12	65	21

N = number of observations

by others. Both expressions of interest and actual replication were classified geographically.

The most frequent expression of interest occurs on the national level (54%), followed by nearby interest (27%), and international interest (14%). Any interest is the union of all three forms of interest, and so taken, 65 percent of the sample had experienced some interest. Actual replication happened most frequently at the local level (27%), then at the national level (24%), and very infrequently at the international level (1%). In all, 42 percent of the entire sample claimed some form of replication. Only 18 percent of the entire sample experienced no expressions of interest in either replication or actual replication. It is not surprising that expressions of interest exceeded actual replications, since interest precedes, but does not always lead to, replication. International interest and replication appear to be quite low—perhaps because there are denser networks of practitioners nationally than internationally or perhaps differences in the nature of problems and institutions make international replication less likely. In any event, Table 6-5 indicates a substantial amount of interest in and replication of these innovations—even before they had received Ford-KSG awards. The Ford-KSG awards themselves could be expected to increase both interest and replication.

A fourth and final way to evaluate innovations is to determine their sustainability, that is, to note whether they are still in operation. Failure

TABLE 6-5   REPLICATION OF INNOVATIONS
(Table Entries are Percentages)

	GROUP								
Extent of Replication	All	IT	OC	EE	P	H	EC	Soc Serv	Edu
Nearby interest	27	26	35	32	25	29	25	22	24
National interest	54	62	70	57	69	21	42	49	62
International interest	14	23	22	19	31	0	8	5	0
Any interest	65	72	76	65	75	43	58	60	71
Nearby replication	27	28	19	30	38	21	25	27	29
National replication	24	36	16	35	38	7	17	15	29
International replication	1	2	3	3	0	0	0	2	0
Any replication	42	51	32	51	63	29	25	39	43
No interest or replication	18	13	19	5	6	57	8	25	10
Total (%)	272	313	295	297	345	197	208	244	268
N	217	47	37	37	16	14	12	65	21

N = number of observations

to pass this test is one of the points raised by Osborne and Gaebler's critics (particularly Winnick, 1993), just as it was raised some years earlier by critics of Peters and Waterman (1982). The latter group seemed particularly to enjoy pointing out instances when any of America's so-called best-run companies went bankrupt.

Notwithstanding its importance, measuring for sustainability would have gone beyond my opportunistic research design. It would have involved an additional survey of the 217 programs in my sample. Such cases would have been still more difficult to trace. Therefore, another route has been taken. The Ford-KSG awards staff have measured the sustainability of the ten winners each year the awards have been given.[4]

Sustainability results are shown in Table 6-6. I find it particularly impressive that almost 92 percent of the award-winning programs are still in operation. A knowledge of organizational ecology would lead one to expect that the survival rate would be lowest for the oldest programs, and this is in fact the case for winners in 1986, the first year of the program. Survival rates for the other early years are surprisingly high.

Taken together, these different verification measures indicate that the results achieved by most of the Ford-KSG semifinalists have been verified by external evaluators, by peer review (i.e., awards) and media attention, by being replicated, and by their continued existence. An innovator with integrity would seek verification in all these ways and would be proud to have achieved it.

TABLE 6-6   SUSTAINABILITY OF FORD-KSG AWARD WINNERS

	WINNERS' STATUS AS OF DECEMBER, 1996	
Year Award Won	Number in Operation	Number Not Operating
1986	6	4
1987	10	0
1988	9	1
1990	8	2
1991	10	0
1992	10	0
1993	9	1
1994	10	0
1995	15	0
TOTAL	87	8

Percentage of Total in Operation = 91.6%
Source: Walters, 1996c.

DETERMINANTS OF AWARDS AND REPLICATION

Two of the verification measures used in the preceding analysis are inter-related. That is, replication is a factor in determining which innovations win awards, and innovations that win awards receive attention and pub-licity that increase the likelihood of their being replicated. The judges of innovation awards do not, however, choose winners at random, but on the basis of how persuasively an applicant makes the case that his or her program embodies the characteristics the award intends to recognize. Thus, we would expect that applications that have produced well-docu-mented outcomes would be most likely both to win awards and to be replicated. Put differently, if we assume that what economists call "ratio-nal expectations" exist in the market for both innovation awards and for replication, then award judges and potential imitators would be looking for innovations that achieve results and document these results convincingly.

Given this rational expectations hypothesis, I tested the determinants of both awards and replication in multiple regression analyses. The results are presented in Table 6-7a and b.[5]

The first two equations are efforts to explain which innovations receive awards. The dependent variable is defined as having received any award (the first line in Table 6-4). The two outcome variables that have a statistically significant influence on winning any innovation award are (1) growing demand for the program's services, which increases the probability of winning an award by 12 to 14 percent; and (2) reduced cost, which increases the probability by 16 or 17 percent. Three variables indicating the strength of the evidence are also statistically significant, and with the expected signs. Thus, having a formal survey increases the probability of winning an award by 18 percent; using an experimental design increases it by 26 to 29 percent, and having no formal evaluation *decreases* the probability of winning an award by 19 to 21 percent.

I also used both any actual replication (the second last row in Table 6-5) and any interest in replication (the fourth row in Table 6-5) as indepen-dent variables. Interest in replication is not significantly different from zero but actual replication—the real thing—is positive and significant. This correlation suggests that innovation award judges put more weight on actual behavior than expressions of intent. Because of the simultaneity between awards and replication, I omitted replication as an independent variable in the second equation. In that equation, the coefficients on all the other independent variables are virtually unchanged.

TABLE 6-7a   REGRESSION ANALYSIS OF AWARDS AND REPLICATION
LINEAR REGRESSIONS

Dependent Variable	Any Award	Any Award	Actual Replication	Actual Replication
Independent variables				
Intercept	.50	.54	.29	.37
	(6.6, .0001)	(7.5, .0001)	(4.1, .0001)	(6.8, .0001)
Formal survey	.18	.18	—	—
	(2.3, .02)	(2.3, .02)		
Experimental design	.26	.29	.23	.26
	(1.9, .06)	(2.1, .04)	(1.6, .11)	(1.8, .07)
Growing demand	.12	.14	.15	.16
	(1.9, .06)	(2.2, .03)	(2.2, .02)	(2.5, .01)
Reduced cost	.16	.17	—	—
	(2.0, .05)	(2.1, .04)		
No formal evaluation	−.19	−.21	−.11	−.14
	(3.0, .004)	(3.1, .002)	(1.5, .13)	2.0, .05)
Any interest	.02	.02	—	—
	(.30, .77)	(.26, .79)		
Any actual replication	.12	—	—	—
	(1.8, .07)			
Any award	—	—	.13	—
			(1.8, .07)	
R^2	.14	.12	.08	.06

The third and fourth equations are efforts to explain whether the innovations have been replicated anywhere. The results are similar to the two equations explaining awards. One outcome variable, growing demand, is significant; it increases the probability of an innovation being replicated by 15 or 16 percent. Two variables indicating the strength of the evidence are also significant: using an experimental design increases the probability of an innovation being replicated by 23 to 26 percent and having no formal evaluation decreases the probability of an innovation being replicated by 11 to 14 percent. Receiving any innovation award increases the probability of replication by 13 percent. Because of the simultaneity between awards and replication, I omitted awards as an independent variable in the fourth equation; the coefficients on the other variables were virtually unchanged, as was the case in the comparison of the first and second equation. Finally, it is interesting to note that the coefficients for experimental design, growing demand, and no formal

TABLE 6-7b   REGRESSION ANALYSIS OF AWARDS AND REPLICATION
LOGIT REGRESSIONS

Dependent Variable	Any Award	Any Award	Actual Replication	Actual Replication
Independent variables				
Intercept	−.06	.13	−.92	−.55
	(.04, .85)	(.16, .69)	(8.2, .004)	(5.3, .02)
Formal survey	.88	.85		
	(5.0, .03)	(4.8, .03)	—	—
Experimental design	1.8	1.95	.98	1.1
	(2.8, .09)	(3.3, .07)	(2.3, .13)	(3.0, .08)
Growing demand	.60	.68	.65	.71
	(3.6, .06)	(4.9, .03)	(5.0, .03)	(6.1, .01)
Reduced cost	.80	.80		
	(3.7, .05)	(3.9, .05)	—	—
No formal evaluation	−.88	−.93	−.47	−.60
	(7.9, .01)	(9.2, .003)	(2.3, .13)	(3.9, .05)
Any interest	.06	.08		
	(.04, .88)	(.06, .80)	—	—
Any actual replication	.59			
	(3.4, .07)	—	—	—
Any award			.5	
	—	—	(3.3, .07)	—

evaluation are similar both for awards (the first and second equations) and for replication (the third and fourth).

Table 6-7b repeats the regressions for the logit specification. The results are very similar to the linear regressions shown in Table 6-7a. The same variables are significant (or insignificant); the coefficients on the other independent variables are not affected when replication is omitted from the equation explaining awards and vice versa; and the coefficients for experimental design, growing demand, and no formal evaluation are similar in the equations explaining awards and in the equations explaining replication.

These regressions lead to an important conclusion: the processes of replication and award-giving display a great degree of rationality. ʾnnovations that produce outcomes, such as growing demand or reduced ʾost, are more likely to win awards and be replicated. Innovations that ʾroduce strong evidence of their outcomes, through experimental design, formal surveys, or formal evaluations are more likely to win awards and be replicated.

CONCLUSION

The evidence presented in this chapter should speak clearly to public sector innovators.

- First, the journey toward innovation may properly begin by setting goals. In part, this message is a standard one based on the psychological literature on goal-setting. Goals focus attention, enable groups and individuals to evaluate their performance, and stimulate effort (Locke and Latham, 1984). The importance of goal-setting is not, however, an abstract message; the vast majority of innovators—70 percent of the programs in this sample—had some kind of goal.

  The goals varied by the type of program, but they still had goals. The goals these programs set included: increasing the demand for the program and/or reaching a certain percentage of a target population; improving the health, education, safety, or some other aspect of the well-being of that target population; improving some measure of service (e.g., frequency, convenience, certainty) for a target population; reducing the cost of providing a service; increasing revenue for programs that operate on the basis of user fees; and improving the morale and/or productivity of public servants.

- Second, innovators must decide early to use a rigorous or formal evaluation to determine how well their programs are doing. Surveys, experimental or quasi-experimental designs, program or environmental audits are typical of such procedures. But others are available, and the one chosen should be appropriate to the nature of the program. In addition, an unbiased outsider should always be involved in the evaluative process.

  Evaluation has both intrinsic and extrinsic benefits. An intrinsic benefit is to determine with more certainty whether the program is achieving its goals and to help provide "mid-course correction." In a world of constrained public sector resources, we can expect that funding agencies will demand evaluation, especially for innovative programs.

The extrinsic reason for evaluation is that programs that are formally evaluated, especially if the formal evaluations are done by outsiders, are more likely to be replicated and win innovation awards. Innovation award judges and practitioners are perhaps skeptics by nature, like citizens from the "show me" state of Missouri; they ask local heroes the by now classic questions: "show me the evidence," and "where's the beef?"

- Third, an important message emerges from the differences between the programs' outcomes and the local heroes' identification of their achievements. Achieving the program's goals—the destination—is essential. How these goals are achieved—the journey—is also important; the local heroes took pride in a number of aspects of the journey, such as enabling people and organizations to work together, putting a theory into practice, educating people about a problem or initiating a dialogue, and using their innovation in unforeseen ways.

- Fourth, the evidence shows that innovations are both replicable and sustainable. Almost half the innovations in this sample had been replicated *before* they were semifinalists, finalists, or winners of the Ford-KSG awards. Presumably, after winning the competition, the number replicated and the frequency of replication increased. Between 1986 and 1997, the Ford-KSG program honored ninety-five innovative programs; 87 or 92 percent of these programs are still in operation. The evidence is cumulative and encouraging, and concerns both replication and sustainability: these programs are surviving, and they are making a difference.

*   *   *

This chapter completes the first section of *Integrating with Integrity*. It completes, that is, our concentration on characteristics that can be gleaned from the entire sample of state and local government innovations. We turn now to the discussion of instances in which one or more of the policy areas stood out from the entire sample. As we explore the sources and implications of these exceptions, our goal will be to develop in finer detail our images of what exactly it means to innovate in different policy areas.

PART 2

On Being an Innovator

The characteristics of innovation presented in the preceding chapters were drawn from programs spanning the entire field of public sector management. In the chapters that follow, we will revisit these characteristics in, and probe more deeply into, specific policy areas. Public sector managers tend to develop their careers in specific areas; though they may be interested in public management innovation in general, they are probably more interested in innovations of a particular kind. Accordingly, the chapters that follow address six types of public management innovation. I will begin with the two most general types of innovation: information technology and organizational change. Though each is a discrete policy field with its own proper content, information technology and organizational change innovation also occur in other policy areas. The other four policy areas are energy and the environment; policing, housing, and economic development; social services; and education. The uniqueness of the different policy types was foreshadowed in the tables in the first part of the book, in which the results for one area were often very different from the others.

I begin each chapter by categorizing the innovations that are currently at work within that specific policy area. These introductory sketches are, in fact, short outlines of the quintessential shape of particular programs and provide a sense of direction—they let us know where the innovations in a specific policy area are tending. The bibliographic references specify the identity of the organization or agency in which the innovation occurred. Readers who want to follow a particular innovation more closely can use these references to contact the organizations or agencies involved for additional information.

The chapters then profile the local heroes in more depth. Here, I will present each one against the background and defining features of the area in which they work and its differences relative to the entire sample. For example, the local hero in information technology will likely be a front-line worker or middle manager with technical expertise; the initiator of organizational change will probably be a director or agency head. Once the setting is established, however, my focus will be on the unique challenges faced by these innovators. Partners and opponents alike are among these challenges, which include the innovators' response to the roles of private sector corporations and individual volunteers; the management of interorganizational cooperation; the use of theories as inspiration for programs; and the most frequent types of resistance to change. The chapters then present examples of the results these innovations have achieved and conclude with advice to practitioners and other potential innovators in that specific policy area.

As statistical analysis was a key tool in chapters 1 through 6, so chapters 7 through 12 lean heavily on qualitative analysis. In these chapters we will focus on the narratives contained in the Ford-KSG semifinalist questionnaire and the experts' site visit reports, where applicable. The latter are available for each of the twenty-five Ford-KSG finalists chosen each year.

DISTINGUISHING POLICY AREAS

How do the different policy areas differ from one another? Two tables, based on responses to the Ford-KSG questionnaire address this issue (Appendix, q. 5). Table I-1 shows that the areas serve a diversity of target populations. Information technology initiatives most often reach the general population, businesses, and government bodies; however, some are targeted at low income groups and the young. Until recently, access to the information highway was assumed to depend on income and education. But innovation in information technology may change this perception as some programs are providing access for those who cannot provide it for themselves. Organizational change initiatives have a wide variety of targets, from the general population to institutions and occasionally to public servants (the "other" category observed in 22% percent of the sample). Environment and energy initiatives are most often

Target Population	All	IT	OC	EE	P	H	EC	Soc Serv	Educ
					GROUP				
General population	29	45	30	51	50	36	42	6	5
Businesses	15	9	16	38	6	21	42	2	10
Government bodies	9	15	22	16	0	0	8	2	0
Nonprofit institutions	4	2	14	3	0	0	0	0	19
High risk individuals	17	4	0	8	19	0	0	34	29
Low income individuals	23	23	8	3	25	64	0	40	19
Young people	21	11	14	0	6	0	0	40	81
Old people	3	2	3	0	0	0	0	6	0
People with disabilities	3	0	0	0	6	0	0	9	0
People with dysfunctions	5	2	3	0	0	0	0	17	5
Other	13	3	22	5	6	7	8	15	5
Total (%)	141	116	132	124	118	128	100	171	173
N	217	47	37	37	16	14	12	65	21

Notes: N = number of observations.
General population includes groups that form a large proportion of population (e.g. drivers), business includes professionals, non-profit institutions include hospitals and schools. IT (information technology), OC (organizational change), EE (environment, energy), P (policing), H (housing, neighborhoods), EC (economic development, transportation), Soc Serv (social services), Educ (education).

aimed at the general population, at business, and at government bodies, and almost never directed at disadvantaged groups. Economic development programs have a similar profile. Policing programs serve the general population, but some specifically target low-income and high-risk individuals. While many housing programs also serve the general population and business, their strongest focus is on low-income households. Social service programs almost exclusively target disadvantaged groups: the young, the poor, the old, those at risk, and those with disabilities or dysfunctions (i.e., prison populations). Not surprisingly, education programs concentrate on the young, on high risk individuals, and schools as institutions.

Table I-2 shows the average number of people reached by innovations in the different areas, the average percentage of the target population reached, and the average operating budget per person reached. Consider the innovations in information technology: the introduction of improved information technology into operations

TABLE I-2   INNOVATIONS' TARGET POPULATIONS
(Number of people reached × 10^3; number of cases are in parentheses)

	GROUP								
	All	IT	OC	EE	P	H	EC	Soc Serv	Educ
Average number	202	299	850	130	103	96	1066	34	5
reached	(157)	(38)	(21)	(14)	(11)	(11)	(7)	(58)	(18)
Average percent of									
target population	48%	61%	64%	63%	49%	30%	54%	35%	36%
reached	(116)	(31)	(19)	(14)	(9)	(6)	(4)	(38)	(14)
Average operating									
budget per	3600	300	13700	800	700	7200	100	1900	2100
person ($)	(135)	(33)	(18)	(9)	(10)	(9)	(6)	(54)	(18)

Note: Average number reached refers to the number of people reached *per year* in the program's *most recent* year of operation.

like paying taxes, automobile registration, or the management of highways will affect large numbers of taxpayers, car owners, and drivers. These innovations reach large populations (an average of 299,000), a high percentage of the target population (61%), and have a low operating cost per person reached (an average of $300). Organizational change innovations often encompass entire organizations; thus they show both large populations reached and large per person budgets. The policy areas that reach by far the smallest numbers of people are social services and education. These programs are *least* often designed for the general population, and often focus on smaller segments of their small target populations. They often involve counseling or other interventions that can be quite expensive on a per-client basis.

DESCRIBING POLICY AREAS

In addition to this statistical glimpse of the differences between the six types of innovation to be discussed, the following brief descriptions may serve as a map of the chapters to come.

- **Information technology.** Innovations in information technology demonstrate the speed at which technology is evolving. New technologies appear from one year to the next.

126

The local heroes in this policy area are most often middle managers and front-line staff who not only understand a technology but also have a knack for explaining it to their often technologically challenged superiors. Most information technologies are holistic in the sense that they can deliver a variety of services; thus, an issue for the local hero in this policy area is how to get other departments involved. They must also struggle to find ways to increase staff and user comfort with the technology. Finally, government use of information technology is growing so rapidly that, in addition to developing innovative applications, governments are now confronting the broader question of the overall management of information technology.

- **Organizational change.** Organizational change is a rubric that includes turnarounds; new ways of managing, particularly by redesigning incentive systems and restructuring agencies to give front-line workers more autonomy; the introduction of competition, either within the public sector or between public and private sectors; initiatives to give the public more ongoing input into the governance of public organizations; and ways of overcoming the inherent problems of large partnerships. These programs, frequently introduced by agency heads, often shake up the agency; front-line workers may be skeptical about empowerment, middle managers may resist ceding authority to front-line workers; unions may see these initiatives as diminishing their representative role; and politicians may feel they are losing control of the organization. The challenge to agency heads is to steer their organization around these shoals without losing too many of the crew.

- **Environment and energy.** Innovative programs in environment and energy stress voluntary compliance, the creation of markets, and the use of new and often simpler technologies. While politicians may strive to maintain a high profile in responding to highly visible problems in these areas, they are usually dependent on the analytic work of public servants. Some of the imperatives that local heroes, whether they are politicians or public servants, must face include thinking systemically about living systems; tapping the willingness of concerned citizens to volunteer; using market incentives, such as user fees; and mediating between environmental interest groups and the corporate sector. In addition, the bureaucracy may be hesitant about new ideas such as voluntary compliance and the creation of markets, preferring the old ways of regulation and litigation.

- **Policing, housing, and economic development.** Programs in these areas are loosely united by their common concern for the community. The new community policing paradigm runs through every policing program in our sample, whether the program is managed within a police department or involves a formal partnership with other departments or community groups. Community renewal and housing renovation programs use similar approaches. Initiators of programs in these areas must learn how to stimulate the interest and support of often skeptical communities, how to get police and other professionals to understand each other's perspectives and function as members of teams, and how to manage large partnerships.

- **Social services.** Initiatives in this policy area deal with difficult social (mostly behavioral) problems in U.S. cities and increasingly in rural America as well: infant mortality, domestic violence, substance abuse, AIDS, and youth delinquency. Innovators in this area are seeking to establish holistic interventions for people suffering from multiple problems, to use prevention strategies, and to engage communal resources to heal troubled individuals. The use of theoretical models as an inspiration for programs, and the ability to find additional support from foundations, the corporate sector, or individual volunteers is crucial to this area. The dilemma social service innovations face is captured in the data on target populations and resource intensiveness presented in Table I-2. Social services treat small populations, often at substantial expense, and their challenge is to find resources—not only to continue functioning, but also to expand their reach and scope.

- **Education.** Education is perhaps the most strongly contested policy area. Educators, parents, the private sector, corporations, and philanthropic foundations all have views as to how to improve the quality of the "system." There are conflicting theories, in particular, the dispute between the "progressive" schools and the advocates of a curriculum based on standards and testing. Educational innovators have the opportunity to seek support for their programs at the political level, from the private sector, and from foundations; however, they must also deal with resistance from these potential supporters—and from teachers and administrators within the system. Educational innovators must respond to the proponents of conflicting theories.

7

Life in the Fast Lane: Innovation through Information Technology

Literature on the New Public Management, whether in North America or elsewhere, seldom grants a large role to information technology. Osborne and Gaebler's *Reinventing Government* (1992) and Osborne and Plastrik's *Banishing Bureaucracy* (1997) hardly mention it. Their silence suggests a serious oversight. Information technology improves the quality of service by increasing accessibility and making possible one-stop shopping; it facilitates the empowerment of front-line workers by giving them the information necessary to make decisions; and it makes measuring performance easier. Many traditional rationales for government intervention, such as public goods, natural monopolies, and externalities are in essence information failures; with improved information, these rationales will no longer exist. Advances in information processing capacity have permitted a variety of public assets to be bought and sold in markets including, for example, clean water and air, landing rights at airports, and access to highways. In fact, rather than ignoring the role of information technology, it would be more appropriate to put information technology at the core of the New Public Management and public sector innovation (Reschenthaler and Thompson, 1996). By recognizing information technology innovation as a generic form of public sector innovation, applicable to many policy areas, this study is according it an appropriate role.

This chapter has a threefold structure. It begins by describing the information technologies observed in the Ford-KSG sample, the broad functions that these technologies perform, and the per-user cost of such innovations; after which it will introduce the local heroes who are responsible for these innovations—their character, the inescapable complexities they face in working with public sector partners and private sector suppliers, and the tactics they use to overcome resistance to new technologies. Finally, this chapter will look at the nature and significance of these innovations—at the results they have achieved and the work they leave unfinished. Do these innovations imply anything about the challenges and the role of information technology in future innovations?

A DIVERSITY OF TECHNOLOGIES

Each of the forty-seven innovations classified under the broad rubric of "information technology" in the Ford-KSG sample used one or more of eighteen different technologies, and no technology appeared in more than seven applications. Table 7-1 lists these technologies and their frequency in the sample; it clearly shows the diversity that characterizes this field. What it perhaps does not show, is how quickly information technology changes. Some of the technologies listed on Table 7-1 are quite old; others are new, and the field is rapidly evolving. Some technologies listed here will no longer be used in a few years' time or may be recombined in new ways. The following comments describe the technologies that appear in Table 7-1.

Geographic information systems (GIS) not only build spatial databases, but use them to explore causal relationships among spatial variables (Cohodas, 1996b). These systems have begun to play a major role in

TABLE 7-1   FREQUENCY OF INFORMATION TECHNOLOGY USE

Type of Information Technology	n	% of Cases
Geographic Information Systems	7	15
Database	6	13
Interactive video, cable TV	5	11
Debit card, smart card	5	11
Electronic data interchange	4	9
Computer/mobile communications	4	9
Computer control	4	9
One-way video	3	6
Hotline	3	6
Barcode	2	4
Electronic kiosk	2	4
Expert system	2	4
Voice mail	2	4
Networked PCs	2	4
Electronic imaging	1	2
Electronic highway pricing	1	2
Photo radar	1	2
Management information system	1	2
Electronic mail	1	2
TOTAL	60	128%

community policing, where they are used to document and analyze patterns of crime and thus help in problem-solving and deployment decisions (City of St. Petersburg, Florida, Police Department, 1994).

Computerized databases have existed for much of this century. Nevertheless, innovations can create new databases, such as Wishard Hospital's Patient Record System, or they can use existing databases in innovative ways, such as Massachusetts' Automated Child Support Enforcement System, which scans all the state's financial databases to find income or assets that can be seized to enforce child support obligations (Massachusetts Department of Revenue, 1993). The initiator of the Massachusetts system, Robert Melia, Director of Strategic Planning in the Massachusetts Department of Revenue, described the essence of his innovation in the following way: "What we've done is to abandon the caseworker approach, and moved to the computer. You don't hire human beings to collect money. You have a system that collects the money" (Cohodas, 1993).

Interactive technologies (video, television, and cable) can be used to bridge distances. The Los Angeles County courts use interactive video to conduct arraignment hearings, thereby eliminating trips between jail and the courthouse for people arraigned on minor charges (City of Los Angeles, California, Municipal Court, 1992). Interactive television, in which students' responses to questions are entered on keypads and transmitted by satellite or microwave relay (in Hawaii) or fibre optic cable (in rural Oklahoma and Kentucky), has been used to enrich distance education (Hawaii Public Television, 1991; Kentucky Education Television, 1991; Beaver County, Oklahoma, Schools, 1990). The electrical utility in Glasgow, Kentucky, has installed a broadband interactive cable network that can be used for interactive cable television, to regulate electrical usage, and pay bills (City of Glasgow, Kentucky, 1994).

Debit cards have been used in Ramsey County, Minnesota, and New York City, where they are given to recipients of public assistance. They can be used at automatic teller machines (ATMs) at participating banks (Ramsey County, Minnesota, Community Human Services, 1990; New York City Human Resources Administration, 1990). Debit cards contain only a small amount of information in their magnetic strip and require on-line interaction with a mainframe. However, smart cards, more commonly used in Europe, contain more information, have processing capability, and permit transactions to be performed off-line (Carnes, 1995). Telephone cards are an increasingly common North American application. Wyoming has been developing a smart card that can be used for a variety of government entitlements, including Medicaid, Aid to Families with Dependent Children, and Food Stamps (Wyoming Department of Health, 1992).

Electronic data interchange (EDI) refers to innovations that make public sector databases readily accessible to citizens by telephone or modem. Two examples are Oregon's Vendor Information Program, in which potential suppliers to government can access information about procurement opportunities (Oregon Department of General Services, 1993) and the Los Angeles County Telecommuting program, in which employees access the computer databases they work with from their homes by modem (Los Angeles County, California, 1993).

Computer/mobile communication is a similar technology, whereby individual public servants carrying laptops can communicate with central databases or information and control systems. For example, the Chicago-area Law Enforcement Radio Terminal Service connects laptop computers in police cars with law enforcement databases by radio (Illinois Criminal Justice Information Authority, 1991).

Computer control refers to computerized decision making, in particular in the operation of transportation systems. The Los Angles Department of Transportation Automated Traffic Surveillance and Control Program, which began as a pilot project (chapter 3), uses computer algorithms to determine the settings of traffic lights so as to optimize the flow (City of Los Angeles, California, Department of Transportation, 1992).

A telephone hotline linked with a database gives operators immediate access to large, agencywide sources of information which they can use to give callers individualized attention. For example, the New York City Human Resources Agency's InfoLine allows callers to gain immediate access to information about their entitlements (New York City Human Resources Administration, 1990).

Barcode technology was used in two very different settings: St. Louis Park, Minnesota, affixes barcodes to household recycling containers to record credits against refuse collection charges and Seminole County, Florida, developed a system whereby clerks used barcodes and scanning equipment to produce minutes for routine court proceedings (City of St. Louis Park, Minnesota, Department of Administration, 1992; Seminole County, Florida, Circuit Court, 1992).

Electronic kiosks are similar to bank ATMs; they permit business transactions from remote places and during nonbusiness hours. For example, transactions with government, such as renewing a driver's license, can be performed at a kiosk, or information about government programs can be received from one. Examples of an innovation using kiosks include Info/California, which was initiated by a middle-level public servant (chapter 3), and Arizona QuickCourt, an innovation established to help the public sector reach its market (California Health and Welfare Data Center, 1993; Arizona Supreme Court, 1994).

Expert systems encapsulate knowledge, and are used in training and decision making. An example is Kentucky's Financial Institutions Expert Examination System, used by its financial institution examiners (Kentucky Department of Financial Institutions, 1994).

An innovation involving voice mail is Seattle's Community Voice Mail for homeless people, mentioned in chapter 3 as an illustration of an idea initiated by front-line staff (Seattle Workers' Center, 1993).

The Rockefeller Institute of Government at SUNY-Albany holds computer-supported problem solving meetings, with participants connected by networked personal computers (State University of New York at Albany, Rockefeller Institute of Government, 1990).

Electronic imaging can reduce the burden of paper files and make information widely available throughout an organization; the Chicago Parking Enforcement Program uses electronic imaging of records to facilitate adjudication of parking appeals at neighborhood offices, rather than in a congested central court, as was the case in the past (City of Chicago, Illinois, 1991).

Electronic highway pricing refers to charging highway tolls to drivers whose vehicles are equipped with a transponder that can be monitored by radio; the Oklahoma Turnpike Authority's Pikepass was one of the first experiments in electronic highway pricing (Oklahoma Turnpike Authority, 1992). Drivers with transponders need not stop to pay tolls.

Photo radar is a technology developed exclusively for the public sector, involving speed limit enforcement using radar and flash photography. An early photo radar system was implemented in the Phoenix suburb of Paradise Valley (Town of Paradise Valley, Arizona, 1990).

This list of innovations contains only one involving electronic mail— Santa Monica, California's Public Electronic Network. Established in the mid-1980s, this program was probably the first E-mail system specifically designed to provide electronic communication between citizens and government both for transactions and policy discussions (City of Santa Monica, California, 1993). It predated the widespread use of E-mail on the Internet; and its lone presence on our list is an indication of how quickly information technology is advancing.

Internet usage began to soar in 1994 and 1995, as I was researching this book. The President, for example, went online in June 1993 (president @whitehouse.gov). By now almost every level of government from the president on down is accessible by E-mail and most government agencies have built, or are building, their World Wide Web sites. This development happened between one year's competition and the next, and spread so rapidly that it is no longer considered innovative for an agency to install E-mail or build a Web site; indeed, any government not already using this system is considered outdated. (On the other hand, the medium has not yet been mastered. A recent survey of Internet use by local governments concludes that many of these sites offer little more than public relations brochures. Where that is the case, we are missing the potential of both electronic transactions and electronic democracy [Martin 1997]).

Future competitions may still involve E-mail systems, but if so, they will be like recent database innovations—outstanding only if they use this well-established technology in an especially creative way.

THE FUNCTIONS OF INFORMATION TECHNOLOGY

Innovations involving information technology perform three major functions: they facilitate transactions between citizens and government; ensure compliance with the law; and provide information to citizens, organizations, and government. These functions are, in some instances, related: for example, performing certain transactions through information technology can ensure compliance because features can be built into the technology to determine whether the transaction is a legitimate one.

Information technology can now be used to pay taxes, prepare legal documents, pay highway tolls, and receive government transfers. To say that transactions are facilitated means that they are improved. Costs are reduced, with savings accruing to the user of the service, the taxpayer, or both. Convenience for the user is increased: electronic kiosks are open longer hours than government offices and in locations such as shopping malls; electronic data interchange and internet communications can be initiated in one's home or office at any time. For recipients of transfer payments, electronic debit cards or smart cards are easier to deal with than checks. They dramatically increase access to benefits and make the delivery of benefits more certain. In some instances, the use of new technology is made mandatory. However, even when the system is voluntary, a high proportion of users will likely switch rapidly to the new way of doing business lured by the ease of the transaction and the reduction in cost—especially if it is passed on to the user.

Information technology facilitates compliance by improving the effectiveness of police work. In the case of traditional policing, in-car computers enable officers to access computer databases or communicate more effectively with headquarters. In community policing, technology has different uses. In addition to using GIS for analysis and deployment decisions, the St. Petersburg, Florida, police department gives officers voice mail boxes to make it easier for citizens to contact them. Information technology is also improving compliance in other areas: Massachusetts' Automated Child Support Enforcement System increased compliance with court-ordered child support obligations; and Phoenix's Bus Card Plus Program issued debit cards to commuters and put electronic fareboxes on buses. The cards are coded so that transit staff can monitor whether employees of any particular business are increasing their use of public transit. Such information is useful, given the municipal passenger-vehicle travel reduction ordinance (City of Phoenix, Arizona, Public Transit Department, 1994).

Information technology provides information—usually about government—to citizens, in more effective ways than in the past. Info/California provided information about government programs organized in a more user-friendly way, namely, on the basis of the information needed (the problem), rather than the agency responsible for the program. In the early 1990s, Texas established a "window on state government" electronic bulletin board that provided a wide range of government data and information. It was a precursor of government web sites, and later became a web site itself (Texas Comptroller of Public Accounts, 1994). Ventura County's Senior Home Share Computer Match Program demonstrates government acting as an information broker to help senior citizens share housing, thus maintaining independent living as long as possible (Ventura County, California Department of Parks and Recreation, 1991).

THE SCOPE AND COST OF INFORMATION TECHNOLOGY PROJECTS

Many information technology innovations reach entire populations or large groups within the population, for example, applications in transportation that improve the efficiency of traffic flow, or programs that increase the efficiency of transactions such as paying taxes, or programs that improve public safety by making policing more effective. While the budgets of these programs are often large, the number of users is also large, so that the costs per user are small. For example, the Los Angeles Automated Traffic Surveillance and Control System serves one million drivers at an annual operating cost of $3.30 per driver and cumulative capital cost of

$103 per driver while Oklahoma Pikepass serves 110,000 drivers at an annual operating cost of $16.00 per driver.

In contrast to projects aimed at the entire population, 23 percent of the information technology innovations in the Ford-KSG sample were designed to serve low income individuals. In some cases, they were intended to help large groups of people. The New York City InfoLine, for example, can be used by anyone receiving social service program benefits. In some instances, the programs seek to give low-income and disadvantaged people access to the same technology or services as the rest of the society. Examples are Seattle's Community Voice Mail Program, the Arizona QuickCourt system, and Lansing, Michigan's, Computer Learning Centers, which provide children in public housing with access to personal computers and educational software (City of Lansing, Michigan, Housing Commission, 1993). Seattle's Community Voice Mail application has eloquently described its mission to help the homeless overcome the disadvantage of being without a telephone:

> Imagine looking for work or an apartment without a phone. Imagine maintaining any critical relationship without a phone. Community Voice Mail is dignified and personalized, providing the missing link between social services case managers and clients, and between clients and the community. Community Voice Mail masks homelessness and other potentially negative connotations that promote bias against persons without phones and stable addresses (Seattle Workers' Center, 1993).

Programs designed to reach large groups of disadvantaged people, like information technology innovations aimed at the entire population, also reach many people at a low per-user cost. New York's Human Resources Administration's InfoLine is used by 900,000 people at an annual operating cost of $2.75 per person. The various programs delivering benefits by debit or smart card reach anywhere from 10,000 to 1,000,000 people, at an annual operating cost of approximately $30 per person.

Programs designed to give disadvantaged people access to mainstream technologies generally reach smaller numbers of people, at a higher per-person cost. Lansing's Computer Learning Centers reach 234 young people at an annual operating cost of $414 per person; Seattle's Community Voice Mail is used by 238 people at an annual operating cost of $277 per person; the Kentucky and Hawaii educational television system both reach approximately 2,000 students in outlying areas at an annual operating cost of $1,100 per student. The per capita costs of these programs are closer to the cost levels of innovations in social services or education.

Programs designed to serve entire groups of disadvantaged people are motivated by efficiency. They are intended to reduce the aggregate transactions costs in social service programs. Programs intended to give the disadvantaged access to technology are different in intention. Recent consumer expenditure surveys have shown that computer ownership is still very income elastic: the disadvantaged do not choose to acquire this technology (Little, 1996; Lewington, 1996). Thus, the programs intended to give them access to technology are social transfers in that someone, either in the public or private sectors, has to buy or donate the technology. These programs exist where donors can be found. The justification given for these transfers is that access to information technology can help adults find work and housing (Community Voice Mail) or give young people constructive alternatives to delinquency (Lansing's Computer Learning Centers) and thus increase self-reliance.

INFORMATION TECHNOLOGY'S LOCAL HEROES

Fully 70 percent of the information technology innovations in the Ford-KSG sample were initiated by career public servants below the political or agency head level (see chapter 3). The applications and the site visit reports filed for finalists and winners paint a vivid picture of some of these local heroes. For example, John Ellwood's site visit report describes Russell Bohart, the developer of Info/California (and director of the California Health and Welfare Data Center):

> [Bohart is] clearly an entrepreneurial manager. He created the legislation to give his agency the ability to direct the funds for the creation of new programs. He has been the head of the center under three governors. He can clearly work with Republicans and Democrats. . . . For a techie he speaks well and does not use computer jargon (Ellwood, 1993).

And David Harrison's report describes the achievement of Rich Feldman and Patricia Barry, two staff members at the Seattle Workers Center who came up with the idea for Community Voice Mail:

> Feldman and Barry have recruited Active Voice Corporation in a partnership to advance this replication further than it would

otherwise have gone. They are both articulate, committed people with a keen sense of program design. They are both effective. . . . [T]hey are both savvy and able to rally support. They convinced the Seattle City Council to designate funds for this project during a low budget year when virtually no new projects were being added (Harrison, 1993).

Terry Williams, the prime mover of Wyoming Smartcard, is also the manager of the Wyoming WIC program (WIC is an acronym for the Special Supplemental Food Program for Women, Infants, and Children). As described by Nicholas Lovrich:

Terry Williams is an extraordinary person by any measure. A Canadian by birth, he was educated in U.S. universities and worked in nutrition and maternal/child health programs in Florida and Wisconsin before coming out to head up the Wyoming WIC program. . . . [H]e is *both* a dreamer . . . and an effective, politically savvy administrator. . . . It was Terry's ability to articulate the vision of a "health passport" and a smartcard broadened to the full range of state programs that caught the attention of Governor Sullivan in his own state, and later the attention of the Governor's associates in Idaho, Oregon, Montana, and North Dakota (Lovrich, 1992).[1]

William Ray developed the Glasgow (Kentucky) Broadband Information Highway. He is the superintendent of the town's Electric Plant board, but Keon Chi's site visit report describes him as sounding "like a visionary and a futurist, rather than an electrical utility representative" (Chi, 1993). Here is Ray's vision in his own words:

Daily feedback on consumption levels, coupled with a new time differentiated rate structure, will allow everyone to alter their lifestyle and thus lower their monthly cost of energy in response to the new flow of information that will be coming into their homes and businesses. . . . Widespread access to video and data connections between all schools, homes, and businesses will put the entire community back into the business of educating children. . . . The City of Glasgow will begin to realize real savings through a decreased need for new streets, highways, and other automobile related infrastructure, as more and more businesses cater to an aging population by offering their services through Glasgow's Broadband Information Highway (City of Glasgow, Kentucky, 1994).

From these quotations a composite drawing of an information technology local hero begins to emerge: he or she is a person close to and knowledgeable about a particular technology and its use in other places, and wants to match, if not exceed, its achievements elsewhere. The information technology innovator has a long-term vision of how the technology will grow to serve new purposes and markets and leadership skills that can be used to communicate this vision to others less familiar with the technology, who control the resources needed to make the vision a reality. Not the average techie!

Support for this portrait comes from a recent survey of government officials in the United States and Canada, who were asked about their perceptions of information technology. Jerry Mechling, technology columnist for *Governing* magazine, reported the survey results. Over 75 percent of respondents rated chief information officers in government and the technology community favorably in terms of their understanding of technology issues; however, the favorable ratings dropped to 36 percent, for budget and finance officers; 28 percent, for government general managers; and 18 percent for legislators (Mechling, 1995b). In short, a critical gap exists between the techies and the political and bureaucratic leadership. Successful innovators are the ones who, through their leadership and communication skills, have been able to transcend it. While the survey refers to chief information officers, it is likely that many of the governments where these innovations occurred did not have such a position, so that the innovator had to be his or her own advocate.

Two major challenges that information technology innovators often faced was getting other government departments to support their projects, and dealing with the private sector. The incentive to get other departments involved is quite strong because the technologies employed are flexible and have great capacity, and thus can simultaneously benefit many departments. Public sector entrepreneurs often want to find partners to help share the fixed costs, and look for other departments and programs to "buy in" to the technology by contributing to development, acquisition, and operating costs. They will try to find partners in the planning phase, because it is usually easier to modify a technology before than after it has been put in place. This intrinsic incentive to get partners involved explains how information technology innovations are holistic. These partnerships can be geographic, in which agencies performing the same function in different locations join a network; or interdepartmental, in which different departments in one location or jurisdiction share the technology. For example, Russell Bohart's goal was that Info/California's kiosks would provide "a single face and access point to all government." Conversely, his worst nightmare was a row of incompatible electronic kiosks, one for each agency (Simon, 1994).[2]

The importance of building partnerships within government surfaced again when innovators were asked to name the single most significant achievement associated with their innovations. Rather than simply getting the technology to work, they frequently said, it was getting organizations to work together on a particular project, or having laid the groundwork for cooperation on future projects. These responses are consistent with the impressions the site visitors reported; the visitors were impressed as much with innovators' communication and political skills as with their technical mastery.

As the public sector acquires more information technology, innovators become increasingly enmeshed with the private sector. Two private sector roles figure in the development of information technology innovations: the contractor who supplies the hardware or software, and the donor who gives hardware, software, cash, or goods in kind. Generally, the public sector does not produce its own hardware. The innovator must choose between producing software or buying it from the private sector. The innovators who introduced their own software were in organizations that had expertise in the area, or their projects were reasonably small, or they simply adapted a software program that was purchased off-the-shelf. The Minneapolis Public Works Department wrote its own user-friendly GIS software; the researchers at the Rockefeller Institute of Government at SUNY Albany developed their own decision conferencing software; and the Kentucky Department of Financial Institutions adapted general purpose expert system software to its own design.

Government agencies went to the private sector when the technology was already available (e.g., the banking system's ATMs were available for distributing income support payments) or being developed (e.g., electronic kiosks), to avoid the difficulty of maintaining and updating the system (e.g., electronic highway pricing technology in Oklahoma and the parking enforcement database and hardware in Chicago), or because they lacked expertise. Further, the provider of the hardware tends to have an advantage in providing the related software and systems integration. Innovators who buy technology from the private sector need to have the appropriate technical, negotiating, and contract management skills. If by chance an agency is among the first to experiment with a technology, the innovator may be able to persuade the private sector firm to give it the technology for free. For example, IBM provided $500,000 of the $1 million development funding for Info/California's electronic kiosks. The gift gave IBM a head start on the bidding when it was time to expand the system. Similarly, the expertise IBM acquired through its involvement helped it win a contract with the Ontario Ministry of Transportation to establish ServiceOntario. ServiceOntario is a system of electronic kiosks that permits transactions, such as renewing a vehicle registration. In this case, IBM contracted to provide the kiosks, with its investment to be recovered by a $1 per-transaction convenience charge. By fall 1996, IBM was advertising the system in *Governing* magazine.

Innovators establishing projects to help the disadvantaged will have an edge if they are also skillful fund-raisers. Almost half the operating budget for Community Voice Mail ($27,000 of $66,000) came from corporate and nonprofit donations, that is, from the Boeing Good Neighbor Fund and from Junior League and the March of Dimes. In addition, Boeing donated the computer, and Active Voice Corporation provided the software. Kentucky's educational television initiative received 10 percent of its operating budget ($193,000 of $1.8 million) in grants from Bell South, the Goethe Institute (to support German courses), and its own fundraising efforts. The Beaver County Interactive Television Cooperative in rural Oklahoma received slightly less than half ($150,000 of $335,000) of its five-year operating funding from two local foundations. The pattern of giving in these examples is consistent with the finding reported in chapter 5: they are either large portions of relatively small budgets (Community Voice Mail, Beaver County Interactive Television) or small portions of much larger budgets (Kentucky Educational Television). The Lansing Housing Commission presents another take on this issue. Although it could have had donor support, it chose not to, fearing that if it were given businesses' and schools' outdated computers, the children it hoped to reach would not be drawn to the program (Lemov, 1993).

IMPLEMENTING CHANGE

Convincing staff and clients to accept the new technology was by far the most common problem that information technology innovators experienced in setting up their programs. In response, the innovators modified the technology to make it user friendly, trained the staff who would be using the new technology, marketed the program incorporating the technology to the public, and—as always—sought additional resources for development (see Table 4-3). Often training and modifying the system occurred together because the staff came up with ideas about how to improve the technology. For example, the Arizona QuickCourt involved court staff in the system's design and encouraged them to practice on the system; and the Seminole County, Florida, courts established a "courtroom of the future," to train staff and involve them in designing the system of barcodes that would eventually be used to produce court minutes.

Innovators also worked hard to get and hold interorganizational cooperation, often using co-optation as the glue. Establishing user groups or user committees, for example, got many people involved in systems design. Bohart established an advisory group of departmental public information officers who, of all people in the government, had the greatest interest in Info/California. Among other examples: Oregon's Vendor Information Program established an advisory committee of business and government leaders to build external support, and the program also consulted frequently with professional and trade groups whose members also used the system. The Ramsey County, Minnesota Electronic Benefit System established a community advisory committee, whose membership included benefits recipients, banks, and the contractor.

The Kentucky Financial Institutions Expert Examination System (FIXX) provided a comprehensive discussion of how training, cooptation of staff, and marketing the technology to financial institutions worked together to reduce opposition to change:

> [T]he project managers addressed [staff concerns] by direct examiner involvement in creating the expert knowledge base, providing training in small groups with individualized training when needed, and involving examination staff in FIXX demonstrations for bankers and other bank regulators. By using FIXX, examiners realized that it was not a means for replacing them but rather of enhancing their professional performance. . . . When field testing of the preplanning module revealed what many examiners described as its "non-user friendly nature," the module was reengineered to address these criticisms. . . . There was initial industry concern that FIXX would be a "black box" examination process deemphasizing human judgment. An extensive outreach program by the Department to the industry has proven these fears to be groundless. . . . Since banks are billed for examiner hours, the industry welcomes the savings due to better examination preplanning and higher quality examinations (Kentucky Department of Financial Institutions, 1994).

ACHIEVING RESULTS

The results achieved by information technology innovations include improvements in the quality of service delivered by public sector organizations, lower costs of operating public sector organizations, and increases in the productivity of public sector workers.

Improvements in Service Quality

The Community Voice Mail Program found that 80 percent of its jobseekers found work within two months and 50 percent of its housing clients were settled within 30 days. Caseworkers observed that these rates were much higher than for homeless people without voice mail. The program used its Innovations award to establish the Community Technology Institute, which has helped replicate Community Voice Mail in 15 other cities throughout the United States (Seglin, 1995; Walters, 1996c).

The Lansing Housing Commission reported that 80 percent of eligible children continue to participate in its Computer Learning Center program, their performance in school has improved, and drug activity in the housing projects has virtually ceased.

Studies of several electronic transfer experiments involving the Food Stamps Program indicate that total operating costs, including administration, lost benefits, retailers' cost, recipients' cost, and financial institutions' cost, decline by as much as 50 percent (Abt Associates, 1993; Kirlin, 1995). In addition, participants in the projects preferred debit or smart cards to food stamps by large majorities (by 91% in one case) because of increased convenience and security (Kirlin, 1995). Cards have dramatically reduced the frequency of lost or stolen benefits; for example, New York's Electronic Payment File Transfer Program went from 100,000 complaints per year to 372 complaints per year.

The Los Angeles Automated Traffic Surveillance and Control system reduces traffic delays in its area of operation by 32 percent (i.e., by 50,000 motorist hours per day) and auto air emissions by 26 percent (350 tons of pollutants per day).

Lower Cost of Government

Info/California reduced the cost of transactions (e.g., producing a birth certificate) by an order of magnitude, from $10 to $1 (Simon, 1993). Despite this and other achievements, Info/California lost its funding in 1995, a victim of political opposition from the right, which wanted it privatized, and the left, which preferred cutting technology to cutting social programs (Swope, 1995). The state has, however, established a system of 164 Welcome California kiosks that can be used to book hotel rooms, rent cars, or buy tickets at major tourist attractions (California Telecommunications Projects Web Site, 1996). In addition, electronic kiosks are operating in Colorado, Kansas, Pennsylvania, Texas, Washington, and the Province of Ontario, Canada (Swope, 1995; Stevens, 1995).

The Arizona QuickCourts pilot project was so popular that 150 new kiosks were being added statewide in 1997. New York and Utah are also developing electronic kiosks for transacting business with the courts. Utah's technology will be the most advanced because it will also, unlike the others, provide for electronic filing of the forms it provides (Lemov, 1997).

Oregon's Vendor Information Program achieved a savings of 10 percent on the cost of goods purchased, and reduced the cost of purchasing by 20 percent. A similar electronic procurement initiative produced a 7 percent overall reduction in cost for the Los Angeles Metropolitan Transit Authority (Newman, 1996).

Chicago's Parking Enforcement Program increased parking ticket revenues from $35 to $40 million in its first year of operation (1991), while reducing costs by $5 million. By 1994, revenues were $60 million per year and its collection rate had increased from 10 to 65 percent (Mahtesian, 1994a). A sixfold increase in the collection rate and only a doubling of revenues indicates that more vigorous enforcement has resulted in less illegal parking.

Improved Productivity

Massachusetts' Automated Child Support Enforcement Program collected 10 percent more money in 1992 than in 1991 with a reduction of 7.5 percent of the jobs in enforcement. After two years in operation, 85 percent of the collections were obtained without caseworker involvement, and the payment compliance rate had increased from 59 to 76 percent (Mechling, 1994).

Results That Matter

Notwithstanding these results, a skeptic may still ask whether they really matter to the clients they serve or the general public. Different types of results matter in different ways. Some programs avert or mitigate catastrophes for large numbers of people (Florida's marine spill GIS system). Other programs (the New York Electronic Payment File Transfer System) serve a similar purpose for individuals. We cannot identify by name the individual New Yorkers who may have had their benefits lost or stolen save for this program; we only know that the likelihood of such an unpleasant event has decreased.

Perhaps the best analogy for this type of innovation is a vaccine. Vaccines eliminate the suffering of individuals who would otherwise have fallen ill. Again, since the suffering was averted, we cannot know their names. Nevertheless, judging by the honors extended to medical innovators like Salk and Sabin, eliminating catastrophes, even for small numbers of people, is something society deems important.

Many information technology innovations that do not avert catastrophes provide small but widespread improvements in social well-being, whether in terms of pollution abated, taxes reduced, or travel time saved. Removing 350 tons of pollutants per day from the air over Los Angeles is a marginal improvement in that city's air quality problems. Saving 10 percent of the cost of state purchases in Oregon or increasing parking ticket revenue by $30 million in Chicago permits either location to lower its taxes slightly or to divert those funds to other more valuable purposes.

Innovations that improve traffic flow may reduce travel time by a few minutes a day for large numbers of motorists. These innovations bring slight improvements to most of us, but transform the lives of no one. In what sense are they valuable? Sometimes a range of actions, all at the margin, can add up to a major change, as appears to be the case with pollution abatement policy. But what if these innovations with marginal impacts are not part of a concerted strategy to achieve greater than marginal impact? Do they have merit on their own?

In the private sector, great companies have been born and personal fortunes amassed as a result of entrepreneurs making innovations that bring relatively small benefits to many people—as long as the benefits are sufficiently noticeable the innovation passes the test of market acceptability. In the public sector, the economists' tool of benefit-cost analysis is most applicable to these improvements because it assumes that marginal impacts take place over a small, and thus linear, range of people's utility functions, so that the resulting benefits can be valued in terms of dollars.

On the other hand, critics of this analysis think that economists are attempting to value impacts that are below a threshold of psychological significance. I think such critics have a point: are these impacts large enough to be noticed? For example, do we notice a difference—an improvement—if traffic control technology reduces our trip to work by three minutes? If not three minutes, then what about five? Or ten? Obviously, at some point we do start to notice. In addition, when an innovation improves life for a large number of people by a small average amount, it is likely the case that the improvement is much greater than the average for some of the population—and they will surely notice.

Further, even if the impacts on *all* people were equal to the average, it would still be worthwhile to support innovation in the public sector. We need such local heroes to continue to strive for the small improvements in convenience or air quality that will benefit large numbers of people. We won't notice the results as much as we noticed the results of Salk's work, and the innovators will still be local, rather than global, heroes. Still, the work is well worth doing.

CONCLUSION

The information technology innovations discussed in this chapter are reasonably small systems, with average operating and capital budgets on the order of $6 million. They also share some important characteristics that have implications for public sector innovators. The following principles are twofold; they refer to the various innovations on a case-by-case basis and to the role of information technology in the public sector generally.

- To begin with the planning stage, the most immediately evident characteristic of these programs is that information technology is changing very rapidly. As a consequence, it is essential to build open systems that can keep up with change without having to be constantly reconfigured.

  Consider the rationale for open systems in terms of the dichotomy between groping and planning. Information technology innovators will most likely plan their systems, especially if the systems require large sums of capital. In addition, many information technology projects can and do serve multiple users, which also requires planning. Nonetheless, innovators should build some flexibility into their systems to take advantage of new technological developments.

- Information technology innovations are a potential resource for reengineering work processes. However, not all customers will want the most advanced technology. Thus, a registry of motor vehicles will almost certainly maintain walk-in offices, even as it installs electronic kiosks and establishes a web site. The organization will have preferences about which technology to use, and it may impose differential prices that reflect its costs *and* encourage the public to accept the preferred technology. Still, it will likely be necessary for an organization to manage several technologies at once, which places limits on the extent to which it can reengineer.

- Information technology innovators are not only technologically competent; they are also good communicators who overcome the chasm between technically sophisticated middle managers and technically naive politicians, agency heads, and central agency staff (Mechling, 1995b). It is essential for information technology innovators to be able to communicate their vision to those who are not technically proficient.

- If the information technology innovator's challenge looking up the organizational hierarchy is communications, then the challenge looking across and down the organizational structure is consultation and participation. We have seen that successful information technology innovators have gotten those who will be working with a new technology, either as producers or customers, involved in its design. Training is also an important incentive and can result in process refinements.

- Innovators in information technology will promote the private sector's involvement in public sector information technology— and to the fullest extent. The private sector may be present as contractor, donor, or partner, since the first question an innovator faces is whether to produce the system in-house or hire a private sector contractor. The public sector tends to design its own small systems and outsource larger systems, particularly if hardware is involved. But in cases where new systems are being developed or if the innovation is at the technological forefront, the private sector may want to get involved on a partnership basis, bearing some or all of the program's development costs, in return for the right to market it elsewhere.

Donations are a second form of private sector involvement. Since computer usage is to some extent income elastic, donors have recognized that providing access to computer technology can be an effective way to fight poverty, for both adults and children. That said, innovators must think carefully about the donations they are likely to receive and how they may affect the project. Sometimes the rejection of donations of outdated equipment may be in the program's best interest.

The relationship between public and private sector information technology goes beyond the roles of contractor or donor. We are now seeing technological convergence between the public and private sectors, in the sense that both sectors are using the same technologies, such as electronic mail, debit or smart cards, electronic data interchange, or expert systems. For example, government-issued debit cards can be used for payment at private sector ATM systems and private-sector debit cards can be used for payment at the public sector's new electronic kiosks.

User perceptions of the quality of technology-based public services will be influenced by their experience with technology-based private services. While one might argue that the public sector's services should be somewhat less technologically advanced because they emphasize equity rather than novelty, user sentiment may not permit the public sector to lag behind (Fountain et al., 1993).

Information technology has become so important to the public sector that governments have begun thinking systemically about it. By early 1996, 38 states had formulated long-range plans for the acquisition of information technology and 18 had submitted their plans to legislative review (National Conference of State Legislatures, 1996). In addition, many states and cities have appointed chief information officers responsible for overseeing these plans and advocating information technology development (Gurwitt, 1996).

Information technology innovations that work well in one state are rapidly being replicated, and the federal government often uses powerful incentives to get them adopted everywhere. For example, in 1988 the federal government passed legislation requiring states to develop automated systems for child support collection, disbursement, and enforcement, but offering to pay 90 percent of the cost. Massachusetts' Automated Child Support Enforcement System is among the leaders; other states are having difficulty meeting the standards (Gurwitt, 1995b). The first experiments in electronic transfer systems have led to a federal Interagency Task Force working to create a unified national system of electronic transfer of all government funded benefits (Carnes, 1995).

Another important issue is how information technology systems, particularly large ones, will be funded. Traditionally, they have been handled through regular capital budgeting and acquisition processes. The *National Performance Review* has argued that these processes are inappropriate because technologies are changing at a faster rate than the processes can move (Gore, 1993). Recently, some jurisdictions have tried to overcome the inadequacies of the traditional capital budgeting process. The Commonwealth of Massachusetts and Santa Clara County, California, have both issued technology bonds; $100 million in 1993 and $240 million in 1996 for the former, and $18 million for the latter. In both jurisdictions the bonds are for seven years, comparable to the useful life of the technologies that will be acquired (Lemov, 1996). The managers of these information technology funds must decide which projects to support. For example, they may decide that projects must cover interest payments with savings achieved. However, if the projects do not deliver promised savings, the bondholders must still be paid because the bonds are backed by the "full faith and credit" of the city, county, or state. This puts an onus on the managers of the technology funds to ensure that the technology investments are well planned and properly implemented.

Ensuring an appropriate return on technology investments is no trivial matter. A growing body of evidence from the United States, Canada, Australia, and the United Kingdom suggests that large information technology projects, such as a national air traffic control system, can be characterized by one or more of three failures: cost overruns, failure to meet deadlines, and failure to deliver promised performance (Gurwitt, 1995b; Kouzmin and Korac-Boisvert, 1995). This finding accords with a good deal of private sector experience. Smaller information technology investments, such as those discussed in this chapter, appear to have avoided similar implementation problems.

To outline a set of guidelines on how to manage an entire government's information technology portfolio, or how to run an internal information technology investment fund, or how to manage major information technology projects would take me far beyond the scope of this chapter. However, as information technology becomes an increasingly important factor of production in the public sector, it is reasonable to conclude that innovation award competitions will not only include more individual projects, but also innovations in the strategic management of information technology.

8

Revolution from Within: Organizational Change

We were burdened for so long by the ways of thinking and meta-phors that came out of the industrial age, when the idea of the machine convinced us to organize our efforts as if the individuals who worked together were parts in a mechanism, who could most usefully be employed doing the same specific thing over and over and over again, without change, until there was some decision made high up the organizational pyramid.

Then all of a sudden, a few leaders of organizations understood that their greatest asset was the unused creativity and brainpower of the men and women in those organizations. And they experimented with new systems to make those individuals understand that their ideas were of value ... and enlist them in the effort to implement their ideas.

VICE PRESIDENT ALBERT GORE
*1996 Innovations in
American Government Awards Ceremony*

Organizational change initiatives, the second generic group of innovations, improve the performance of an organizational unit or function, or even the entire organization. Such changes are usually accomplished by some form of restructuring or change in the incentive system. By contrast, the innovations classified under specific policy areas (e.g., education or policing) are new programs. Organizational change initiatives are some-times found in discussions of specific policy areas (chapters 9 to 12); however, the focus then is on their program or policy characteristics. Here our focus is on their structural aspects.

Organizational change is a broad category that encompasses five types of innovation: turnarounds; new ways of managing; increasing competition; innovations in governance; and large partnerships.

- First, turnarounds are relatively rare instances in which political or public recognition that a public sector organization has been performing poorly leads to a change of leadership and a comprehensive revision of its organizational mandate and programs.
- Second, under the rubric new ways of managing, the Ford-KSG sample includes initiatives that delegate increased authority to local units or use performance outcome measures or gainsharing—and comprehensive organizational change initiatives that include all of these elements. These new management initiatives are closely related to one another and to turnarounds; these types of innovation do not appear frequently in the sample, but when they do appear, they are together.[1]
- The third, fourth, and fifth types of organizational changes, namely, increasing competition within the public sector, innovations in governance (particularly to increase direct citizen input), and the involvement of large partnerships were sufficiently represented in the Ford-KSG sample to provide us with several examples of each.

The elements of interest in each example include its characteristics, the organizational change process, and its results. The conclusion to this chapter provides a repertoire of actions that enterprising local heroes or potential innovators can ponder in their effort to make effective and lasting changes in the structure of incentives in their organizations.

TURNAROUNDS

Cases about organizational turnarounds have assumed substantial visibility in New Public Management literature.[2] They are rarely described as such, but are cited as examples of the heroic application of principles in particularly difficult situations. For example, Fallows (1992) criticized Osborne and Gaebler for implying in their case studies that the application of their principles invariably leads to a turnaround. As Fallows put it: "Every story is a success story. Before the change everything is bad. After the change everything is good."

Despite the emphasis public sector turnarounds have received in the literature, my research indicates that few are evident at any point in time. Table 2-2 (chapter 2) shows that only 5 (or 2.5%) of 217 Ford-KSG semifinalists and only 12 (or 3.5%) of 339 IPAC award recipients were classified as turnarounds.[3] Nevertheless, turnarounds attract our attention precisely because the actions of the turnaround leader are heroic; the individuals chosen by *Governing* magazine as its "public officials of the year" are frequently those who have led turnarounds. In addition, turnarounds seem to have the same mythic structure as biblical or literary tales of redemption or deliverance (Frye, 1982).

Given the significance of turnarounds, it seems reasonable to include in this chapter a review of the private and public sector literature on turnarounds—along with four tales of organizational redemption and deliverance that were included in the Ford-KSG sample. But first, a note of caution: it can be dangerous to model behavior too closely on the behavior of turnaround leaders. Their situations call for an extraordinary effort to overcome major problems. If the model that results from their undertaking is inappropriately applied, the drastic action that results may destroy what incremental change could have accomplished.

Private Sector Literature

The private sector literature on turnarounds is relatively large and includes single and comparative case studies, studies based on interviews with turnaround leaders, and cross-sectional statistical studies to determine the factors most strongly associated with sustained improvements in corporate performance. Bibeault (1982) has the best general definition of a turnaround as

> . . . a substantial and sustained positive change in the performance of a business. In most cases a turnaround follows several years of declining profitability. In its most severe form, this decline usually culminates in substantial losses that threaten the financial viability of the firm. In its mildest form, declining performance may not threaten the financial viability of the firm, but it has serious negative impacts on market competitiveness, customer confidence, and employee morale (p. 81).

Hoffman's (1989) survey of the empirical studies of corporate turnarounds shows a very strong agreement that most turnarounds involve a change in corporate leadership very early in the process. A turnaround CEO will make major changes in senior corporate personnel or organizational structures and may, especially if the corporation faces a liquidity crisis, temporarily centralize power. In addition, new leaders attempt to create a more confident and positive corporate culture, and to inject new values and vision.

Following leadership changes, the turnaround process is usually characterized by a number of strategic moves beginning with retrenchment. Retrenchment includes various tactics, such as reducing inventories, collecting receivables faster, laying off personnel, restructuring debt, shutting down plants, and selling assets or businesses if the firm has become too diversified. This stage is particularly critical for firms that have filed for, or are attempting to avert, bankruptcy. The effect of these steps is to improve the firm's cash flow, either to maintain solvency or to create cash reserves that can be used for subsequent strategic moves.

The next stage in a turnaround involves refocusing and restructuring. In this stage, firms are likely to change their marketing strategies and eliminate unsuccessful products. They may reposition their products, diversify, or refocus, depending on the new leader's strategic vision. It is difficult to develop generalizations about these strategic moves because they are contingent on the firm's competitive situation. At this point, the study of turnarounds rejoins business strategy.

By and large, studies of private sector turnarounds focus on the role of the CEO and other senior executives who provide the firm's visible leadership and make strategic decisions. Very little has been written about the impact of turnarounds at lower levels of the organization, other than to observe that discontinued product lines and closed factories create hardship for the workers involved.

Public Sector Research

With one notable exception, hardly any research has been done on public sector turnarounds. Mark Moore, however, devoted almost a third of *Creating Public Value: Strategic Management in Government* (1995) to a very fine-grained analysis of two turnaround cases. The first describes Harry Spence's takeover of the Boston Housing Authority; the second, Lee Brown's takeover of the Houston Police Department. Moore referred to the situations confronting both men as "the public sector equivalent of bankruptcy" (p. 207), and extracted from his analysis the following repertoire of strategic moves for turnaround managers:

1. Embrace external political accountability to raise performance expectations of your organization and win the trust and support of the authorizing environment.
2. Either bring in your own top management team (Spence) or give the existing team important assignments, the results of which can easily be assessed (Brown).
3. Match structure to strategy by elevating the importance of units charged with new priorities.
4. Enhance internal accountability, for example, through budgeting and planning processes.
5. Build on initial successes and better relations with the authorizing environment to gain additional resources to devote to priorities.
6. Undertake major, publicized initiatives that will concretely represent the organization's new vision and priorities.
7. Reengineer the basic processes of the organization. Spence, for example, got tenants involved in maintaining the properties and selecting tenants more likely to maintain them; and Brown redesigned operating procedures to introduce community policing.
8. Replace centralized functional organizations with geographically decentralized organizations that give front-line workers and local managers more autonomy but also demand accountability for results.

My research on public sector turnarounds has focused on an analysis of eight cases, two of which (the New York City Bureau of Motor Equipment In-House Research and Development Network and the Washington State Workers' Compensation System) are discussed in this chapter.[4] The following conceptual model of public sector turnarounds is based on this analysis.

- *Visible problems.* Frequently, the turnaround process begins with an external review of the organization's problems. The reviews are conducted in a number of settings including the media, auditors' reports, public hearings of legislative committees, or election campaigns. Ultimately, they put organizational failure on the public agenda and help create the perception that the organization is involved in widespread instances of poor service delivery or crises that lead the public to infer major problems.

- *New leadership*. Reviews are often followed by the appointment of a new CEO, most often because the previous CEO was fired or reassigned. Frequently, other members of the senior management team who identified closely with the previous CEO or who are unable to adapt to the new CEO's approach are also let go.

  The new leaders have a number of common characteristics. They are energetic, dynamic, and often relatively young for the post. They either know the business well, or they are well acquainted with one or more of the major stakeholders. Knowing the business is important because immediate action is necessary. Expectations are high, and the turnaround leader cannot spend the first six months learning on the job. Knowing key stakeholders is also important because gaining their support is often the critical first step in the reform process.

  The leaders in my sample were not all charismatic leaders.[5] They did, however, display an unusual ability to create vision and inspire others, certainly to a greater extent than their predecessors. Nevertheless, it is unlikely that they would have been equally successful in any setting, or would have chosen to lead in other settings. Their expertise in the business or their knowledge of the stakeholders appears to have been the critical factor.

  The tenure of successful turnaround leaders is generally quite long, between four and fifteen years. (The four year term is still twice the average for a deputy minister in the Canadian federal government.) The major reason these CEOs stay in place is that a turnaround in a large organization is not instantaneous and requires a long commitment. Moreover, bringing about a turnaround can be immensely rewarding, so much so that the CEO prefers to stay. Though my study did not identify any, the public sector does contain some "turnaround artists" who, like their private sector counterparts, move from one turnaround situation to another. Earl Phillips has been in charge of public housing agency turnarounds in Houston, Miami, and Atlanta (Gurwitt, 1992) and Harry Spence went from the Boston Housing Authority to the financially bankrupt Boston suburb of Chelsea (Petersen, 1994).
- *Organizational change*. Turnaround leaders initiate a variety of organizational changes, including
  1. The development of a mission statement and strategic plan. The mission statement will reflect a new organizational

philosophy or self-definition; the strategic plan will elaborate on the new philosophy.

2. A reform or modification in organizational governance. Some organizations become more closely integrated with their authorizing environment; others seek more autonomy from political decisions and imperatives so that they can be managed on a business-like basis. The latter is often done by establishing a private sector style board of directors.

3. A reorganization of work at the front lines. In some instances, front-line jobs are broadened so that workers can handle complete processes rather than parts of a process, or became case managers, responsible for all interactions with clients. Workers can be encouraged to make suggestions and begin to play a larger role in continuous improvement.

4. A decentralization of power. The organization may be divided into smaller and more autonomous units. In some instances, the decentralization is geographic, but in other instances it will be done in a given workplace by replacing a functional approach with multifunctional teams.

5. Outreach to, and increased consultation, with clients. Such openness ensures that services will be designed to better meet their needs.

6. The use of information technology. Turnaround leaders are open to new ways to improve internal operations and enhance client service.

In my research, all six of these changes were often observed, and every turnaround involved more than one of them. The reorganization of the front line appeared most frequently—indeed, in every case, and appears to be the key component in turnarounds undertaken to improve client service and to increase staff commitment and morale. Strategic redefinition was important in organizations that had lost focus, but organizations that did not change their mission or philosophy also improved performance dramatically as a result of reorganizing their work.

- *Results*. Improved performance will be evident in every turnaround, though how this improvement is measured will vary. Some organizations will use outcomes, such as lower accident rates for workers' compensation agencies or fewer incidents of equipment failure for maintenance facilities. Others will use efficiency measures, such as reduced cost or greater productivity. In addition, progress can be measured by benchmarking, and, of course, some successful turnarounds will win innovation awards.

Sample Cases

Four programs included in the Ford-KSG sample illustrate various aspects of the turnaround models that Moore and I have sketched.

New York City Child Health Clinics. In brief, this turnaround expanded the mandate of the clinics operated by the New York City Bureau of Child Health—from a narrow focus on infant health and traditional preventive services (e.g., inoculations and dispensing public health information) to delivering primary child care from birth to age twelve. The clinics adopted this mandate to meet the previously unaddressed medical needs of poor urban children. Following the restructuring process, children were assigned to one doctor, rather than made to see whoever was available. Doctors were encouraged to become more involved with local hospitals and to provide more effective referrals for secondary care. An initiative was launched to help families manage their asthmatic children, a dramatic improvement on the past in which doctors had simply dispensed bronchodilators and referred children to hospitals for acute episodes. Finally, the Bureau convinced the city's Office of Management and Budget to fund renovations for some of the clinics.

Dr. Katherine Lobach, the bureau's director, fits the model of a turnaround leader perfectly. She was brought in by the Commissioner for Health who was "dissatisfied with the dilapidated facilities, outmoded procedures, and limited effectiveness of the department's 55 child health stations." Lobach knew the business and the stakeholders. She had been a professor of pediatrics at Albert Einstein College of Medicine, and she "had extensive experience in the Bronx developing and operating a model primary comprehensive health program for children" (New York City Bureau of Child Health, 1994). She has stayed in her position at the Bureau of Child Health since 1987, turning down several offers of promotion. As Hale Champion describes her:

> Dr. Lobach's breadth of vision, energy, and commitment [stand out] in the normal bureaucratic sea of intellectual and managerial inertia. . . . I met a number of other first class public servants during my site visits, some of whom were there simply because of Dr. Lobach

and her ability to lead and communicate her sense of possibility. They were unanimous on one subject—Dr. Lobach. In my judgement, [the program] wouldn't have happened without her, and would lose momentum, if not character, if it lost her leadership in the near future. Fortunately, she seems committed to seeing it through. . . . She does not appear to be charismatic or even remarkable, but she is quietly articulate, persuasive, responsible, and gifted with good managerial temperament and sense. Her political instincts in her own area of expertise and responsibility seem sure and successful (Champion, 1994).

The Ford-KSG application described the process that Dr. Lobach used to win staff acceptance of the changes. The new vision was developed in a series of retreats and follow-up meetings. Most staff members welcomed the changes as long overdue, some accepted them passively, and a few actively resisted. Dr. Lobach replaced the resisters, and retrained the remaining staff.

The turnaround improved performance in several areas. The percentage of children who regularly see the same physician increased from 43 percent in 1989 to 88 percent in 1993. The percentage of all visits accounted for by sick visits increased from 16 percent in 1991 to 55 percent in 1994. Kept appointment rates increased from 54 percent in 1989 to 65 percent in 1993. While these indicators are not health indicators per se, they do show the center's success in bringing comprehensive health care closer to children of the urban poor. In 1993, Dr. Lobach won a prestigious Sloan Public Service Award for excellence among career public servants in New York (Teltsch, 1993).

New York City Bureau of Motor Equipment. By 1979, the performance of New York's Bureau of Motor Equipment, which is responsible for servicing New York's 4,500-truck sanitation fleet had deteriorated so badly that the city was virtually unable to pick up garbage. At any given time, 50 percent of the trucks were out-of-service. Operations were maintained by paying overtime for repairs and night garbage collection. Labor-management relations within the bureau were strained to the breaking point. Discredited, the entire senior management team resigned. Ronald Contino was appointed Deputy Commissioner of Sanitation in charge of the Bureau of Motor Equipment, with a mandate to achieve a rapid turnaround (Contino and Lorusso, 1982).

Contino began by rejecting the traditional approach to fleet maintenance operations in which "innovative ideas, if any, are generated by management and/or professionals, while trades workers are relegated to daily maintenance routines," with the result that their "primary objectives are getting through the workday and retiring as soon as possible. The quality of services they provide is marginal at best and undermines the long-term viability of the equipment they are charged with maintaining" (New York City Bureau of Motor Equipment, 1992).

Contino took immediate steps to implement a new philosophy of front-line worker involvement in the essential innovative work of the organization. He established a labor-management committee structure and set up an operations improvement unit to analyze and implement ideas coming from the committees. He also formed a research and development group to find ways to improve the equipment and eliminate maintenance problems.

Additional steps involved staffing the research and development unit almost entirely with tradespeople rather than engineers, negotiating late delivery penalties in contracts with suppliers, establishing sole-source contracts (so that suppliers would have an incentive to work with the bureau to improve equipment), and replacing piece work for individual tradespeople with internal profit centers for groups. Union leaders supported the changes, rather than risk further deterioration and privatization. Middle managers, on the other hand, initially perceived the labor-management committees as a competing power structure. They were coopted, however, by being offered places on the committees.

The results of this turnaround are both dramatic and sustained. Between 1979 and 1992, the average daily out-of-service rates for trucks decreased from 46 percent to 16 percent and for sweepers from 51 percent to 21 percent. Productivity gains have been substantial. The number of vehicles increased over the period by 40 percent, from 4,500 to 6,200, but the staff stayed virtually constant at 1,100. A 1989 audit showed that the bureau's employees, though only 1 percent of the city's total workforce, contribute 14 percent of all suggestions. Numerous suggestions have been incorporated in the vehicle design, and some ideas have been patented. Contino stayed for 11 years, and was replaced by Roger Liwer, who had been his deputy. Liwer maintains that the success of his agency depends on its management style, saying in an interview, "if I were to leave tomorrow and some autocrat were to come in, this [program] would die in a day" (Mechling, 1994).

City of Chicago Parking Enforcement Program. I have already referred to the City of Chicago Parking Enforcement Program to exemplify a systems approach to problem solving and a politically driven comprehensive planning process. It also exemplifies various aspects of our model of a turnaround. Before the turnaround, parking enforcement in Chicago was a failure. People parked illegally and paid only 10 percent of the tickets. As described in the Ford-KSG questionnaire, "the old system was so bad that there was widespread public and legal community sentiment in favor of junking it and beginning afresh." Despite public sentiment, the bureaucracy was unable to rethink the problem and "there was also a general disbelief among city employees, as well as among the public, that plans would be translated into action" (City of Chicago, Illinois, 1991). Two critical elements led to the turnaround: a strong political will from the newly elected Mayor Daley, and the decision to bring in an outside team.

Parking reform appealed to Daley, given his temperament and approach to politics. According to political scientist Paul Green, "Daley hates waste. He hates inefficiency. . . . In many ways, he's a policy nerd" (Mahtesian, 1994a, p. 26). Daley made parking reform a priority and set deadlines for action (see chapter 3). The Parking Enforcement Program also had strong support from the business community because it would improve the traffic flow in downtown Chicago. Nevertheless, a number of organizations had pieces of the parking problem, and they had to be persuaded to go along with the new system. Thus, when 42 data entry clerks in the police department were made redundant by the new system, new positions were found for them. The position of parking administrator was created directly for the program, which meant that no one had to be fired. The administrator, a former state attorney and her top staff, were brought in from the management consulting world; while they did not have experience in the parking business, they did have experience in systems analysis and information technology, which constituted the core of the new business of parking enforcement.

Results were swift. The new system increased revenue and reduced cost (see chapter 7), and travel speeds in the Loop increased by 15 percent between 1988 and 1990, at least partially because the parking enforcement program was keeping more lanes open.

Washington State Workers' Compensation System. The Washington State Workers' Compensation System (WCS), a public sector monopoly provider of no-fault insurance for work-related injury or illness, serves two million workers in Washington State. It has 2,500 employees and an administrative budget of $67 million.

In the early 1980s, WCS was in dire straits. It ended the 1985 fiscal year with a $144 million operating loss, even after rate increases of 17 percent in 1983 and 33 percent in 1984. Its major problem was a mandatory vocational rehabilitation law that had dramatically increased the time injured workers were away from work and the number of vocational rehabilitation specialists practicing in the state. Business was demanding an end to this expensive monopoly. Labor was embarrassed by the system because, despite mandatory vocational rehabilitation, injured workers were receiving inadequate or inappropriate medical care. By all measures, customer service was poor and staff morale low. Republican gubernatorial candidate Booth Gardner was elected in 1984 on a platform of running government in a more business-like way, and WCS was his prime example of inefficiency (Washington State Workers' Compensation System, 1992).

Gardner's first step in turning WCS was to appoint new senior managers, one each from business and labor. Richard Davis, a marketing executive for Pacific Northwest Bell, who had previously directed Oregon's Department of Human Resources, was appointed director. His deputy director was Joe Dear, a research director for the Washington State Labor Council. The Governor next introduced legislation ending mandatory vocational rehabilitation and reducing benefits; organized labor accepted the legislation in return for a promise from the business community to end its lobbying for a private insurance system.[6] This agreement paved the way for a financial turnaround.

Once the financial turnaround was in place, Davis and Dear began building an organizational culture that would be receptive to innovation— a culture, according to John Ellwood: "in which the WCS sees itself as an insurance company with a social conscience. That is, its goal is to outperform private insurers in terms of the standard measures of efficiency while at the same time maintaining its social goals" (Ellwood, 1992).

Under Davis and Dear's leadership, WCS engaged in a number of innovative processes. For example, it improved its health cost containment rate by analyzing physician and chiropractor bills, invested in management information systems to speed claims processing, and established incentives for firms to increase workplace safety and programs to shorten the time taken by injured workers to return to work. WCS also found ways to get close to the customer. It now has field staff to help educate companies about safety and filing claims, staff at AFL-CIO headquarters to answer workers' questions, and Spanish-speaking staff to work with

Latino farm workers in eastern Washington. In addition, front-line work has been restructured so that each claim is the responsibility of a single case manager (Davenport and Nohria, 1994). Claims managers work in teams and competition has been encouraged among teams.

The results of this turnaround can be measured various ways. WCS has moved from being a high-cost provider to a medium-cost provider. Premiums as a percentage of payroll were slightly less in 1992 than in 1985; while nationwide, premiums had increased by 70 percent. WSC's contingency reserve (assets minus liabilities) improved from a deficit of $225 million in 1985 to a surplus of $330 million in 1992. Various measures of customer service have improved. About 95 percent of customer calls are returned within 48 hours; first payment of claims is made within two weeks in 86 percent of cases. Partnerships with the private sector have reduced accident rates; for example, the number of fatalities in construction fell from 30 to 40 per year in the 1970s to 9 per year in 1991.

Davis stayed as director of WCS until 1987; Joe Dear succeeded him, and stayed until 1993, at which time he was appointed to head the Occupational Safety and Health Administration in the Clinton Administration. Ellwood described Dear as "a labor leader who has fallen in love with modern management literature and techniques" but who "retains the respect of organized labor."

Each of these innovative programs displays the characteristics of the turnaround model. Each was an organization in crisis or, at the very least, performing inadequately; and each one had a new leader, and often a new management team; a new vision and mission for the organization; and a strengthened relationship with the authorizing environment (often resulting in additional resources). Other aspects of the model exemplified by these cases are their emphases on reorganizing front-line work (to encourage creativity and improve service) and improving the organization's overall performance. Finally, each of the new leaders stayed long enough to see the turnaround through.

NEW WAYS OF WORKING AND MANAGING

Those who practice the second broad category of organizational change—new ways of working and managing—have no shortage of ideas. Many initiatives are underway all over the country. To the extent that a common denominator can be found in this category, it is a belief in the potential of front-line workers. A recent study by the National Association of State

Budget Officers reported that thirty-nine states have undertaken TQM or other quality initiatives, twenty-seven are developing performance outcome measures, eighteen are eliminating management layers, and ten are attempting to link pay to performance (National Association of State Budget Officers, 1995).

Skeptics of these initiatives complain that though many government programs readily embrace a host of new theories and techniques, they are equally likely to discard them—including TQM, managing for results, benchmarking, reengineering, downsizing, and competitive contracting. In some instances, states disseminate information about the many programs available to managers but do not get actively involved in organizational change; in others, initiatives begun by one administration may be dropped or deemphasized by their successors, as Governor Pataki dropped Governor Cuomo's Quality Through Partnerships (Walters, 1996a).

But whether their practice is robust or short-lived, these initiatives appeared less frequently in the Ford-KSG sample than we expected—perhaps for two reasons. First, the Ford-KSG sample includes the early years of the decade, before these managerial initiatives became rampant, indeed almost faddish. Second, the judges are likely to have weeded out routine applications of management techniques and entries that have not produced results. Thus, the initiatives in this category that are included in the sample, though few, are likely to be imaginative and successful. Their themes include increasing local autonomy (geographical decentralization), transforming front-line work, measuring and benchmarking performance, gainsharing, and comprehensive organizational change.

The cases that follow are presented in outline only as examples of each new management theme, with one exception. Following the description of the two cases that exemplify gainsharing, I will discuss the fifth theme, namely, comprehensive organizational change, in more detail. In it, I will comment at length on David Osborne and Peter Plastrik's new book, *Banishing Bureaucracy*, which makes an argument for the primacy of comprehensive organizational change. Our final summary will include all four themes—to establish a broader view of their implications for innovation in the public sector (e.g., the obstacles their champions faced and with what results). As unwieldy as it may seem to divide the discussion this way, it befits the inclusive character of comprehensive organizational change. Innovations so classified have their own particular content but also reprise the other themes.

Four Themes, Five Sample Cases

Local autonomy. For many years, the New York City Transit Authority faced a massive set of problems: aging subway cars, graffiti, decaying track, and crime-ridden, dilapidated stations. During the 1980s, its priority had been simply to improve the trains and track. The stations' problems remained and were exacerbated by the Transit Authority's organizational structure in which all staff at the stations reported through functional units (e.g., cleaning, repairs, and safety). There was neither leadership or coordination at the stations (Kelling and Coles, 1996; Spicer, 1995). Customers voiced the common complaint that "no one was in charge."

New York City's Station Manager Program, a Ford-KSG finalist in 1993, was the Authority's attempt to deal with these problems by creating the position of station manager. The station manager was to be a "visible, proactive, front-line individual accessible and responsive to our customers and empowered to coordinate all station activities." Station managers were empowered to work directly with support divisions to improve safety and cleanliness in the stations. The program also had an outreach component, so that station managers could work closely with transit riders, community organizations, public officials, and private developers (Metropolitan Transportation Authority, 1993).

Transforming the front line. The Massachusetts' Department of Environmental Protection's Blackstone project, a Ford-KSG winner in 1991, involved a new approach to environmental regulation. The standard method of environmental regulation for industrial sites at that time was to have a separate inspection for each medium (e.g., air quality, hazardous waste management, and water pollution). Separate inspections are not able to deal effectively with what regulators call "the pollution shell game," the tendency of some factory operators to transfer pollution from one medium to another.

The Blackstone Project was a pilot program that inspected all media simultaneously. The project included twenty-six factories in the Upper Blackstone Water Pollution Abatement District and required a substantial reorganization of work at the front lines. Inspectors were trained to "examine a facility as a series of production units with raw material inputs, processing operations, products and wastes and emissions" (Massachusetts Department of Environmental Protection, 1991). Next, the inspectors were to develop strategies for reducing pollution at its source.

Measuring and benchmarking performance. As an example of Osborne and Gaebler's principle of results-oriented government, or the funding of outcomes rather than inputs, the State of Oregon developed a comprehensive set of 272 benchmarks (also called quality of life or performance indicators) in such areas as infant health, elementary and secondary student achievement, air and water quality, housing affordability, crime, employment, and per capita income (Oregon Progress Board, 1994). Since then, priorities have been established: twenty-seven items on the list are identified as urgent, such as reducing teen pregnancy and increasing access to health care; another eighteen as core, for example, enhancing educational attainments (Walters, 1994). Oregon Benchmarks, one of few such programs in the country in the late 1980s, is now widely copied. In fact, twenty-seven states are developing performance outcome measures for programs (Walters, 1994; National Association of State Budget Officers, 1995).

Gainsharing. William Niskanen's *Bureaucracy and Representative Government* (1971), explores the hypothesis that bureaucrats tend to maximize their budgets. The hypothesis implies that a bureau's output will be produced at more than minimum cost. Niskanen's suggestions to induce more efficient behavior include the notion that a bureaucrat should be allowed to keep a portion of the money saved if products or services can be delivered at less cost than expected. This incentive is, in effect, gainsharing.[7]

In recent years, numerous organizations have experimented with gainsharing. Two implementation problems must be dealt with. First, how does a program manager (or other authority) determine a fair allocation of the gains between the public and the bureaucrats, so as not to reward historical inefficiency? Second, savings must not be made by delivering goods and services of unacceptably low quality (Walters, 1995).

The Shared Savings Program is a case in point. Robert Soderberry, director of the Public Services Department in Pittsburg, California, originated this program at a time when the city was under intense pressure. During the 1980s population growth was up but taxes were down (the latter as a result of Proposition 13); and Soderberry had already replaced retiring civil service employees with hourly workers who, unlike civil service employees, can be hired to work for lower wages and no benefits or job security. They were also hired only if there was work to do.

Soderberry believed that the workforce has two types of employees: clock-punchers and go-getters. Frustrated with the time he spent monitoring and disciplining the former, Soderberry wanted to motivate the go-getters. He offered a small group of go-getter hourly employees in the parks maintenance division an opportunity to participate in a gainsharing program. They would be paid a full forty hours every week, but would relinquish any overtime. They were given control over a budget that included variable costs such as labor, materials, and supplies. If they produced savings by increasing productivity or innovating, 40 percent of the savings would go to the city, but the remaining 60 percent would go the employees as bonuses.

To ensure that employees did not keep costs down by doing substandard work, Soderberry imposed financial penalties on such work. Members of the program were given the right to decide whether other employees could join. Between 1987 and 1993, the program grew from eight employees in one division to twenty-four employees in nine divisions covering such functions as parks, maintenance and repair of public buildings, streets, sewers, and water lines (City of Pittsburg, California, Public Services Department, 1993; Simon, 1992).

Marion County, Oregon's Model for Controlling Wage and Benefit Costs also has a gainsharing component. This program, which effectively changes the collective bargaining practices between the county and its labor unions, emerged from the county's 1988 mission and vision statement. Its goal is to improve the relationship between the county and organized labor unions. The Oregon Public Employees Union, which represents two-thirds of the county's workforce became a key supporter, and other unions followed (Marion County, Oregon, Department of General Services, 1994). The parties first negotiate the size of the total compensation package. Once agreement has been reached about the size of the total package, then negotiations can begin on its components (e.g., salaries, merit increases, benefits).

Critical to the second stage of negotiations is the sharing of information so as to reach agreement on how much different components (e.g., health care benefits) are expected to cost over the life of the contract. This process gives the unions more flexibility to substitute among different components and to share in any savings resulting from reductions in the cost of any component in the total compensation package.

Comprehensive Organizational Change

Discrete cases of new management initiatives lead inexorably to the fifth of its categories, comprehensive organizational change, which must also contain the theoretical underpinnings for this type of innovation—and perhaps for reinventions generally.

A theoretical aside. Osborne and Plastrik tell us from the outset that *Banishing Bureaucracy* (1997), unlike *Reinventing Government*, is prescriptive. It begins, therefore, with a definition of reinvention:

> [It is] the fundamental transformation of public systems and organizations to create dramatic increases in their effectiveness, efficiency, and capacity to innovate. This transformation is accomplished by changing their purpose, incentives, accountability, power structure, and culture (p. 14).

The authors also stress the comprehensive nature of reinvention and sound almost Maoist in their insistence that it goes beyond business process reengineering, TQM, and privatization: "Reinvention is large-scale combat [that] requires intense, prolonged struggle in the political arena, in the institutions of government, and in the community and society" (p. 28).

Their prescription for reinvention includes five strategies:

- a core strategy in which an agency focuses on its own key purposes,
- a consequences strategy that changes the incentive system (to reward performance);
- a customer strategy that creates internal markets and promotes accountability to the customer and competition with the private sector;
- a control strategy that forgoes central agency oversight in favor of empowering public servants; and
- a cultural strategy that builds a more entrepreneurial organization.

Osborne and Plastrik urge reinventers to use as many of these five strategies as possible.

Banishing Bureaucracy cites fewer cases than *Reinventing Government*. Those it does cite are almost all comprehensive change programs. It includes initiatives in the United Kingdom and New Zealand (two of the earliest and most comprehensive New Public Management reformers); the City of Hampton, Virginia; and the City of Indianapolis, which is a leader in using competition between public and private sector suppliers.

I am uncomfortable with Osborne and Plastrik's maximalist position for several reasons. By glorifying *comprehensive* organizational change, they deemphasize numerous other types of public management innovation; for example, those that use only one or two of the five strategies. There are many programs that introduce these elements of organizational change one at a time, and they are also producing results.

By concentrating on *organizational* change, Osborne and Plastrik pay too little attention to other types of public management change, such as the introduction of information technology or innovations in particular policy areas. That is, they seem to be advocating radical surgery where less intrusive therapies are called for. The trap they have fallen into is the very one I cautioned us to avoid: beware of taking drastic action where incremental change would be more effective.

Finally, by focusing on the efforts of major figures, such as Margaret Thatcher or other politicians and agency heads, in reinventing government—Osborne and Plastrik ignore the local heroes who are responsible for so much public management innovation.

Despite these objections, we may yet learn something by looking briefly at one of Osborne and Plastrik's illustrations of comprehensive organizational change.

A city takes charge. In the mid-1980s the mayor and city council of Hampton, Virginia, a city of 130,000 people, conducted a review of the city's condition. The results were troubling: higher taxes than most other cities in Virginia, a stagnant local economy, and low per capita incomes. Quickly, and with a sense of urgency, they began an economic turnaround for the city, deciding at the same time to create a more innovative and flexible city government, consistent with their economic strategy. When the city manager retired, they hired a new city manager, Robert O'Neill, with a mandate for comprehensive organizational change (Osborne and Plastrik, 1997).

O'Neill moved simultaneously on many fronts: flattening the hierarchy, encouraging greater coordination on cross-cutting issues, stimulating employee suggestions for cost-savings and performance improvement, and rewarding employees on the basis of performance. He established six task forces, chaired by assistant city managers or department heads, to deal with the broad issues that cross departmental boundaries, such as economic development, public safety, and citizen services. As well as these ongoing task forces, the city set up numerous ad hoc task forces and encouraged employees at all levels to participate in them. This approach demands a great deal of individual flexibility, and was supported by investing heavily in training (Walters, 1996b).

O'Neill also established performance measures for each department and put department heads on performance contracts with bonuses for exceptional performance. Departments began to design their own performance appraisal systems and programs to reward cost-saving suggestions. An annual citizen satisfaction survey was established, and its results also influence bonuses.

A "vision and mission" statement was developed in consultation with the city council. The vision committed them to making Hampton "the most livable city in Virginia." The initiatives launched a decade ago are still in operation, and Hampton is regarded as an exemplar of progressive public management (Osborne and Plastrik, 1997). O'Neill attributes the city's managerial success in part to a willingness on the part of politicians to leave management to the managers and on the managers' willingness to adopt, and adapt, theories to practice (Walters, 1996a). The city's economic performance has also improved. With more downtown development, it can lower taxes and pay back debt.

New Ways of Working and Managing: A Summary

Overcoming opposition. Initiatives to develop new ways of working and managing create small revolutions in the internal politics of the organizations. It is no surprise that they often face opposition; sometimes from workers who don't want to be empowered, sometimes from middle managers who don't want to cede authority to front-line workers, and similarly from union leaders whose representational role would be diminished if staff were empowered.

Thus, the Hampton, Virginia, initiative found that some workers could not adapt to the new, more participatory, and less structured environment. Some supervisors resented the loss of control and some front-line workers were not comfortable with empowerment and additional accountability. The City invested heavily in training; nevertheless, some employees, including department heads, left (City of Hampton, Virginia, Department of Human Resources, 1990; Osborne and Plastrik, 1997).

The New York Station Managers Program faced reluctance on the part of the transit police to share the responsibility for maintaining order with station managers. Their reluctance and opposition to change were overcome by running customer service training workshops for all employees. The workshops emphasized their roles as members of a problem-solving team.

The Blackstone project, while making inspectors' work more challenging, created problems for the supervisors, who continued to have a single program focus. As a result, multimedia inspection reports had to be circulated from supervisor to supervisor. The Department of Environmental Protection responded by training supervisory staff; however, this tactic simply moved the problem to a higher level. The U.S. Environmental Protection Agency, for the most part, still operates on a "one-pipe-at-a-time" basis. This problem demonstrates graphically the tendency of innovations to create pressure for change on related programs; either the pressures will bring about change, or the status quo may overwhelm the innovation.

In the California Shared Savings Program, the major challenge was to integrate new members into the group. Both time and training are necessary before new members can begin to "develop management attitudes and learn to see themselves as general partners in the service delivery business" (City of Pittsburg, California, Public Services Department, 1993).

In addition, these initiatives encountered external opposition—from those who find it inappropriate for public servants to behave in an entrepreneurial manner. The Shared Savings Program was initially concerned about public criticism because paying bonuses to employees might be seen as a radical departure from traditional civil service practices. However, the severity of the city's financial crisis facilitated an explanation of the program and disarmed any local opposition. Despite that, similar criticisms of it have been expressed by public administrators at state and national conferences.

More serious is the challenge to Marion County, Oregon's Model for Controlling Wage and Benefit Costs. As a result of the county's success at controlling some payroll costs, such as health insurance, employees received wage increases two percentage points higher than the Consumer Price Index. As a result, some voters felt that the employees were being overpaid. Consequently, two initiatives to cut public service salaries and benefits were placed on the ballot in 1994. If such initiatives succeed, the employees will obviously be unwilling to continue to work within the model.

Achieving results. To evaluate its program of extensive organizational change, Hampton, Virginia, used customer satisfaction surveys from 1987 to 1989. Over 93 percent of those surveyed said they were satisfied or very satisfied with the performance of city employees. There were employee-generated savings of over $3 million from 1987 to 1989 on an annual budget of $170 million, and 1,100 employees worked on fifty-three different task forces and focus groups in 1989.

The Station Manager Program has achieved a 10 percent higher cleanliness rating for participating than for nonparticipating stations and slightly higher turnstile availability (97 percent as compared with 95 percent). Kelling and Coles (1996) argue that the program has worked together with a number of policing initiatives to reduce crime rates in the subways. The station managers, in a sense, own the stations and have an interest in preventing crime. In addition, the program has had favorable newspaper coverage and the public has requested that it be extended to all stations.

The Blackstone Project demonstrated the viability of whole facility inspection. In sixteen of the first twenty-six inspections, violations were caught that would have been missed under the old system of single-program inspections. Even so, whole facility inspections took 10 to 50 percent less time. New source reduction strategies have been developed as a result of these cross-media inspections, and the department has expanded the program statewide (Innovations in State and Local Government, 1992).

The Shared Savings Program demonstrated cost savings of $212,000, or 7 percent of a $3 million budget in 1991–1992; these savings resulted because empowered employees generate many productive and cost-saving ideas, such as taking better care of the equipment and putting more effort into comparative shopping for new equipment (Simon, 1992). Fully 70 percent of residents surveyed in 1993 indicated that they were somewhat or very satisfied with the parks. A substantial number of program participants take part in training programs. Nancy Dunn's site visit report also gives the program high marks. She writes: "About the other positive effects of the program—high quality work and improved employee motivation and morale—I have no doubts whatsoever. I simply have not seen such pride, self-determination and team spirit elsewhere" (Dunn, 1991).

Marion County's Model for Controlling Wage and Benefit costs has resulted in closer relations between management and labor, as evidenced by numerous joint conference presentations; more accurate budgeting because total compensation costs have been anticipated; and stronger incentives to reduce benefit costs such as health, dental, and workers compensation premiums.

Oregon's Benchmarks, a winner of the 1994 Innovation Award, were incorporated by an increasing number of state and local government agencies into their planning and budgeting processes during Barbara Roberts' term as governor. Her successor, John Kitzhaber, has retained the Oregon Progress Board, but the benchmarks do not appear as valuable to him as they were to Roberts (Osborne and Plastrik, 1997). Still, Robert Behn, who did the site visit report on Oregon Benchmarks, noted that benchmarks were being adopted by local government, nonprofits, and the private sector, though none of them were compelled to use them. All this led Behn to conclude:

> Ten years from now, will we look back on Oregon Benchmarks as another well-meaning but naive governmental fad? Or will it be seen as the beginning of another seminal reform in the history of American government? . . . In the future, we may be using performance indicators for some purposes or in some jurisdictions, but not everywhere or for everything. Nevertheless, if a decade or two from now, governments, civic organizations, and society are using outcome benchmarks to motivate performance, to measure success, and to establish accountability, there will be little doubt that much of the initial practical effort to make the concept a success will have been done in the 1990s in Oregon (Behn, 1994).

COMPETITION WITHIN THE PUBLIC SECTOR

Another way to improve organizational performance is by the introduction of competition, the third broad category of organizational change. Competition may be within the public sector or between the public and private sectors. Competition among bureaus was also proposed by Niskanen (1971) as a way of reducing bureaucratic efficiency; indeed, he puts competition ahead of creating incentives to efficiency through gainsharing.

Competition does operate in a fundamentally different way from the other techniques. Other techniques assume that public sector organizations will retain their monopoly status and then seek ways to increase the efficiency of the monopoly, for example, through performance measurement or gainsharing. The competitive approach attacks the assumption of monopoly, using competition to force efficiency gains, with the threat that inefficient public sector suppliers will face—to use Moore's terminology—not the public sector equivalent of bankruptcy, but the public sector equivalent of liquidation. The following examples of comprehensive initiatives to create competition between the public and private sectors are from the Ford-KSG semifinalist applications between 1990 and 1994. I also discuss the city of Indianapolis, Indiana, which won a Ford-KSG innovation award in 1995 for its initiatives in this area.

Minnesota's Consolidated Chemical Dependency Treatment Fund, a 1993 finalist, pools all state and federal sources of funding for substance abuse treatments for financially eligible clients. Counties and Indian reservations receive an allocation from the Consolidated Fund which they can then use to purchase treatments from state-licensed public or private vendors, at negotiated rates. Thus, the program relies on competition among vendors to control costs and ensure access. Its most important achievement has been to implement a system of chemical dependency treatment that allows the "dollar to follow the client" to the most appropriate program (Minnesota Department of Human Services, 1993).

Texas's Child Care Management Services, a 1993 innovations award winner, takes a similar approach to child care. Funding from fourteen federal programs for twenty-two eligible groups is consolidated, and twenty-seven regional contractors help parents choose an eligible child care provider. The program can also be considered an information technology innovation because its management information systems match funding sources with eligibility criteria, manage waiting lists, switch children seamlessly from one funding source to another, and generate billings and payments (Texas Department of Human Services, 1993).

These programs have identical characteristics: funding consolidation; choice, made by or on behalf of a service recipient; state certification of vendors, to maintain quality; and competition among vendors. The repertoire is similar to the much-publicized reforms of the British National Health Service, in which local health boards or general practitioners, acting on behalf of their patients, choose secondary care services from competing hospitals (Lacey, 1997). The programs are, in addition, examples of Osborne and Gaebler's principle of competitive government.

Such programs were initially opposed by agencies that were forced to compete. Legislation proposing Minnesota's Fund failed the first time in 1985, primarily as a result of opposition from state hospital labor unions, particularly the American Federation of State County and Municipal

Employees (AFSCME), which feared potential job losses. Private hospitals also feared a loss of business if they had to compete with nonhospital programs. In 1986, the law was passed with modifications that addressed these concerns, including cash flow assurances for state hospitals and the establishment of four pilot projects to precede statewide implementation in 1988. As site visitor William Grinker described the politics of the legislation: "Republicans liked it because it increased competition and efficiency; Democrats liked it because it broadened services, and the Indian community liked it because it increased their control and resources for treatment" (Grinker, 1993).

Despite their fears, the state-run programs were able to cope with the new environment. Though their admissions decreased by 50 percent, they have stayed in operation by downsizing, creating specialized programs (e.g., for women and minorities), and marketing (Minnesota Department of Human Services, 1993). The Texas program also reported that it was criticized by some contractors who feared the marketplace, but they also adjusted to the new dynamics of competition (with the program's help). Vendors who previously had local monopolies were given gradually decreasing enrollment guarantees and training in marketing (Texas Department of Human Services, 1993).

The strategy of increasing competition has achieved results, and the successes of these programs are notable. Minnesota reported that between 1989 and 1992 the average cost per placement for chemical dependency rose only 7 percent, while the average cost of medical services during the same period rose by 28 percent. The fear that the poor and minorities would lose access to treatment was unfounded, as overall placements under the Consolidated Chemical Dependency Treatment Fund rose 8 percent and the proportion of those placements accounted for by minority clients rose from 26 to 32 percent.

Texas reported that its Child Care Management Services Program allowed the state to take full advantage of federal funding, so that between 1991 and 1992 expenditures on child care more than doubled, from $64 to $135 million. Improved automation also decreased the error rate on claims from 12 percent to 1 percent. Finally, as a result of competition, the number of child care providers increased from 2,000 to over 4,000. More recently, Texas has been emulating this innovation by building a computer system to integrate intake, eligibility determination, and enrollment procedures for twenty-five public benefit programs (Enos, 1997).

Indianapolis Mayor Stephen Goldsmith, elected in 1991, was initially an advocate of privatization as a way of reducing the cost of government.

However, he became convinced that public servants could compete with the private sector, if the burden of traditional management control was removed (Gurwitt, 1994b). His conviction gave rise to the City's Competition and Costing Program, which won an Innovation Award in 1995 (City of Indianapolis, Indiana, Department of Administration, 1995).

Competition and Costing involves three steps: first a volunteer advisory committee from the business community helped identify services that would present good opportunities for competition. Second, a consulting firm costed out the services as conducted in the public sector, in particular identifying overheads, to ensure a fair comparison of private and public sector bids. Third, and finally, the services were opened up to bids from both the private and public sectors. In addition, AFSCME helped workers prepare their bids (Husock, 1995).

Some services stayed in the public sector (street repair, trash collection, vehicle maintenance) while others were outsourced (wastewater treatment) or privatized (abandoned vehicle service, the municipal golf course). When public sector employees were the winning bidders, they were allowed to keep some of the cost-savings, in essence gainsharing (Osborne and Plastrik, 1997). The end result of the program has been a cost savings of $10 million in annual operating expenses, a reduction in the nonpublic safety workforce of 30 percent, and the identification of one-time savings of $123 million. Goldsmith was also chosen by *Governing* magazine as one of its "officials of the year" in 1995 (Perlman, 1995).

The most significant opposition to the program came from middle management, because they were found to be a major contributor to overhead costs in the public sector. For public sector bids to be competitive, middle management positions had to be substantially reduced. Though middle management's criticism continues, according to the award application, the program is popular and has not been halted or reversed.

INNOVATIONS IN GOVERNANCE

Innovations in governance, the fourth type of organizational change, include several initiatives to increase citizen input, one through the use of information technology; and the others, through the establishment of public consultative bodies. Oregon Benchmarks, discussed previously as an exemplar of outcome-based management, also represents an innovation in governance through its use of consultation. This process began with the publication of the state's strategic plan in 1989. This plan, written by the Governor's Office and Economic Development Department on the basis of an extensive public consultation, recommended the establishment of an oversight board to ensure that the state's actions would accord with the vision outlined in the plan—which the Ford-KSG application described as "building a world-class workforce and maintaining a social and natural environment attractive to competitive enterprises and workers." In response to the recommendation, the legislature created the Oregon Progress Board, an independent, nonpartisan agency of nine people, chaired by the Governor, with the other members appointed by the Governor with Senate approval. As an example of bipartisanship, Governor Barbara Roberts, a Democrat, appointed her defeated Republican opponent to the Board (Roberts, 1994). In addition to its oversight role, the board conducts extensive public consultations (Oregon Progress Board, 1994).

North Dakota's Consensus Council is somewhat similar to the Oregon Progress Board. Its objective is to provide a forum for public discussion and consensus-building on important but difficult policy issues, such as life-sustaining medical treatment and health care reform. The Council, now a private nonprofit corporation with a board of directors, represents a wide spectrum North Dakota society—the Chamber of Commerce, AFL/CIO, rural electric cooperatives, Native Americans, both political parties, the executive branch, the judicial system, and, ex-officio, the Governor's Office (North Dakota Consensus Council, 1994).

The three other governance initiatives are more local in nature:

- The Indiana Department of Corrections has established county corrections advisory boards of fifteen to nineteen members, who represent a wide range of interests: law enforcement agencies, the judiciary, prosecutors and defense attorneys, municipal government, probation officers, correctional agencies, victims of crime, ex-offenders, mental health professionals, and the public. The boards help identify priorities for local corrections spending, allocate state grants to support local programs, and have been developing community-based alternatives to incarceration (Indiana Department of Corrections, 1994).
- The Santa Barbara County Department of Social Services, faced with increasing case loads and shrinking resources, established a volunteer business advisory team, representing the local business community. The team advises on policy and program issues, such as establishing a family preservation program; management issues, such as the design of a computerized information system to match recipients with the twenty-six different programs the

department administers; and partnership opportunities, for example, finding work for recipients with local businesses (Santa Barbara County, California, Department of Social Services, 1993).
- Santa Monica, California's Public Electronic Network, was an early
  version of electronic democracy, initiated before widespread use
  of the Internet.

Governance innovations expand participation in public policy discussion and debate and have, on occasion, given rise to the unruliness that
often characterizes direct democracy. New viewpoints have on occasion
drawn criticism from existing viewpoints. For example, Oregon Benchmarks has been criticized as too ambitious and idealistic, and some critics
have also questioned the benchmarks selected as priorities. The North
Dakota Consensus Council has been criticized for usurping the preroga-
tives of the executive agencies and the state's legislative assembly.

Santa Barbara's Business Advisory Team aroused the Department
of Social Services' suspicion that it was really a form of outside oversight—
which the elected county board of supervisors thought necessary because
that bureaucracy had become self-interested and unimaginative. Opposition also came from advocacy organizations for the disadvantaged, who
saw it as an attempt to reduce entitlements. The director responded to
these criticisms by holding departmental meetings to allay suspicions
about the team and broadening the team's membership to include the
advocacy organizations. Similarly, Indiana's Community Corrections Advisory Boards were opposed by those who preferred incarceration to
alternative sentencing and community-based programs.

Some city council members in Santa Monica, unwilling to be the
object of flaming, no longer use the Public Electronic Network (Conte,
1995). The broader question regarding such experiments in electronic
democracy is how the virtues of free access and instant responsiveness
can be reconciled with the requirement for calm deliberation that was
the original justification for representative, rather than direct, democracy
(Wright, 1995). Internet user groups—for example, through the use of a
moderator—have begun to find ways to temper their discussions. Much
progress, however, will be needed to establish the protocols for electronic democracy.

What then do innovations in governance achieve? Even if the governments or organizations they affect have become more participatory, have
their decisions become any better? The North Dakota Consensus Council
has been able to find publicly acceptable solutions to the problems it has

dealt with, such as policies on life-sustaining medical treatment. The Santa Barbara Department of Social Services Business Advisory Team has helped the department work with the computer industry to develop an expert system to apply eligibility rules for different programs, and has helped the department communicate more effectively with the public. The growth of Indiana's prison population dramatically slowed from 1990 to 1993, in contrast to continued growth in the rest of the country; this was, in part, due to alternative corrections programs that the advisory boards had a hand in establishing. Despite its problems, Santa Monica's Public Electronic Network was used for a discussion about homelessness that resulted in the establishment of a program to provide showers, washers, and lockers for homeless people. The discussions facilitated by these innovations in governance have had an impact on public policy.

LARGE PARTNERSHIPS

Pressman and Wildavsky's path-breaking book *Implementation* (1979) delivered a pessimistic message about why good policies and programs often do not come to fruition:

> ... the apparently simple and straightforward is really complex and convoluted. We were initially surprised because we did not begin to appreciate the number of steps involved, the number of participants whose preferences have to be taken into account, the number of separate decisions that are part of what we think of as a single one. Least of all did we appreciate the geometric growth of interdependencies over time where each negotiation involves a number of participants with decisions to make, whose implications ramify over time. . . . Given these characteristics, the chances of completing the program with the haste its designers had hoped for—and even the chances of completing it at all—were sharply reduced (1979, pp. 93–94).

They demonstrated this point mathematically by showing that if a program has a large number of *consecutive* steps to be cleared, even if the chance of getting a clearance on any one step is high, the probability of successfully getting through the entire sequence of steps is much lower. In essence, they argued that Lindblom's (1965) model of partisan mutual adjustment breaks down when the number of parties becomes very large. However, three large partnerships in this sample show how it is possible to overcome the implementation problem posed by Pressman and Wildavsky.

The Joint Urban Mobility Program (JUMP Start) is a partnership of thirty-six government agencies involved in transportation in the San Francisco Bay Area. It was organized by the Metropolitan Transportation Commission to expedite high-payoff yet low-cost projects to improve traffic flows, encourage the use of alternatives to automobile commuting, reduce auto emissions, and streamline the planning process. How difficult those tasks task might be can be seen from the program's response to the Ford-KSG questionnaire, which noted that JUMP Start "brought to the fore a largely hidden problem—the multiplicity of owners and operators responsible for the transportation network in any metropolitan region (at least 150 agencies in the Bay Area alone!) which presents a roadblock to interjurisdictional projects" (Metropolitan Transportation Commission, 1993).

The Task Force on Fast-Tracking Road and Bridge Projects is a similar initiative, though less complex. The three agencies with shared jurisdiction for road and bridge projects in greater Cleveland (Ohio Department of Transportation, Cuyahoga County engineer's office, City of Cleveland Department of Public Service) created this task force to speed the completion of transportation projects (Build Up Greater Cleveland, 1994).

The Urban Bay Action Teams have the object of reducing and preventing pollution in the bays in the Puget Sound Area. An interagency work group, consisting of representatives of federal, state, county, city and tribal governments, port authorities, and regional planning bodies, is formed to encourage commitments to deal with the environmental problems of each particular bay. In addition, citizens advisory committees consisting of representatives of environmental groups, industry, chambers of commerce, recreational users, and neighborhood associations are formed to comment on the interagency work plans, identify public concerns, disseminate information to their members, and ensure public accountability of program participants responsible for performing remedial actions (Washington State Department of Ecology, 1992).

Overcoming Barriers to Partnership

Partnerships are generally created to facilitate collective action. That is, they institutionalize their efforts to prevent inaction. They work to ensure that all members of the partnership participate in its support, to compensate potential losers, and to prevent turf fights among agencies.

Large partnerships have used a number of tactics to overcome these barriers.

JUMP Start describes its partnership as "loose-knit but effective," and in its 1991 annual report, Lawrence Dahms, executive director of the Metropolitan Transportation Commission, wrote that "the partnership has no hierarchy, no legal documents—just mutual interest. No logos, no letterheads—just project sponsors and results." In addition, the partnership has "a blue ribbon advisory council that draws its membership from a virtual *Who's Who* of transportation research and professional organizations, and environmental and business groups, as well as prominent community groups." Both the advisory council and the partnership meet quarterly on the same day, with the advisory council putting pressure on the partnership to overcome institutional barriers to action. In addition, each project is managed by a subset of the partnership composed of the sponsoring agencies with one of the agencies' staff, or if necessary MTC staff, taking the lead (Metropolitan Transportation Commission 1993).

Cleveland's Task Force on Fast Tracking Road and Bridge Projects also commented on the importance of frequent informal meetings of the participants and the role played by a private sector facilitator:

> The principal challenge was to get Cuyahoga Country's principal road and bridge players in the same room often enough to see problems and solutions together as partners. This diverse group of individuals, often with conflicting opinions, procedures, and agendas began meeting regularly in "shirt sleeve" sessions for eleven months in 1989 and 1990 to fashion a set of recommendations, which was published in September 1990. The group successfully set aside its differences and gradually evolved into a cohesive unit. . . . The deft leadership of a private sector volunteer, Richard Donaldson, as chair of the task force enabled personnel from the three agencies to focus their collective efforts on a goal of community betterment as the rationale for fast tracking instead of more parochial organizational goals (Build Up Greater Cleveland, 1994).

In addition, this Ford-KSG semifinalist also reported that the city, the county, and the state all used project managers, who are described as "empower[ed] to act within their home agency as facilitator, expediter, coordinator, advocate and trouble shooter for projects under their control . . . [and] accountable for the success of failure of projects under their supervision." Thus, the city, county, and state project managers for any project all had an incentive to work together to see it through.

The Urban Bay Action Teams' application also mentions the importance of clearly defined mandates for immediate action and of bringing enough parties to the table that it is difficult for any participant to evade their responsibility:

> The program's uniqueness, that action teams work within a focused geographical area, provides a framework for public and private entities to voluntarily commit to participation in an action plan. The program's design emphasizes immediate actions that achieve results through the use of existing data on pollution sources. The action plan assists in performance accountability by identifying the specific action and whose responsibility it will be to complete that action. Accountability is then achieved through peer pressure to complete assigned elements of the action plan (Washington State Department of Ecology, 1992).

Thus, innovative partnerships do find ways to avoid the dilemma Pressman and Wildavsky identified. Because the organizations involved recognize that they will have overlapping interests on many similar issues, they can form partnerships to bring all relevant interests to the table *simultaneously*, not as consecutive steps. The "geometric growth of interdependencies" that Pressman and Wildavsky bemoan is still there, but partnerships permit these interdependencies to be worked out together, at the same time in the same room, and using a number of tactics to sort them out successfully. Thus, meetings are informal; clients who have a strong interest in seeing the partners reach agreement also sit at the table, sometimes chairing the meetings, and often expressing appropriate impatience at seeing the public good being held hostage to interminable interagency turf wars. The partnerships have focused on immediate and tangible results. Finally, when agreements have been reached, lead agencies or individuals are clearly designated and given responsibility for implementation.

Achieving Mutual Objectives

JUMP Start reports numerous collaborative projects that came to fruition in its first year in operation, including convincing the last holdout municipalities to participate in a system of freeway call boxes, initiating a demonstration project for a universal bus/rail transit ticket, and synchronizing lights along a nine-mile stretch of an arterial passing through five different cities. Nevertheless, the program describes its main achievement as one thing:

> the proliferation of new interagency alliances to implement the JUMP Start projects. Almost overnight, offices that at best politely ignored each other, or at worst were prone to open warfare, are working harmoniously to remove project roadblocks. . . . This new spirit of partnership is percolating beyond JUMP Start to other aspects of planning and programming. For instance, in the fall of 1992, Metropolitan Transportation Commission convened a freight advisory council made up of representative of trucking, shipping and rail interests.

The Task Force on Fast Tracking Road and Bridge Projects reported that it had reduced the time a typical federal-aid highway project required from initiation to contract letting from 88 to 49 months and, as a consequence, the value of road and bridge contracts let had increased from $40 million in 1988 to $192 million in 1993. The Puget Sound Urban Bay Action Teams have recorded decreases in the levels of metals in several urban bays, have eliminated the dumping of 28 million gallons of polluted wastewater, and have cleaned up fourteen sites and fifty-six leaking underground storage tanks.

CONCLUSION

Innovations in all five types of organizational change suggest a repertoire of strategic moves that innovative managers can use to overcome internal and external difficulties and achieve performance results in keeping with their organizational mission and strategic plan.

- First, the cases of turnarounds support the theoretical models presented in this chapter. It is, of course, unlikely that managers will make the first move in this category. Instead, a political figure or board will hire the turnaround manager. They should hire someone from outside the organization who knows the business or stakeholders, and who is relatively young and energetic; and they should make sure that this person is willing to commit to staying for the reasonably long time required to make a turn-around work.

Once a turnaround manager is in place, he or she must make a number of strategic moves, including closely monitoring senior staff or possibly replacing them, redefining the organization's mission, developing a strategic plan, enhancing internal accountability, and building on early successes to make a claim for additional resources. Other strategies are similarly important, such as consulting with the organization's customers, initiating internal decentralization, and reorganizing work at the front lines. The reader should be aware, however, that this repertoire does not constitute a detailed recipe. Some moves will be appropriate in some organizations, but not in others. Even if all these moves are appropriate, there are many possible sequences in which they may be undertaken, and following the right sequence may be critical to success.

- Second, while many new ways of working and managing characterize public sector organizational innovations, a number of messages appear to be applicable to all. These messages are addressed to agency heads since, as we have seen, they are the leaders most likely to undertake initiatives of this kind. Notwithstanding the variety of innovations, flavor-of-the-month management, in which techniques are rapidly embraced and quickly discarded, is terribly destructive. Based on a careful analysis of the organization, adopt the most appropriate technique or set of techniques. It may be that different techniques are more appropriate to different parts of the organization.

Note, too, the variety of views about how extensive change ought to be. In most of the cases surveyed here, only one or two techniques were adopted, but in a few, most notably, the Washington State Workers' Compensation System and the Hampton, Virginia, city government, a large number of techniques were implemented. My suggestion here is that the agency head exercise his or her judgment about how comprehensive a set of changes to introduce. The question to be asked in particular circumstances is whether a menu as extensive as Osborne and Plastrik's is appropriate.

New management techniques may, and indeed, based on this analysis, often arouse opposition, both from outside the government and from within. Opposition from outside results from the public's unwillingness to accept entrepreneurship by bureaucrats. Yet, we also saw cases in which politicians were either proponents of management reforms themselves (e.g., Richard Daley in Chicago, Stephen Goldsmith in Indianapolis) or supporters of public servants who were implementing management reforms (e.g., the city council in Hampton, Virginia). Political support for management change can help overcome public opposition.

Likewise in this category (new management techniques), the innovator may find it useful to be especially attentive to patterns of internal opposition. When workers are asked to do their jobs differently, they will need training. Individuals who ultimately cannot accept reforms investing them with more authority will need attention and help, perhaps to retire or go elsewhere. While unions initially resist these reforms, they will support them when it becomes clear that the membership supports them.

Middle management has a more problematic role. Empowering front-line workers, whether through geographic decentralization, gainsharing, or competing for contracts, changes the lives of middle managers. Some people can adapt by changing their role from supervisor to coach. The inescapable truth is, however, that fewer middle managers are needed. An inevitable consequence of many changes described here is that people—either the middle manager who is no longer needed or the front-line worker who resists empowerment—leave the organization. These transitions should be handled with dignity and with appropriate compensation.

- Third, managers of organizational change programs that introduce competition into the provision of public services must use a number of tactics to minimize the opposition of public servants or firms who believe that they will be hurt by competition. Indeed, it may be possible and desirable to emulate the tactics that were used in the cases just analyzed. For example, a certification process can ensure that competitors provide an appropriate level of quality. Similarly, if the competition is for services, such as health care or education, purchased for, rather than by individuals, the delegated purchaser should also be involved in maintaining quality. We have also seen in these cases the value of providing a level playing field, for example, by doing cost studies to ensure that appropriate overheads were taken into account for all competitors. Finally, programs introducing competition may need to provide some transitional assistance for competitors, especially at the outset. These measures may include help in preparing bids, such as AFSCME gave to public sector workers in Indianapolis, or training in marketing and strategy, as the Texas Child Care Management Services Program did for child care providers.

- Fourth, innovations in governance increase citizen input. Still, it appears that in organizational change involving governance innovations, we are left with a repertoire of questions, rather than answers. Which groups and individuals are to be consulted? How can the program be made nonpartisan? Which issues will consultative bodies address? If the consultative process is on the Internet, how can problems often afflicting discussion groups be avoided? How can the frequent unwillingness of the bureaucracy to take outside advice be overcome?

- Fifth, and finally, the analysis of innovations involving large partnerships does generate a repertoire of actions to guide the behavior of public sector innovators who may plan on convening similar partnerships. Innovators in this situation should invite organizations that repeatedly deal with issues on which they have overlapping interests. Keeping the setting for such meetings informal and bringing in client groups who have a strong interest in the outcome and little patience with turf fights can build support; so can asking a representative of these groups to act as chair. Focus on immediate and tangible results. Finally, make sure that a lead agency or individual is designated to implement decisions.

9

Dances with Business: Environmental and Energy Management

Environmental pollution and energy shortages first emerged on the policy agenda twenty-five years ago. Since then much legislation has been enacted and regulatory agencies have been established for both environmental protection and energy. In many instances, however, legislation intended to prevent pollution has instead created complicated, expensive, and time-consuming procedures to clean up past environmental failures or to assess the environmental impact of new projects. Since the original environmental and energy legislation, attitudes toward the private sector have also changed. Many people initially regarded business as "them," as the enemy. But it is clearer now that business is part of "us." The private sector produces goods that citizens value and jobs that citizens desire. The former naive attitude is further contradicted by a growing awareness that pollution is produced not only by point sources—like smokestacks and sewage treatment plants—but also by thousands of small businesses and millions of citizens. The regulatory approach used for point sources may be less effective for multiple point (diffuse, or "non-point") sources of pollution, such as highway and urban stormwater runoff, and agriculture.

Public sector innovators in the environment and energy policy areas show a willingness to work with the private sector to achieve results while also reducing complexity, delay, and expense. In addition, although environmental legislation and regulations are enacted at the federal level, they are generally administered by state and local agencies, and it is at this level that most of the efforts to streamline enforcement will be found. Dewitt John's *Civic Environmentalism* (1994) summarizes this approach to environmental policy:

> In contrast to the traditional command-and-control model, the relationships that characterize civic environmentalism are not primarily

hierarchical—orders do not come down from EPA to states to polluters. Rather, these three key players relate to one another at almost
the same level. . . . Most of the links involve nonregulatory "carrots"
like information, education, subsidies, and economic incentives.
However regulatory "sticks" are still important at times (p. 14).[1]

In this chapter, we will look more closely at public sector innovations
involving environmental and energy issues to determine their objectives
and meaning, and to discover who is proposing them, why, and with
what success. What approaches do we have, or what tools and methods
work best to affect practice in these important matters?

Innovations in the environmental and energy policy area—at least
those included in the Ford-KSG sample used for this study—involve
three main themes. Thus, some public sector innovators seek greater
cooperation with the private sector and, in some cases, voluntary compliance. Others encourage public involvement in the creation of new markets
to pursue policy objectives, such as recycling; and still others are interested
in using new technologies to solve environmental and energy problems.

The identity of local heroes and innovators in the environmental
and energy area also illuminates practice in this field. Table 3-1 shows
that compared to the overall sample, there is a very high incidence of
innovation initiated by politicians (30%), and a high incidence of initiation
by middle managers or front-line workers (42%), but a very low incidence
of initiation by agency heads (11%). This pattern merits a more detailed examination.

While approaches vary, innovations in the environment and energy
area are often holistic. Many, that is, will use a catchment basin, watershed,
or ecosystem-based approach to resource management; and they will
often pull together creative partnerships of diverse organizations or use
volunteers in their programs. The public is commonly involved in these
innovations as committee members and volunteers but also as consumers.

Environmental and energy innovations employ user fees to finance
the operating costs of programs more frequently than in any other policy
area (41% of environmental and energy programs included in the Ford-
KSG sample involved such fees). They must respond to a wide range of
opponents and critics, from environmental zealots, on the one hand, to
narrow profit-maximizers on the other. Sometimes, the critics include an
entire bureaucracy that is still wedded to the command-and-control
model. The chapter concludes with recommendations for would-be innovators in the environmental and energy areas.

VOLUNTARY COMPLIANCE

Voluntary compliance is often written off as an oxymoron, but is it? Citizens or businesses must first know the law before they can be expected to comply with it, and often knowing the law—especially in nonburdensome cases—is sufficient to gain compliance. The alternative—a strict command-and-control approach—implies that compliance can only be achieved through inspection and litigation. Inspection consumes public sector resources, and litigation is both expensive and time-consuming, especially if there are thousands, or indeed millions, of sources of pollution.

Programs that involve voluntary compliance and cooperation may have a number of components: the provision of information in plain English so that firms or individuals can know their obligations and the technologies available to help them meet these obligations; the use of economic incentives for compliance, for example, rebates against trash disposal fees for those who recycle; and, finally, the threat of sanctions or litigation. Sanctions and litigation should be seen as an instrument of last resort; the objective of these innovative programs is to achieve compliance without resorting to them. The following two programs provide information about environmental standards and how to comply with them.

California's Air Resources Board (part of the California Environmental Protection Agency) through its Compliance Assistance Program provides information about state and federal air quality standards. Technical manuals are provided to inspectors in local air pollution control districts and "comic book" style handbooks are provided free of charge to industry to encourage self-inspection and to train equipment operators. Between 1988 and 1994, 12,000 technical manuals and 350,000 simplified handbooks were distributed (California Air Resources Board, 1994).

A Vermont law passed in 1978 offered to pay 80 percent of the capital cost incurred by communities that had mandatory recycling programs in place by 1991. The City of Burlington planned to meet that deadline; however, it was not picking up recyclables from businesses or institutions. To help businesses comply with mandatory recycling by making their own arrangements, the City began to provide informational brochures, free workshops, and technical advice. Eventually, the city did more than provide information; it decided to pay 75 percent toward the cost of recycling containers and to award a Business Recycling Seal of Approval to businesses in compliance before the enforcement deadline (City of Burlington, Vermont, Solid Waste Division, 1993).

The cost and complexity of the Superfund program (authorized as the Comprehensive Environmental Response, Compensation, and Liability Act) is a strong incentive to voluntary action in cleaning up polluted industrial sites (Cuciti et al., 1994). James Gutensohn, a former Commissioner of the Massachusetts Department of Environmental Management and site visitor for the City of Wichita environmental cleanup project wrote

> . . . [T]he Federal EPA as an institution is unable for many reasons to approach an environmental clean-up in a community with clarity of purpose. EPA has multiple agendas set by Congress, the executive branch and interest groups. They see local superfund projects through the confusing kaleidoscope of precedent for other sites, mandates to achieve certain numerical goals, enormous workload, scientific uncertainty, and inexperience and act only hesitantly, begrudgingly, and tentatively. The program in many communities across the country has been the story of protracted haggling and endless studies with little relief in sight (Gutensohn, 1994).

Two programs in our sample were designed to avoid this legal and regulatory quagmire. Minnesota's Voluntary Investigation and Cleanup program provides technical assistance and liability assurance for businesses or individuals involved in cleaning up contaminated urban land (and thereby circumventing Superfund cleanups). The program uses the same cleanup standards as Superfund, but is less bureaucratic (Minnesota Pollution Control Agency, 1994).

The City of Wichita Environmental Cleanup (chapter 4) was also a creative way of circumventing Superfund and overcoming legislative obstacles. The city played the leadership role in structuring a multiparty partnership, in which a local manufacturer responsible for a significant portion of the pollution agreed to accept responsibility for its share of cleanup costs and other property owners in the area continued paying property taxes based on property values before, rather than after, discovery of the contamination. The city used the additional tax revenues to help finance the cleanup and banks agreed to resume lending in the area in exchange for release from cleanup liability.[2] The voluntary nature of the agreement avoided expense and litigation and led to a much faster cleanup than would have been the case if Superfund had been invoked (City of Wichita, Kansas, 1992; Rosegrant, 1992).

These programs all had the support of regulatory sticks, which former EPA Administrator William Ruckelshaus often referred to as the "gorilla in the closet" (John, 1994). Other programs with no such sticks have found other ways of influencing behavior. Two Iowa programs, the Leopold Center for Sustainable Agriculture and the Agricultural-Energy-Environmental Initiative, teach their constituents how to minimize the negative environmental impacts associated with farming practices, in particular, by using techniques that require less nitrogen-based fertilizer (Iowa Department of Natural Resources, 1993; Leopold Center for Sustainable Agriculture, 1993). Both programs originated in the Iowa Groundwater Protection Act of 1987. DeWitt John's *Civic Environmentalism* (1994) includes a case study of the history and effects of this act, which he regards as a classic example of civic environmentalism. It does not regulate fertilizer or set standards for groundwater but supports demonstration projects, research, and education intended to persuade farmers to use less fertilizer.

The Texas Water Commission's Ground Water Protection Program (chapter 2) uses incentives rather than regulation. Any public water system can inform the Water Commission of its desire to participate and provide maps indicating the location of its wells. The Water Commission then investigates the system and ultimately produces a report about how that particular public water system can manage its resources to prevent groundwater contamination. The Commission does create some pressure on these local water systems by publicizing its reports and enlisting citizen volunteers to help inventory potential sources of contamination and serve on task forces to ensure that the recommendations are implemented (Texas Water Commission, 1992). This program was undertaken in the context of a turnaround in which the Water Commission took a tougher regulatory stance toward major point sources of pollution (Arrandale, 1992).

CREATING MARKETS

The Coles Levee Ecosystem Preserve was discussed in chapter 3 as an example of an innovation that emerges from opportunity, rather than necessity. It is also an illustration of an innovation that creates a new market. Coles Levee is the result of an agreement between Atlantic Richfield (ARCO) and the California Department of Fish and Game, in which ARCO promised to acquire a mitigation land bank of 6,000 acres on the

Coles Levee in return for permission to drill numerous oil wells in the Bakersfield, California, area. (Absent the agreement, ARCO would have been responsible for mitigating the impact of the wells on endangered species on small parcels of land near each of the new wells.)

The land bank is large enough that ARCO can sell acreage to other developers with similar obligations. Altogether, the project reduces regulatory cost for government and the private sector and improves protection for endangered species (California Department of Fish and Game, 1994). The practice of mitigation banking is spreading; for example, Bank of America runs an endangered species conservation bank near San Diego, and the state and local water management districts in Florida run wetlands mitigation banks (Fulton, 1996).

A number of programs involved the creation of markets for recycled materials. The Multi-State Procurement of Recycled Xerographic Paper initiative (chapter 3) began as a demonstration project, but eventually stimulated a demand for 30 million pounds of recycled paper, thereby giving producers an incentive to solve technical problems and set standards for recycled paper. The same states are cooperating to create demand for other recycled products, such as retreaded tires, re-refined oil, computer forms, and envelopes (Wisconsin Department of Administration, 1993). The Pennsylvania Governor's Recycled Materials Market Development Task Force (chapter 4) creates markets for recycled materials, by hosting conferences that bring buyers and sellers together and by maintaining an electronic bulletin board (Pennsylvania Department of Administration and Public Affairs, 1991).

USING APPROPRIATE TECHNOLOGY

Energy and environment is the second most frequent user of technology, according to the Ford-KSG sample where it appeared in 30 to 35 percent of the programs in this area (see Table 2-1). Three of the applicants noted their use of information technology: Florida's Marine Spill Analysis Program and the Maricopa County Notice of Flood Hazard Determination Program use geographic information systems (Florida Department of Environmental Protection, 1994; Maricopa County, Arizona, Flood Control District, 1994) and St. Louis Park, Minnesota uses barcode technology for its recycling program.

The Maricopa County program records a notice of flood hazard on properties located within floodplains, assuming that if owners and buyers are more aware of risks, they will be more likely to purchase appropriate insurance. The properties at risk were initially determined manually, but managers later realized this could be done automatically by using a geographic information system to overlay flood insurance rate maps on land assessment maps. To accomplish their goal, they adapted a system that the county had bought for another purpose.

Collectors in the St. Louis Park, Minnesota, curbside recycling program also began by compiling a manual record of the households that recycled (as each of them was to receive a credit against their refuse collection bill). A consultant hired by the city suggested barcode technology. Now, residents put a barcode sticker on their containers and collectors use handheld scanners built to withstand temperatures of −20 °F and equipped with miniature ice scapers (City of St. Louis Park, Minnesota Department of Administration, 1992).

Many innovations involving environmental or energy technology per se use simpler, less expensive, and more appropriate technologies. Georgia's Dry Hydrant Assistance Program provides information for municipalities about drilling dry hydrants (i.e., nonpressurized pipes permanently installed in lakes, farm ponds, and streams) that can be used to provide an unprocessed water supply for firefighting. Dry hydrants are a much cheaper alternative to building pressurized water systems or using tanker trucks (Georgia Governor's Office of Energy Resources, 1991). Similarly, the Loxahatchee River Environmental Control District in southern Florida has established an irrigation quality (IQ) water program, whereby it provides wastewater treated to irrigation quality for golf courses, thereby conserving potable groundwater (Loxahatchee River, Florida Environmental Control District, 1990).

Georgia's No-tillage Assistance Program provides advice and equipment rental so that small farms can take advantage of no-till planting technology. No-till technology enables farmers to plant new crops directly into the previous year's crop residue thus leaving the maximum amount of undisturbed residue on the surface between crops and during the growing season. It uses less fuel than conventional technology, but more important, it helps control erosion (Georgia Governor's Office of Energy Resources, 1991). Finally, New York State's Self-Help Support System helps small towns find inexpensive alternatives to purification plants (New York State Department of State, 1994).

Programs involving waste treatment also employ new technologies that are simpler, less expensive, and more protective of the environment than the technologies they replace. The town of Harwich, Massachusetts, worked with private sector investors to build a plant using solar aquatics to treat septic tank sewage. The sewage is treated with sunlight, water, oxygen, plants, and animals in greenhouses rather than with chemicals in concrete superstructures (Town of Harwich, Massachusetts, Board of Health, 1991). Other small communities throughout the United States are experimenting with artificial wetlands, wet and dry detention basins, and other natural treatments of wastewater (Arrandale, 1995a). The Arcata, California, Wetland Wastewater Treatment Program, one of the earliest winners of an innovation award, pioneered this technology (Walters, 1996c).

ENERGY AND ENVIRONMENT'S LOCAL HEROES

Fully 30 percent of innovations in energy and environment are initiated by politicians, though politicians initiate only 18 percent of programs in the entire sample. This high incidence of political involvement in this field is not surprising, however, given the political visibility of these problems. In some cases, the innovation occurred as a direct response to a visible crisis; in other cases, individual politicians helped place the issue on the public agenda. Environmental and energy issues are usually so complicated and technical, however, that politicians soon call in public sector staff to advise them. And in some cases, this order was reversed, and the staff provided the information that led to the political initiative.

Groundwater pollution in Iowa was first discovered by environmental experts, who then formed a multiagency task force to study the problem. Water quality monitoring programs had detected pesticide and nitrate residues in both surface and groundwater throughout Iowa— largely as a result of agriculture practices. The experts soon realized that a rural environmental crisis was brewing: a combination of soil erosion, off-farm impacts of agricultural chemicals, water-quality degradation, habitat destruction, and loss of natural predators. Efforts to involve the U.S. Environmental Agency (EPA) were unsuccessful because that agency had no clear mandate to deal with groundwater pollution. A number of Iowa legislators were interested, however, and one of them, Paul Johnson, entered politics in 1984 primarily to legislate a reduction in the use of agricultural chemicals. Johnson and a number of other legislators built a coalition powerful enough to overcome the opposition of the chemical industry and enact Iowa's Groundwater Protection Act of 1987 (John, 1994).

Seattle's recycling program is also a good example of a coordinated response to a crisis. In this case, the mayor and city council provided leadership, the bureaucracy did the planning, and the public responded. The crisis had several elements: the City's two landfills reached capacity in 1983 and 1986, and ceased operation. The federal government then designated these landfills as Superfund sites, thus raising the closure costs to about $100 million. The city's reliance on more distant landfills, together with closure costs, had already doubled solid waste disposal assessment rates. Then began the interplay of political leadership, public pressure, and bureaucratic planning that led to innovation:

> With direction from the Mayor and the City council to "gain control" of the situation, the Solid Waste Utility developed an array of disposal options ranging from the status quo (recycling at drop boxes and buy back centers, landfilling the rest) to the "balanced approach" (40% recycling, incineration, and landfilling of the ash and noncombustible materials). Citizens questioned the need for incineration and the level of commitment to recycling. The City Council directed the Solid Waste Utility to conduct an in-depth study to answer the following question: "How much diversion could the city accomplish if it spent the same amount in recycling programs as is planned for incineration?"
>
> Staff redesigned garbage contracts, redesigned the rate structure, designed curbside yard waste and recycling programs, developed a household hazardous waste plan and gained control over landfill closure. . . . The Mayor, with the support of the City Council, directed that curbside recycling be initiated and also set a goal in late 1988 for the city to recycle 60 percent of its waste by 1998 (City of Seattle, Washington, Engineering Department, 1990).

In other instances of energy and environmental innovation, middle managers or front line workers were the sole initiators, especially if the innovations were technical or procedural, and middle managers or front line workers knew the relevant technology. Under such conditions, they often saw ways to improve operations that agency heads or politicians may not have been aware of. The Coles Levee Environmental Preserve, for example, was the idea of an employee of the Fish and Game Department, who suggested that "instead of developing individual permits for each project, ARCO request an areawide permit and establish a mitigation bank" (California Department of Fish and Game, 1994).

The California Air Resources Board's Compliance Assistance Program also had its origins at the operating level, as its response to the Ford-KSG questionnaire shows:

> CAP was begun as a result of inspections we conducted showing widespread noncompliance in many industries ... the majority of sources told us their noncompliance problem stemmed from the fact they did not know how to comply. We also learned by working with local district inspectors that they had difficulty interpreting, and thus verifying compliance with, regulations. Through staff level contact and with the support of organizations such as the California Air Pollution Control Officers Association, we conceived the Compliance Assistance Program (California Air Resources Board, 1994).

Similarly, the Massachusetts Department of Environmental Protection's Blackstone Project originated from a suggestion by Manik Roy, then a doctoral student at the Kennedy School of Government and one of the department's head office staff. Roy's idea to combine source reduction and cross-media inspection won the support of Kenneth Hagg, the Department's Deputy Commissioner. He encouraged Roy to put the idea in writing and began promoting it to the line offices (Scott, 1993).

Local heroes in the energy and environmental bureaucracies are very similar to those working in information technology (chapter 7). They, too, are working day to day on the routine problems of regulation or management. They are familiar with environmental or energy technology, both in their own jurisdiction and its state-of-the-art possibilities. They are not only equipped to discover a better process or technology, but also to interest their superiors in the innovation and, ultimately, to persuade them to support it. In the process of innovation and persuasion, local heroes in energy and environment use a variety of practices, management styles, and structural techniques to prevent pollution, restore disturbed landscapes, and make their projects work (politically and environmentally). The common elements in their innovations are a thought process that is ecosystem-based, a proper evaluation of the role of volunteers, and a recognition that new vigor can often be found in creative partnerships and that innovative programs can sometimes be financed by user fees.

Systems Analysis

The attempt to understand the behavior of ecosystems is intrinsic to the environmental movement. Innovators in this policy area think systemically not only about the natural environment, but about their program's role in it. For example, Iowa's Leopold Center for Sustainable Agriculture described itself as supporting research, demonstration, and education projects "to improve management and reduce the environmental impact of agricultural chemicals, to develop alternative crops, and to expand biological pest control . . . emphasiz[ing] a holistic, integrated approach to reflect the systemic nature of farming" (Leopold Center for Sustainable Agriculture, 1993).

The Massachusetts Department of Environmental Protection's Blackstone Project results from conceptualizing the production process and its relation to environmental regulation systemically, as its Ford-KSG applications suggests:

> . . . circumventing cross-media transfer of pollutants by integrating compliance assurance inspections; making reduction of industrial wastes at the source an explicit goal of compliance assurance efforts [thus] coordinating the Commonwealth's technical assistance (carrot) and regulatory (stick) programs, without compromising either. . . . (Massachusetts Department of Environmental Protection, 1991).

Cross-media transfers of pollution were well known to environmental authorities as far back as the 1970s; the Blackstone Project was one of the first projects to work through the organizational implications of dealing with the problem.

Other examples of thinking systemically include the Harwich, Massachusetts, solar aquatic wastewater project, which created an ecosystem in its greenhouses to support aquatic plant propagation, fish farming, and the production of compost from septic tank sludge; and Seattle's Recycling Program, which was based on thinking systematically about waste management. In this case, waste stream analysis, waste generation and recycling forecasts, rate-setting, marketing and public relations, program development and implementation were used successfully to reconfigure the city's program (City of Seattle, Washington, Engineering Department, 1990).

The implications of ecosystem-based planning are clear. Efforts to prevent pollution or to maintain an entire ecosystem require governments to integrate across traditional programs, one of the elements of holism introduced in chapter 2.

Encouraging Volunteers

The strength of the environmental movement and the importance of environmental causes to certain segments of the population, particularly youth, presents an additional opportunity for innovation. Environmental initiatives can take advantage of this support by promoting programs in which this interest and support can be channeled by using activists as program volunteers. The Texas Water Commission's Ground Water Protection Program uses volunteers to help inventory potential sources of contamination. Louisville, Kentucky's Operation Brightside (chapter 3) uses citizen volunteers, in particular children and community groups, in environmental and cleanup projects. The city attempts to maintain the commitment of the volunteers through written maintenance agreements for small parks or greenspaces, and fosters their enthusiasm through a variety of recognition celebrations, such as donor parties and the mayor's annual appreciation breakfast (City of Louisville, Kentucky, Department of Community Services, 1993).

Yet a third program using volunteers is Seattle's Master Home Environmentalist Program in which volunteers assist people, in particular low income households and households renovating older homes to deal with sources of indoor air pollution such as lead-based paint. This program had to be adapted to the use of volunteers; for example, its heavy emphasis on technical information, which was better suited to professional inspectors, had to give way to a greater emphasis on community outreach, ideas that are easy to communicate, and cultural sensitivity (City of Seattle, Washington, Planning Department, 1994).

We may speculate that financially strapped governments will, in the future, encourage volunteers to participate in other aspects of environmental programming. For example, volunteers are increasingly being used to operate environmental monitoring equipment; the ideological commitment of activists ensures that the monitoring is done zealously. Another promising approach is that monitoring can become a project for science classes in the schools. Daniels (1995) mentions programs using volunteers to monitor streams in Montgomery County, Maryland; and in Missouri. The government will continue, no doubt, to employ scientists for project management and quality control, but the simpler tasks may be given to volunteers.

Forming Creative Partnerships

The Ford-KSG sample contains at least two innovations in which the collaborating organizations had entirely different missions. The environmental projects, however, provided opportunities for both to advance their missions. These collaborations call to mind the classic illustration of the advantages of bilateral trade.(e.g., British grain for Portuguese wine). Levin and Sanger (1994) also noticed such partnerships, and referred to them as instances of interest convergence.

The Hennepin County Household Battery Management Program in Minneapolis-St. Paul is a collaboration between the County, which recycles batteries, and a nonprofit organization that employs clients from the County's mental health program to sort the batteries by chemical composition (Hennepin County, Minnesota, Department of Environmental Management, 1992). New York City's Materials for the Arts Program is a collaboration between the Department of Cultural Affairs and the Department of Sanitation, in which the Department of Cultural Affairs encourages the donation of art materials, administrative supplies, and office furniture and equipment to needy arts and cultural organizations, and the Department of Sanitation picks up the materials and holds them in a warehouse to be picked up by the recipients (New York City Department of Cultural Affairs, 1993).

Employing User Fees

The environmental and energy areas employ user fees more often than any of the other policy areas (41% of the innovations in the Ford-KSG sample). In a number of cases programs are supported, entirely or in part, by designated user fees rather than through budget appropriations. The economic rationale for user fees is that they make citizens more cognizant of the cost of a service, such as waste disposal, and thus more likely to economize. In some cases, user fees involve including the disposal cost in the purchase price of the good. In other cases, more sophisticated pricing schemes have been used to strengthen the incentive to recycle.

Examples of user charges vary. The Minnesota Voluntary Investigation and Cleanup program's administrative expenses are financed by user fees to participating organizations; the Hennepin County Household Battery Management Program is financed by the county's user fee for solid waste collection, and the No-tillage Assistance Project's operating costs (fuel and labor) are funded by a user fee of $12 to $15 per acre.

The Wichita Environmental Cleanup was also financed by user fees. In this instance, the fees were in addition to damages paid by the major responsible party. Other property owners' taxes (based on property values before, rather than after contamination) paid for $500,000 of the $2,000,000 cost of the cleanup in 1992. The total cost of the cleanup is expected to be $20 million. Additional costs after 1992 will be negotiated and shared among the city, the major polluter, and other property owners.

For years, many state energy conservation programs have been financed by oil overcharge funds. These funds originated from fines that federal courts levied on major petroleum companies for overcharging during periods when gas and petroleum prices were federally regulated. Instead of trying to compensate the millions of consumers involved, the courts allowed the federal government to pass some of these funds to state governments for energy conservation programs (John, 1994). For example, 80 percent of the funding for Iowa's Agricultural-Energy-Environment Initiative came from oil overcharge funds; similarly, Georgia's Dry Hydrant Assistance Program and the capital cost of its No-Tillage Assistance Program were funded by oil overcharge payments. However, with deregulation of energy prices, these fines are no longer being collected, and most of the funds collected in the past have already been spent.

In some cases, taxes on an environmental hazard were used to pay for research to eliminate it, which can be seen as including in the purchase price of a good part of the long-run cost of disposing of it. A small tax of .5 percent on nitrogen fertilizers and pesticides pays for 65 percent of the operating budget of Iowa's Leopold Center for Sustainable Agriculture. Pennsylvania's Municipal Waste Planning, Recycling, and Waste Reduction Act of 1988, which led to the creation of the Recycled Material Market Development Task Force, specified that recycling initiatives were to be revenue neutral. The state's contribution to recycling was drawn from a fund generated by a $2 per-ton surcharge on all solid waste disposal.

In some instances, user fees for waste disposal are partially rebated to encourage recycling. The St. Louis Park, Minnesota, program integrating barcode technology with curbside recycling rebates refuse collection fees by $6.60 quarterly—if residents recycle. Similarly, the City of Seattle Recycling Program uses increasing marginal cost pricing: it charges households the cost of service for the first can of garbage and more for subsequent cans. Seattle also introduced a low-priced "mini-can" (19 gallons) to encourage aggressive waste reduction and recycling (City of Seattle, Washington, Engineering Department, 1990). The pricing strategy practiced by St. Louis Park and Seattle has caught on, and more than a thousand local governments are now charging by the bag or can for picking up trash (Arrandale, 1995b).

OVERCOMING OBSTACLES

The two most predictable sources of opposition to environmental and energy initiatives are from environmental activists, who say that such programs don't go far enough, and from regulated entities, who say they go too far. The Coles Levee Ecosystem Preserve was criticized by members of the Mountain Lion Foundation, who did not think that the management of endangered species and their habitats should be placed in the hands of private enterprise. Minnesota's Voluntary Inspection and Cleanup program was criticized by activists who felt that "voluntary cleanup" was an oxymoron meaning an "inadequate" cleanup. The Texas Ground Water Protection Program was also criticized by activists because it was voluntary.

These programs also faced criticism from those who found their behavior constrained or feared that their opportunities and incomes would be reduced. For example, Minnesota's Voluntary Investigation and Cleanup program was attacked by groups who argued that the cleanup of hazardous waste sites should not be a national priority. Initially, the Burlington, Vermont, business community was opposed to mandatory recycling, citing it as yet another example of how Burlington was bad for business. The Leopold Center for Sustainable Agriculture was criticized by the agricultural chemical industry and the Farm Bureau Federation: the former believed that "sustainable agriculture" would reduce fertilizer sales; the latter, that it would increase farmers' costs. The Multi-state Procurement of Recycled Xerographic Paper program was criticized by the paper industry and copy centers, who doubted that recycled paper could be developed to an acceptable standard for copying machines, and by purchasing agents, concerned about increased costs. The Maricopa County Notice of Flood Hazard Determination program was criticized by home owners whose property was affected and who assumed that the designation would lower their property values and make it harder to sell. (By contrast, real estate brokers were ambivalent, depending on whether they were acting for vendors or purchasers.) Finally, some attorneys were critical of the Wichita's Environmental Cleanup, because it eliminated the possibility of lucrative lawsuits resulting from the determination of liability under the Superfund.

The third source of opposition to many of these innovations is the environmental bureaucracy itself. Some environmental professionals opposed the initiatives included in the Ford-KSG sample on philosophical grounds, because they believed in a regulatory, rather than voluntary approach. They also opposed the initiatives on self-interested grounds, because reducing the extent of regulation could put their jobs in jeopardy. Thus, the California Association of Professional Scientists criticized the Coles Levee Ecosystem Preserve because it didn't want ARCO carrying out an activity—ecosystem management—that it felt rightly belonged to its members. The Compliance Assistance Program of the California Air Resources Board was opposed by local air pollution control districts which, according to the Ford-KSG applicant, "felt stringent enforcement only, not user-friendly handbooks, was the answer to educating industry about air pollution."

Environmental and energy innovators generally respond to their external critics with persuasion—pointing out the benefits of their projects or programs—and accommodation—consulting private sector critics and modifying the projects to allay their concerns. They dealt with the internal critics in the bureaucracy by training them to work in a changed environment and accommodating some of their concerns.

Another obstacle frequently affects environmental and energy programs, namely, the difficulty bureaucracies sometimes have in dealing with new technologies. Florida's Loxahatchee River District was initially opposed by the local office of the State Department of Environmental Regulation because no regulations had been formalized regarding the use of irrigation quality water on golf courses. The River District overcame this obstacle by working with the proponents of other similar initiatives to convince the state to issue new regulations that would directly encourage innovative projects (Loxahatchee River, Florida Environmental Control District, 1990).

The Harwich, Massachusetts, Solar Aquatic Wastewater Project faced a similar obstacle in the regional office of the Department of Environmental Protection, which, according to Michael O'Hare's site visit report, "is not structured or staffed to oversee innovative alternative technology programs," and is most comfortable regulating "known, tested technologies operating within standard limits" (O'Hare, 1991). Ultimately, the state agency took the responsibility for oversight of the plant away from the regional office. It is ironic that the Massachusetts Department of Environmental Protection had two very different offices, the conservative regional office dealing with the Harwich Project and the innovative office launching the Blackstone Project.

ACHIEVING RESULTS

Innovative environmental and energy programs achieve changes in human activity regarding the environment, reduce the costs and delays associated with regulation, and increase compliance. Many programs encourage socially desirable behavior, such as recycling, or they encourage the use of a new technology, such as no-till planting. The impacts of these programs are usually measured in terms of their diffusion within the target population, on the assumption that programs having high takeup rates are good programs. Yet few of these programs measure their impacts using cost-benefit analysis to compare resources foregone with resources saved. The most notable exception to this pattern in the Ford-KSG sample was the Seattle Recycling Program, which did compare the cost of recycling with the skyrocketing cost of landfill disposal. The following programs achieved high or increasing takeup rates.

The City of Seattle estimated that participation in its curbside recycling program reached 78 percent of the eligible population by 1989, and by 1990, 44 percent of the residential waste stream was being recycled or composted. In addition, the program contributed to a significant behavioral change in the general population, at a time when basic attitudes were receptive to such change. According to its description in the Ford-KSG sample:

> Nine years ago the average customer [produced] three and a half 30-gallon cans [of waste per week]. Today, 86 percent of the City puts out only one can or less each week. Now a "peer pressure" ethic is in place. If you are one of the few on your block *not* recycling—everyone knows. . . . It is significant that our programs have led to such substantial public behavior changes in less than two years. Citizens of Seattle were ready to be asked to make this change for the environment (City of Seattle, Washington, Engineering Department, 1990).

Iowa estimates that its Agriculture-Energy-Environment initiative reduced the state's use of nitrogen fertilizer for growing corn 20 percent between 1985 and 1992, while fertilizer use in the bordering state of Illinois continued to increase. Despite the reduction in fertilizer, yields in Iowa have been comparable to those in Illinois (John, 1994). The Leopold Center for Sustainable Agriculture describes its achievement as "generating a large and growing body of basic and applied scientific knowledge about agriculture's interaction with the environment and ways to reduce its impact" (Leopold Center for Sustainable Agriculture, 1993).

St. Louis Park, Minnesota, estimates that the participation rate in its curbside recycling program is 88 percent. Florida's Loxahatchee River District saw golf courses more than double their use of irrigation quality water—from 400 million gallons in 1987 to over 900 million gallons in 1989. Burlington, Vermont, estimates that more than 80 percent of businesses there are complying with the state's recycling law. And, by 1992, the No-Tillage Assistance Program was operating in 117 of Georgia's 159 counties (Innovations in State and Local Government, 1992).

Environmental and energy innovations also report a second type of achievement: reduced regulatory costs and fewer, less lengthy delays. Consequently, these programs also improve compliance, particularly if the programs specifically involve voluntary compliance or improved procedures. Thus, the Wichita Environmental Cleanup Project reported that many businesses participated in the program, that property values in the affected area remained stable, and that banks continued to make loans and businesses continued to invest in the downtown area.

California's Compliance Assistance Program measured its effectiveness with an experiment. In two of its pollution control districts, service station owner/operators instituted a training program for their employees on self-inspection of vapor recovery equipment using the relevant handbook. At the end of three months, notices of violation related to standards for this equipment declined by 73 percent in one district and 90 percent in the other. It is not clear, however, how much effect the training program had on these declines.

Minnesota's Voluntary Inspection Program notes that between 1983 and 1993, 210 sites had been added to the Superfund list and 73 had been cleaned up. In the five years between 1988 and 1993, 372 sites had entered the Voluntary Inspection Program and action had been taken on 196 of these sites, including 65 cleanups to Superfund standards, and 1,000 acres had been returned to productive use.[3] Thus, the program is cleaning up sites at a faster rate and at lower cost than the Superfund program.

The immediate result of the Coles Levee Ecosystem Preserve is that ARCO is selling conservation credits to willing buyers—which is clearly a sign that the innovation is being used. In addition, the California Department of Fish and Game sees the preserve as a precedent in breaking a stalemate between business and government, and demonstrating that preserving a habitat and its biological diversity can co-exist with economic development (California Department of Fish and Game, 1994).

Finally, New York State's Self-Help Support System measures its achievement in cost reduction. By demonstrating the use of simpler technologies, the program has saved 150 participating towns more than $17 million, or 35 percent of the estimated cost of new sewage treatment facilities (Finkel, 1995b).

CONCLUSION

This chapter has shown that the environmental and energy programs responding to the Ford-KSG semifinalist questionnaire are emphasizing voluntary compliance, information, economic incentives, and the devolution of power to state and local government—in place of federal regulation and litigation. Their activities and viewpoint are, then, consistent with DeWitt John's model of "civic environmentalism." This approach still generates considerable controversy. While some people laud the increased cooperation with business in environmental management, others argue that dancing with business is really dancing with wolves. While the EPA feels many states are doing a good job of environmental enforcement, it feels that others have been too lenient (Cushman, 1996).

Looked at from the point of view of a would-be innovator in the environmental area, it means that criticism can be expected from environmentalists and business and possibly from EPA as well. That said, there are several things to learned from the local heroes in this policy area that may perhaps be taken as guidelines to help one become actively engaged in environmental and energy innovations.

- **First,** environmental programs are holistic; they increasingly involve systemic thinking about the management of entire ecosystems. Consequently, successful programs will require integration across government departments. Thus, the Blackstone Project may be considered in the vanguard, simply because it helped integrate the work being performed in the regional office of an environmental protection department. True ecosystem management will require even more extensive integration. An example of this, at the planning level, was the interdepartmental task force established in Iowa to develop policy for groundwater contamination. However, for organizational reasons, it is often harder to integrate practice than planning.
- **Second,** environmental activists can be a valuable resource and support to local heroes. Their research and advocacy help design

effective programs and counter the arguments of industry groups. It is not uncommon for program managers to mobilize activists as, for example, the Texas Water Commission did by establishing citizens' task forces to pressure local water systems to implement the Commission's recommendations. Mobilizing activists as volunteers can also supplement diminishing budgets in this policy area (i.e., by getting activists interested in environmental monitoring). I expect that this encouragement of volunteer action will happen more frequently in the future. If so, then training the volunteers, or the need for such training, will likely require bringing the educational system on board.

- **Third,** innovators should turn to market mechanisms and user fees to support and enforce these programs. These tools are more powerful than voluntary compliance, because polluters can*not* just say no. They must respond by paying the fee or changing their behavior. The virtue of market mechanisms and fees is that they force people to make comparisons between the value to society of a cleaner environment, which the fees are set to approximate, and the cost of changing their behavior. For example, over a thousand cities are now charging for garbage collection on a per bag basis, a market mechanism that has clearly extended the incentive to recycle down to the household level.
- **Fourth,** environmental and energy initiatives tend to involve politicians and public servants in different ways, with substantial permeability across the boundary between the bureaucratic and political worlds. The public is interested in environmental and energy issues and, as a consequence, so are legislators. Oil spills and groundwater contamination are examples of issues that have come to matter to legislators. In this respect, environmental and energy issues are different from information technology and organizational initiatives. In information technology, the innovators' problem was often getting politicians to understand a technology; in organizational change, it was getting them to be supportive but without intervening.

At the bureaucratic level, the picture is mixed. On one hand, local heroes seek to improve compliance or to develop new technologies. Consider the inspectors of the California Air Resources Board who developed an information program to achieve voluntary compliance, the staff of the California Department of Fish and Game inventing mitigation banks, or a doctoral student in

the Massachusetts Department of Environmental Protection conceptualizing the Blackstone Project. Similarly, initiatives in the use
of irrigation quality water, barcodes on recycling containers, slow-
sand filtration, dry hydrants, and no-till technology all originated
at the staff level. New technological or program ideas are not
missing at the front lines.

On the other hand, opposition to these innovations is also
located in the bureaucracy—often at the same front-line level.
Many have worked their entire careers in the compliance regulation and enforcement for individual media. Their philosophical
world view and economic self-interest have sometimes led them
to resist cross-media integration or voluntary compliance. Retraining is essential to win their support: it may be technical—to help
them understand the dynamics of pollution in other media, or
organizational—for example, in the negotiation skills necessary
to persuade people to comply voluntarily (Arrandale, 1996).

One may question whether training is sufficient. If it is not,
we can imagine environment departments initiating early retire-
ment programs in a scramble to change their organizational culture. In addition to changes in culture, changes in organizational
structure may be needed. For example, rather than organizing by
media, environmental departments might organize geographically
and train generalists to deal with all media in a given region.

• **Fifth,** planning and policy analysis play an important role in the
environment and energy areas. The question concerning the type
of analysis undertaken before the program is put in place showed
that 68 percent of the innovations in this area were the result
of comprehensive planning (see Table 3-5). Some cases, such as
Seattle's recycling program, had a very thorough planning process.
By contrast, some other programs in the Ford-KSG sample presented their ideas and achievements with less rigor. It is important
to know that more people are recycling or that more businesses
are voluntarily complying. However, it is also important to understand the resource implications of these programs. Thus, it would
be useful to have more cost-benefit analyses in support of these
applications.

Such measures would also help respond to criticisms that
have been made about many of these programs. We also know
that environmental or recycling programs have diminishing re-
turns; that is, it often becomes very expensive to achieve the last

bit of cleanup. Environmental innovations have often been criticized by their opponents for going too far and spending too much to achieve the last bit. Leaving a program vulnerable to such criticism is unfortunate, because it diverts attention from the value of the cleanup up to its last questionable increment. Cost-benefit analyses are useful ways of making marginal decisions about how far to go.

Programs considered for Innovations Awards in the environment and energy areas have illustrated the strength of "civic environmentalism" and a holistic approach; the challenge for would-be local heroes is to learn from their experience how to make future programs more effective.

10

We Are Family:
Community Building

This chapter deals with innovations in three seemingly disparate policy areas—policing, neighborhoods and housing, and economic development and transportation. Though distinct, these policy areas are united in a common theme: each is a type of community building. In the programs described here, the public sector and the community it serves are mutually reinforcing. The public sector sometimes strengthens the community; sometimes the resources of the community help the public sector do its work.

A theme heard frequently in this chapter is empowerment, the notion that individuals and community groups, by claiming a larger role in making public decisions, can improve in self-efficacy. Empowerment most frequently appears as a tool and goal of community building in policing and housing initiatives. In the Ford-KSG data, it was present in more than 70 percent of the policing initiatives and in approximately 60 percent of those in housing (see Tables 2-1 and 2-2).

We begin this chapter by looking back at the policing initiatives included in the Ford-KSG data. Those that involve police departments only are examples of community policing. All other policing initiatives in our sample involve partnerships between police departments and other government departments or community groups.

The second group of community building programs reviewed in this chapter concern housing issues, that is, they seek to rebuild the urban ghetto. Some of these initiatives involve more effective provisions of public services generally; others, the actual creation of new housing or the rehabilitation and maintenance of existing housing. The chapter then touches on a third group of community building initiatives, which includes measures to increase the supply of low to moderate income housing and other economic development and transportation programs that affect urban residents.

In each of these policy areas, discussion will center on the origins and organizational structure of the various initiatives; the obstacles to community building that each one confronted, and the results—achievements or progress—attributed to each program. The chapter then concludes with suggestions for potential innovators in these fields.

POLICING

The extent to which the movement, philosophy, or paradigm known as community policing, problem-solving policing, or neighborhood-oriented policing has become dominant in policing innovation is clearly seen in the Ford-KSG data: a total of 16 policing initiatives are included, each of which exemplifies some aspect of this paradigm, which both Sparrow (1994) and Moore (1995) have described. Sparrow provides a succinct list of its major characteristics:

> This movement emphasizes the formation of closer relationships between police departments and the communities they serve; recognizes that traditional police views as to priorities do not necessarily accord with those of the public; puts a high value on more personal and personable service, often through provision of "beat officers"; rejects the traditional reliance on incident-by-incident, after-the-fact responses in meeting public needs for security and safety; and seeks to establish more intelligent and analytical approaches to persistent problems (p. xiv).

This definition sharply contrasts with the notion of scientific policing that developed in the 1930s. Scientific policing advocated the abandonment of service-related activities and concentration on law enforcement, severing links with the community in favor of motorized patrols, centralizing power within the police department (e.g., central assignment of officers in patrol cars to respond to 9-1-1 calls), and the development of specialized units such as narcotics and forensics, which are also controlled centrally (Kelling and Coles, 1996). Scientific policing was influenced by F. W. Taylor's "scientific management," and, by routinizing police work, turned officers into workers who exercise little or no discretion.

I have argued elsewhere (Borins, 1995b) that the same approach was found in many other public sector bureaucracies—and to such an extent that one defining characteristic of the New Public Management is its empowerment of front-line workers. In this respect, community policing is simply a part of the New Public Management, and its innovations are similar to organizational initiatives that increase the autonomy of front-line workers (see chapter 8). Community policing stresses that police should spend more time out of their patrol cars and in direct contact with citizens; officers are expected to analyze the pattern of criminal activity and calls for service to understand the community's underlying problems. Then, working with other government agencies or community groups, they can attempt to solve these problems (Moore, 1995).

Five innovations in the Ford-KSG sample focus on activities of the police department itself. The Madison, Wisconsin, Experimental Police District, a semifinalist in the 1990 and 1991 competitions, was a pioneer in community policing—a program actually initiated in 1981. The program began with the creation of an elected Officer Advisory Council to represent front-line employees and the writing of a departmental vision and mission statement in 1985. These developments culminated in a decision to test emerging community policing ideas in one experimental district located in downtown Madison. The district had several minority populations (black, hispanic, and native American) and a substantial off-campus student population. The experiment involved establishing a neighborhood office, community meetings, customer satisfaction surveys, and problem-oriented policing (City of Madison, Wisconsin, Police Department, 1990; 1991).

The Reno, Nevada, Police Department, also a pioneer in community policing, is represented twice in our study. Its 1993 response to the Ford-KSG questionnaire dealt with the frequent use of surveys concerning public perceptions of crime and the performance of the police department. The applicant recounted that even though gang related incidents account for less than 1 percent of all crimes, youth gangs (and their graffiti) were a major source of fear among citizens. This information led to the creation of a team specializing in gang enforcement, the enactment of a graffiti removal ordinance, a significant reduction in the public's fear, and improved feelings of public safety (City of Reno, Nevada, Police Department, 1993).

Reno's 1992 entry dealt with the application of community policing principles to traffic services. In 1986, the police department purchased 21 traffic radar units; the result, after thousands of tickets during three months of use, was a dramatic increase in complaints about the police, but no reduction in accident rates. The radar program was suspended. As the department was then implementing community policing, it decided to apply that philosophy to traffic enforcement. The new approach led to partnerships with other government departments to increase safety by making physical changes (e.g., adding sidewalks and removing obstructing trees), changing regulations (parking signs and one-way streets), and working with schools to emphasize driver education (City of Reno, Nevada, Police Department, 1993).

St. Petersburg, Florida, a 1994 Ford-KSG semifinalist, described its technology-enhanced and community problem-solving policing model. The department divided the city into 48 community policing districts, in each of which a team of police officers conducts surveys and identifies and addresses problem-oriented policing projects. The technological aspects of this program include using a geographic information system that tracks crime data on a district basis and providing voice mail for each officer to facilitate contact with the community. The database is used by officers and the public to help solve problems (City of St. Petersburg, Florida, Police Department, 1994; Finkel, 1995a; Gurwitt, 1995a).

The San Diego Police Department's Refugee Program involved the creation of a class of noncommissioned and unarmed officers recruited from refugee groups. These recruits carry out community policing projects and conduct resettlement education programs based in storefront offices. Some community service officers have been promoted to regular officer positions. In addition, the department has established a multilingual information hotline and appointed an Asian community relations adviser to the police chief (City of San Diego, California, Police Department, 1992).

Many policing initiatives involve partnerships between the police and other government departments or community groups. These programs attack crime, especially drug use, by denying criminals access to their preferred locations. Three programs in the San Francisco area focused on shutting down drug houses. Safe Streets Now! is an Oakland, California, program and a 1993 finalist. It helps a citizens group fight drug use by having its members launch numerous suits in small claims court against the owners and occupants of drug houses. By collectivizing individual action, the group overcomes the fear that prevents individuals from acting alone, thus empowering them (Safe Streets Now!, 1993). That program appears to have influenced how the Oakland Police Department deals with drug houses. The department's Drug Nuisance Abatement Program was a semifinalist in 1994. Described as "operat[ing] on a location-based theory of crime prevention to target deviant places not people," it mobilizes utilities and other government departments (housing, public works, the FBI) to take action against drug houses (City of Oakland, California, Police Department, 1994).

San Francisco's Code Enforcement Task Force, a semifinalist in 1993, also uses rigorous code enforcement against owners of properties used for drug activity. Staff from the housing, building, fire, public health, planning, police, and city attorney's departments inspect suspected drug houses that have been identified by neighborhood residents (City of San Francisco, California, Office of the City Attorney, 1993). Both the Oakland and San Francisco programs are backed by California's Narcotics Nuisance Abatement Act, which places an affirmative duty on property owners to abate drug-related nuisances. The San Francisco program also appoints receivers who are responsible for the rehabilitation of properties that owners have consistently failed to repair.

The Portland, Oregon, Landlord Training Program (chapter 3) advises landlords about occupant screening, signs of drug activity, and eviction options, and provides tips on working with neighbors and police (City of Portland, Oregon, Police Bureau, 1992). It has been replicated in Oakland, California (as part of the Drug Nuisance Abatement Program), in Milwaukee, Wisconsin, and Mesa, Arizona. In Mesa, landlords now require tenants to sign an addendum to their leases acknowledging that they can be evicted for criminal activity (Gurwitt, 1994a).

Still other collaborative programs attack crime problems more broadly. Aurora, Colorado, a suburb of Denver, established a Gang Task Force that mobilized the community to deal with the growth of gang violence. Its activities include police raids on gang strongholds and clubhouses, advocacy for local gun control legislation and tougher prosecution and sentencing, the development of alternative activities for youth, and community education (City of Aurora, Colorado, Police Department, 1993). The Tacoma, Washington, Safe Streets Campaign also used a variety of tactics to fight a major crime problem, including block-by-block community organizing, surveillance of drug dealers and crack houses by both police and block organizations, graffiti removal, and youth organizations that provide alternatives to substance abuse and gang activity (City of Tacoma, Washington, Executive Branch, 1992).

Columbia, South Carolina, has a Police Homeowner Loan Program that provides subsidized financing to police officers so that they can live in low-income neighborhoods where they work. This initiative began as a partnership between the city's community policing program and its housing program, which had committed $30 million to new housing and rehabilitation (City of Columbia, South Carolina, Community Development Department, 1993).

In Syracuse, New York, the Sheriff's Handicapped/Ambulatory Parking Enforcement Program delegated the responsibility for enforcing restrictions on parking spaces reserved for the handicapped to a nonprofit organization for people with disabilities. This program gives them the satisfaction of working for their own cause as well as easier access to stores (Onondaga County, New York, Sheriff's Department, 1994).

Program Origins

Policing programs have by far the lowest incidence among all policy areas (19%) of being initiated by middle management and front-line workers (see Table 3-1). The reason may be that traditional "command and control" organizations train their front-line workers in a culture that rewards those who routinely follow orders. However, one of the basic tenets of community policing is that front-line officers will become involved in finding and solving problems. This tenet is an explicit call for officers to become innovators. The Oakland Police Department's Drug Nuisance Abatement Program provides an excellent example of an innovative officer. In this case, the information needed was provided to Robert Crawford, a patrol sergeant, during a meeting with a car dealership that was considering moving out of Oakland after twenty-five years. A mechanic told Crawford that it seemed as though a lot of drug dealing and prostitution was happening at one nearby house. Crawford investigated the house and found a broken sewer and an unconventional electric meter. He began telephoning housing, sewer, and electric company inspectors, and with their help made the owner aware that the house needed repairs and more suitable tenants. The owner complied, the illegal activity ceased, the dealership remains in the neighborhood, and Crawford has begun to use the same approach elsewhere (City of Oakland, California, Police Department, 1994). If community policing is successful, we can expect to see more officers like Sergeant Crawford, and more of their initiatives among the Ford-KSG finalists. Thus, an indirect measure of the success of the problem-solving component of community policing will be whether the frequency of innovations initiated by front-line officers increases in the future.

The policing programs display a wide variety of initiators other than front-line officers. Many were initiated by organizations. Table 3-1 shows that 26 percent of policing programs were originated by citizens groups or individual citizens, a higher proportion than for any other group except education. For example, Molly Wetzel started Safe Streets Now! in 1989 when she organized her neighbors and took successful civil action against one drug house. Her action attracted a great deal of interest, and she founded a nonprofit corporation to replicate it. Site visitor Hubert Locke described her as a "highly articulate, personable individual who launched Safe Streets Now! while serving as an administrative aide to one of Oakland's long-time city councilmen" (Locke, 1993).

Sometimes the initiator will be an agency head. For example, the St. Petersburg, Florida, community policing program was spearheaded by Police Chief Ernest Curtsinger, who went to St. Petersburg from Los Angeles, where he had directed a high profile community-policing pilot project (Gurwitt, 1995a). Given the visibility of drug-related crime, elected officials will occasionally take the lead, as was the case for San Francisco's Code Enforcement Task Force, which was initiated by City Attorney Louise Renne in response to complaints by neighborhood groups that standard enforcement procedures had failed to close several crack houses. Bruce Gould, a housing judge in New York City, described Renne in his site visit report as "in command, knowledgeable and clearly outfront in her backing and support for the Code Enforcement Task Force and Receivership Program. She certainly appears to be a seasoned campaigner and has taken on this program because it provides her office with an affirmative role" (Gould, 1993).

In one case, Tacoma's Safe Streets Campaign, the recognition that the city was facing a crime crisis led to an initial meeting of community leaders in politics, law enforcement, the schools, and the black community and then to an open public meeting attended by 2,200 people.

Policing innovations account for the highest incidence (56%) of groping as a method for analyzing a program's possibilities (see Table 3-5). For example, Madison, Wisconsin's Experimental Police District; Oakland's Drug Nuisance Abatement Program; Safe Streets Now; and Portland's Landlord Training Program were characterized by groping. These programs were relatively early attempts at community policing. However, even after the process of doing problem-oriented policing has been clearly articulated (Goldstein, 1990), the actual problems discovered and the solutions devised may still come from groping. If this is so, groping may be more characteristic of policing than of other policy areas.

Organizational Structures

Community policing initiatives transform the police departments that initiate them. Community policing leads to geographic decentralization as neighborhood units are given more freedom to identify and solve neighborhood problems. In addition, individual officers are assigned to specific neighborhood units long enough to get to know the neighborhood and its problems. In this context, the Columbia, South Carolina, Police Homeowner Loan Program can be seen as an additional attempt to promote identification between the police and the neighborhoods they serve. St. Petersburg's community policing program is, in effect, a matrix organization: front-line officers are responsible both to a team sergeant (the traditional line of authority) and to a community policing adviser (also at the rank of sergeant). The community policing sergeants are located in each area, but are also responsible for coordinating community policing efforts throughout the entire city.

The programs involving collaboration within the government or between government and community groups often use interdepartmental teams and/or steering committees as coordinating mechanisms. The San Francisco Code Enforcement Task Force has representatives of all the agencies involved in its activities, and is coordinated by the city attorney's office. The Aurora Gang Task Force has several committees, each concerned with a specific part of the program (education, legislation, public affairs, youth) and composed of representatives from both the public sector and interested voluntary organizations. The committees report to a task force appointed by the mayor and consisting of a politician, the city manager, chief of police, and the executive director of the regional medical center.

Community Roles

Given that community policing is predicated on collaboration between the police and the community, people in the community play a number of roles. The most important one is that of (unpaid) consultant—the public tells the police what it thinks the major crime problems are, and whether they (the police) are doing a good job in confronting these problems. For example, 31 percent of the policing programs included in the Ford-KSG data listed public consultation as one mode of analysis. This percentage is far higher than was the case for any other type of innovation (see Table 3-5); and 44 percent of these initiatives indicated that a formal client survey was used to measure the impact of the program, again a far higher percentage than was reported in other policy areas (see Table 6-1).

Volunteers are occasionally involved in policing innovations. They work, for example, in the Sheriff's Handicapped/Ambulatory Parking Enforcement Program in Syracuse; administer client surveys for the Reno police; and advise San Francisco's Code Enforcement Task Force about where the drug houses are.

Some collaborative programs receive financial support from the private sector. Oakland's Safe Streets Now! receives half of its $240,000 annual budget from government, with the other half coming from foundations and corporations (37%), individual donations (4%), and fees for its seminars (9%). Over half of the $1.9 million annual budget for Tacoma's Safe Streets Campaign comes from the private sector in the form of in-kind support from advertising agencies, television stations, and newspapers; and from the United Way and individual donations. Some community groups raise money themselves—for example, groups in Los Angeles and Philadelphia have paid for building or renovating neighborhood police stations (Daniels, 1996).

Overcoming Obstacles

Community policing affects work patterns in a police department in a number of ways, as was made clear in both the Madison and Reno applications. The change in the officer's work from catching lawbreakers to working with diverse groups and individuals takes some adjustment, as in this description of Reno's use of community policing principles to improve traffic enforcement:

> [Officers] were now being asked to manage a social program that they believed was the responsibility of other agencies or individuals. Officers had to expand their skills in order to develop working relationship with other city departments; interact with citizens and neighborhood groups; get along better with the local media; and develop some expertise in areas of traffic engineering, public education, and public speaking (City of Reno, Nevada, Police Department, 1992).

When the Reno police department increased its use of surveys as an element of community policing, both officers and senior management had difficulty understanding and using the information produced, an obstacle ultimately overcome with training in statistical methods. The Madison department found that middle managers had difficulty ceding authority to geographically defined policing units. They found it hard to move from close supervision to coaching roles. Involving middle managers in the planning process, however, reduced their resistance to change.

The Reno Police Department also found that its efforts to work directly with citizens led to resistance from politicians. As Ross Sandler, a former New York City Commissioner of Transportation, pointed out in his site visit report, direct police contact with citizens "becomes a threat to elected officials who see themselves as the primary provider of constituent service. With the success of the police program, there is less for elected officials to do, and some elected officials have been jealous of the community support for the police" (Sandler, 1992).

The politicians' response to community policing in Reno is not unique. It also happens in other client service initiatives that characterize public management innovation. Traditional representative democracy accords politicians primacy in dealing with citizens, and critics of these innovations are concerned about bureaucrats usurping this prerogative (Goodsell, 1993; Savoie, 1995). It can be argued, however, that government has grown too large and complex for politicians to perform this role throughout the entire public sector; as a consequence, public servants must expand their role.

For the initiatives involving collaboration between police, other government departments, and the community, motivating cooperation was the biggest challenge. For example, the Oakland Drug Nuisance Abatement Program found that individuals from other agencies, particularly in social services, were uncomfortable working with the police. However, these problems were overcome in various ways. The San Francisco Code Enforcement Task Force found that its participants began to respect one another once they saw each other's strengths. For example, the police became the Task Force's "eyes and ears" on the street. It also helped to have the city attorney's office designated as the central filing point for all problem properties (City of San Francisco, California, Office of the City Attorney, 1993). The participants in Oakland's Drug Nuisance Abatement Program had a similar experience:

> Success in abating drug nuisance locations gave agency members a sense of accomplishment. . . . Personal contact with dedicated police officers and civilian personnel dispelled negative impressions of the police. Finally, knowledge that the team could accomplish much more than any individual agency alone developed eager participants (City of Oakland, California, Police Department, 1994).

In sum, difficulties in collaboration were largely overcome by the partners' learning to respect each other's organizational culture, by devoting substantial effort to communication, and, in some cases, by designating a lead agency. Once programs began to achieve results and to recognize that everyone had participated in the result, cooperation became easier (an example of Weick's [1984] idea of small wins).

Achieving Results

The main objectives of policing innovations are to reduce actual crime and the public's perceptions that no one is safe. The community policing initiatives in our sample made progress on both fronts. For example, St. Petersburg experienced a 15 percent reduction in recorded crime; its surveys showed increased citizen satisfaction with the work of the police, and fewer repeat calls to the same location. Madison's experimental police district achieved an 18 percent reduction in reported property crime though the same crime increased 9 percent in Madison's other districts over the same four years. Questionnaires showed higher public satisfaction with the police in the experimental district than in the rest of the city as well as higher levels of job satisfaction within the police force working the district. Similarly, Reno's surveys show that public perceptions of police performance have gone from 41 percent positive in 1987 to 93 percent positive in 1993, which is surely evidence that the police are responding to citizen issues.

The community-based initiatives to close down drug houses have also made great progress. Oakland's Safe Streets Now! has closed down 175 drug houses, reduced crime rates in those neighborhoods by 60 percent, and increased their property values by $15,000 to $25,000. The Drug Nuisance Abatement Program has closed another 1,300 drug houses since 1988 and an evaluation study reports less trafficking at targeted sites and areas. San Francisco's code enforcement task force also reported fewer police calls near targeted buildings as well as an abatement of code enforcement violations. Tacoma's Safe Streets Campaign has virtually eliminated gang-related graffiti and closed 250 crack houses. Further, the number of 9-1-1 calls regarding complaints and emergencies fell 25 percent between 1989 and 1990, and participation in youth programs increased 33 percent between 1990 and 1991.

Other programs have also reported significant results. Columbia, South Carolina, experienced a 15 percent decrease in crime, though it is not clear how much of this improvement is the result of its police homeowner loan program. However, this program has been replicated by 71 municipalities or agencies nationwide (Walters, 1996c). Portland's Landlord Training Program has reached 4,000 primarily small landlords— about 20 percent of the rental housing stock—and 91 percent of participants in the course took some recommended action within six months. Syracuse's handicapped parking enforcement program reports that restrictions on handicapped parking are violated only 7 percent of the time in the malls participating in the program, while in a comparable mall that doesn't participate in the program, violations occur 48 percent of the time.

In addition to these results, 13 percent of the policing initiatives included in the Ford-KSG sample cited as their most important achievement the fact that they had implemented a theoretical model—community policing—and 25 percent of the policing applicants noted their achievement in educating people about problems such as drug houses and gangs and how to overcome them.

In addition to these achievements, the advocates of community policing feel that it creates a climate supportive of other community development initiatives:

> The result [of community policing] is that the police create room for other forces to take hold. By reducing the fear of crime or violence in a neighborhood, they give neighborhood associations the confidence they need to begin mobilizing residents, they give city agencies on-the-ground support, and they make it more likely that the kind of private money needed to turn a neighborhood around will ultimately show up. . . . "I would advise any city that's contemplating revitalizing neighborhoods by geographical area like we have, make sure you've got community policing first," says [St. Petersburg mayor] David Fischer (Gurwitt, 1995a).

In recent years, sharp declines have been reported in major crimes in New York, San Diego, Houston, and Dallas—all cities that have adopted various community policing practices (Anderson, 1997). Finally, the policing initiatives receive by far the highest level of interest expressed in replication (75%) and actual replication (63%). This interest suggests that community policing is indeed a new paradigm (see Table 6-7).

RECLAIMING THE GHETTO

Community policing initiatives often deal with drug use by targeting the houses where it happens. This section look at housing innovations more broadly, namely, in terms of rehabilitation and maintenance or in some cases, the provision of new housing. In addition, programs in housing often work with other initiatives to affect the look of a neighborhood, such as removing litter and abandoned automobiles, and with initiatives to improve all public services in urban ghettoes. The intellectual basis for these initiatives is the "broken windows" hypothesis of Wilson and Kelling (1982), namely, that broken windows and other instances of poor maintenance of public or private property are indicators that no one in a neighborhood cares about preserving order, which then invites criminals into the neighborhood: "Just as physicians now recognize the importance of fostering health rather than simply treating illness, so the police—and the rest of us—ought to recognize the importance of maintaining, intact, communities without broken windows" (Wilson and Kelling, 1982, p. 38).

Improved public safety is a precondition for these development initiatives, and collective action is another. A well-known problem is the disinclination of individuals to upgrade or maintain their own properties if their neighbors are not so inclined. Neighborhood organizations are a way of achieving collective action on the part of all neighbors. Thus, increased safety, better housing, and improved public services can be seen as components of an attack on the whole set of problems that plague the urban poor. William J. Wilson (1987) has eloquently made the point that these communities suffer from a steady out-migration of middle- and working-class families, with the consequences that adults who remain in them "experience a social isolation from the job network system that permeates other neighborhoods" and the youths who remain have no role models of adults who have received an education and who have meaningful employment (pp. 56-57). Housing initiatives attempt to reverse the malaise and out-migration that characterize urban ghettoes by encouraging residents to care for one another—to be a community—and to have confidence in their ability to take action—to be empowered.

The Massachusetts Housing Finance Authority, landlord to 150,000 residents of public housing, redefined its approach to housing management by thinking of its projects as neighborhoods and its task as empowering residents and rebuilding communities. To accomplish this task, the housing authority began to outsource security, often to local firms. It also initiated a tenant assistance program to deal with issues like violence, AIDS, and single parenting; developed a youth program that includes computer workshops, self-esteem seminars, and entrepreneurship courses; and established a program to support minority business (Massachusetts Housing Finance Agency, 1994). These initiatives carry on the directions established in Harry Spence's turnaround of the Boston Housing Authority (Moore, 1995).

Savannah, Georgia, had two Ford-KSG semifinalists in this group, Showcase Savannah and Grants for Blocks/Leadership Training. Showcase Savannah, a finalist in the 1992 competition, is a neighborhood revitalization program for nine low to moderate income neighborhoods with a total population of 4,000 households. The program began with meetings between the planning department and the residents to identify substandard conditions and set priorities; then the city and residents signed informal contracts about their commitments to improving the quality of life, with the city acting first to make specific improvements (e.g., improving street lighting or sidewalks) and the residents promising to ensure that the revitalization becomes self-sustaining (City of Savannah, Georgia, Bureau of Public Development, 1992). Grants for Blocks, a Ford-KSG semifinalist in 1994, is a program of small grants (up to $500) for community development projects designed by inner city residents. It was funded from the $20,000 finalist's award for Showcase Savannah (City of Savannah, Georgia, Bureau of Public Development, 1994).[1]

Government Action on Urban Land is a Cleveland redevelopment program that dramatically speeds the process of assembling vacant land and approving its development. The essence of the innovation is that when property taxes are delinquent, the county quickly searches for and notifies the owner. If the owner cannot be found or does not pay, the county forecloses and puts the land up for auction with a minimum price equal to the delinquent taxes plus costs. This pricing policy discourages speculators, including the original owner, from buying the property and not paying tax again. If no one buys the property, it reverts to the county, which assembles the land for housing or business redevelopment. The city participates in the program by helping the developer move through the financing and approval processes quickly (Cuyahoga County, Ohio, Prosecutor's Office, 1993). This program requires substantial interorganizational cooperation, which is facilitated by a task force headed by the County Prosecutor and Treasurer, with representatives of the seven county agencies involved as well as the city's Community Development Department.

Baltimore's Community Development Financing Corporation is similar to Cleveland's program in objectives, but it is not involved in land assembly. It has a $41 million line of credit—$10 million from the public sector, and $31 million from the private sector—which it uses to make loans at subsidized interest rates for low and moderate income housing. The housing is available primarily through the restoration of some of the 6,300 vacant houses in the inner-city. While the public sector provides the subsidies, the participating banks accept some of the default risk (Baltimore, Maryland, Community Development Financing Corporation, 1992).

Time of Jubilee is a Syracuse, New York, program that is revitalizing an inner-city neighborhood by providing loans for the construction of low and moderate income single-family housing. Its innovation is the establishment of a community land trust to own the land; purchasers buy the houses with a 99 year renewable lease on the land. This feature reduces the cost of the houses, provides assurance of long-term affordability which counteracts possible gentrification, and promotes the viability of the community (City of Syracuse, New York, Community Development Department, 1993).

The City of Scottsdale, Arizona, established a Friendly Enforcement Program designed to replace the complaint-driven, reactive, and litigious zoning code enforcement process with one based on communication and cooperation between code enforcement staff and citizens. Staff attempt to identify problems before violations occur, and if violations occur, to deal with them immediately as civil, rather than criminal, cases. This program is similar to voluntary compliance initiatives in the environmental area. In addition, it has a community-building component because staff work with the police to implement block watches and other community policing programs and, where appropriate, refer people to social services agencies (City of Scottsdale, Arizona, Planning and Community Development Department, 1993).

Housing Code Certificate of Compliance is a Manchester, New Hampshire program that was initiated to deal with the problem of speculators flipping substandard rental properties during the real estate boom of the mid-1980s. The city undertakes a comprehensive inspection of each rental property and if all requirements are met, issues a certificate of compliance. In addition, it prohibits the sale or transfer of a property without a certificate of compliance (City of Manchester, New Hampshire, Housing Code Department, 1992).

Initiating Urban Reclamation

The obvious visibility of the urban problem has prompted politicians, agency heads, and front-line staff to initiate programs, and examples of all three appeared in the Ford-KSG data. Baltimore mayoral candidate Kurt Schmoke called for the creation of a city development bank to fund the restoration of vacant houses and to "provide credit to credit-starved neighborhoods." Establishing the Baltimore Community Development Financing Corporation was one of his priorities, just as improving parking enforcement was one of Chicago Mayor Richard Daley's. Cuyahoga County Treasurer Francis Gaul recognized the implications of a massive tax delinquency of $85 million for Cleveland's credit rating, got a task force working on the problem, and led the effort to lobby for state legislation to enable the county rapidly to foreclose on and resell tax-delinquent property.

Showcase Savannah was the brainchild of Arthur Mendonsa, a long-time city manager. (In the 1970s, Mendonsa established a program called Responsible Public Service Analysis, which used a variety of indicators to quantify the effectiveness of city service delivery in various parts of the city.) Remarking on his latest initiative, site visitor Howard Husock wrote:

> Year in and year out the same neighborhoods continued to rank poorly on the numerical index. It was this data which inspired Mendonsa to try a different approach. If neighbors did not report drug activity to police, no increase in police patrols would, Mendonsa believed, be effective. Thus was hatched the idea of linking city service delivery with community organizing (Husock, 1992b).

Mendonsa's approach to evaluating the effectiveness of public services is similar to one of the central tenets of community policing: to gather data and use it to identify problems and seek solutions. And this emphasis on gathering data is likewise a key theme of many initiatives, in particular those involving performance indicators.

Scottsdale's Friendly Enforcement Program was initiated by front-line staff, inspired by individual citizens. Two code enforcement staff members, Randy Grant and Jeff Fisher, noticed that several volunteers were calling in detailed listings of potential violations. Recognizing that private individuals were interested in revitalizing their neighborhoods, Grant and Fisher conceptualized the Friendly Enforcement Program, and developed a property maintenance ordinance for the City Council (City of Scottsdale, Arizona, Planning and Community Development Department, 1993).

Obstacles to Change

To make these projects work, managers had to overcome three obstacles to change: first, all relevant government agencies had to work together;

second, the larger and more skeptical community had to be convinced that the innovation would actually affect conditions in the ghetto; and third, the residents of these neighborhoods had to be empowered to grasp the opportunities being given them.

Francis Gaul, Cuyahoga County's treasurer and founder of Government Action on Urban Land, was aware of the potential for conflict over turf and credit among the seven county government agencies that would be involved in the program. A task force approach proved to be an effective structure: "Once everyone [on the task force] realized how much potential this project contained, the usual petty bickering ceased and was replaced with enthusiasm, cooperation and excitement. After the first meeting, the project became a total team effort." (Cuyahoga County, Ohio, Prosecutor's Office, 1993).

In addition, as Amy Anthony reported in her site visit, Gaul was effective in making participants understand the effect on the city's credit rating of having a major uncollectible tax balance. As a result of his low-key leadership, there was "no visibility, no public face, no public agendas in the early days of this innovation, and therefore little competition for the spotlight. Now they bathe in the reflected glow of the city's success in the drive to move people into the city" (Anthony, 1993). Government Action on Urban Land displays the characteristics of successful large partnerships such as informality, strong leadership, and a focus on immediate and tangible results.

Savannah's initiatives were championed by the city manager—with political support. Mendonsa made his department heads aware that the Showcase Savannah neighborhoods were special. He also communicated this message by assigning the program to a team of five planners in the Planning and Community Development Department. They are responsible for planning and coordinating the efforts of other government departments to improve service delivery and support neighborhood organizations. Mendonsa insisted that measurable objectives based on the residents' concerns be formulated and distributed to city department heads and field personnel. The city's task was then to develop strategies to meet these objectives. In addition, departments were expected to coordinate their actions to meet the objectives. The process was described in the Ford-KSG application:

> Police officers work closely with the nuisance property abatement manager, sanitation code inspectors and housing code inspectors to share information, and the housing rehabilitation and private industry council departments have combined their efforts to inform

the community of their services. The Showcase Savannah program is now a model for teamwork in the city (City of Savannah, Georgia, Bureau of Public Development, 1992).

In many community-based housing initiatives, external skepticism had to be overcome. Time of Jubilee had to convince both banks and potential purchasers of the viability of the land trust concept. The city agreed to take a mortgage on the first house built to establish a basis for future appraisals, and persistent marketing, with the help of some clergy, was needed to convince potential purchasers that the program was not simply another rental scheme. New Hampshire's Housing Code Certificate of Compliance survived a court challenge by a group of property owners. While the case was in the courts, the program continued to operate without being draconian or detrimental to the real estate market. To reach hispanic minorities, Scottsdale's Friendly Enforcement Program offered its service in Spanish and worked hard to develop "cultural sensitivity to attain the higher level of diplomatic skills required to ensure the rights of several clashing cultural practices."

Savannah's managers discovered that residents who were to be empowered were initially suspicious. They did not trust government to help them and lacked the confidence, motivation, and resources to help themselves. The challenge for staff was not to provide too much guidance, but to act as consultants to the neighborhoods, recognizing that the essence of the program was residents working together to develop skills and confidence. Once the process began working, residents voiced some immediate concerns, such as crack houses or overgrown lots, at meetings with planners. When the city responded to these concerns, trust began to develop, and neighborhood residents became willing to discuss their long-term goals and vision for their communities with the planners (City of Savannah, Georgia, Bureau of Public Development, 1994).

Measurable Outcomes

Most of the ghetto revitalization programs included in the Ford-KSG data reported measurable impacts, such as reduced crime rates, crack house closings, units of housing built, tons of litter removed, building code violations corrected, and abandoned cars towed away. These outcomes result from government activity, though with some element of community support (e.g., community organizations helping police to identify crack houses and inspectors to identify violations). In some programs, another outcome or achievement was noted: residents of blighted neighborhoods began to feel more empowered or efficacious.

The Massachusetts Housing Finance Authority reported that resident surveys showed fewer concerns about safety, improved internal risk assessments of many of its inner city projects, and more people participating in its courses. It cited as its most important achievement "the sense of trust and empowerment that is developing among residents."

By 1992, Government Action on Urban Land had completed 1,760 foreclosure cases, eliminated $13.6 million in tax delinquency, and enabled 650 units of new housing to be built on assembled land. A foreclosures process that once took seven years now takes only one.

The Showcase Savannah program eliminated 125 crack houses in two years, secured 500 vacant buildings, and demolished 150 others. The program also removed 500 abandoned vehicles, litter (and helps control littering), and achieved a 40 percent reduction in house fires. Consistent with the city manager's philosophy, all these accomplishments have been measured meticulously. The Grants for Blocks program documented 76 projects involving 464 residents. However, it described its impact by quoting residents who said that they personally felt that they had more influence now than in the past, and that trust and closeness were developing in their communities. Howard Husock wrote in his site visit report that the program, in addition to its measurable impacts, had gone some distance toward the intangible goal of building community:

> By seeking to rebuild community structure as a prerequisite for a more effective delivery of city services Mendonsa, perhaps unconsciously, has revisited the impulses which underlay War on Poverty programs (with their "maximum feasible participation" of the poor) but done so in a common-sense way, without creating new paid positions or programs. It is moving to attend ceremonies in which the Showcase program designates a newly renovated home as "house of the month," or a well-kept yard as "yard of the month." Such modest, symbolic steps clearly reinforce the essence of the community which is fundamental to the program: a local minister delivers an invocation, neighbors take photographs, a sign designating the honoree is unveiled to applause (Husock, 1992b).

Scottsdale's Friendly Enforcement Program has led to a dramatic increase in the productivity of housing inspectors. The department has gone from 4,000 to 13,000 cases per year with the same number of inspectors. Previously, 25 percent of these cases ended up in court; the program has reduced that to 2 percent. Compared to other Arizona cities, Scottsdale has the highest number of cases per inspector, the highest compliance rate, and the lowest percentage going to court.

The Baltimore Community Development Financing Corporation, in two years of operation, approved a total of $30 million in loans toward 1,000 units of housing. Manchester, New Hampshire in 1991 issued 1000 certificates of compliance and recorded the correction of 13,000 individual code violations. Time of Jubilee built 22 houses in its first two years in operation, and cited as its major achievement the acceptance of its Community Land Trust by lenders, government, and purchasers.

The measurable impacts of these programs are impressive, but questions remain. How big a dent are they making in the entire problem? For example, the Baltimore Community Development Finance Corporation was renovating 1,000 units of housing but it still had over 5,000 abandoned units to deal with; Government Action on Urban Land foreclosed on properties representing a delinquency of $13.6 million, but the total delinquency is about $85 million. Do these programs make enough of a difference to turn neighborhoods around? To replace the vicious cycle of decay with a virtuous cycle of renewal?

Housing innovations rely on the notions of community and empowerment to create the virtuous cycle. Are the fledgling community organizations that are being developed (within these initiatives) robust enough to supplement and ultimately replace special efforts, such as housing subsidies or targeted neighborhoods? On the other hand, the Savannah program recognized the possibility that other neighborhoods would resent the concentration of city resources on showcase neighborhoods, and in his site visit report, Howard Husock asked whether there would be a white backlash to a program helping mainly black neighborhoods. The Savannah program expressed the hope that its initiatives would lead to the establishment of one or more community development corporations, with their own staff, and able to seek grants or loans for projects independently of the city. Similarly, Scottsdale's Friendly Enforcement Program expects that when less government revenue is available, the program will require more participation by citizen volunteers.

Housing innovators recognize the limits of their programs and know that patching up houses may be more tractable than healing the occupants. For example, the Massachusetts Housing Finance Authority expects that it will in future years be dealing with a greater proportion of elderly people, the homeless, and those with psychiatric disabilities—and with additional demands to expand its security and youth programs. Time of Jubilee would like to expand its program to rehabilitate rental housing, to provide housing for the elderly and disabled, and to play a broader role in community development. Government Action on Urban Land has found that it must contend with environmental concerns on some sites, and it has established a "Brownfields Committee" to analyze the problem. Perhaps this program will become—will be forced to become—an environmental as well as a housing innovation. The bottom line in all cases is that housing programs are moving toward becoming more holistic initiatives.

OTHER HOUSING INITIATIVES

The housing initiatives discussed in this chapter have so far been intended to reclaim the ghetto; however, the Ford-KSG sample also contained a number of other programs that also attempt to increase the supply of low to moderate income housing, but not necessarily in the ghetto. For example, Maryland's Partnership Rental Housing Program is a partnership initiative whereby local governments provide land, off-site improvements, a waiver of taxes and development costs; state government pays for the housing; and the residents do the project maintenance and participate in community service, such as crime watch and recycling. The projects are small, a maximum of 45 units, and designed to blend in with existing communities (Maryland Department of Housing and Community Development, 1994).

West Virginia's Low Income Assisted Mortgage Program, a winner in the 1993 Ford-KSG competition, creates a secondary market for mortgages for low income housing built by Habitat for Humanity and similar groups. These groups build the homes and sell the mortgages to the state housing finance agency, which then resells them to banks. The housing finance agency, the nonprofit builder, and the banks subsidize the mortgages, and the nonprofit builders advise the homeowners on budgeting and house maintenance (West Virginia Housing Development Fund, 1993). These initiatives, like community development programs in general, involve partnerships among different levels of government or between government and the private sector as well as community empowerment.

ECONOMIC DEVELOPMENT AND TRANSPORTATION

Economic development and transportation initiatives in the Ford-KSG sample also fit broadly within the framework of community development. They do not have the thematic unity of the policing initiatives, nor were they aimed specifically at reclaiming the ghetto. However, they do have some common characteristics. Three quarters of these applications involve partnerships within the public sector or between the public and private sectors,which is by far the highest incidence of partnerships for any type of innovation (see Table 2-2). Organizationally, they also have the highest incidence of formal coordinating mechanisms (58%), use advisory committees most frequently (also 58%), and most often cite "maintaining the partnership" as their biggest shortcoming (33%) (See Tables 5-2 to 5.5). And, finally, these initiatives describe their most important achievement as "operationalizing a theoretical model" (25%) or as "educating people to think about a problem" (also 25%), and do so by conceptualizing new models of economic development and educating people about the pollution and congestion problems created by the automobile (see Table 6-2). The following initiatives are indicative of the richness in this area.

The Regional Alliance for Small Contractors is a large partnership of many government agencies and major construction firms in the New York City/New Jersey metropolitan area. It provides technical assistance to small, minority, and women-owned firms through courses and seminars, loaned executives, help in obtaining financing, and access to information about bidding opportunities. It originated in response to a 1989 Supreme Court Decision (*Croson* v. *Richmond*) that invalidated minority procurement programs such as "set asides." The key organization starting the program was the Port Authority of New York and New Jersey and the local hero was a middle-level public servant, Rebecca Dogget, the director of the Office of Business and Job Opportunity, who conceptualized and designed many of its components (Regional Alliance for Small Contractors, 1994).

Littleton, Colorado, a Denver suburb, is working on actualizing an alternative philosophy of economic development based on the development of an information infrastructure. Its plan is to educate indigenous small businesses to become competitive in the information economy, rather than lure jobs from outside with promises of subsidies and low taxes (which they refer to as the "hunter" and "dealmaker" theories of economic development). Activities include giving seminars about the information economy at the local community college, particularly for blue collar workers; consulting on techniques such as GIS and TQM; and working with a local cable television company to wire the city (City of Littleton, Colorado, Business/Industry Affairs Department, 1992).

Revival of the Traditional Tribal Economy, an initiative of the Santa Ana tribe in New Mexico, involves the restoration of traditional collective agriculture using a diverse selection of crops and crop rotation (blue corn is one of the most successful crops). Crop diversity enables the tribe to provide year-round rather than seasonal agricultural work. The applicants feel that the initiative has begun to restore the prominence of agriculture, and, as a result, the tribe's traditional culture (Santa Ana Tribe Agricultural Enterprises, 1992).

Two transportation projects, Cleveland's Task Force on Fast-Tracking Road and Bridge Projects and the San Francisco Bay Area's JUMP Start program, are examples of large partnerships (see chapter 8). A third, Go Boulder, is a Boulder, Colorado, initiative to increase the use of public and alternative transit through consciousness-raising and incentives, rather than regulation. Its programs include marketing bus passes, in particular to students at the University of Colorado; building bicycle paths and bus shelters; and promoting carpooling and telecommuting (City of Boulder, Colorado, Public Works and Transportation, 1993).

These economic development and transportation initiatives frequently involve partnerships, both among governments, and between business and government. Government participation was necessary for some of these initiatives, but not sufficient. In addition, they displayed new ways of conceptualizing economic development and transportation. For example, the Regional Alliance for Small Contractors arose as an alternative to court-invalidated "set aside" programs; the Littleton, Colorado New Economy Project is an alternative to old models of economic development; Revival of the Traditional Tribal Economy is an alternative to ubiquitous Indian bingo and other gaming ventures; and Go Boulder promotes alternatives to the automobile.

CONCLUSION

Some common conclusions emerge from the experience of community builders (whether in policing, housing, economic development, or transportation) that should provide guidance to potential public sector innovators in these areas.

- First, many of the programs discussed in this chapter demonstrate the importance of research and analysis. Community policing initiatives depend on customer surveys and on the analysis of patterns of incidents and calls for service. Savannah's City Manager has put a great deal of effort into establishing a set of urban indicators and evaluating programs in terms of their effect on these indicators. And this emphasis on gathering and analyzing data was also characteristic of Oregon's benchmarking program. If these cases are, as we think, indicative of the reinventing government movement, then that movement contains a strong management or "policy wonk" component. Consequently, curricula in the graduate schools of public policy or management (see chapter 3) should continue to include a strong component of data analysis techniques.

Note that the Reno, Nevada, Police Department recounted that one of the obstacles it had to overcome in implementing community policing was the lack of familiarity of its front-line and senior staff with statistical methods. Obviously, there is still a role for analytically oriented graduates of a public policy program. However, such a role must include skills for communicating results and training others.

- Second, even the most troubled communities harbor some strong individuals and neighborhood groups that programs can call on. Such groups include people who care about the community and want to make it better, some who have time to devote to volunteer efforts—and some may even have money to contribute. Further, community policing depends on the willingness of residents to provide information to the police.

  Other programs also depend on the willingness of communities to mobilize to fight crime or to improve the urban environment. In fact, neighborhood groups are forming throughout the United States. Thus, though Putnam (1995) may be correct in his analysis of the decline of social capital in the United States, it is also the case that the neighborhoods most in need of social capital have begun to reconstruct it. One implication of this reawakening of communities is that when a community is empowered, the role of public servants should change from leading to listening.

- Third, these initiatives suggest that a great potential exists for using process redesign as a type of innovation. For example, Cleveland's Government Action on Urban Land redesigned the foreclosure process for tax delinquency, Safe Streets Now! uses the small claims court in an innovative way, Manchester's Housing Code Certificate of Compliance changed the process for transferring real estate, and Syracuse, New York's, Time of Jubilee developed a land trust that separates ownership of housing from ownership of land to make housing more affordable.

  Legal processes are not sacrosanct and can be redesigned to

serve social needs different than those that existed when they were established. Such process redesigning is not, however, immediate or costless. Cuyahoga County had to lobby the state to pass enabling legislation and Manchester's Housing Code Certificate of Compliance had to fight off a court challenge. The would-be innovator should, if process redesign is the option chosen, work with a good attorney to implement it.

- Fourth, cooperation among individuals and institutions is key to making these initiatives work. Cooperation among individuals is necessary because these initiatives change the pattern of work at the front lines. Both community policing and neighborhood development initiatives require geographic decentralization, the former because officers are given more authority to identify and solve neighborhood problems, and the latter because these initiatives attempt to integrate the delivery of services on a neighborhood basis.

Police and other public servants must become more effective at communicating with the community. All public servants involved in these integrative programs have to become more effective at working together as members of multifunctional teams. This conclusion entails understanding more about one another's work, having more respect for one another's work and where it fits into a program, and ultimately cross-training to be able to perform one another's tasks should the need arise. These initiatives give front-line workers more autonomy to respond to public needs; and they, in turn, modify existing programs to meet needs identified by specific neighborhood and community groups.

In addition to multifunctional teams at the front lines, these integrative programs will require coordinating structures at the managerial level. In some cases, such as the St. Petersburg Police Department, the innovation may involve a matrix structure in which front-line staff are responsible to both a functional unit and a geographic unit. As there are already structures to share information across and coordinate functional units, structures should be created to share information across and coordinate the geographic units.

Other programs involve cooperation and the coordination of different organizations, usually achieved by a task force. Such a force will often have a clearly defined leader. The work of the program may actually occur in the task force (for example, Cleve-

land's Government Action on Urban Land) or the task force may
include the managers of the front-line staff who do the work of
the program (for example, San Francisco's Code Enforcement Task
Force). Some programs that have a large community participation
component, such as the Aurora Gang Task Force or Safe Streets
Campaign, may have public-private task forces working on different parts of the problem, coordinated by a board of directors or
executive group. Thus, while there are several variants the theme
is clear, namely, that coordinating structures are necessary.

- Fifth, innovators in these policy areas must expect resistance and
know how to overcome it. At the front lines, training will be
necessary. It may involve cross-training in the work of other professionals involved in the partnership (which is a good way of
increasing respect and understanding for their work); training in
statistical analysis as a part of problem-solving or performance
measurement methodologies, or training in communications skills
to work more effectively with neighborhood groups.

Many programs will find that as people from different pro-
fessions began to work together, they also begin to understand
the unique contribution each profession can make to the success
of the project. Beginning to see the success of the project, as a
result of some quick, easy wins early on, facilitates cooperation
and reduces opposition (Weick, 1984; Levin and Sanger, 1994;
Mechling, 1994; and Moore, 1995).

In sum, the strength and growth of the community-building approach to
problems of safety, housing, and economic development can help potential innovators realize that communities have resources that can and
should be tapped in designing the next generation of initiatives.

11
Facing the Toughest Challenges: Social Services

This chapter is about optimism in the face of adversity. The initiatives discussed here deal with some of the toughest challenges facing American society: reducing infant mortality, healing the victims of violence, overcoming youth violence and delinquency, preventing the spread of AIDS and dealing with its devastation,[1] and using the criminal justice system to prevent recidivism. The innovators are optimists: they see themselves as struggling against problems that can be overcome, rather than as passively accepting conditions that cannot be remedied.

In this chapter, we will discuss the problems that these initiatives address, major characteristics of the initiatives, and community and private sector roles in their implementation. We will also note several sources of resistance to the changes embodied in these innovations and present a brief outline of their results. Finally, we will conclude this chapter with a discussion of the future of these initiatives, in particular, whether they can be undertaken on a larger scale; and the recommendations they hold for potential public sector innovators in the social services.

The two characteristics most frequently observed in innovative social services programs—at least in the Ford-KSG sample—are holism and an emphasis on prevention. Two other characteristics of social service initiatives are evident in this study: (1) many of them are attempts to operationalize theories, and (2) academic research plays a predominant role in program evaluation. In social service initiatives, the term "community," is used more broadly than in previous chapters. Here it refers not only to geographic neighborhoods but also to the broader ethnic and linguistic communities that give rise to neighborhoods. The role of the community is likewise broadened; its responsibility in these innovations is not only to build social capital but to use its strength to help individuals overcome personal dysfunctions.

TYPES OF SOCIAL SERVICE INNOVATIONS

Social services is, by far, the policy area with the greatest number of innovative programs—at least as measured by their appearance in the semifinal ranks of the Ford-KSG Awards. In our analysis, 65 of 217 programs were drawn from this area. Had we looked at all the data (i.e., had we coded all semifinalists from 1990 to 1994 instead of concentrating on those in 1993 and 1994), the number and proportion of social service programs in the total sample would have been larger. However, a subsample of sixty-five is sufficient to illustrate the depth and diversity in this policy area. The sixty-five initiatives included in the analysis developed as responses to eleven different social problems. The list that follows categorizes selected programs according to the problems they were designed to limit or eradicate. Sometimes programs addressing the same problem are similar to one another; sometimes they use a variety of different approaches.

Reducing Infant Mortality and Ensuring Healthy Births

- The Child and Mothers Parenting Project is a San Francisco program in which specially trained public health nurses undertake aggressive outreach to substance-abusing low-income women during and following pregnancy, often treating the women at home (City of San Francisco, California, Department of Health, 1993).
- The Baltimore Project (see chapter 6) uses neighborhood health workers, rather than health professionals, to visit at-risk women. It then deals with the entire range of issues (e.g., substance abuse and poor nutrition) responsible for infant mortality or low birthweight (City of Baltimore, Maryland, Health Department, 1993).
- The Hospital-based Initiative to Reduce Infant Mortality and Morbidity is a Connecticut program in which hospitals provide medical care for uninsured women during and following pregnancy. Its $3 million annual cost is charged to other hospital functions, and it too has an outreach component to identify potential clients (Connecticut Association for Human Services, 1993).
- Not every initiative of this kind takes place in an urban setting; Non-Emergency Medical Transportation, located in seven poor rural counties in southern Illinois, provides transportation to

hospitals for women during and following pregnancy (Southern Seven Health Department, 1993).

Healing the Victims of Violence

- The Quincy, Massachusetts, Model Domestic Abuse Program empowers the victims of domestic abuse by making the court process faster and more user-friendly to them (see chapter 2). In addition, it imposes strict sanctions on abusers such as tight pretrial probation, confiscation of weapons, and alcohol and drug abstinence orders enforced by random testing. The program also provides constant contact for victims with probation officers, to ensure that abusers are obeying court orders (City of Quincy, Massachusetts, District Court, 1992).
- The Tulsa, Oklahoma, Sexual Assault Nurse Examiners Program provides immediate and compassionate medical examinations of people who were sexually assaulted. The examinations are conducted by trained nurses supported by volunteer advocates (City of Tulsa, Oklahoma, Police Department, 1994).
- The Orange County, California, Child Abuse Services Team (chapter 2) reduces trauma for abused children by having a specialized examiner, also supported by a volunteer advocate, conduct a comprehensive examination. This examination replaces several incomplete examinations (Orange County, California, District Attorney, 1993).
- In the Boston, Massachusetts, Child Witness to Violence Project, the police and mental health professionals work together to provide immediate counseling to children who have been traumatized by witnessing violence in their families (Boston City Hospital, 1994).

Reducing Youth Violence and Delinquency

- The Philadelphia Anti-Drug Anti-Violence Network and the Aurora Gang Task Force are attempts to reach young people, particularly those at risk, to prevent violence and drug use (City of Philadelphia, Pennsylvania, Anti-Drug Anti-Violence Network, 1994; City of Aurora, Colorado, Police Department, 1993).

- The Little Rock, Arkansas, Fight Back! program provides assessment, education, and treatment for drug abuse for all 26,000 children in the Little Rock public schools (City of Little Rock, Arkansas, Office of the City Manager, 1992).
- Families and Schools Together is a Madison, Wisconsin, program that uses the schools to reach four to nine year-olds whose behavior patterns predict potential delinquency problems. The program then works with the children's families to change those behaviors (Families and Schools Together, 1994).
- Baltimore's Counseling Unit is a police department program that uses noncommissioned officers to work with families who report their children missing or incorrigible. The program provides short-term counseling or referrals for longer term treatment (Baltimore County, Maryland, Police Department, 1994).
- In Boston, Massachusetts, Common Ground is a program where police and community workers establish youth centers for nine to thirteen year olds identified as gang wannabes (City of Boston, Massachusetts, Dorchester Youth Collaborative, 1994).

Preventing AIDS and Its Devastation

- The Cermak Health Education and HIV Related Services Program involves HIV education, testing, and treatment for inmates in a major Chicago prison (Cook County Department of Corrections, 1993). For a definition of HIV, see note 1 for this chapter.
- Alaska's Mobile HIV Testing Program does HIV testing on an outreach basis in gay bars (Municipality of Anchorage, Alaska, 1994).
- New York City's Early Permanency Project provides placements with foster parents for children whose parents are terminally ill with AIDS while the parents are still able to be involved in child care (New York City Child Welfare Administration, 1993). Project Home AIDS is a Maryland initiative to place single people with AIDS in certified private homes, with supportive case management (Maryland Department of Human Resources, 1994).
- AIDS Facilities Financing Program gives guarantees for New York State's tax-exempt bonds to provide credit to developers of residential facilities for people with AIDS (New York State Medical Care Facilities Finance Agency, 1993).

Using the Criminal Justice System to Prevent Recidivism

- In Pennsylvania, Pittsburgh's Community Intensive Supervision Program is a half-way house that uses community-based monitors to model participant behavior but also imposes graduated penalties for antisocial behavior (Allegheny County, Pennsylvania, Court of Common Pleas, 1994).
- Young Men as Fathers is a California program of culturally sensitive parenting education for incarcerated young men (California Youth Authority, 1994).
- Indiana's Community Corrections Grant Program established county corrections advisory boards to help find ways of increasing the use of alternatives to incarceration (Indiana Department of Corrections, 1994).[2]

Maintaining Health and Providing Meaning for the Elderly

- Elderly Services is a Spokane, Washington, program to provide comprehensive home-based health services to the elderly; its most innovative component is Gatekeepers, a program that trains employees of institutions dealing with the elderly (postal workers, bank tellers, librarians, police, apartment managers) to identify symptoms of Alzheimer's and dementia among isolated elderly people living alone and to refer them to health professionals (Eastern Washington Area Agency on Aging, 1992).
- The New York State Partnership for Long Term Care brings private sector insurers into the market to offer coverage for long-term care for elderly middle-income people, thus giving them an alternative to spending down or giving away all their assets to become eligible for Medicaid (New York State Department of Social Services, 1994).
- The Adult Day Service Program, is a Nashua, New Hampshire, initiative that provides day services to senior citizens at a vocational-technical high school, thereby providing recreational and therapeutic activities to the elderly and training in geriatric care for the students (City of Nashua, New Hampshire, Housing Authority, 1993).
- Senior Citizen Tax Workoff is a South Carolina program that permits seniors to reduce their property tax obligations by doing part-time work for the government, thus giving them an opportu-

nity to remain active professionally (Aiken County, South Carolina, 1994).

Substance Abuse

- The Columbus, Ohio, Miracle Village is a substance abuse program in which participating women are provided safe and clean renovated apartments in public housing while receiving treatment (Ohio Department of Alcohol and Drug Addiction Services, 1994).
- New York State's Health Care Intervention Services identifies alcohol or other substance abuse problems that people who enter hospitals for other reasons may have been able to mask. Once the problem is known, the clients/patients can begin treatment for the abuse problem as well as for the physical or other ailment that brought them to the hospital (New York State Office of Alcoholism and Substance Abuse Services, 1994).

Mental Health and Disabilities

- New York State's Surrogate Decision-Making Committee uses committees of knowledgeable volunteers to speed and simplify medical decision-making on behalf of the mentally disabled (New York State Commission on Quality of Care for the Mentally Disabled, 1993).
- Alaska's Community Resource Network finds family, friends, or neighbors to serve as volunteer case managers for people with disabilities (Alaska Family Resource Project, 1993).

Job Training

- Pennsylvania's Job Centers (chapter 2) provide a variety of skills development and job search services to the unemployed—in a "one stop shopping" context (Pennsylvania Department of Labor and Industry, 1992).
- NETStops is a Lynn, Massachusetts, program that places unskilled and unemployed clients in local businesses, especially convenience stores (City of Lynn, Massachusetts, Northshore Employment Training, 1993).

Helping Troubled Families (Child Support and Family Preservation)

- Programs to ensure, and increase, child support payments have two approaches, tougher enforcement and/or improving the employability of noncustodial parents (more colloquially referred to as "deadbeat dads.") Massachusetts's Automated Child Support Enforcement Program calls for tougher enforcement. It accesses financial databases to attach liens against the income and/or assets of delinquent noncustodial parents (Massachusetts Department of Revenue, 1993).

- The Parents' Fair Share Program, an example of the second approach, is a Minnesota initiative to provide counseling, parenting skills, and employability skills training for delinquent noncustodial parents (Anoka County, Minnesota, Job Training Center, 1994).

- The Children First Program is a similar Wisconsin initiative, in which Goodwill Industries works as a contractor to develop employability skills for noncustodial parents (Wisconsin Department of Social Services, 1993).

- Family preservation programs attempt to improve the functioning of troubled families as an alternative to foster care. They have become increasingly important throughout the country.[3] Examples are the Los Angeles Black Family Investment Project and the Massachusetts Parenting Partner Program. The former uses community organizations, particularly churches, as partners; the latter uses "parenting partners," that is, experienced foster parents, to help client families by functioning as parent aides (Los Angeles County, California, Department of Children's Services, 1994; Massachusetts Department of Social Services, 1994).

Poverty

- New York State's Child Assistance Program is an experiment combining economic incentives to work with case management focusing on skills development for low-income single parents (New York State Department of Social Services, 1992).

- The Arlington, Virginia, Bilingual Outreach Program provides a range of services to low-income immigrants in five Asian and Central American languages (Arlington County, Virginia, 1992).

CHARACTERISTICS OF SOCIAL SERVICE INNOVATIONS

Holism

Two-thirds (66%) of the Ford-KSG semifinalists who worked in social services described their innovation as holistic. While this measure is only slightly higher than the mean for the entire sample, 46 percent of the programs in social services provide multiple services to their clients; whereas the policy area that ranked second in providing multiple services reported this characteristic in only 25 percent of its programs. This pattern is not surprising, since social problems rarely occur alone. People who had a troubled infancy and childhood are more likely than others to have educational problems, substance abuse problems, problems finding and holding a job, and health problems. To help clients with one of these problems often involves helping them with other problems simultaneously.

Social service agencies realized this necessity a long time ago. Governments initially attempted to achieve this integration by ambitious mergers of agencies and programs; however, these efforts have not been very successful (Kusserow, 1991; Mahtesian, 1994b). It now appears that more modest efforts—using existing organizations and programs but integrating services through a collocation of providers and case managers—may be more successful (Meyers, 1993; U.S. General Accounting Agency, 1992). Many programs described in this chapter are examples of these more modest initiatives. In *Within Our Reach* (1988), Lisbeth Schorr listed the characteristics of successful initiatives to help disadvantaged children and families. These programs provide a broad spectrum of services; they cross traditional professional and bureaucratic boundaries and, if necessary, find ways to circumvent traditional professional and bureaucratic practices or rules; and they see children in the context of their families and families in the context of their communities (pp. 256–259).[4] Professionals working in these programs often redefine their roles to respond to client needs and, by caring about and respecting clients, win their trust. The social service innovations in our sample also display these characteristics.

The first of these characteristics—providing a broad spectrum of services to clients—occurs in almost half of the social service programs in our sample. Pennsylvania's Job Centers program describes its ultimate objective as "providing a one-stop shop for all services that citizens need to overcome barriers to employment and obtain suitable employment."

Thus, the centers offer a wide range of training, placement, counseling, and rehabilitative services. This diversity is accomplished by collocating local offices of the Department of Labor and Industry's Job Service with the Bureau of Unemployment Compensation Benefits and Allowances, the Office of Vocational Rehabilitation, and the federal Veterans' Administration and Job Training Placement Act representatives.

In addition to programs that involve many agencies in a program to help solve multiple problems, our sample contained several pairs of unrelated departments that codesigned new programs to advance their mutual objectives. For example, to get foster care placements for the children of individuals who have AIDS, New York City's Early Permanency Planning Project required collaboration between the Division of AIDS Services and the Child Welfare Administration, two previously unrelated units of the New York City Human Resource Administration.

Living in Family Environments, a Michigan program run by a nonprofit organization, places individuals with developmental disabilities in the foster homes of people who were formerly on public assistance. In this instance, the organizational structure is more complicated, since the nonprofit organization acts as a broker between the state departments of mental health and social services (Judson Center, 1994).

Boston's Child Witness to Violence Project involves cooperation between police and mental health professionals, also groups who had not worked together before. The Ford-KSG applicant describes the benefits for both: "police officers acquire increased awareness and sensitivity to the emotional needs of traumatized young children, and child clinicians gain more timely access to children who witnessed violence, allowing for much earlier and more effective interventions" (Boston City Hospital, 1994).

Prevention

The second characteristic most frequently appearing in social service innovations is prevention, occurring in 25 percent of these data. In this context, prevention is planned and implemented to avert more serious problems. The notion of prevention is in some sense rhetorical; many advocates use it to justify funding their programs. Such claims can be evaluated, however, by comparing the cost of the prevention program to the cost of dealing with more serious problems in the future, the latter weighted by the probability that problems will occur in the absence of a prevention program. For example, Schorr (1988) compared the cost per child ($1,000) for a prenatal care program with the hospital care cost per child ($100,000) for each premature birth; and the same researcher reports that the $2,600 per family cost of an intensive family support program (Homebuilders) was less than 30 percent of the long-term cost of foster care.

The prevention argument is often made by youth and criminal justice system programs. We know that the futures of young people are still undecided, and it is a great value to society if bad outcomes, such as crime and drug addiction, can be averted. We also have good statistical evidence that certain groups—for example, the children Wilson (1987) identified as growing up in neighborhoods that lack adult role models (i.e., adults who have received an education and are holding steady jobs)— are more at risk of these bad outcomes than others.

The ultimate objective of programs aimed at reducing substance abuse among pregnant women and improving birthweight (e.g., the Baltimore Project; Hospital-based Initiative to Reduce Infant Mortality and Morbidity; and Child and Mothers Parenting Project) is to prevent the serious health problems that have been traced back to poor birth outcomes. The Hospital-based Initiative, which was funded by taxing other hospital admissions, is most revealing because it successfully used the prevention argument to gain the cooperation of private sector insurers, whose support was vital:

> We had to convince private insurers of the program's value as it is financed with a cost-shift onto other hospital services for which they pay. Their lobbying of the General Assembly could easily have killed the initiative. Instead, we convinced them that investing in prenatal care "up front," in the form of a cost-shift, wold pay off in the long-term as hospitals would eventually reduce the more expensive de facto cost-shift associated with the intensive care required by low birthweight uninsured babies (Connecticut Association for Human Services, 1993).

Similarly, the Bilingual Outreach Program in Arlington, Virginia, convinced landlords that if the program were given on-site space, it would help tenants improve their use of the landlords' properties and reduce landlords' maintenance expenses and unit turnovers (Arlington County, Virginia, 1992). A number of youth programs attempt to prevent substance abuse by persuading a broad spectrum of kids not to start (Philadelphia Anti-Drug Anti-Violence Network, Aurora Gang Task Force); other programs (e.g., Families and Schools Together, Common Ground) are more narrowly focused on youth who are most at risk of joining gangs or participating in other antisocial behaviors. Finally, programs based in the criminal justice system also involve prevention, such as the Cermak HIV Program, which educates prisoners about HIV and how to avoid contracting it; and California's Young Men as Fathers Program, which seeks to reduce recidivism by instilling in inmates responsibility for their families.

Involving the Community

Many social service programs use the community in some way to ameliorate the problems of individuals. The community's involvement in implementing a program or delivering a service can have several senses: the community may be consulted about program design, or it may help deliver a program through grant-supported community organizations, or the service may be provided by members of the same ethnic or linguistic group as the client. The unifying thread behind these types of community involvement is the notion that communities can provide services in more caring and effective ways than public bureaucracies. Indiana's Community Corrections Grants Program illustrates the community's role as a consultant for program design. Its county advisory boards work with the Department of Corrections to develop community-based programs such as restitution and half-way houses. An example of a community organization involved in program delivery is Alaska's Community Resource Network, in which neighbors or friends of people with disabilities volunteer to serve as their case managers.

Numerous programs in this sample were designed so that services could be provided by members of the client's own local community or ethnic group and in the client's mother tongue. In some cases, the service providers were public servants while in other cases the service was provided by the staff or volunteers of a community organization. The Baltimore Project trains health workers from low-income neighborhoods and pays them to work in the neighborhood. The Philadelphia Anti-drug Anti-violence Network uses indigenous workers in their own communities, Wisconsin's Families and Schools Together matches the ethnicity of social workers and clients, and Los Angeles' Black Family Investment Project uses black churches and professionals. These cases exemplify Schorr's notion of treating families in the context of their communities.

Linguistically, the most ambitious project in the Ford-KSG sample is the Arlington, Virginia, Bilingual Outreach, which provides services to Asian and Central American immigrants in five languages. The rationale for multilingualism was eloquently explained in this program's response to the Ford-KSG questionnaire:

Because of experiences with political upheaval in their own countries, concerns about immigration status and encounters of prejudice, immigrants can initially view Americans with suspicion, fear and self-consciousness. Many are also reluctant to visit public buildings. . . . The solution of hiring bilingual technicians with similar backgrounds to provide on-site delivery of services was crucial to Bilingual Outreach's success (Arlington County, Virginia, 1992).

Using Volunteers

Volunteers are active in approximately 15 percent of the social service programs—a higher incidence than in most other areas. Many community organizations (chapter 10) mobilize large numbers of volunteers for collective activities such as marches or street patrols. But in social service programs, smaller numbers of well-trained volunteers supplement the professional staff and work individually in roles that are critical to the program design.

Programs for victims of violence often involve volunteers this way:

- Tulsa's Sexual Assault Nurse Examiners Program has female volunteer rape crisis advocates who accompany victims during examinations and male volunteers who meet with the family of the victim;
- the Child Abuse Services Team uses volunteer child advocates to accompany children through examinations; and the
- Quincy Model Domestic Abuse Program is supported by volunteer victim advocates who accompany victims of domestic violence to court and stand between them and the accused attackers.

In each of these programs, professionals, no matter how solicitous or kindly their demeanor, must investigate, make professional judgments, and move on to the next case. The volunteer's role is to provide ongoing sympathy and support.

Finally, in one program, all authority has been delegated to volunteers, albeit volunteers who have appropriate backgrounds. New York's Surrogate Decision Making Committees are panels that make binding decisions about major medical treatment for the mentally disabled.

Volunteers staffing these committees are lawyers, health care professionals, and health advocates.

Private Sector Supporting Roles

The private sector plays important if supporting roles in social service innovations. In some cases the private sector may assume the lead role, but such cases are exceptional and usually involve a nonprofit foundation's having provided the startup funds for the project. The Minnesota Parents' Fair Share Program, for example, received a major three year grant from the McKnight Foundation as part of its Aid to Families in Poverty initiative. (In sum, the McKnight Foundation committed $10.5 million to 34 projects between 1988 and 1991).

The Robert Wood Johnson Foundation provided major funding for a number of health-related innovations, including Little Rock's Fight Back!; New York's Health Care Intervention Services, to which it gave $800,000 for evaluative studies; and the New York Partnership for Long-Term Care, to which it gave $2 million, 50 percent of operating cost over six years. Similarly, Schorr (1988) reported that the Robert Wood Johnson Foundation awarded grants of $12 million to twenty cities to establish school-based adolescent health care programs.

These foundations serve as an alternative locus of power to the public sector because their funding of projects based on certain models or philosophies helps put on the public agenda policy approaches that government may not favor. If such projects are successful, government may be persuaded to adopt them. Just as state and local governments represent, in Brandeis's phrase "laboratories of democracy," so these foundations represent policy laboratories.[5]

Looking at the entire sample of social service initiatives, 40 percent received some private sector support to put toward their operating budgets—a higher incidence of private support than most other policy areas obtained (see Table 5-1)—and where private support was received, it covered an average of 16 percent of the annual operating budget. The average level of private sector support was $100,000. Its source was mainly corporate philanthropy, funding from the United Way, or donations from individuals. Wisconsin's Families and Schools Together appears to be a typical case; it received $74,000, or five percent of its operating budget, from the United Way and Oscar Meyer Corporation. Given that social service initiatives are usually intended to help the poor, they rarely receive any revenue from user fees. As a consequence, their major source of funding was from the public sector itself (i.e., budgetary appropriations), with a small amount of assistance from the private sector.

A third mode of private sector support is a supply of in-kind services without charge. Two job training examples are NETStops, in which convenience stores provided the jobs, and Wisconsin's Children First Program, where Goodwill Industries did training and placement for noncustodial parents. The Gatekeepers component of Spokane's Elderly Services program relies on hundreds of private and public sector employees, such as bank tellers, apartment managers, librarians, and postal workers, to identify at-risk cases. The Arlington, Virginia, Bilingual Outreach program locates its offices in space provided without charge by apartment owners.

THE INFLUENCE OF THEORY

Fully 25 percent of the social service programs in the Ford-KSG sample described their most important achievement as having operationalized a theoretical model. A variety of theoretical models, usually originating in social psychology, lie at the heart of their innovations.

Families and Schools Together was consciously designed on the basis of family systems theory. Its founder, a former social work professor, conceived the program using research from the National Institute of Mental Health (Families and Schools Together, 1994). In addition, the program design included various psychological tests to see whether the behavior of participants was improving.

Family systems theory has also influenced family preservation programs. These programs try to strengthen troubled families so that children can stay in the family, instead of being placed with foster parents or institutions. For example, the Black Family Investment Project described its focus as "strengthening the family's level of functioning, and community participation in these families' lives by bringing services to homes and neighborhoods . . . removing the risk from the child rather than removing the child from risk" (Los Angeles County, California, Department of Children's Services, 1994). Similarly, Massachusetts' Parenting Partner Program uses foster parents to reinforce troubled families:

> . . . The Parenting Partner approach gives these families the one-on-one attention that they need, without monopolizing the social workers' time. Biological parents learn to view foster care as a support in strengthening the family, rather than an intrusion. Social workers have likewise learned that foster parents can assist them

in working towards reunification and have begun to view foster parents as paraprofessionals and partners (Massachusetts Department of Social Services, 1994).

Minnesota's Parents' Fair Share Program paradoxically applied the idea of preservation to families that had broken down. The program assumed that noncustodial parents still care about their children, and argued that this assumption was different from traditional thinking about the child support problem, and would therefore lead to a different program design:

> When the program was in its initial conceptual stage, staff heard the question . . . "why bother with deadbeat dads?" Unemployed noncustodial parents were viewed as just another of many inevitable and unsolvable social conditions. Critics claimed that investing any employment and training resources (even private foundation resources) in this population was equal to throwing scarce resources to the wind. . . .
>
> County staff took the view that there was a mutual obligation at work: both parents should support their children and the government should provide services to both parents to promote self-sufficiency. County staff, private industry council members, and the county Board of Commissioners moved a step further with a key assumption that most noncustodial parents care about their children, and with the appropriate support, will work actively to provide for them (Anoka County, Minnesota Job Training Center, 1994).

Another idea in evidence among social service innovations is the combination of positive and negative sanctions. Miracle Village, the Columbus, Ohio, substance abuse program, combines the stick of treatment with the carrot of living in a renovated public housing unit. If, however, participants return to drug use or dealing, they are evicted. In addition, this program

> combines elements of traditional residential drug treatment with elements of recently popularized family preservation programs. . . . Miracle Village borrows from and reconfigures both concepts with a short intensive up-front treatment followed by an extended more modest system of aftercare. The follow-up services are more than

just therapy and counseling however. Additional job-related services are introduced for the parent such as vocational training and remediation. Continual outreach to the child occurs both though in-school and after school programming (Grinker, 1994).

Another example of mixed positive and negative sanctions is Pittsburgh, Pennsylvania's, Comprehensive Intensive Supervision Program; it combines the carrots of probation monitored by members of the prisoners' own community and African-American history courses, with the stick of graduated penalties for antisocial behavior, for example, counseling and extra work assignments for missing homework through to boot camp for a lengthy absence without leave.

The Robert Wood Johnson Foundation describes the prenatal care programs that it has supported as transmedical because they deal with social factors that lead to high infant mortality and low birthweight, and also help parents prepare to focus on the responsibilities of parenthood. The Baltimore Project (chapter 6) also shares this view and thus adopted an outreach rather than a purely medical approach. In fact, it conceptualized outreach about prenatal care as a means of community mobilization, and successfully trained neighborhood residents in outreach and case management for pregnant women. As a result of the Baltimore Project's success, the city's new Healthy Start Program is using its approach to train and hire forty-five residents of Sandtown-Winchester as case workers, thirty-five of whom were women on welfare. This approach brings income into the neighborhood and provides a basis for community organizing (City of Baltimore, Maryland, Health Department, 1993). Penny Feldman, Director of the Center for Home Care Policy and Research in the Visiting Nurse Service of New York, supports this philosophy. In her site visit report, she writes:

This is a superbly designed program. It combines four key components—intensive, neighborhood-based outreach; ongoing support and case management; off-site referrals supplemented by site-based social and educational services; and administration by a publicly sponsored but independent corporation—to launch a broad-based attack on social conditions and risk behaviors that jeopardize mother and infants. In addition, it builds on and reinforces a broader community development strategy in a severely disadvantaged neighborhood (Feldman, 1993).

New York State's experimental Child Assistance Program is based on a new philosophy of how to lift single mothers out of poverty. It combines positive economic incentives to work (i.e., minimal reduction of benefits when participants begin to earn money) with a case management system that encourages finding work, getting child support orders against noncustodial parents, and behavioral changes, such as better budgeting and self-management.

Seeing so many theories applied to these problems demonstrates the ferment in current thinking about social services. In addition, by bringing theory to bear on a problem, the initiators of these innovations were thinking clearly about what they were doing and planning carefully, since operationalizing a theory is positively correlated with comprehensive planning (chapter 3). A second benefit of having a theory is that it leads one to think about how to test it, in particular against alternative theories. Thus, we can expect programs that actualize theories to be more likely to design rigorous evaluations to determine if their innovations are having the predicted impact. Indeed, social services have the highest frequency (among all policy areas) of using experimental designs to measure program impacts (Table 6-1).

RESISTANCE TO CHANGE

Resistance to change in the realm of social services came most frequently from social service professionals. These professionals were skeptical that community organizations or volunteers could replace or supplement them; they were opposed to new theories being espoused by innovators; and they found that some of the innovations adversely changed their work patterns and redefined their jobs.

The Baltimore Project encountered "the resistance of the professional community to the use of untrained and unskilled neighborhood residents to carry out outreach and case management services." It overcame this resistance by convincing local decision-makers that the ideas deserved to be tried (i.e., piloted); then by building community support for the project, and ultimately by demonstrating that the project had succeeded (City of Baltimore, Maryland, Health Department, 1993). Alaska's Community Resource Networks reported that traditional disability service providers initially viewed a project using volunteer case managers as the state's attempt to take a potential source of case management income away from them. They were also worried that it was a first step in a larger effort to reduce financial support for disability programs. In addition, the program felt that these professionals were attempting to "hold onto their self-image and 'need to be needed' " (Alaska Family Resource Project, 1993).

The Baltimore Police Counseling Unit was criticized for its philosophical approach and its impact on the work of the police inside the department and professional counselors outside. It began in the early days of community policing when many officers did not think that counseling juveniles should be part of their job. Professionals working in youth treatment agencies had criticisms that were both philosophical and interest-based. They preferred psychodynamic or psychoanalytic treatment to the behavioral reality therapy used by the police department's counseling unit. In addition, they criticized the police for using lower paid non-licensed counselors, instead of psychiatrists or psychologists (Baltimore County, Maryland, Police Department, 1994).

New York's Healthcare Intervention Services reported a similar resistance from doctors:

Some physicians were reluctant to have their patients assessed and/or intervened with. Sometimes such reluctance arose out of clinicians' stereotypic view of alcoholics. . . . Other factors also inhibited physician recognition including fears of losing the patient and an inability to acknowledge an area where they lacked expertise. . . . [In responding to this problem] the most effective agent of change has been staff education. A major component of the program is educating nurses and physicians to increase their awareness of alcohol and other drug issues, the understanding of addictive disease, how it causes or contributes to patients' medical conditions, and the efficacy of early intervention" (New York State Office of Alcoholism and Substance Abuse Services, 1994).

Finally, an aspect of these programs that might have been expected to have engendered resistance was the provision of service in languages other than English. Some states have declared English to be their sole official language, and the U.S. Congress debates similar legislation from time to time. This debate is part of a cluster of problems related to mainstreaming, affirmative action, equal opportunity, educational philosophy, and changing patterns of immigration in the United States. It may also be fueled by the appalling ethnic violence in the former Yugoslavia and the specter of linguistic separatism in Canada. However, none of the programs in our sample recounted any criticism of their programs for their use of other languages. If other languages were necessary to reach their clients more effectively, their use was seemingly accepted.

ACHIEVING RESULTS

Because social service innovations are often about reducing the incidence of a problem in an at-risk population, their impacts are measured in terms of that goal. Some programs in the Ford-KSG survey were evaluated by means of a quasi-experimental design that compared the incidence of the problem in a control group. A measure of success for programs that are optional is how rapidly the program is accepted by the target population. The following list provides selected results on a problem-by-problem basis.

Reducing Infant Mortality

- The Baltimore project reported an enrollment rate of over 85 percent of its target population (pregnant women in the Sandtown-Winchester district), no infant deaths, and a retention rate in the program of over 90 percent.
- Connecticut's Hospital-Based Initiative found in its first year that participating women were receiving more prenatal care than previously and that 88 percent of their children were born with no more than minimal intensive care required.
- The Non-Emergency Medical Transportation Program contributed to a reduction in infant mortality from 15.6 per thousand in 1986 to 8.9 per thousand in 1989 and a record of not a single infant death due to preventable diseases during that period in the seven southern Illinois counties it serves.

Healing the Victims of Violence

- Quincy's Domestic Abuse Program doubled the number of women seeking protection orders under the program between 1986 and 1991, and 36 percent of batterers completed treatment, a higher rate than for self-referral or other programs. Also, only 18 percent of the 1,500 women in the Quincy program dropped their protective court orders, as compared with 45 percent in a neighboring town.

- Tulsa's Sexual Assault Nurse Examiner Program served 500 women, or 58 percent of all reported rapes in Tulsa between 1992 and 1994; and all cases of sexual assault prosecuted using evidence provided by nurses in the program resulted in convictions.

Youth Violence

- Families and Schools Together demonstrated that participating children improved 20 to 25 percent on measures of conduct disorder, attention span, and anxiety withdrawal. They also received improved ratings based on teacher and parent observations of their behavior.

Maintaining Health for the Elderly

- As a result of Spokane's Elderly Services program, 40 percent of referrals of elderly people for mental health services were made by Gatekeepers, and this program has helped reduce Spokane's geriatric suicide rate from twenty-eight to sixteen suicides per 100,000.
- The New York State Partnership for Long-Term care sold 2,000 policies in its first year of operation, which is 30 percent of the total market for long-term care insurance. In addition this partnership led to a better working relationship between the state government and the insurers.

Substance Abuse

- Miracle Village reported that 75 percent of the women who entered the program stayed sober over two years, and drug-related crime in the housing project also declined.
- New York's Healthcare Intervention Services found 15 percent of 57,000 people tested in 1989 had some alcoholism problem, and that its program helped deliver interventions in 90 percent of those cases. Further benefits identified in the site visit are that it reaches people whose substance abuse problem would otherwise be undetected at a time when they are receptive and at a place where treatment is available. It reduces the cost of diagnosis and treatment; has spillover benefits (i.e., it reaches people who have other addictions); educates doctors and nurses about these problems,

and motivates them to embrace a more holistic treatment of patients (Levin, 1992).

Helping Troubled Families

- Wisconsin's Children First Program recounted that in both participating cities, Fond du Lac and Racine, total child support payments increased by 28 percent and 145 percent, respectively, and
  the number of people paying child support increased by 44 percent
  and 94 percent, respectively.

Poverty

- New York's Child Assistance Program found that its participants
  were earning 50 percent more income and receiving more money
  on child support orders than women in the control group.

THE DILEMMA OF SOCIAL SERVICE INNOVATIONS

The generally held view of social service innovations is that they reach
only a small number of people, and are therefore expensive in cost per
person. The data presented in the introduction to the second part of this
book are generally consistent with that image. Social services innovations
reach an average of 34,000 people, the second lowest of all policy areas,
at a cost of $1,900 per participant, the third highest for all areas. They
reach about 35 percent of their intended populations, the second lowest
of all areas.

When social service programs are looked at in detail, it is clear that
they bifurcate: either they reach a large number of clients by dealing with
a specific problem at a reasonably low cost per client; or they provide
specialized and ongoing treatment or counseling to smaller populations
at a greater per-person expense. Examples of programs reaching larger
numbers at lower cost per person (based on annual cycles) are the Tulsa
Sexual Assault Nurse Examiner Program treating 200 victims at $600 per
examination; Bilingual Outreach serving 460 families at $400 per family;
the Non-Emergency Medical Transportation Program providing trips for
1,300 clients at $140 per client; and the Cermak HIV Education Program
providing education and/or testing for 19,000 inmates, at a cost of $32
per inmate.

Examples (also on an annual basis) of programs providing expensive specialized treatment are Miracle Village helping 110 women with 285 children at $21,000 per woman, Connecticut's Hospital-Based Initiative to Reduce Infant Mortality and Morbidity reaching 285 women with 202 children at $10,500 per woman; the Parenting Partner Program helping twenty families at $6,000 per family; Common Ground helping forty youths at $4,000 per youth; Families and Schools Together serving 580 families at $2,600 per family; the Baltimore Project reaching 270 women at $2,400 per woman; and Young Men as Fathers counseling 235 inmates at $1,600 per inmate.

Even with this bifurcation, the most frequently identified shortcoming of social service programs is a lack of resources. This finding affects 51 percent of the programs in this area, which again yields a higher incidence than in all the other areas (see Table 4-5). The programs' most frequent expectation for the next five years is that the problems that they are dealing with are not going to disappear—a response given by 77 percent of them, more frequently than most other policy areas (Table 4-6). Finally, two-thirds or about 66 percent of the program initiators would like the problem to be dealt with through the provision of more resources. This finding is also among the highest incidence of all the policy areas (Table 4-7).

Despite their limited resources, the innovators often had dreams about how they could extend their programs. The Parenting Partners Program would like to use the concept in families where parents are suffering from AIDS. The Philadelphia Anti-Drug Anti-Violence Network and Families and Schools Together would both like their programs to be the basis of community organizing. Boston's Child Witness to Violence Project sees its future as becoming a component of an overall community policing approach. New York's Healthcare Intervention Services would like to extend testing to other forms of substance abuse. Maryland's Project CARE would like to develop a continuum of housing options for people with AIDS. Miracle Village would like to use its approach as a basis for making public housing drug-free. Connecticut hopes to use the Hospital-Based Initiative to Reduce Infant Mortality and Morbidity as a model for financing other public health programs by shifting the costs to the private insurers.

Are these hopes realistic? Sometimes the innovators themselves recognize the difficulty of their challenges. They often use the rhetoric of prevention, claiming that the programs will avert greater expense in the future. However, the difficulty in justifying expenditures on prevention is that today's expenses are much more visible than tomorrow's savings, especially in the budget process. Further, expenses often occur in different agency budgets than the savings. Madison, Wisconsin's Families and Schools Together vividly described the difficulty in making such arguments:

> Nobody wants to pay for prevention: schools educate children, counseling centers do therapy, treatment facilities provide substance abusers treatment, police/prisons care for criminals, child welfare workers service problem children, and courts are involved with delinquents. The systems have their missions and goals, and in a society with escalating social problems, they are crisis driven and do not invest in early intervention/prevention. In addition, the arguments that money spent early is a fraction of dollars spent later falls on deaf ears during a recession. It is hard to generate a passion about future problems which translates into funding choices (Families and Schools Together, 1994).

A second widespread problem is expanding programs, not simply because more resources are required, but because the care that went into program design and implementation is hard to replicate.

Pat Wong, the site visitor to Michigan's Living in Family Environments, highlighted this difficulty in his site visit report: "to attain quality control and avoid adverse publicity, heavy creaming of foster parents and intensive staff/foster parent relationships must be in place," both factors that will limit the size of the program (Wong, 1994). Similarly, Schorr included among her list of characteristics of successful interventions having "competent, caring, and flexible" professionals who are willing to go beyond the boundaries of their job descriptions, and who can win their clients' trust. The programs described in this section have attempted to do this in a number of ways, for example by visiting clients in their homes rather than at an office, or by attempting to match the race, ethnicity, or language of the client and the professional staff. Still, this might not go far enough; we have seen that some programs use volunteers to add a level of caring that goes beyond that which professionals are able to give. Paradoxically, we have seen that much of the resistance to these programs comes from professionals who are unable to go beyond the boundaries of their job descriptions, or who feel threatened by volunteers.

CONCLUSION

Despite these dilemmas, optimists will continue to establish innovative social service programs, and the experience of the public sector programs discussed in this chapter may provide some advice to them.

- First, they must recognize that social service innovations are intrinsically holistic. When they attempt to deliver multiple services to a target population, they should think about collaboration in terms of such questions as how the program will be structured, how it will be financed, and how front-line staff will be affected. The collaboration will likely involve existing organizations working together, rather than merging into a new organization.
- Second, innovators should be creative in looking for partner organizations; many social service innovations came about when two organizations that thought they had nothing in common realized they could help each other.
- Third, innovators must recognize that many social service innovations have been inspired by theory. They should consult the relevant social science literature to see whether its theories or models are relevant to their program, and to consider how their program could help test the validity of the theories.
- Fourth, innovators should use prevention as an argument in seeking funding for their programs and develop the best possible measures of the cost of problems that their programs will avert. They should, moreover, make these arguments to the parties who will bear these costs and bring them in as partners (e.g., as private sector insurers in Connecticut were convinced to support a program to improve prenatal and neonatal care).
- Fifth, social services innovators should think about how best to reach the client. Techniques may involve home visits, program delivery by members of the client's racial, ethnic, or linguistic group, or the use of volunteers to add a measure of caring that professionals cannot provide.
- Sixth, innovators should look to the private sector for some support for the program. Foundations may provide seed money if the program is consistent with their agenda; innovators must recognize that foundations are interested in testing and evaluating new models of program delivery. In addition to foundation support, individual or corporate philanthropy may be available to

cover a small portion of the budget, and, in some cases, in-kind support may be more valuable than philanthropy.

- Seventh, innovators in this policy area should look to the community for some support in implementing the program. This support may involve consultation in program design and participation in program operation.
- Eighth, innovators should be aware that there will be resistance to change, particularly by professional groups. They may be unwilling to go beyond the jobs they learned in basic training or graduate school and they may be threatened by or dismissive of volunteers. As in other policy areas, training staff is important; in this case, staff must learn how to do tasks that are not in their original job description or to receive additional information about their clients which, by breaking down stereotypes, might increase their capacity for caring. Their resistance might also be to the use of volunteers; clearly, they will be more willing to accept volunteers if they are seen as supplementing the work of staff, rather than replacing them. Also, achieving some early successes is a way of breaking down resistance.
- Ninth, innovators should not only plan to do evaluation, but actually do it—as rigorously as possible. It will be essential to the program's survival, improvement, and replication.

Despite the challenges social service innovations face, they are clearly making progress. They are achieving identifiable benefits. Some of them are being replicated. They are leaders in important new trends in American social policy, such as the establishment of programs to respond to the needs of victims of violence, family preservation programs, and programs to improve the health of infants. They are meeting the toughest challenges.

12

Everybody's Business: Innovation in Education

As a nation that believes in equality of opportunity, Americans care passionately about education and about whether their schools do, in fact, provide equal opportunities to all students. Even if equal opportunity were not an issue, however, Americans would still be concerned about the overall quality of their educational system, certainly in comparison with the systems of other countries. More recently—as the basis of international economic competition began to shift inexorably toward knowledge-intensive production—managers and workers have put additional pressure on schools to ensure that they equip all Americans with the skills needed to be employable in the new economy. Indeed, everyone has spent some time in the educational system, and many adults have children at some stage in the system now. Therefore, everyone considers him or herself an expert, and few are willing to defer to those with credentialed expertise.

Thus, intense and passionate public interest characterizes the educational innovations discussed in this chapter. They stand out from all other groups of innovations in a number of ways: more educational innovations were new programs (62%, Table 2-2); more received some financial support from the private sector (also 62%, Table 5-1); more were initiated in response to a current or anticipated crisis (about 50%, Table 3-2); and more educational innovations were initiated by interest groups (about 43%, Table 3-1) than was the case in any other area. The next highest incidence of interest groups initiating innovations was in housing (social services), and involved only 14 percent of the innovations in that area (Table 3-1).

Again, in relation to the other policy areas, more educational innovators (29%) claim that their major achievement was operationalizing a theoretical model. With so much passion, and so many interest groups attempting to implement specific reform agendas, it is not surprising that educational innovators also received the highest incidence of criticism by professionals (38%). Innovations in education appear to be the battle-ground for persistent clashes between reformers and the educational es-tablishment, which, of course, enfolds the previous generation of reformers.

This chapter illustrates some of the educational innovations that people care so passionately about. We begin by looking at the types of educational innovations represented by these programs, their client populations, and the resources they use. We will also demonstrate how much education is on everyone's agenda by reviewing cases in which the innovators have come from within the educational system, cases in which interest groups or the private sector played the major role, and cases in which politicians have become high-profile supporters of cer-tain innovations.

Educational reform, like social service initiatives (chapter 11), tends to be theory-driven, and this chapter will contain some innovations that were intended to operationalize new pedagogic theory. Theories have their supporters and their opponents, and clearly, some opposition to educational innovation emerges from doctrinal disputes about what con-stitutes effective education. Some opposition, on the other hand, is interest-based, as various participants in the educational system worry that they may be materially disadvantaged by the innovations. Our discus-sion of the methods used to overcome opposition leads us directly to consider the results of these initiatives and to the conclusion of this chap-ter, the advice contained in these innovations for potential educational innovators.

TYPES OF EDUCATIONAL INNOVATION

Educational innovations encompass five very diverse themes: making learning possible for students; developing better teachers; introducing new technology to the classroom; improving vocational education; and comprehensive reform of secondary education.

Programs to make learning possible attempt to improve children's circumstances outside the classroom, so as to make them physically and psychologically able to focus when in the classroom.[1] Abolish Chronic Truancy (ACT) is a program run by the District Attorney's office in Los Angeles. It requires the parents of students who are chronic truants to meet with officials who can explain the seriousness of truancy. School representatives and relevant social service agencies may also be called in to help the family deal with other problems. The program then monitors the attendance of these students. If attendance doesn't improve, they are referred to truancy mediation (Los Angeles County, California District Attorney, 1994).

Student Conflict Resolution Experts, a Massachusetts program, trains high school students in conflict resolution skills (see chapter 2). It reduces violent incidents and gang activity in the schools and transforms the student mediators, some of whom might otherwise have been involved in violence themselves (Massachusetts Attorney General's Office, 1994).

The City of Seattle's Families and Education Interlocal Agreement provides for a special levy of $10.8 million each year between 1991 and 1998 to fund early childhood education, services for out-of-school youth, and comprehensive health services for students and their families. This program is directed to those most in need, and was described in our sample as "coordinat[ing] social and health services in the community to support educational goals and ensure that every child is safe, healthy, and ready to learn" (City of Seattle, Washington, Public Schools, 1993).

Programs to develop better teachers deal with a variety of situations. The New York City Peer Intervention Program engages experienced teachers to provide counseling and skills development for teachers rated as unsatisfactory—a group containing fewer than 1 percent of New York's 45,000 teachers—and thus the most troubled in the system (New York City Board of Education, 1993).

The Michigan Partnership for New Education includes both government and the private sector in programs to improve the quality of the state's primary and secondary schools. The partnership involves twenty-five professional development schools in sixteen communities working in collaboration with the educational faculties of twelve universities to restructure curriculum, develop teacher skills, and disseminate best practices (Michigan Partnership for New Education, 1994). The Center for the Enhancement of Science and Math Education (CESAME), based at Northeastern University in Boston, supports innovations in math and science education that are created and implemented by individual teachers (Bay State Skills Corporation, 1993).

The information technologies included in educational innovations are interactive television (in Kentucky, Hawaii, and Beaver County, Oklahoma) and providing personal computers for students of underprivileged backgrounds living in public housing in Lansing, Michigan. Interactive television was introduced in Kentucky to improve the quality of education in the poorest and most remote school districts as part of a 1990 educational reform package passed in response to a state Supreme Court ruling that the educational system was unconstitutional because of gross inequities (Kentucky Educational Television, 1991).

Other educational innovations are designed to improve vocational education. The Omaha Job Clearinghouse is a business-education partnership that targets noncollege-bound students (juniors and seniors) and provides counseling, job and life skills' training and job shadowing (Metropolitan Community College, 1994).

CityWorks, a program at a comprehensive high school in Cambridge, Massachusetts, is an example of fundamental reform in vocational education. The program integrates academic and vocational education to give students a broad range of basic skills (rather than technical training in one narrow occupation) and to link vocational education to community economic development. It takes the City of Cambridge as a "text" and requires students to work in teams to research the city and create "artifacts," such as maps, tapes, oral histories, and three-dimensional models. These artifacts are presented to real audiences as a motivation to do high-quality work (Rindge School of Technical Arts, 1992).

A number of other initiatives are achieving comprehensive educational reform in academic high schools. Humanitas, a program in the Los Angeles Unified School District, describes itself as an "interdisciplinary thematic team-taught writing-based model of teaching humanities to diverse and urban high school students." Teams of faculty advise groups of students who do not use textbooks, but read books, view works of art, write extensively, and often produce integrative essays or video documentaries (Los Angeles Unified School District, 1992). Michael O'Hare describes in his site visit report how Humanitas incorporates the traditional humanities curriculum: "students are given things to think about . . . , and discover quite quickly that writing, spelling, logic, and [a] chronology of events help them do a challenging and grownup thing" (O'Hare, 1992).

The Coalition for Essential Schools is a movement to reform secondary education on the basis of principles developed by Theodore Sizer in *Horace's Compromise: The Dilemma of the American High School* (1984). Key ideas include having students work on projects in which they are coached by teachers, assessing students for graduation on the basis of portfolios (similar to the integrative essays or videos in Humanitas or the artifacts in CityWorks), an interdisciplinary curriculum, classes small enough to give individual attention, and parental involvement in the governance of the school.[2]

Two of the most successful members of the coalition were Ford-KSG Award winners, Central Park East Secondary School (in New York City) and Thayer Junior/Senior High School in Winchester, New Hampshire. Thayer's unique contribution is that it established a program to disseminate its innovations by creating and marketing videos, hosting visitors and conferences, and satellite broadcasts of televised workshops (Thayer, New Hampshire High School, 1994; Sizer, 1996, 18–22).

In its application for the Ford-KSG award, Central Park East described its pedagogic approach as follows:

> [It includes seeing the] teacher as coach and student as worker, personalization, interdisciplinary curriculum, and outcomes-based assessment. Every CPESS student engages in weekly community service, and prior to graduation participates in a career-oriented apprenticeship as well as a college-based course. Students graduate when they can successfully demonstrate through publicly defended portfolios their mastery of important intellectual and social competencies. Developing such performance standards has been a major focus of its work, as well as pioneering ways to demonstrate such standards (New York City Board of Education, 1993).

Central Park East was able to provide smaller classes by covering fewer elective subjects than a traditional high school. The school is organized in units of eighty students and five teachers. Academic governance is the responsibility of a tripartite body of teachers, students, and parents. The school's unique contribution is its demonstration that the principles of intellectually rigorous, performance-based education can be implemented in a school serving largely poor African American and Latino families (see also Sizer, 1996).

TARGET POPULATIONS AND RESOURCE-INTENSIVENESS

The majority of these innovations are designed to help students who are in some way disadvantaged. Such students may come from low-income backgrounds or from African-American, Latino, and native American minorities, or they may be students with disabilities. Thus:

- the Massachusetts Student Conflict Resolution Experts mediates conflicts in low income areas;

- Seattle's Families and Education Interlocal Agreement reaches the city's most needy students;
- the Black Feet Tribal Head Start Program (Black Feet Tribal Business Council, 1993), provides bilingual education in English and Blackfoot for preschool children;
- Lansing's Computer Learning Centers serves children living in public housing projects;
- Omaha's Job Clearinghouse is for students who are not college bound; and
- Kentucky's Educational Television Initiative focuses on the state's poorest and most remote districts.

The programs that are not specifically designed to serve disadvantaged students focus on teachers (New York City Peer Intervention Program) or embrace comprehensive reform (Michigan Partnership for New Education; Humanitas; Here, Thayer, and Everywhere). Even some comprehensive educational reforms are set in the context of disadvantaged schools such as Central Park East Secondary School. The challenge to educational innovators is to bring their reforms to fruition in under-resourced schools serving disadvantaged children.

Table I-2 shows that educational programs reach an average of 5,000 people, the smallest client population among all areas, and 36 percent of their potential population, the second lowest percentage among the policy areas. Yet these programs cost an average of $1,900 per person reached, the third highest of all areas. On first impression, therefore, educational innovations are small and expensive. Looked at in more detail, the impression changes; they are smaller than they are expensive.

Of course, some are quite expensive on a per-person per-annum basis: for example, the New York City Peer Intervention Program at $10,000 per teacher assisted and Central Park East Central School at $3,800 per student. However, the cost of Central Park East is similar to a year in an average high school, and the New York City Peer Intervention Program is comparable to the intensive social service interventions discussed in the previous chapter. After these outliers are taken into account, most of the other applications on a per-student basis cost less than $1,000. CityWorks is the most expensive of this group, at $1,700 per participating student, but it covers a major part of the curriculum for participating students. Massachusetts's Student Conflict Resolution Experts costs $1,000 per mediation. However, the cost of a mediated settlement is quite small in comparison to the potential costs of an unmediated conflict.

In size, although a few outliers reach large populations (e.g., 15,000 students participate in Michigan's Partnership for New Education, and 4,500 Los Angeles-area students participate in Humanitas), most other programs are small. For example, the New York City Peer Intervention Program reaches eighty-five teachers each year, Central Park East Secondary School serves 450 students, and CityWorks has a student enrollment of 100.

PART OF MANY AGENDAS

Educational innovations are influenced by (and bear the indications of) various groups' agendas. In many instances, the innovators themselves— the local heroes who initiated these programs—came from outside the public sector, from foundations, businesses, or interest groups; still, in many instances, they originated within the educational sector. In some cases the innovations were initiated by politicians, or politicians very quickly became champions of the innovation. In addition, 62 percent of these innovations—a higher percentage than for any other area—received some private sector support, either monetary or in-kind.

Philanthropist Alfred Taubman worked with Judith Lanier, Dean of the College of Extension at Michigan State University, and Michigan Commerce Secretary Doug Ross to develop the Michigan Partnership for New Education. Taubman emphasized business and community collaboration with the school system; and Lanier, higher standards for teaching. The Rockefeller Foundation was the prime mover for Humanitas, following its 1981 report on the humanities in American life. In 1985, the foundation's search for innovative programs in the humanities led to the Humanities Magnet Program at Cleveland School in Los Angeles, which became the model for Humanitas. The Omaha Job Clearinghouse began as a pilot project in job shadowing and placement initiated by the Omaha Chamber of Commerce, local businesses, public schools, and a local community college; its initial funding came from a grant from the U.S. Department of Education.

The programs also provide some good examples of change resulting from the efforts of groups and individuals within the educational system. The New York City Peer Intervention Program resulted from a 1987 needs-assessment questionnaire distributed by the teachers' union. A majority of respondents recommended a program using stronger teachers to help less effective ones. President Sandra Feldman then put such a program on the negotiating table.

The program at Central Park East Secondary School had its origins in a 1974 decision by then superintendent of schools, Anthony Alvarado, to create a system of small schools of choice at the elementary level. Deborah Meier was the principal of the first such school, Central Park East Elementary School. The program there included a curriculum characterized by the use of themes, independence for teachers in choosing themes and organizing their classes, a heavy emphasis on reading, and supportive parental involvement. The school was very successful by all traditional criteria: it maintained order, its students performed well on standardized reading tests, and its graduates did well in high school (Schorr, 1988, 241-245). Meier reported that much of her inspiration for the elementary school "came from the independent school movement, which had a history of serving New York City's elites, but whose work had too long been ignored as irrelevant to the education of the disadvantaged." In 1985, Meier founded Central Park East Secondary School to incorporate the ideas she had experimented with in the elementary school and Sizer's theories in the Coalition for Essential Schools.

The originator of CityWorks was Larry Rosenstock, who first trained as a lawyer, then taught carpentry for eleven years in Boston and at the Rindge School of Technical Arts in Cambridge, and afterwards worked in Washington as an advocate for vocational education reform. He lobbied for the Carl Perkins Vocational Education and Applied Technology Act of 1990, which required states and school districts to revamp vocational education programs in two ways: by providing better academic training, and by including in vocational training all aspects of the trade, including management, financing, and marketing (Sylvester, 1992). Rosenstock then returned to Cambridge as Executive Director at Rindge, and began to realize his vision with the establishment of CityWorks.

Politicians have also been initiators of educational reform. Seattle's Families and Education Interlocal Agreement resulted from Mayor Norman Rice's initiative in response to a crisis in the school system. Against a background of poor student performance (low test scores, high dropout rates, declining enrollment, growing concern about student safety), a controversial initiative eliminating mandatory busing for racial balance was passed by the voters in November 1989. Mayor Rice made improving education a major campaign theme and began a response to the busing initiative. He proposed that the city convene an education summit. Prior to the summit, over 2,000 Seattle citizens met in community meetings, and developed a consensus on ways to improve education in Seattle, which was then ratified at the summit held in May 1990. The Families and

Education Interlocal Agreement was thereafter approved in a referendum (City of Seattle, Washington, Public Schools, 1993).

In other cases, politicians who did not initiate a program recognized its consistency with their visions, and quickly became its champions. In Massachusetts, for example, Scott Harshbarger, elected Attorney General in 1990, and a strong supporter of mediation, took a special interest in the Student Conflict Resolution Experts program, mentioning it in numerous speeches. Because the program relies on local matching funding, the intent of his advocacy was to gain attention for the program and therefore additional money for its expansion (Massachusetts Attorney General's Office, 1994).

Similarly, the Michigan Partnership for New Education began during the administration of Democratic governor John Blanchard, but it received strong support from his Republican successor, John Engler.

> Governor Engler has made the Partnership one of the cornerstones of his effort to reform education. He is a strong advocate of educational innovation and has fought hard in the legislature for financial support for the innovation system despite adverse economic conditions and a substantial state budget deficit (Michigan Partnership for New Education, 1994).

The private sector, whether or not it had been present at the beginning of these reforms, has provided financial or in-kind support for a substantial portion of them. The Michigan Partnership for New Education received one-third of its support from the private sector. The initiative budgeted $49 million over five years, and by 1994, $13 million of the required $16 million in private sector support had been pledged by foundations (e.g., Taubman, Kellogg, and Rockefeller) and firms (e.g., General Motors).

In many other cases, private sector and foundation support provided approximately 10 to 20 percent of the funding, and enabled the programs to undertake projects or purchases that would otherwise have remained on their wish lists. For example, Central Park East Secondary School received between $75,000 and $125,000 of its $1.7 million budget in grants from foundations such as EXXON and Panasonic, and has used this money to fund enrichment programs (art, music, Saturday classes, camping trips) and staff development. Thayer High School in New Hampshire received $300,000 of its $2 million budget in foundation support; Humanitas received $615,000 of its $3.7 million budget in corporation and foundation grants; and businesses contributed $47,000, or 16 percent, of the funding of the Omaha Job Clearinghouse and also provided the sites for job shadowing. Finally, CityWorks received in-kind support from Polaroid Corporation, namely, film and cameras and an employee of Poloroid on loan as a teacher. Polaroid also produced photo ID cards for students to use during their forays into the community.

The attractiveness of educational innovation to corporate supporters throughout the United States has increased in recent years. For example, substantial corporate support is behind President Clinton's initiative to provide every school with access to the Internet. This support was amply demonstrated on California's 1996 Net Day, when corporate sponsors (MCI, Netcom, and America On-Line) and 20,000 volunteers began wiring that state's schools (Purdum, 1996) and a year later when Net Day was launched nationally (Associated Press, 1997). Skeptics may argue that corporations are contributing to this initiative simply to win the loyalty of future generations of consumers or to enhance their image as supporters of popular government programs. But to an educational innovator who is attempting to cobble together resources, such support is clearly welcome.

THEORY-DRIVEN INNOVATION

Fully 29 percent of the educational programs included in the Ford-KSG sample—a higher percentage than occurs in other policy areas—cite the actualization of a theoretical model as their major achievement. The Los Angeles District Attorney's Abolish Chronic Truancy program combines the carrot of treatment for the problems that underlie truancy with the stick of sanctions for the behavior itself. In this combination of positive and negative sanctions it is similar to programs dealing with drug abuse and delinquency (chapter 11):

> [Abolish Chronic Truancy] demonstrates that the prestige and power of the District Attorney can facilitate and enhance the efforts of other social institutions which are trying to deal with a variety of social problems, not truancy alone. The most significant impact of these programs lies in their ability to empower families to reestablish parental authority (Los Angeles County, California, District Attorney, 1994).

A comprehensive model of education was presented by Central Park East Secondary School and Thayer Junior/Senior High School, involving

interdisciplinary curriculum, individualized learning, and the use of portfolios. Humanitas does this in a more limited way, dealing solely with the
humanities curriculum. All three of these programs cite as an important
achievement the widespread application of this model. Deborah Meier
described Central Park East Secondary School's achievement:

[Central Park is] demonstrating to a wide range of sometimes doubt-
ing audiences that the kind of serious, thoughtful, and creative education normally associated with private elite progressive schools
was feasible for schools in which a majority of the students had a
history of average or even low academic achievement, were of low
or modest incomes, and predominantly African American and Latino. . . . CPESS has shown that a school that reaches out far enough
and provides useful feedback can indeed make an alliance with
most, if not all, families regardless of their socioeconomic histories
and circumstances (New York City Board of Education, 1993).

CityWorks created a new model of vocational education, breaking
down the segregation between it and academic education and building
linkages between the school and the community. Like Humanitas and
Central Park East, CityWorks incorporates publicly presented interdisciplinary student research projects requiring the mastery of important skills.
As evidence that its model is successful, the program notes that more
academic students are taking CityWorks, more vocational students are
taking art and other nonvocational electives, and more nonvocational
students are enrolled in junior and senior apprenticeship programs. Similarly, evidence that the school is building links between itself and the
community is that Rindge students helped design and build the Erikson
Center, a multigenerational residence for senior citizens and adolescent
mothers (Rindge School of Technical Arts, 1992).

Another model for strengthening the relationship between the
schools and the community was described in the Black Feet Tribal Head
Start Program, whose major innovation is the use of the Blackfoot language, in addition to English, in its preschool program. This innovation
enables preschool students to gain an insight into their cultural background and encourages parents to play a more active role in their children's education. Dorothy Still Smoking, director of the program,
describes its ultimate achievement as the "destruction of the fallacy that
tribal elements are not worthy for use in the classroom" (Black Feet Tribal
Business Council, 1993).

Finally, a number of programs identify their innovation's achievement as changing the role of the teacher by providing more scope for teachers to develop innovative curricula. For example, according to the Humanitas program:

> [Our] single most important achievement is the raised expectations that teachers have set for themselves because that has resulted in raised expectations for their students—all their students and not just a select few. . . . [T]eacher empowerment means teachers assuming a greater responsibility for the development of meaningful curricula and, in the process, learning more themselves (Los Angeles Unified School District, 1992).

The Center for the Enhancement of Science and Math Education supports the innovations of individual science and math teachers, describing its model of educational reform in the following way:

> We believe that teachers are in the best position to serve as change agents—able to develop the programs necessary to inspire students and spark educational reforms. . . . Traditional educational systems develop and disseminate new approaches from the top down. . . . Unfortunately, this imposition of information from above eliminates the use of a teacher's practical knowledge of what works in the classroom, which is vital to the development of teaching innovations (Bay State Skills Corporation, 1993).

Thus, a consistent set of themes characterize these educational innovations: interdisciplinary work and student projects that incorporate basic skills as the basis of evaluation; teacher empowerment; strengthened linkages between the school and the community; and the application of this approach in all schools, not just elite schools. In that sense, these innovations are similar to Barzelay's (1992) description of the postbureaucratic paradigm as a set of closely related ideas.

OPPOSITION TO EDUCATIONAL INNOVATION

In his overview of *Bureaucracy*, James Q. Wilson (1989) argued that organizations resist innovations that threaten to alter core tasks. As an example, he claims that the educational reforms that have been most readily accepted over the last 50 years were "add ons," such as vocational education, drivers' education, remedial reading courses, health education, teacher aides, school lunch programs, and special classes for those with limited English or learning problems. Conversely, innovations that have been resisted include team teaching, individualized instruction, computerized instruction, and the use of television in the classroom. However, Wilson believes that innovations that redefine core tasks can succeed if the teachers can be monitored, and if strong constituencies support the innovation. While Wilson would classify some of the innovations discussed in this chapter as add-ons (e.g., those involving readiness to learn), there are many others, such as the comprehensive educational reform efforts and distance education programs, that do involve reconfiguring core tasks. It is therefore interesting to observe the patterns of opposition to these educational innovations.

Educational initiatives engender three types of opposition. The first type is, as Wilson predicted it would be, the difficulty of injecting new programs into existing institutions. They disrupt the internal balance of power and are perceived by some teachers and administrators as diminishing their role. The second is burnout: some of these innovations demand time and energy over the long term, and participants can become tired— especially if they are constantly fighting battles. Finally, opposition arises to the theories themselves.

Disrupting the System

Massachusetts' Student Conflict Resolution Experts program would, at first glance, seem to have met no opposition. It responded to a crisis of violence in the schools, had demonstrated results, and strong political support. Nevertheless, it was resisted in the schools because, "schools can be very closed systems and very resistant to 'outsiders'." High school administrators see mediation as a threat to their turf or power base, and as a way for offenders to avoid suspension. Similarly, teachers resist releasing student mediators from class for training and mediation sessions, particularly since some of the students selected to be mediators are considered to be "at risk."

The program attempts to overcome these obstacles in a number of ways. Its coordinators work to build trust with the schools by going to sports events, chaperoning dances, and attending faculty meetings. They search for a supportive "insider" who can educate them about a particular school's culture and how things are done. Coordinators reinforce the administration by using mediation *after* suspension rather than *instead of* suspension. They try to find out the needs of disciplinarians—for example, which situations cause them the most headaches—and then offer to take these problems off their hands. They take whatever cases they can get and build gradually to the cases they want. They also train at least twenty students per school each year so that no one mediator will be used too much. Finally, they try to demonstrate the benefits of the program by inviting similarly trained students from other schools to demonstrate their skills and speak about the effect that involvement in mediation has had on them personally (Massachusetts Attorney General's Office, 1994).

The program's plan for the future builds on its efforts to overcome opposition within the schools and to thoroughly integrate conflict mediation into the institution. Such objectives involve training administrators, teachers, and custodians in conflict resolution and working with teachers to build conflict resolution into the curriculum. Ironically, at this point, Wilson would probably advise keeping the mediation program as an add-on.

The New York City Peer Intervention Program faces two obstacles. First, it must build the trust of the teachers it is trying to help, which it does by not having supervisors present during interventions. However, support for the teachers often creates difficulties with the teachers' supervisors, usually assistant principals or department chairs, who argue that only licensed supervisors with credentials should assist teachers. The intervention threatens these supervisors who see it as a judgment that they are not "doing enough" for struggling teachers. Some critics have even suggested that the program is motivated solely by financial concerns because peer intervenors' salaries are lower than those of supervisors (New York City Board of Education, 1994). Humanitas had a similar problem. Because it began and was then replicated within the Los Angeles Unified School District on a teacher-helping-teacher basis, some administrators resented it, and in some cases left the system as a result.

The Michigan Partnership for New Education spends $10 million per year to work with 750 teachers and 15,000 students in twenty-five schools. It is clearly a major initiative, and it is just as clearly opposed by many within the system. Its response to the Ford-KSG semifinalist questionnaire noted that the State Board of Education regarded them as interlopers, that the state and local governments were unwilling to collaborate in the ways recommended by the partnership, and that many parents and educators think that the schools' problems should be solved by working harder in traditional ways, rather than through innovations proposed by the partnership. Local union leaders resist changes in collective agreements that would allow innovators flexibility, and university faculty have also been difficult participants, because they prefer doing research, rather than collaborating with practicing educators at school sites. Further, many of the partners in the coalition have their own agendas. For example,

> some in the business community seek immediate results as measured by employability skills and standardized tests and have little patience for long-term attempts at systemic reform. Politicians who live by the election cycle are also inclined to quick fixes. Some educators and business people believe that we are too strongly focused on academics and don't pay sufficient attention to vocational education (Michigan Partnership for New Education, 1994).

The partnership has worked to overcome opposition and bring its critics on board in numerous ways. Collaborations with the State Department of Education in curriculum, professional development, leadership, performance indicators, and technology have begun to overcome the department's suspicions and convince it that the partnership and the department are working toward shared goals. The partnership's board of directors and the governing bodies of local partnerships reflect the breadth of participants. Finally, they have responded to the dispersed responsibility of the educational system by working with all key stakeholders to set coherent goals, develop strategic plans, and implement program objectives. This emphasis on planning in a collaborative context exemplifies a situation in which planning is preferable to groping (see chapter 3).

One would not expect the Central Park East Secondary School to face teacher opposition since its teachers are self-selected devotees of its educational philosophy. However, it too faces major difficulties as it struggles to be innovative within a school system that operates as a machine bureaucracy:

> Obstacles to school reform (quite aside from the lack of funds) have been well-documented—local, state and federal rules, laws and regulations, union contracts, custodial agreements, to mention just a few. We face(d) each and every one: hiring procedures, ways of reporting and monitoring, testing and assessment systems that our students were obliged to undergo, the materials we could order, the inflexibility of funding categories, the scheduling and calendar. All operate on the assumption that teachers and students are interchangeable parts and schools are institutions with identical structures, visions and needs (New York City Board of Education, 1993).

Burnout

One innovation—Here, Thayer, and Everywhere—is itself a response to burnout. Other school systems were so interested in Thayer's program that staff were frequently asked to speak and give workshops. When this interest began to disrupt their work within the school, they began to produce and broadcast television programs so that they could continue their work as change agents more efficiently.

Humanitas teachers have also felt burnout because they had to work harder in classroom preparation for a team-teaching setting. They did not express intrinsic opposition to team-teaching, though they wanted additional resources to sustain it. Abolish Chronic Truancy also faces burnout. The commitment of school personnel to monitor attendance and follow-up with families fades as it becomes apparent that serious truancy problems cannot be solved overnight. In its response to the Ford-KSG questionnaire, this program noted that "it is a constant challenge to keep some of the schools focused and working on the project, although as positive results occur it becomes easier to motivate school personnel" (Los Angeles County, California District Attorney, 1994).

Opposing the Theory

Not only do innovative schools like Central Park East Secondary School face difficulties in dealing with the educational bureaucracy, but they are in the center of debates over how education should be reformed, as Deborah Meier reported:

> The kind of criticism CPESS is likely to engender would include those of reformers J.D. Hirsch and Bill Bennett who argue for a standardized external curriculum backed by a national system of monitoring and assessment. They would view CPESS's focus on "habits of mind" and depth over "coverage" as dangerous ("It's okay for Meier and her crew," they'd probably say, "but too risky in the hands of others.") On the local scene many colleagues believe that in some way we have fudged the data, or had unusual breaks— hidden monies, "better" kids. . . . (New York City Board of Education, 1993).

Meier adds that Jonathan Kozol "while praising CPESS, argues that choice and school-based reform creates a dangerous illusion in the absence of more fundamental equity reform."

Humanitas has also been criticized within the school system from the viewpoint that Deborah Meier here attributes to Hirsch and Bennett, namely by "teachers who value coverage . . . every day, date, name, and event, rather than . . . concepts in which the particulars gain significance within context." However, the success of Humanitas has tended to deflect this criticism (Los Angeles Unified School District, 1992).

In recent years, the advocates of national standards have become increasingly critical of "progressive education," a category that covers at least some of the practices of the Coalition for Essential Schools. For example, Sara Mosle, in a recent *New York Times Magazine* article advocating standards, argues that "though as a means of learning portfolios are wonderful, as a means of testing they are too subjective, too labor-intensive, and consequently too costly to implement on a national scale" (Mosle, 1996b).[3] In addition, Mosle notes that some experimental schools, such as the Science Skills Center in Brooklyn, are providing a rigorous education aimed at producing high achievement on standardized tests such as the SAT and New York State Regents exams, and have been quite successful with the same low-income black and hispanic population as Central Park East Secondary School (Mosle, 1996a). These schools belong to a movement started by Hirsch and other advocates of national standards, known as Core Knowledge Schools (Hirsch, 1996).

While resisting the educator's temptation to digress at length on this issue, I do think that the differences between these views are exaggerated by their advocates. For example, even during the creation of the Coalition for Essential Schools, Sizer (1984) wrote:

> The existence of final "exhibitions" by students as a condition to receiving their diplomas . . . combined with a variety of external examinations, such as the Advanced Placement Examinations of the College Board . . . would give outside authorities, like regional accrediting agencies, a good sense of the quality of work being done (p. 138).

Schools in the Coalition for Essential Schools continue to measure their performance in terms of their students' performance on standardized exams (Sizer, 1996); and advocates of national standards do not reject all elements of "progressive education." For example Mosle (1996b) wrote:

> Still, progressive educators are right to point out that too many American classrooms remain dull and lifeless. But standards

advocates are not arguing for a return to rote learning. The sensitivity to children's needs and differences, the ability to inspire intellectual curiosity and excitement exist independent of method. Schools should be allowed to use whatever approach they like and then to be held accountable for the results on substantive, content-based exams that are geared to curriculum.

Hirsch (1996, 251, 263) also finds merit in both exhibitions and performance-based assessment, two techniques at the heart of the Coalition for Essential Schools:

> Exhibitions are excellent, though subjective, devices for motivating students at the classroom level. . . . An advantage of performance-based assessment is that it requires the student to integrate the various sublearnings which make up a skill. This encourages both teachers and their students to stress such integration in the course of teaching and learning. Another advantage is said to be heightened student motivation, since such realistic modes of assessment directly exemplify the practical uses to which learnings are to be put. . . . The best use of performance tests are as lower-stakes "formative" tests, which help serve the goals of teaching and learning within the context of a single course of study.

In Mosle's and Hirsch's writings, exams are a goal intended to motivate the exceptional performance shown, for example, in the documentary dramatization *Stand and Deliver* in which passing the Advanced Placement calculus exam was the goal used by one instructor to motivate his mathematics class in an inner-city Los Angeles school. But while having a goal may be necessary, it is equally necessary to have a strategy to reach it.

Larry Rosenstock's CityWorks had to deal with the class bias leading to negative perceptions of vocational education. His response has been, not only to create a high quality program, but also to change public perceptions of vocational education. CityWorks sent direct mailings to parents, went to the local press, developed a slide-show for academic teachers, eighth grade students, and their parents, and had faculty and students design and build a new attractive "common room" and set of offices. Rosenstock also invited the chief state officer for vocational education to the school early on to support the initiative (Rindge School of Technical Arts, 1992).

How can educational innovators respond to these three types of obstacles? In cases of opposition by the educational system, they can show that innovations, such as student conflict resolution or peer intervention, can make life easier for middle managers (e.g., assistant principals) and in the case of burnout, by bringing in additional resources. In addition, some innovations, such as Humanitas, involve retraining teachers, which takes both time and money. When the opposition is philosophical, the answer is straightforward. The best way to respond is for an innovation to succeed; that, at least, will increase its claim on resources. In addition, because society at large holds a diversity of views about educational reform, some innovators can mobilize external supporters, whether in politics, the private sector, or among the consumers of their program.

ACHIEVING RESULTS

Consider first the comprehensive reform initiatives. Wilson is skeptical about the prospects for educational reforms that are more than add-ons. Is his skepticism about the comprehensive initiatives justified? Are they working? What have they accomplished?

At Central Park East Secondary School, 73 percent of students graduate on time, compared to a citywide average of 47 percent; ultimately, 95 percent of their students graduate, and 90 percent go on to college. In addition, the school's average performance on the SATs is equal to the national average, which is very good given that its students are predominantly disadvantaged. In Humanitas, evaluative studies have shown that, compared to a control group, student performance, particularly in writing, has improved, the dropout rate has declined, and teachers report higher job satisfaction. Here, Thayer, and Everywhere measured its initial success by the diffusion of its materials: 550 sites tune in to its televised workshops, it sells 600 tapes a year, and 200 people attend its conference. That said, this program also recognizes that a better—but more long-term—measure would be the extent to which educators who learn from it change their own schools.

The Michigan Partnership for New Education found that universities and schools were joining the partnership faster than had been expected and, in the classrooms themselves:

[A]lthough it is too early to provide definitive data on these issues, initial signs are very encouraging. Test scores and student attendance are already up in a number of sites, and some classrooms are exhibiting strong evidence of higher order critical thinking skills and problem solving capacity that are not yet measured by standardized norm referenced tests (Michigan Partnership for New Education, 1994).

Programs to make learning possible by improving circumstances outside the classroom also report successes. The Seattle Board of Education was able, as a result of new funding received from the Families and Education Interlocal Agreement, to reduce class size and improve attendance in the schools receiving additional money. Their students are achieving higher test scores. Abolish Chronic Truancy reported a success rate of over 90 percent, that is, attendance is improving without having to refer students to truancy mediation through the court system. The Massachusetts Attorney General reported that in the 1992-1993 school year, Student Conflict Resolution Experts reached agreements in 512 of 525 mediations and schools were referring fewer conflicts involving fights and racial disputes to mediation, which is interpreted as evidence that more and earlier mediations are occurring, thereby preventing fights. Parties were required to evaluate the mediation and students to evaluate their conflict resolution training; in both cases satisfaction was near 100 percent. In addition, student mediators report that their skills have helped them avoid conflict situations in contexts other than school. By 1996, 24 school districts in Massachusetts had established conflict-resolution programs modeled on SCORE (Walters, 1996c).

Vocational education programs have also achieved results. City-Works was evaluated when it applied for the Ford-KSG Award. Its successes included better attendance and improved academic performance for participating students and increased engagement by older vocational arts teachers, as evidenced by many working overtime without pay. Of the students participating in the Omaha Job Clearinghouse, 99 percent graduated from high school, 80 percent either went on in school or were employed, and 27 percent of the job sites offered employment to the students who visited them.

CONCLUSION

Clearly in a field that is everybody's business, there will be many innovations. Indeed, 25 states have passed laws to facilitate the creation of public charter schools free from constraints such as union seniority rules (Mosle, 1996b). These schools provide scope for experimentation, and may serve as pedagogic laboratories. They also contain a number of lessons that potential public sector innovators may want to emulate.

- First, educational innovation is clearly theory-driven. So innovators should either choose a theory they believe in from the many that are competing in the marketplace of ideas, or develop a theory of their own that overcomes the weaknesses they find in other people's theories.
- Second, they should look for private sector resources. Educational innovations are more likely to receive such support than any other type of innovation. However, it is unlikely that this support will amount to more than 20 percent of their program's budget; still, that is enough money to fund many of the items on any program's wish list. Of course, the supply of support also stimulates demand. Certain firms, particularly in the computer industry, have been approached so often that they have developed standard procedures to give any legitimate applicant some support, but not a great deal. The challenge is to find untapped sources of funds and to develop programs that are so innovative and well-thought-out that they surpass others in the competition for funding.
- Third, innovators should take the charter school route, if it is available. In comparison to creating a charter school, internal reforms in the public school system are more difficult to achieve, and may meet resistance from the academic system's middle managers, the unions, or the teachers themselves. Innovators working within the public school system will have to find strategies to gain the support of these groups, to retrain teachers where necessary, to find funding, and to achieve enough early successes that opposition can be neutralized.

   This chapter has shown that educational initiatives are controversial and that they may arouse considerable opposition within the educational system. To some extent, charter schools may be spared that opposition, since the staff who choose to work in them will be supporters of their philosophies. They may be committed to team teaching, computerized instruction, and other innovations that Wilson cites as changing the traditional core of teaching. Or they may be committed to academic rigor by affiliating with Hirsch's Core Knowledge Foundation.

   In the case of these charter school experiments, the first question is whether they will survive; the second, is whether they will be replicated. The existence of the Coalition for Essential Schools and the interest in Thayer High School's achievements would seem to answer both questions in the affirmative, though it is far from clear that they will become as prevalent as information technology innovations or community policing initiatives.

I also have some skepticism as to whether the proponents of national standards will ever achieve their goal in a country as diverse as the United States, but they appear to be on the way to creating a coalition of schools that use a variety of methods to achieve the goal of high performance on standardized examinations.

- Fourth, educational innovations, in common with those in other policy areas, must be properly evaluated. Therefore, immediately after having developed a theory, innovators should also develop ways to test it. Educational innovations will be expected by their funding sources, whether they are private or public sector or parents empowered to choose among competing schools, to show results.

13

Some Final Words for
Practitioners and Academics

Innovation is at the heart of our American culture, from be-bop to the light bulb, from Pop Art to the World Wide Web. American innovation stems from our faith that a single individual can change the world, and our willingness to work hard day after day and night after night to make our dreams come true.

VICE PRESIDENT ALBERT GORE
1996 Innovations in American
Government Awards Ceremony

I have come now to the end of my study. But it is not an absolute ending. Instead it is an opportunity to apply what we have learned and to plan additional research. Accordingly, this chapter presents my conclusions— first, in the form of advice to practitioners: to public sector front-line workers, executives, and others who will be the next wave of innovators and local heroes—and second, as my version of the research agenda on public management innovation. The theme of my advice to practitioners is integrity in innovation; the findings are intended for both practitioners and academics. The research agenda, though it contains some ideas of interest to policy discussions, may be of more interest to academics than to practitioners.

INTEGRITY IN INNOVATION

I began this book by asking what characteristics we would likely associate with someone who displays integrity in innovation. The programs in our sample and our analysis provide some answers. The characteristics we can expect are both intellectual—in terms of how one solves the conceptual puzzles inherent in designing a program that works on a practical level—and moral—in terms of how one deals with the interests and sensitivities of clients and coworkers. Marc Zegans (1990), former executive director of the Ford-KSG awards, describes the winners as "managers who pursue humble, hands-on problem solving approaches" and who "view themselves not as 'innovators' but as caring practical people who saw a problem that needed solving and determined that they would do something about it."[1] Similarly, by integrity in innovation, I mean intellectual honesty in designing and testing one's program and empathy in one's relationships with clients and co-workers—qualities that shine through the work of many of these innovators.

Encouraging Heroism in Public Service

Our research has shown that innovative programs are initiated at many levels in the organization, most frequently—almost half the time—by career public servants in middle management and at the front lines. If our traditional public sector model is one of command at the top and implementation at the lower levels, this finding brings us closer to the private sector model of innovation bubbling up from below. And it is surprising, given the ideological and structural constraints on public sector entrepreneurship. The implication for public sector organizations is to encourage, rather than suppress, the innovative ideas of middle management and front-line staff. I propose that we offer encouragement, not simply as a human resources ploy or item of faith, but as a conclusion grounded in evidence. Many public sector agencies are changing their structures and adopting programs that give front-line workers more responsibility. Gainsharing, for example, encourages front-line workers to take initiatives to control costs, and the community policing model encourages rank and file officers to identify and solve problems. As these trends continue, we should expect to see an increase in the amount of innovation coming from the career public service.

Our research did not support the widespread notion that externally visible crises are a royal road to public sector innovation. Many innovations in our sample began as a response to internal problems or new opportunities. Public servants who innovate are proactive; they solve problems before they become crises. Indeed, the data support a trichotomy of initiators and circumstances: politicians initiate in times of crisis; agency heads, when they take over the reins or in an organizational change context; and middle-level and front-line public servants develop innovative responses as needed to solve internal problems or take advantage of opportunities.

An Intellectual Discipline

Our sample of innovative public sector programs revealed a much higher incidence of comprehensive planning than of groping, as the process that leads to innovative programs. Circumstances associated with planning include large capital investments, inter-organizational partnerships, applications of theory, and political input, while groping more often involves new programs, new leadership, and the absence of circumstances associated with planning. Each model has its place, however, in practice and in the public management curriculum.

Among related conclusions:

- A noticeable percentage of the programs included in our study operationalize theoretical models—many of them derived from research. Consider, for example, the prevalence of psychological theories, such as family systems theory, in the social services; or pedagogic theories, such as either the progressive model or standards-driven education in the schools—or the community policing model, or civic environmentalism.
- A high percentage of the programs in our sample established quantitative goals and measures; in fact, many of them depended on data analysis to help them determine their clients' needs and measure their own performance (as exemplified in Oregon Benchmarks).
- A substantial percentage of the programs in our sample were evaluated by outsiders, such as auditors, central agencies, and academics; and finally,
- Regression analysis confirms that programs that were formally evaluated and whose outcomes were clear were more likely to be replicated and to receive awards.

Based on these findings, practitioners are well advised—and I would urge them—to follow the mental discipline of consulting the theoretical literature in their field—and in related fields—when looking for inspiration, to plan their programs as carefully as possible, and to design evaluation protocols at the outset.[2]

Another conceptual element of many innovations is process redesign, especially if the innovator's objective is to deliver a service faster, more accurately, more sensitively, and less expensively than before. Sometimes process redesign involves the use of information technology; on many other occasions, however, it simply involves thinking about client needs and being willing to reexamine basic assumptions. In the programs in our sample, process redesign sometimes involved using the legal system in new ways or changing the patterns of interaction among organizations. So again, I would urge practitioners to take note: thinking hard about how to improve processes is another important way of stimulating innovation.

Opponents and Critics

Most of the opposition to public sector innovation comes from within rather than outside the bureaucracy; and while opponents and critics are sometimes motivated by material self-interest, they are more often motivated by philosophies or ideologies that conflict with the ideas espoused by innovators. Sometimes the ideologies are rooted in professional jealousies and an unwillingness, or perhaps an inability, to step outside the professional roles in which we have been educated. Our sample revealed instances in which conflicting professional views led to opposition from within. Taking opponents and critics seriously means respecting their arguments and objections and attempting to win converts by persuasion: that is, by showing how an innovation can further a widely held goal, or by designing an experiment to determine if an innovation is achieving clearly defined goals.

In addition, different types of resistance to change occur at different organizational levels. Sometimes front-line workers are reluctant to be empowered; sometimes they are willing to be empowered but middle-managers have difficulty ceding authority to them; and of course, not only managers but also labor unions have difficulty with arrangements that reduce their representational role. Taking these groups seriously means attempting to accommodate them by consulting with them or involving them in the program's design.

We can, in such cases, provide training or modify a technology to make it more user friendly. To accommodate this process, innovators may want to restrain their haste in asking for declarations of support or shows of force from above. Opponents cannot be simply pushed aside. However, at some point, managers of innovative programs must consider providing exit packages for those who are unwilling or unable to accept change. Finally, taking the opponents to innovation and the critics of change seriously implies an attitude of forbearance—the innovators in our sample were people who had learned to live with obstacles that cannot be completely overcome.

Private Sector and Community Support

Another important finding of our study is that the private sector plays a variety of roles in public sector innovations:

- foundations provide seed money—particularly if the initiative is testing a new theory in the policy area that the foundation typically supports;
- individual or corporate donations make up small portions (generally no more than 20%) of an innovation's operating budget;
- access to private sector resources, either donated or rented, can be an essential component of program delivery;
- corporate funding may support pilot projects, particularly, in information technology and if the project may subsequently be commercialized; and, finally,
- volunteers, acting individually or in groups, may do some of an innovation's work.

In addition, communities have become involved in public sector innovation. They mobilize for common causes (e.g., to fight crime); participate in policy debates (e.g., through surveys and "electronic democracy"); or gather their resources to help troubled members. Innovators can pursue any or all of these options for building support for their programs. Indeed, a major challenge for innovators is to think creatively about how such interests should be pursued.

A related challenge is designing programs that elicit the desired private sector or community support from the beginning. For example, if a foundation is deeply involved in testing new theories, the innovator should have a well-designed and up-to-date research proposal that includes the foundation's perspective. Similarly, many corporations have developed philanthropic strategies designed to support causes that project a desired image (Sweeney, 1994); innovators must know these strategies and present their proposals as a complement to them.

Thinking Holistically—Program Design and Cross-Training

The most frequently observed characteristic of innovative programs is that they are holistic. Holism can, however, be variously displayed, depending on the type of innovation. Information technology programs, for example, can contain a wide range of services, each appropriate to a different audience. Innovators, like entrepreneurs, must use this variety to attract additional sponsors and participants. Similarly, environmental programs are moving away from a narrow focus on cleaner air or water to the management of ecosystems: that is, to a focus on the interactions of various media (air, land and water); problem-oriented policing initiatives inevitably develop solutions that involve other government departments; and social service innovators have discovered that as individuals have multiple problems, programs that treat the whole person are more effective than sending the client from office to office (Davenport and Nohria, 1994).

Innovators who intend to deliver holistic programs must develop integrative organizational structures, such as lead agencies, advisory committees, and task forces. Part of the innovator's "art" is knowing which of these structures to use, and when.

Integrative programs also require cross-training of front-line staff who will be working in multifunctional teams, demonstration projects to convince potential partners of the benefits of collaboration, a vision focused on the results of the collaboration, and partnerships that make participants cognizant of the collective benefits of cooperating and that, at the very least, provide credit for all participants. We have seen examples of large partnerships that succeed because they use client pressure to override parochial agendas, because they were run informally, and because they clearly delegated responsibility to lead players. The evidence is compelling: collective action is possible if innovators are skilled in the techniques that make it happen.

Vision and Commitment

Public sector innovators or local heroes are those who think about changing circumstances, such as new technologies, funding shortfalls, or new national legislative mandates, and how these will affect their programs. More important, they also formulate responses to those circumstances. Sometimes the circumstances will expand the mandates of their programs; sometimes, the programs themselves will be enfolded in larger initiatives. In either case, the local heroes in our survey were primarily committed to the initiative and its survival and then, only secondarily, to its organizational base—it must be so in future innovations.

The epigram from Vice-President Gore, which stands at the head of this chapter, summarizes this advice to practitioners. Innovation, or inventiveness, is an American trait that is universally admired. Its presence in individuals, whether in the bureaucracy or in those who influence the bureaucracy from outside, is sufficient to overcome the status quo and make a difference. No vision, however, no matter how innovative, can succeed unless the innovator also does the hard work of designing intellectually sound programs and persuading and accommodating other people, especially skeptics, to implement them. That is the best way to ensure that the innovations will succeed and endure.

THE RESEARCH AGENDA—QUESTIONS WORTH PURSUING

The field of public administration has enjoyed a dramatic revival of interest in recent years, created largely by the New Public Management. Yet a lively debate continues on whether the ideas that constitute the New Public Management are really new, and whether, collectively, they constitute a new paradigm. I have argued in support of both propositions (Borins 1995b; 1995c, and 1995d); however, this book is not about doctrinal arguments. This book is about evidence, and its role was to provide hard evidence in support of the new paradigm.

I wrote this book to show that a rigorously constructed sample of public management innovations in state and local government in the United States contains a respectable presence and many iterations of the New Public Management themes—themes such as customer focus, empowerment, prevention, results orientation, private sector involvement, and use of market mechanisms, among others, which Osborne and Gaebler championed in their original study (1992). Second, I wrote this book to present clear evidence that many of the innovative programs in this sample have achieved and are achieving results in the locale where they began and elsewhere through replication. In part 2 of this book, the evidence was sifted to show that not only do these themes recur in different policy areas, but also each recurrence illustrates the paradigm of the New Public Management in its own way.

In this book, I have tried to depart from the most commonly used methodology in the study of public management, namely, the case study. Instead, I assembled a large database and used it to test hypotheses developed in the literature, for example, Behn's groping model, and Golden's extension of that model, which looks at circumstances to determine when an innovation is more likely to depend on planning than groping, and vice versa. I have also used the database to test Lindblom's optimistic model of spontaneous coordination through partisan mutual adjustment and Pressman and Wildavsky's pessimistic model of implementation failure. But Lindblom and Pressman and Wildavsky are both found wanting. The conclusion is that coordination can occur if the agencies involved set up formal structures and adopt tactics designed to promote consensus.

I have also used the database to determine where in pubic sector organizations innovations are most likely to be introduced, to determine the factors most likely to lead to innovation, and to identify the most likely sources of opposition and how they can be overcome. I hope that the value of this methodology will convince other scholars that it can and should be used as an alternative to, or in addition to, case studies. Based on this study—on what it does and on what it has not been able to do— I submit the following questions regarding public management innovation as deserving of further study.

The Authorizing Environment

Moore (1995) used the term "authorizing environment" to apply to the political-bureaucratic context that determines whether an innovative program will receive the political and financial support it needs to survive. One controversy in the literature is the importance of winning over the agency heads and their most senior deputies. James Q. Wilson (1989) summarizes the literature:

> As individuals who must balance competing interests inside the agency it is [senior executives] who must decide whether to protect or to ignore managers who wish to promote changes. Almost every important study of bureaucratic innovation points to the great importance of executives in explaining change (p. 227).

Levin and Sanger (1994), however, based on their sample of public management innovations, concluded that the role of senior executives was less significant than Wilson suggests:

> The innovative managers' relationships to their top political executives—mayor, governor, cabinet secretary—were significant, but there was a dual pattern. In some instances—in crises or for large programs—the relationship [between innovative managers and top

political executives] was close and supportive at the outset. In others—indeed, most of them—the relationship with a top political executive proved important only in sustaining an already successful enterprise. These smaller programs, not facing crises, seemed to benefit from the initial freedom to experiment that came from their distance from top political executives (p. 164).

I did not attempt to resolve this disagreement because answers to the Ford-KSG semifinalist questionnaire about who was supportive of, or involved in, planning these programs often included long lists and may have inflated the role of agency heads and political chief executives.

A worthwhile subject for future study would be to trace in more depth how local heroes try to build support in their authorizing environment. Such a study could control for bias in describing the role of agency heads and politicians by checking the innovators' description of these leaders against the way they are described in the site visit reports for finalists and winners, or by excluding programs that claim agency heads and politicians play a major role but do not describe it.

Such a study could also look separately at innovations initiated by politicians, agency heads, middle managers, and front-line staff to look for similarities or differences in the pattern of ways that support is sought and coalitions are built. Interviews would also be useful here.

A related question is whether the New Public Management depends on or helps create a new political vision. For example, in this analysis, several politicians and agency heads were intensely interested in public management: Mayors Richard Daley in Chicago, Illinois; Stephen Goldsmith in Indianapolis, Indiana; Jerry Abramson in Louisville, Kentucky; and City Manager Robert O'Neill in Hampton, Virginia. They seemed, in fact, more interested in efficiency and less interested in distribution than typical politicians or agency heads. Are there others like them? If so, are there other characteristics or interests that would fit into the description? The role of politicians is not well studied in the New Public Management (Behn, 1996c), and an empirical study of their role would contribute greatly to the field as a whole.

Innovative Jurisdictions and Organizations

The private sector literature often refers to the characteristics of innovative organizations or gives prescriptions on how to make an organization more innovative (Kanter, 1988). While the Ford-KSG Awards identify individual innovations, some of these programs represent a series of innovations within a given organization over a long period of time (e.g., the New York Bureau of Motor Equipment In-house Research and Development Network). Similarly, certain organizations, cities, and states seem to produce a large number of innovations (Behn, 1993). In 1993, for example, Phoenix, Arizona, received the Bertelsmann Foundation Award for the best-managed city in the world. We could, therefore, look to it as an example of a city with a high rate of innovation (Ehrenhalt, 1995; Mahtesian, 1994c). We could use applications to the Ford-KSG Awards, the secondary literature, and expert opinion to define a sample of innovative organizations or jurisdictions and then study their common characteristics.[3]

Survival and Replication of Innovations

In writing this book, I used any available published reports, that is, the secondary literature that reports on the fate of programs in this sample. A more direct way to determine whether programs survive and whether if they do, they are also replicated, would be to contact the innovators years after their initial application and ask them. This approach would, moreover, respond directly to the argument made by Osborne and Gaebler's detractors and by critics of the New Public Management, that innovations do not stand the test of time. Such a study should not be undertaken, however, simply to score debating points. It should be undertaken, ultimately, to learn what we can about the diffusion of various public sector innovations. For example, are more environmental bureaucracies now doing cross-media inspections? Are public sector electronic kiosks well established, or are they being displaced by transactions over the Internet? A useful concept in studying the innovative process is the logistic, or S-curve. Where on the logistic curve are these innovations: at the outset when only a few agencies are experimenting; at the stage of rapid diffusion throughout the population; or at saturation? What is the level of saturation? What differentiates innovations that have been rapidly and widely diffused from those that have not?

Role of the Private Sector

We know from this study that the private sector plays many important roles in innovative public sector programs. However, we also have reason to think that the Ford-KSG sample underestimates the role of the private sector since it excludes all programs that receive more than 50 percent of their funding from the private sector. In addition, the Ford-KSG data may miss initiatives that involve privatization and outsourcing. Certainly their incidence seems to be growing in recent years (Kittower, 1997). To include these initiatives, we would need to acquire databases other than the Ford-KSG Awards, for example, a partnerships database. The value of a more inclusive analysis lies in the more complete picture it would give us of private sector involvement.

Extending the Study

The data on which this study is based dealt with state and local government innovations that were semifinalists for the Ford-KSG Awards between 1990 and 1994. The next step would be to apply a similar methodology to semifinalists from 1995 to 1998. A sample of semifinalists drawn from those years would be similar in size to the present sample, but it would also include the federal government. Above all, it would likely demonstrate new waves of innovation. For example, if earlier trends can be trusted, it would contain many benchmarking efforts and public sector applications of the Internet.

Recall, too, that my research design was opportunistic, as I simply used the semifinalist questionnaire as my research instrument. Future researchers may want to develop their own instruments and send them to the Ford-KSG award candidates or to other similar professional lists. Such instruments, because they are not linked to an innovation award, may be more effective at getting unbiased answers to questions of interest to the researcher. The tradeoff is that with no extrinsic award linked to completion of the questionnaire, the response rate may be low. If applicants to the Ford-KSG Awards are used for nonopportunistic research designs, the researcher can probably augment the responses to the semifinalist application with additional questions. One example of a nonopportunistic research design is the questionnaire (based on the Ford-KSG semifinalist questionnaire) that I sent to winners and finalists of the Institute of Public Administration of Canada innovative management award. I added several questions—for example, the lessons the innovators had learned from their experience and whether their innovation had been characterized by planning or groping.

Another valuable extension of this study would be comparative research on public management innovation. Many countries now have public management innovation awards, and applications to these awards could be used to build international databases and then to see whether public management innovations are similar worldwide, or whether they admit differences that stem, for example, from different political systems and bureaucratic cultures.

These paragraphs represent, then, my agenda for additional research on public management innovation involving the creation and analysis of databases, particularly from innovation awards, in addition to the more common case studies. The Ford-KSG Awards have provided an excellent point of departure for this approach; however, much remains to be done.

The Innovations Awards Questionnaire

1. Please describe the purposes, scope, and nature of your program or policy initiative, including the specific problem it addresses.

2. Briefly describe the principal program activities, clients, and resources at the core of your innovation.

3. What makes this program or policy initiative innovative? Compare it with other programs or policies currently operating in your state, region, or nationally that address the same problem. How does your approach differ?

4. Please list, in order of priority, the most important goals or objectives of your program or policy.

5. Please describe the target population served by your program or policy initiative. How does the program or policy identify and select its clients or consumers? How many clients does your program or policy initiative currently serve? What percentage of the potential clientele does this represent?

6. What is the program's current operating budget? What are the program's funding sources (e.g., local, state, federal, private)? What percentage of annual income is derived from each? Please provide any other pertinent budget information. Please note that the applicant is required to substantiate its claim that one or more state, local, or tribal government institutions currently provide at least 50% of ongoing funding. [The last sentence was first used in 1994].

7. Briefly describe the composition, role, and reporting relationships of any government departments, boards, or committees involved in the policy-setting or administration of your program or policy initiative. Include any sub-contractual relationships with outside organizations

or individuals. (Please attach an organization chart to show the current number, responsibilities, and reporting relationships of key program employees or staff.)

8. When and how was the program or policy initiative conceived in your jurisdiction? Please describe any specific incidents or circumstances that led to the initiative. What individuals or groups are considered the primary initiators? Please substantiate the claim that one or more state, local, or tribal government institutions played a formative role in the program's development. (If your innovation is an adaptation or replication of another innovation, please identify the program or policy initiative and jurisdiction originating the innovation. In what ways has your program or policy initiative adapted or improved on the original innovation?)

9. Please identify the key milestones in program or policy development and implementation and when they occurred (e.g., pilot program authorization enacted by State legislature in June 1986; pilot program accepted first clients, September 1986; expanded program approved by legislature in July 1987). How has the implementation strategy of your program or policy evolved over time?

10. Please describe the most significant obstacle(s) encountered thus far in your program. How have they been dealt with? Which ones remain?

11. What other significant individuals or organizations have been most significant in a) program development, and b) ongoing implementation and operation? What roles have they played?

12. What individuals are the strongest supporters of the program or policy initiative and why?

13. What individuals or organizations are the strongest critics of the program or policy initiative and why? What is the nature of their criticism?

14. What are the three most important measures you use to evaluate program success? In qualitative or quantitative terms for each measure, please provide the outcomes of the last full year of program operation and at least one prior year.

15. What would you describe as the program's or policy initiative's single most important achievement to date?

16. What would you characterize as the program's most significant remaining shortcoming?

17. If your program or policy initiative has been formally evaluated or
audited by an independent organization or group, please provide the
name, address, and telephone number of a contact person from whom
the materials are available. Please summarize the principal findings
of the independent evaluator(s) and/or auditor(s).

18. How do you believe the principal problem(s) addressed by your
program or policy initiative will evolve over the next five years and
how is your program going to respond?

19. To what extent do you believe your program or policy is potentially
replicable within other jurisdictions and why? To your knowledge,
have any other jurisdictions or organizations established programs
or implemented policies modeled specifically on your own?

20. Has the program or policy initiative received any awards or other
honors? If yes, please list and describe the awards or honors and the
sponsoring organizations.

21. Has the program received any press or other media coverage to date?
If yes, please list the sources and briefly describe relevant coverage.
[This question was first asked in 1994.]

Notes

Chapter 1.

1. As Osborne and Gaebler did not list their cases, someone else's list may be longer or shorter than mine. I counted only cases that were discussed at some length, as opposed to passing references.

2. Similar lists have been developed by other authors undertaking international comparisons of public management reforms (e.g., Holmes and Shand, 1995; Organization for Economic Cooperation and Development, 1995; and Thompson, 1997).

3. A conversation with Graham Allison helped me recognize this distinction.

4. My research assistants were students at Harvard University, one undergraduate in economics, a second undergraduate in anthropology, a graduate student in divinity, and another graduate student in Eastern European studies. In the early stages of the project, when the code book was being developed, each of us coded every questionnaire; once we had determined the code, each questionnaire was coded by me and one assistant. Any differences in coding were reconciled through discussions.

5. Between 1990 and 1993, the Ford-KSG award had no annual themes. In 1994, however, the application encouraged applicants to address three themes: tapping the creativity of front-line workers, reshaping organizational cultures, and significant policy innovation. These three themes, which are all reasonably broad, were chosen because it was felt that they had been underrepresented in previous years. Nevertheless, the 1994 competition remained open to all innovators "at all levels of state and local government, and from all types of programs." It was not narrowly targeted.

6. In a 1995 research project, I sent a questionnaire based on the Ford-KSG semifinalist questionnaire to finalists in a Canadian public management innovation competition. The Canadian finalists had competed between 1990 and 1994. The response rate after two rounds of follow-up telephone calls was only 35 percent.

Chapter 2.

1. In doing this calculation, the total holistic, total technology, and total process improvement percentages are used, rather than the sum of percentages for the components of each. The reason is that the totals represent the union of their component characteristics.

2. One early example of this type of competition, cited by Osborne and Gaebler (1992), is garbage collection in Phoenix, Arizona; the British government has also introduced this approach, called market testing, in a wide variety of public services.

3. However, one of the award winners in 1995 was the City of Indianapolis's program of competition between the public and private sectors for contracts to deliver services (City of Indianapolis, Indiana, Department of Administration, 1995).

4. This section is based on a paper presented at the 1995 Association for Public Policy and Management research conference (Borins, 1995e).

5. At the federal level, the Government Performance and Results Act of 1993 now requires all departments to develop and use performance-based measures.

Chapter 3.

1. These conditions or challenges are similar to those cited by Zegans (1992) in research based on focus groups with senior civil servants in state and local government.

2. This section is based on a paper presented at the 1995 Association for Public Policy and Management research conference (Borins, 1995e).

3. On first reading, Behn's argument may appear similar to Lindblom's (1959) "science of muddling through," and Quinn's (1980) model of logical incrementalism in business strategy. However, Behn differentiates his model from Lindblom's, arguing that Lindblom's work deals with policymaking whereas he focuses on management—that is, the leadership of government agencies (Behn, 1991). Behn also argues that his model is less incrementalist than Quinn's, because Quinn's private sector managers are less willing to proclaim their goals than were the public managers he studied (Behn, 1991).

4. When the independent variables in a multiple regression are completely uncorrelated with one another (i.e., when the correlation coefficients between all pairs of independent variables equal zero), every independent variable's coefficient in a multiple regression will be identical to its coefficient in a simple regression. The correlation coefficients among the independent variables, while not zero, were quite small, which indicates every independent variable's coefficient in a multiple regression will be similar to its coefficient in a simple regression.

5. This does occur for the linear probability regressions in Table 3-8. Take the case of a hypothetical observation in which all the characteristics that increase the probability of comprehensive planning are present and all the characteristics that decrease the probability of comprehensive planning are absent. For the linear model for comprehensive planning (column 1 of Table 3-8), the predicted probability would be .53 (the intercept) + 1 (.40) + 1 (.28) − 0 (.38) + 1 (.14) + 1 (.09) − 0 (.33) − 0 (.14) = 1.44.

6. A second reason for using a nonlinear search procedure is that observations of the dependent variable are all either 0 or 1, so the natural logarithm of the odds for 0 would be negative infinity and for 1 would be positive infinity. A

search procedure produces regression results by using very small numbers to approximate negative infinity and very large numbers to approximate positive infinity.

7. Pindyck and Rubinfeld (1991, 263) report that "small-sample studies suggest that the signs (and frequently the relative magnitudes) of the estimated parameters obtained from linear probability models and the maximum-likelihood logit estimators are usually the same," so perhaps my result is not surprising.

8. In fairness to Levin and Sanger, I must point out that they do not suggest removing planning skills from the curriculum, and they do recognize the value to the curriculum of including such topics as applied microeconomics, benefit-cost analysis, statistical analysis, and some knowledge of broad policy areas.

9. Lynn (1996) also argues for the importance of analytic skills in the curriculum; he shows how analytic skills and conceptual models can be used to develop better answers to teaching cases and more useful studies of policy problems.

Chapter 4.

1. The program was designed so that students could respond via computer keypad to the distant teacher's questions; the answers received are tabulated and transmitted back to the students.

2. The percentage of times an obstacle was overcome was calculated by coding each obstacle encountered for each applicant (i.e., the responses to question 10). We also coded the obstacles each applicant said remained and generated from these two codings a matrix with the following cells: (1) cases where an obstacle was not encountered (i.e. it was neither initial nor remaining); (2) an initial obstacle that does not remain (i.e. that was overcome); (3) an initial obstacle that was not overcome; and (4) an obstacle not encountered initially but subsequently discovered and still remaining. The percentage of times an obstacle was overcome was calculated as $2/(2 + 3 + 4)$. Cell 4 was included in the denominator because we assumed that if applicants only mentioned an obstacle as remaining, then they had not been successful in overcoming it initially and did not describe there efforts to do so.

3. I could have presented Table 4-3 as a matrix of obstacles and tactics; however, a 270-cell matrix of 15 obstacles and 18 tactics would have been rather unwieldy and would have contained many zeroes or small numbers.

4. Similar views were expressed by James Q. Wilson (1989, 230): "an agency that wishes to implement an innovation over the opposition of some of its members often needs to concentrate power in the hands of the boss sufficient to permit him or her to ignore (or even dismiss) opponents." My study finds that this autocratic necessity happens less often than Wilson suggests.

5. If there is any likely bias in answering this question, it would be the claim that an innovation happened more smoothly than it actually did, which would mean ignoring a program's actual critics altogether. For that reason, I am reasonably sure that the people identified as strong or strongest critics actually were.

6. Writing as a Canadian, it is possible to view innovations in the health sector as attempts to provide care for those who fall between the cracks in the U.S. health care system as it presently exists. One is tempted to say that a more

radical solution—national health insurance—is preferable to all these innovative but marginal improvements on an inadequate system. On the other hand, if national health insurance is not a possibility, then these innovative marginal improvements are still worthwhile. This realization demonstrates that what is innovative in a society is a function of its policies and institutions prior to the innovation. Furthermore, while Canada's system of national health insurance has successfully provided basic service to all citizens, funding constraints have led to queues for some services and a reduction in the number of services covered. I would expect that in a Canadian public management innovation competition, health care applications would address those problems.

7. These cases are discussed in more detail in the first section of chapter 8, dealing with turnarounds.

Chapter 6.

1. The literature on goal-setting advocates "stretch" goals, that is, goals that organizations have a reasonable chance of meeting if they work hard (Locke and Latham, 1984).

2. In some cases, the ideal is unattainable because it is impossible for participants not to know whether they are being treated. In others, if it is thought that a treatment might be helpful, it is politically impossible to withhold it from people who want to receive it.

3. Enabling individuals or groups to work together had the following correlation coefficients, all significant: .28 in instances in which the private sector is used to achieve a public sector purpose; .2 in cases involving partnerships between the public and private sectors; .17 in cases involving the holistic coordination of several organizations.

4. From the twenty-five finalists, a panel of distinguished practitioners and academics chooses ten winners. In addition to reading the semifinalist application and site visit report, the judging process includes a short presentation to the panel.

5. Before doing the multiple regression analysis, I did simple correlation coefficients between the dependent variables (any award and any actual replication) and all the outcomes listed in Table 6-1 and the types of formal evaluation listed in Table 6-3. Because of the simultaneity between replication and awards, I used each as an independent variable with respect to the other. Variables with significant simple correlations were included in the multiple regressions and those with insignificant simple correlations were not. Because the independent variables are not strongly correlated with one another, the parameters estimated in multiple regressions will be very close to those estimated in simple correlations (as was the case in the regressions presented in chapter 3).

Chapter 7.

1. Without in any way derogating from Williams's achievement, as a Canadian I must add that the universal health insurance provided by all Canadian provinces has long been portable among all provinces.

2. However, the goal of a single kiosk for all government services might itself be unworkable. Including all services on a single kiosk would mean putting lengthy transactions together with short ones. Queuing theory tells us that overall waiting is decreased by separating lengthy transactions from short ones (just as supermarkets separate shoppers with few purchases from those with many). Thus there should be at least two types of electronic kiosks, one for a set of quick transactions and the other for a set of lengthy ones; when the question of kiosk design is considered thoroughly, it might turn out that it is optimal to have more than two types.

Chapter 8.

1. The proof of this assertion can be seen in the following positive and significant correlation coefficients between the paired characteristics of innovation originally presented in Table 2-2. Thus, between turnarounds and continuous improvement, .22; between turnarounds and organizational restructuring, .22; between turnarounds and education of staff, .25; between geographic decentralization and continuous improvement, .1; between geographic decentralization and increased client orientation, .21; between participatory management and organizational restructuring, .15; between participation management and client orientation, .12; between participatory management and better systems and procedures, .10; between continuous improvement and organizational restructuring, .15; between continuous improvement and client orientation, .28; between continuous improvement and education of staff, .16; between restructuring and education of staff, .11.

2. This section is based on a report sponsored by the Canadian Government (Borins, 1994a) and a paper presented at the 1994 Association for Public Policy and Management research conference (Borins, 1994b).

3. Mark Moore, in conversation with me about turnarounds, made the point that any public sector organization that has been in operation for a long time has likely experienced at least one turnaround.

4. The others are the Tactical Air Command of the US Air Force (Finnegan, 1987; Creech, 1994); the Swedish National Student Aid Board (Kelman, 1993); and four Canadian cases (the Correctional Service of Canada [Vantour, 1991], the Archives of Ontario, the Ontario Development Corporation, and the Alberta Workers' Compensation Board). In addition, I tested the robustness of the model by applying it to a ninth case. After writing the first version of the paper, I heard a presentation by Ellen Schall about her experiences turning around the New York City Department of Juvenile Justice (Schall and Feely, 1992; Schall, 1996; Varley, 1987). Based on her talk and subsequent correspondence, it was clear that the model fit her experience as well. In addition, Schall's (1996) retelling of the story also makes clear that she and her staff followed a strategy of groping rather than planning, as I would predict in the case of a new agency head taking over a troubled program.

5. Weber's (1959, 245) classic definition of charisma is "natural leaders in distress [who are] holders of specific gifts of the body and spirit; and these gifts have been believed to be supernatural, not accessible to everybody."

6. Similar changes in rehabilitation practices and reductions in benefits have been made in many other states in the 1990s, in response to equally poor financial performance (Cohodas, 1994). Thus, Washington was one of the first to reform.

7. I am indebted to Gernod Gruening for pointing this out to me.

Chapter 9.

1. Similarly, Malcolm Sparrow, in a comparative study of policing, tax collection, and environmental regulation, observed a change from command-and-control to partnership and voluntary compliance approaches in all three areas (Sparrow, 1994).

2. This arrangement is both similar to and different from a process known as tax increment financing that was used by many other cities in the 1980s. Typically, a city would target a blighted area, freeze property taxes, issue a bond to pay for new infrastructure, and intend to pay the interest on the bond from taxes paid by new private investment that would be made in the area. In some cases, this approach was unsuccessful because the investment did not materialize (Lemov, 1994). The Wichita case is different because the partnership agreement ensured that there would be sufficient resources to pay for the cleanup and, as a consequence, no bonds had to be issued.

3. The Voluntary Inspection and Cleanup program counts as a completion either an investigation showing no contamination, a cleanup, or the provision of liability assurance while the Superfund only counts cleanups as completions (Minnesota Pollution Control Agency, 1994).

Chapter 10.

1. Seattle has had a Neighborhood Matching Grants Program in operation since 1988, in which the city makes small grants to neighborhood organizations for improvement projects and the organizations match the grant either with money or labor. Hampton, Virginia has a Department of Neighborhoods which also makes matching grants to neighborhoods. In addition, it is working on a scheme that will enable neighborhoods to exchange assets, trading skills and tasks that will count towards their matching grant contributions. It has also established a training institute for neighborhood leaders and activists (National Civic League, 1996).

Chapter 11.

1. AIDS is defined as "a disease of the immune system characterized by increased susceptibility to opportunistic infections, to certain cancers, and to neurological disorders: caused by a retrovirus transmitted chiefly through blood or blood products that enter the person's bloodstream, especially by sexual contact or contaminated hypodermic needles" (Webster's College Dictionary, 1992). Human immunodeficiency virus (HIV) is defined as the AIDS virus, "a variable retrovirus that invades and inactivates helper T cells of the immune system and is a cause of AIDS and AIDS related complex" (ibid).

2. This program was also mentioned in chapter 8 as an example of an innovation in governance because of its use of advisory boards. As a social service innovation, the relevant feature is the use of alternatives to incarceration.

3. Schorr (1988, 156–63) reported that, by mid-1987, eight states were experimenting with intensive family support programs as an alternative to foster care. She also described one of the best programs at that time, the Tacoma, Washington, Catholic Children's Services Homebuilders Program; it provides intensive and immediate support delivered at home by a team of professionals.

4. See also Schorr (1993).

5. In this context, it is fitting to mention the Ford Foundation's interest in the identification and diffusion of public sector innovation, which supports both the Ford-KSG Awards and research on innovation.

Chapter 12.

1. These programs can be considered exemplars or extensions of the first principle enunciated in the 1989 education summit called by President Bush, namely, that all first graders should enter school "ready to learn" (Hirsch 1996, 217).

2. These principles are listed in Sizer (1996, 154N5).

3. As is consistent with the "everybody's business" hypothesis, the *New York Times Magazine* (1996) reported that this article "generated a vigorous debate among score of letter writers."

Chapter 13.

1. Heifetz (1994) took a similar approach to the broad subject of leadership, by arguing that real leadership—without easy answers, as he put it—involves helping one's organization to confront, rather than avoid, adaptive challenges. The art, or science, required is that of focusing attention on the tough problems and helping one's followers to deal with the problems at a tolerable rate.

2. My exhortations are entirely consistent with those of Lynn (1996). However, we arrived at the same point in different ways. Lynn undertook a careful critique of other authors; I base my conclusions on a rigorous study of successful public sector innovations. Darman (1996) makes a similar point in urging the federal government to invest more heavily in research trials and policy experiments.

3. Light (1996), in his review of Levin and Sanger (1994) makes a similar point in suggesting that the public management field pursue the agenda of creating organizations in which innovation, lower cost, and higher performance naturally thrive and survive.

References

INNOVATIONS AWARD APPLICATIONS AND SITE VISIT REPORTS

Aiken County, South Carolina. 1994. "Senior Citizens Tax Work-Off Program." Semifinalist Application to Innovations in State and Local Government Awards Program. [William M. Shepherd, County Administrator, Administrator's Office, 828 Richland Avenue West, Aiken, SC 29801; (803) 642-2012, fax: (803) 642-2124.]

Alaska Community Resource Network. 1993. "Family Resource Project." Semifinalist Application to Innovations in State and Local Government Awards Program. [Bruce Andersen, Director, Community Resource Network, 700 Katlian Street, Suite B, Sitka, AK 99835; (800) 243-2199, fax: (206)463-8311.]

Allegheny County, Pennsylania Court of Common Pleas. 1994. "Community Intensive Supervision Program." Semifinalist Application to Innovations in State and Local Government Awards Program. [Joseph Daugerdas, Director of Court Services, Allegheny County Court of Common Pleas, Juvenile Section, 3333 Forbes Avenue, Pittsburgh, PA 15213; (412) 578-8210, fax: (412) 578-8279.]

Anoka County, Minnesota Job Training Center. 1994. "Minnesota Parents' Fair Share." Semifinalist Application to Innovations in State and Local Government Awards Program. [Marcia Adkins, Coordinator, Minnesota Parents' Fair Share, Anoka County Job Training Center, 1201 89th Avenue Northeast, Suite 235, Blaine, MN 55434; (612) 783-4826, fax: (612) 783-4844.]

Anthony, Amy. 1993. "Site Visit Report on Government Action on Urban Land." (June 14). Boston, MA. Unpublished.

Arizona State Mine Inspector. 1991. "Volunteer Abandoned Mines Program." Semifinalist Application to Innovations in State and Local Government Awards Program. [Douglas K. Martin, State Mine Inspector, State of Arizona, 1616 South Adams, Room 411, Phoenix, AZ 85007-2627; (602) 542-5971.]

Arizona Supreme Court. 1994. "Arizona 'QuickCourt' System." Semifinalist Application to Innovations in State and Local Government Awards Program. [Jeanie Lynch, Program Manager, Juvenile Justice Services Division of the Administrative Office of the Courts, Arizona Supreme Court, 1501 West Washington, Phoenix, AZ 85007-3327; (602) 542-9554, fax: (602) 542-9480.]

Arlington County, Virginia. 1992. "Bilingual Outreach." Semifinalist Application to Innovations in State and Local Government Awards Program. [Deborah Powers, Chief, Community Resources, Arlington County Parks, Recreation and Community Resources, 2100 Clarendon Boulevard, Suite 414, Arlington, VA 22201; (703) 358-3339, fax: (703) 358-3328.]

Baltimore County, Maryland Police Department. 1994. "Counseling Unit." Semifinalist Application to Innovations in State and Local Government Awards Program. [John R. Worden, Supervisor, Counseling Unit, Baltimore County Police Department, 700 East Joppa Road, Towson, MD, 21286; (410) 887-2201, fax: (410) 887-5337.]

Baltimore, Maryland Community Development Financing Corporation. 1992. Semifinalist Application to Innovations in State and Local Government Awards Program. [Bill Toohey, Director of Public Information, Baltimore Department of Housing and Community Development, 417 East Fayette Street, Room 1337, Baltimore, MD 21202; (410) 396-4563.]

Bay State Skills Corporation. 1993. "The Center for the Enhancement of Science and Mathematics Education." Semifinalist Application to Innovations in State and Local Government Awards Program. [Ephraim Weisstein, Senior Program Specialist, Bay State Skills Corporation, 101 Summer Street, 2nd Floor, Boston, MA 02110; (617) 292-5100, fax: (617) 292-5105.]

Beaver County, Oklahoma Schools. 1990. "Beaver County Interactive Television Cooperative." Semifinalist Application to Innovations in State and Local Government Awards Program. [Jim Bouse, Superintendent, Beaver Schools, Balko, Beaver, Forgan and Turpin School District, P.O. Box 580, Beaver, OK 73932; (405) 625-3444.]

Behn, Robert. 1994. "Site Visit Report on Oregon Benchmarks." (June 2). Durham, NC. Unpublished.

Blackfeet Tribal Business Council. 1993. "Blackfeet Tribe Head Start Program." Semifinalist Application to Innovations in State and Local Government Awards Program. [Dorothy M. Still Smoking, Director, Blackfeet Tribe Head Start Program, P.O. Box 537, West Boundary Street, Browning, MT 59417; (406) 338-7370, fax: (406) 338-7030.]

Boston City Hospital. 1994. "Child Witness to Violence Project." Semifinalist Application to Innovations in State and Local Government Awards Program. [Betsy McAlister Groves, Director, Child Witness to Violence Project, Division of Development and Behavioral Pediatrics, Boston Medical Center, Mat 5, 1 Boston Medical Center Place, Boston, MA 02118; (617) 534-7915.]

Build Up Greater Cleveland. 1994. "Task Force on Fast Tracking Road and Bridge Projects." Semifinalist Application to Innovations in State and Local Government Awards Program. [Dr. Jack A. Licate, Director, Build Up Greater Cleveland, 200 Tower City Center, Cleveland, OH 44113-2291; (216) 621-7220, fax: (216) 621-6013.]

California Air Resources Board. 1994. "Compliance Assistance Program." Semifinalist Application to Innovations in State and Local Government Awards Program. [Bruce Oulrey, Outreach Liaison, California Air Resources Board, Exec. Office, California Environmental Protection Agency, 2020 L Street, Sacramento, CA 95814; (916) 445-3187, fax: (916) 323-0764.]

California Department of Fish and Game. 1994. "Coles Levee Ecosystem Preserve." Semifinalist Application to Innovations in State and Local Government Awards Program. [Ronald D. Rempel, Program Supervisor, Habitat Conservation Planning, California Department of Fish and Game, 1416 9th Street, Room 1341, Sacramento, CA 95814; (916) 654-9980, fax: (916) 653-2588.]

California Health and Welfare Agency Data Center. 1993. "Info/California." Semifinalist Application to Innovations in State and Local Government Awards Program. [Russell Bohart, Director, Health and Welfare Agency Data Center, 1651 Alhambra Boulevard, Sacramento, CA 95816; (916) 739-7700, fax: (916) 451-0780.]

California Youth Authority. 1994. "Young Men As Fathers." Semifinalist Application to Innovations in State and Local Government Awards Program. [Sharon J. English, Assistant Director, California Youth Authority/Executive Office, 4241 Williamsborough Drive, Suite 214, Sacramento, CA 95823; (916) 262-1392, fax: (916) 262-1446.]

Champion, Hale. 1994. "Site Visit Report on New York City Child Health Clinics." (June 2). Cambridge, MA. Unpublished.

Chi, Keon. 1993. "Site Visit Report on Glasgow Electric Plant Board's Fully Interactive Communications and Control System." (June 1). Lexington, KY. Unpublished.

City of Aurora, Colorado, Police Department. 1993. "The Aurora Gang Task Force: A Total Community Approach to Gangs." Semifinalist Application to Innovations in State and Local Government Awards Program. [J. Michael Stiers, Division Chief, Investigative Division, Aurora Police Department, 15001 East Alameda Drive, Aurora, CO 80012; (303) 341-8598, fax: (303) 341-8656.]

City of Baltimore, Maryland, Health Department. 1993. "The Baltimore Project." Semifinalist Application to Innovations in State and Local Government Awards Program. [Barbara Squires, Director of Healthy Start Policy, Baltimore City Health Department, 303 East Fayette Street, 2nd Floor, Baltimore, MD 21202-3418; (410) 347-7602.]

City of Boston, Massachusetts, Dorchester Youth Collaborative. 1994. "Common Ground." Semifinalist Application to Innovations in State and Local Government Awards Program. [Emmett Folgert, Program Director, Dorchester Youth Collaborative, 1514A Dorchester Avenue, Dorchester, MA 02122; (617) 288-1748, fax: (617) 288-2136.]

City of Boulder, Colorado, Public Works and Transportation. 1993. "Go Boulder." Semifinalist Application to Innovations in State and Local Government Awards Program. [Tracy Winfree, Transit Planner, GO Boulder, 2018 Eleventh Street, Boulder, CO 80302; (303) 441-4260, fax: (303) 443-8196.]

City of Burlington, Vermont, Solid Waste Division. 1993. "Burlington, Vermont Commercial Recycling Program." Semifinalist Application to Innovations in State and Local Government Awards Program. [Thomas E. Moreau, Division Head, Solid Waste Division, Burlington Public Works Department, 33 Kilburn Street, Burlington, VT 05401; (802) 862-6404, fax: (802) 864-7653.]

City of Chicago, Illinois. 1991. "Parking Enforcement Program." Semifinalist Application to Innovations in State and Local Government Awards Program. [John Holden, Public Information Officer, Department of Revenue, City of Chicago, 11 North LaSalle Street, Chicago, IL 60602; (312) 744-2604.]

City of Columbia, South Carolina, Community Development Department. 1993. "Police Homeowner Loan Program." Semifinalist Application to Innovations in State and Local Government Awards Program. [Richard J. Semon, Director, Community Development Department, 1225 Laurel Street, Columbia, SC 29201, (803) 733-8315, fax: (803) 733-8212.]

City of Glasgow, Kentucky. 1994. "Broadband Information Highway." Semifinalist Application to Innovations in State and Local Government Awards Program. [William J. Ray, Superintendent, Glasgow Electric Plant Board, 100 Mallory Drive, Glasgow, KY 42141; (502) 651-8341, fax: (502) 651-1638.]

City of Hampton, Virginia, Department of Human Resources. 1990. "Retooling the Public Organization: A Working Prototype." Semifinalist Application to Innovations in State and Local Government Awards Program. [Tharon Greene, Director of Human Resources, Department of Human Resources, City of Hampton, 22 Lincoln Street, Hampton, VA 23669; (804) 727-5407.]

City of Indianapolis, Indiana, Department of Administration. 1995. "Competition and Costing." Semifinalist Application to Innovations in American Government Awards Program. [David A. Lips, Special Assistant, Department of Administration, Mayor's Office, 200 East Washington Street, Suite 2501, Indianapolis, IN 46204; (317) 327-3744, fax: (317) 327-3980.]

City of Lansing, Michigan, Housing Commission. 1993. "Computer Learning Centers." Semifinalist Application to Innovations in State and Local Government Awards Program. [Christopher Stuchell, Executive Director, Lansing Housing Commission, 310 Seymour Avenue, Lansing, MI 48933; (517) 487-6550, fax: (517) 487-6977.]

City of Little Rock, Arkansas, Office of the City Manager. 1992. "City of Little Rock Fight Back! Insure the Children." Semifinalist Application to Innovations in State and Local Government Awards Program. [Wendy Salaam, Executive Director, Fighting Back Department, Office of the City Manager, City Hall, Room 120W, 500 West Markham Street, Little Rock, AR 72201-1499; (501) 399-3420, fax: (501) 399-3425.]

City of Littleton, Colorado, Business/Industry Affairs Department. 1992. "Littleton, Colorado's New Economy Project." Semifinalist Application to Innovations in State and Local Government Awards Program. [Christian Gibbons, Director, Business/Industry Affairs Department, 2255 West Berry Avenue, Littleton, CO 80165; (303) 795-3760.]

City of Los Angeles, California, Department of Transportation. 1992. "Automated Traffic Surveillance and Control." Semifinalist Application to Innovations in State and Local Government Awards Program. [Robert R. Yates, General Manager, Los Angeles Department of Transportation, City Hall, Room 1200, 200 North Spring Street, Los Angeles, CA 90012; (213) 485-2278, fax: (213) 237-0960.]

City of Los Angeles, California, Municipal Court. 1992. "Central Courts Video Arraignment Project." Semifinalist Application to Innovations in State and

Local Government Awards Program. [Edward M. Kritzman, Court Administrator, Los Angeles Municipal Court, 110 North Grand Avenue, Room 428G, Los Angeles, CA 90012; (213) 974-6171.]

City of Louisville, Kentucky, Department of Community Services. 1993. "Operation Brightside." Semifinalist Application to Innovations in State and Local Government Awards Program. [Michael T. Stegeman, Director, Operation Brightside, Louisville Department of Community Services, 200 South Seventh Street, Suite 200, Louisville, KY 40202; (502) 574-2613, fax: (502) 574-4227.]

City of Lynn, Massachusetts, Northshore Employment Training. 1993. "NETstops—Community Business Ventures." Semifinalist Application to Innovations in State and Local Government Awards Program. [Harry MacCabe, Executive Director, Northshore Employment Training (NET), 20 Wheeler Street, 4th Floor, Lynn, MA 01902; (617) 595-0484, fax: (617) 599-8550.]

City of Madison, Wisconsin, Police Department. 1991. "Madison Wisconsin Experimental Police District." Semifinalist Application to Innovations in State and Local Government Awards Program. [Michael F. Masterson, Captain of Police, Madison, Wisconsin, Experimental Police District, 211 Carroll Street, Madison, WI 53703; (608) 266-4664.]

City of Manchester, New Hampshire, Housing Code Department. 1992. "Housing Code Certificate of Compliance." Semifinalist Application to Innovations in State and Local Government Awards Program. [Anthony F Simons, Director, Manchester Housing Code Department, 50 Bridge Street, Room 270, Manchester, NH 03101-1621; (603) 624-6453.]

City of Minneapolis, Minnesota, Public Works Department. 1994. "Cookbook/GIS." Semifinalist Application to Innovations in State and Local Government Awards Program. [Brad Henry, Engineer III, Minneapolis Public Works Department, 309 Second Avenue South, Room 300, Minneapolis, MN 55401; (612) 673-3620, fax: (612) 673-2948.]

City of Nashua, New Hampshire, Housing Authority. 1993. "Adult Day Service Program." Semifinalist Application to Innovations in State and Local Government Awards Program. [Jadine M. Stockley, Director of Resident Services, Nashua Housing Authority, 101 Major Drive, Nashua, NH 03060-4783; (603) 883-5661, fax: (603) 598-3750.]

City of Oakland, California, Police Department. 1994. "Beat Health Unit (Drug Nuisance Abatement Project)." Semifinalist Application to Innovations in State and Local Government Awards Program. [Diane Dickstein, Program Coordinator, Beat Health Unit, Oakland Police Department, 455 Seventh Street, Oakland, CA 94607; (510) 238-6368, fax: (510) 238-2297.]

City of Philadelphia, Pennsylvania, Anti-Drug Anti-Violence Network. 1994. Semifinalist Application to Innovations in State and Local Government Awards Program. [James J. Mills, Executive Director, Philadelphia Anti-Drug/Anti-Violence Network, 121 North Broad Street, 6th Floor, Philadelphia, PA 19107; (215) 686-2121, fax: (215) 977-2856.]

City of Phoenix, Arizona, Public Transit Department. 1994. "The Bus Card Plus Program." Semifinalist Application to Innovations in State and Local

Government Awards Program. [Neal Manske, Deputy Public Transit Director, Phoenix Public Transit Department, 302 North First Avenue, Suite 700, Phoenix, AZ 85003; (602) 262-7242, fax: (602) 495-2002.]

City of Pittsburg, California, Public Services Department. 1993."Shared Savings Program." Semifinalist Application to Innovations in State and Local Government Awards Program. [Robert Soderbery, Director, Pittsburg Public Services Department, 357 East 12th Street, P.O. Box 1518, Pittsburg, CA 94565; (510) 439-3600 and 439-4850, fax: (510) 439-0469.]

City of Portland, Oregon, Police Bureau. 1992. "Landlord Training Program." Semifinalist Application to Innovations in State and Local Government Awards Program. [Gregory Clark, Commander, Community Policing Support Division, Portland Police Bureau, 1111 Southwest Second Avenue, Room 1552, Portland, OR 97204; (503) 796-3126.]

City of Quincy, Massachusetts, District Court. 1992. "Quincy Model Domestic Abuse Program." Semifinalist Application to Innovations in State and Local Government Awards Program. [The Honorable Charles E. Black, Presiding Justice, Quincy District Court, One Dennis F. Ryan Parkway, Quincy, MA 02169; (617) 471-7653.]

City of Reno, Nevada, Police Department. 1992. "Community Policing: An Approach to Traffic Services." Semifinalist Application to Innovations in State and Local Government Awards Program. [Jim Weston, Chief of Police, Reno Police Department, 455 East Second Street, P.O. Box 1900, Reno, NV 89505; (702) 334-2100, fax: (702) 334-2097.]

————. 1993. "Quality Assurance." Semifinalist Application to Innovations in State and Local Government Awards Program. [Ronald W. Glensor, Deputy Chief of Police, Patrol Division, Reno Police Department, 455 East Second Street, Reno, NV 89503; (702) 334-3860, fax: (702) 334-2157.]

City of San Carlos, California, City Manager's Office. 1994. "Cost Avoidance Reserve." Semifinalist Application to Innovations in State and Local Government Awards Program. [Brian Moura, Assistant City Manager/Finance Director, Finance Department, City Manager's Office, City Hall, 666 Elm Street, San Carlos, CA 94070-3085; (415) 802-4210, fax: (415) 595-2044.]

City of San Diego Police Department. 1992. "City of San Diego Police Department Refugee Program." Semifinalist Application to Innovations in State and Local Government Award Program. [Donna J. Warlick, Grants Analyst, San Diego Police Department, 1401 Broadway, MS 796, San Diego, CA 92101; (619) 531-2221.]

City of San Francisco, California, Office of the City Attorney. 1993. "Code Enforcement Task Force and Receivership Program." Semifinalist Application to Innovations in State and Local Government Awards Program. [Ilene Dick, Deputy City Attorney, Fox Plaza, Suite 250, 1390 Market Street, San Francisco, CA 94102; (415) 554-3920, fax: (415) 554-4318.]

City of San Francisco, California, Department of Health. 1993. "Children and Mothers Parenting Program (CHAMP)." Semifinalist Application to Innovations in State and Local Government Awards Program. [Barbara Giles-Wallen, Director of Nursing, Health/Community Public Health Services,

San Francisco Department of Public Health, 101 Grove Street, Room 204, San Francisco, CA 94102; (415) 554-2755, fax: (415) 554-2746.]

City of Santa Monica, California. 1993. "Public Electronic Network (PEN)." Semifinalist Application to Innovations in State and Local Government Awards Program. [Jory Wolf, Manager of Information Systems, Information Systems Department, 1685 Main Street, Santa Monica, CA 90401; (310) 458-8381, fax: (310) 395-2343.]

City of Savannah, Georgia Bureau of Public Development. 1992. "Showcase Savannah Program." Semifinalist Application to Innovations in State and Local Government Awards Program. [Henry J. Moore, Assistant City Manager, Bureau of Public Development, City of Savannah, P.O. Box 1027, Savannah, GA 31402; (912) 651-6520, fax: (912) 651-6543.]

———. 1994. "Grants for Blocks." Semifinalist Application to Innovations in State and Local Government Awards Program. [Henry J. Moore, Assistant City Manager, Bureau of Public Management, City of Savannah, P.O. Box 1027, Savannah, GA 31402; (912) 651-6520, fax: (912) 651-6543.]

City of Seattle, Washington, Engineering Department. 1990. "City of Seattle Recycling Program." Semifinalist Application to Innovations in State and Local Government Awards Program. [Nancy Glaser, Director, Seattle Recycling Program, Engineering Department/Solid Waste Utility, 505 Dexter Horton Building, 710 Second Avenue, Seattle, WA 98104; (206) 684-8086.]

City of Seattle, Washington, Planning Department. 1994. "Master Home Environmentalist Program." Semifinalist Application to Innovations in State and Local Government Awards Program. [Richard Conlin, Master Home Environmentalists, Metrocenter YMCA, 909 Fourth Avenue, Seattle, WA 98104; (206) 382-5013.]

City of Seattle, Washington, Public Schools. 1993. "Families and Education Levy Interlocal Agreement." Semifinalist Application to Innovations in State and Local Government Awards Program. [Jay D. Iman, Grants Manager, Office of External Funding, Seattle Public Schools Division of External Relations, 815 Fourth Avenue North, Seattle, WA 98109; (206) 298-7220, fax: (206) 298-7201.]

City of Scottsdale, Arizona, Planning and Community Development Department. 1993. "City of Scottsdale's Friendly Enforcement Program." Semifinalist Application to Innovations in State and Local Government Awards Program. [Jeff Fisher, Code Enforcement Manager, Development Services, Planning and Community Development Department, One Civic Center, 7447 East Indian School Road, Scottsdale, AZ 85251; (602) 994-2546, fax: (602) 994-7781.]

City of St. Louis Park, Minnesota, Department of Administration. 1992. "Integrating Bar Code Technology with Curbside Recycling." Semifinalist Application to Innovations in State and Local Government Awards Program. [Clint Pires, MIS Coordinator, St. Louis Park City Hall, 5005 Minnetonka Boulevard, St. Louis Park, MN 55416-2290; (612) 924-2517.]

City of St. Petersburg, Florida, Police Department. 1994. "Technology Enhanced Community Problem-Solving Policing Model." Semifinalist Application to

Innovations in State and Local Government Awards Program. [Donald S. Quire, Major, Vice and Narcotics Section, St. Petersburg Police Department, 1300 First Avenue North, St. Petersburg, FL 33705; (813) 824-5940, fax: (813) 824-5918.]

City of Syracuse, New York, Community Development Department. 1993. "Time of Jubilee." Semifinalist Application to Innovations in State and Local Government Awards Program. [The Honorable Vito Sciscioli, Commissioner, Department of Community Development, City Hall Commons, 201 Washington Street, Syracuse, NY 13202; (315) 448-8700, fax: (315) 448-8705.]

City of Tacoma, Washington, Executive Branch. 1992. "Safe Streets Campaign." Semifinalist Application to Innovations in State and Local Government Awards Program. [Lyle Quasim, Executive Director, Safe Streets Campaign, 934 Broadway, Tacoma, WA 98402; (206) 272-6824, fax: (206) 272-9586.]

City of Tulsa, Oklahoma, Police Department. 1994. "Sexual Assault Nurse Examiners Program (SANE)." Semifinalist Application to Innovations in State and Local Government Awards Program. [Kathy Bell, Coordinator, Sexual Assault Nurse Examiners (SANE) Program, Tulsa Police Department, 600 Civic Center, Tulsa, OK 74103; (918) 596-7608, fax: (918) 596-9210.]

City of Wichita, Kansas. 1992. "Environmental Cleanup Project." Semifinalist Application to Innovations in State and Local Government Awards Program. [Chris Cherches, City Manager, Office of the City Manager, City Hall, 13th Floor, 455 North Main Street, Wichita, KS 67202; (316) 268-4351, fax: (316) 268-4519.]

Connecticut Association for Human Services. 1993. "Hospital-Based Initiative to Reduce Infant Mortality and Morbidity." Semifinalist Application to Innovations in State and Local Government Awards Program. [Robyn Hoffman, R.N., C.S., M.S.N., Director, Family Health Division, Connecticut Association for Human Services, 880 Asylum Avenue, Hartford, CT 06105; (203) 522-7762, fax: (203) 520-4234.]

Cook County Department of Corrections. 1993. "Cermak Health Education and HIV Related Services." Semifinalist Application to Innovations in State and Local Government Awards Program. [Delia Johnson, Director, Health Education and HIV-Related Services, Cermak Health Services, 2800 South California, Chicago, IL 60608; (312) 890-6293, fax: (312) 890-7177.]

Cuyahoga County, Ohio Prosecutor's Office. 1993. "Government Action on Urban Land." Semifinalist Application to Innovations in State and Local Government Awards Program. [Michael M. Sweeney Jr., Supervisor, Delinquent Tax Department, Cuyahoga County, County Administration Building, 1219 Ontario Street, Cleveland, OH 44113; (216) 443-5872.]

Dunn, Nancy. 1991. "Site Visit Report on Shared Savings Program." (June 6). Long Beach, CA. Unpublished.

Eastern Washington Area Agency on Aging. 1992. "Elderly Services." Semifinalist Application to Innovations in State and Local Government Awards Program. [Nick Beamer, Director, Eastern Washington Area Agency on Aging, West 1101 College Avenue, Room 365, Spokane, WA 99201-2096; (509) 458-2509, fax: (509) 324-1507 and Raymond Raschko M.S.W., Director, Elder Services, West 1101 College Avenue, Room 365, Spokane, WA 99201-2096.]

Ellwood, John. 1992. "Site Visit Report on Workers' Compensation Program, Washington State." (June 5). Berkeley, CA. Unpublished.

———. 1993. "Site Visit Report on Info/California Pilot." (May 28). Berkeley, CA. Unpublished.

Families and Schools Together. 1994. Semifinalist Application to Innovations in State and Local Government Awards Program. [Dr. Lynn McDonald, Program Originator, Families and Schools Together, Family Service, 128 East Olin Avenue, Suite 100, Madison, WI 53713; (608) 251-7611, fax: (608) 251-4665.]

Feldman, Penny. 1993. "Site Visit Report on the Baltimore Project." (June 1). Boston, MA. Unpublished.

Florida Department of Environmental Protection. 1994. "Florida Marine Spill Analysis System." Semifinalist Application to Innovations in State and Local Government Awards Program. [Christopher A. Friel, Research Administrator II, Division of Marine Resources, Florida Marine Research Institute, Florida Department of Environmental Protection, 100 Eighth Avenue Southeast, St. Petersburg, FL 33701-5095; (813) 896-8626, fax: (813) 823-0166.]

Georgia Governor's Office of Energy Resources. 1991. "The No-Tillage Assistance Program." Semifinalist Application to Innovations in State and Local Government Awards Program. [Paul Burks, Head, Energy Resources Division, Georgia Planning and Budget Office, 254 Washington Street Southwest, Suite 614, Atlanta, GA 30334; (404) 656-5176, fax: (414) 656-7970.]

———. 1993. "Dry Hydrant Assistance Program." Semifinalist Application to Innovations in State and Local Government Awards Program. [Paul R. Burks, Executive Director, Georgia Environmental Facilities Authority, 100 Peachtree Street Northwest, Suite 2090, Atlanta, GA 30303-1901; (404) 656-5176, fax: (404) 656-6416.]

Gould, Bruce. 1993. "Site Visit Report to Code Enforcement Task Force and Receivership Program." (June 1). Unpublished.

Grinker, William. 1993. "Site Visit Report on Consolidated Chemical Dependency Treatment Fund." (May 31). New York, NY. Unpublished.

———. 1994. "Site Visit Report on Miracle Village." (June 2). New York, NY. Unpublished.

Guttensohn, James. 1992. "Site Visit Report on City of Wichita Environmental Cleanup Project." (June 1). Boston, MA. Unpublished.

Harrison, David. 1993. "Site Visit Report on Community Voice Mail for Phoneless/Homeless Persons." (June 4). Seattle, WA. Unpublished.

Hawaii Public Television. 1991. "Hawaii Interactive Television System." Semifinalist Application to Innovations in State and Local Government Awards Program. [C.J. Baehr, Director, Distance Learning Services, Hawaii Public Television, 2530 Dole Street, Honolulu, HI 96822; (808) 955-7878.]

Hennepin County, Minnesota, Department of Environmental Management. 1992. "Hennepin County Household Battery Management Program." Semifinalist Application to Innovations in State and Local Government Awards Program. [Linda Gondringer, Program Analyst, Hennepin County Department of Environmental Management, C-2200 Hennepin County Government Center, 417 North Fifth Street, Minneapolis, MN 55401-1309; (612) 348-4788.]

Husock, Howard. 1992b. "Site Visit Report on Showcase Savannah." (June 2). Cambridge, MA. Unpublished.

———. 1994. "Site Visit Report on Self-Help Support System." (May 20). Cambridge, MA. Unpublished.

Illinois Criminal Justice Authority. 1991. "Area-Wide Law Enforcement Radio Terminal System (ALERTS)." Semifinalist Application to Innovations in State and Local Government Awards Program. [Terrance Gough, Illinois Criminal Justice Information Authority, 120 South Riverside Plaza, Suite 1016, Chicago, IL 60606; (312) 793-8550.]

Indiana Department of Corrections. 1994. "Community Corrections Grants Program." Semifinalist Application to Innovations in State and Local Government Awards Program. [Robert Ohlemiller Jr., Deputy Commissioner, Division of Community Services, Indiana Department of Correction, E-334 Indiana Government Center South, 302 West Washington Street, Indianapolis, IN 46204; (317) 232-5763, fax: (317) 232-5728.]

Iowa Department of Natural Resources. 1993. "Iowa's Agricultural-Energy-Environment Initiative." Semifinalist Application to Innovations in State and Local Government Awards Program. [Larry J. Wilson, Director, Iowa Department of Natural Resources, Wallace State Office Building, East 9th and Grand, Des Moines, IA 50319-0034; (515) 281-5385, fax: (515) 281-6794.]

Judson Center. 1993. "Living in Family Environments." Semifinalist Application to Innovations in State and Local Government Awards Program. [Mounir W. Sharobeem, President and Chief Executive Officer, Administration, Judson Center, 4410 West Thirteen Mile Road, Royal Oak, MI 48073; (810) 549-4339, fax: (810) 549-8955.]

Kentucky Department of Financial Institutions. 1994. "Financial Institutions Expert Examination System (FIXX)." Semifinalist Application to Innovations in State and Local Government Awards Program. [Don Brothers, Department of Financial Institutions, Kentucky Public Protection and Regulation Cabinet, 477 Versailles Road, Frankfort, KY 40601; (502) 573-3390, fax: (502) 573-8787.]

Kentucky Educational Television. 1991. "KET Star Channels." Semifinalist Application to Innovations in State and Local Government Awards Program. [Virginia Gaines Fox, Executive Director and Chief Executive Officer, Kentucky Educational Television, 600 Cooper Drive, Lexington, KY 40502-2296; (606) 258-7100, fax: (606) 258-7399.]

Leopold Center for Sustainable Agriculture. 1993. Semifinalist Application to Innovations in State and Local Government Awards Program. [E. Anne Larson, Communications Specialist, Leopold Center for Sustainable Agriculture, 126 Soil Tilth Laboratory, Iowa State University, Ames, IA 50011-3120; (515) 294-3711, fax: (515) 294-9696.]

Levin, Martin. 1992. "Site Visit Report on Hospital Intervention Services." (June 12). Waltham, MA. Unpublished.

Locke, Hubert. 1993. "Site Visit Report on Safe Streets Now!" (June 3). Seattle, WA. Unpublished.

Los Angeles County, California. 1993. "Telecommuting Program." Semifinalist Application to Innovations in State and Local Government Awards Program. [Evelyn Gutierrez, Chief, Office of Special Programs, Chief Administrative Offices, Los Angeles County, 500 West Temple Street, Room 588, Los Angeles, CA 90012; (213) 974-2616, fax: (213) 680-2450.]

Los Angeles County, California Department of Children's Services. 1994. "Black Family Investment Project." Semifinalist Application to Innovations in State and Local Government Awards Program. [Saundra Turner-Settle, Director, Black Family Investment Project, Bureau of Specialized Programs, Department of Children's Services, 2444 South Alameda Street, Room 111, Los Angeles, CA 90058; (213) 846-2144, fax: (213) 846-2134.]

Los Angeles County, California District Attorney. 1994. "Abolish Chronic Truancy." Semifinalist Application to Innovations in State and Local Government Awards Program. [Mia A. Baker, Special Assistant District Attorney, District Attorney Bureau of Management and Budget, 320 West Temple Street, Suite 540, Los Angeles, CA 90012; (213) 974-3521, fax: (213) 626-6922.]

Los Angeles Unified School District. 1992. "Humanitas." Semifinalist Application to Innovations in State and Local Government Awards Program. [Barbara Golding, Co-Director, Humanitas, Senior High Schools Division, Los Angeles Unified School District, 644 West 17th Street, Los Angeles, CA 90015; (213) 622-5237, fax: (213) 629-5288.]

Lovrich, Nicholas. 1992. "Site Visit Report on Wyoming Department of Health WIC Program and Maternal Child Health Service." (May 30). Pullman, WA. Unpublished.

Loxahatchee River, Florida, Environmental Control District. 1990. "I.Q. Water: The Smart Way to Conserve a Limited Resource." Semifinalist Application to Innovations in State and Local Government Awards Program. [Richard C. Dent, Executive Director, Loxahatchee River Environmental Control District, 2500 Jupiter Park Drive, Jupiter, FL 33458-8964; (407) 747-5700.]

Maine Department of Risk Management. 1991. "VDT Safety in the Workplace." Semifinalist Application to Innovations in State and Local Government Awards Program. [David Fitts, Director, Risk Management Division, General Services Bureau, Maine Administrative and Financial Services Department, Maine State House, Station 78, Augusta, ME 04333, (207) 289-2341.]

Maricopa County, Arizona, Flood Control District. 1994. "Notice of Flood Hazard Determination." Semifinalist Application to Innovations in State and Local Government Awards Program. [Jim Phipps, Public information Coordinator, Flood Control District of Maricopa County, 2801 West Durango Street, Phoenix, AZ 85009; (602) 506-1501, fax: (602) 506-4601.]

Marion County, Oregon, Department of General Services. 1994. "A Model for Controlling Wage and Benefit Costs." Semifinalist Application to Innovations in State and Local Government Awards Program. [Randy Curtis, Director, Department of General Services, Senator Building, 220 High Street Northeast, Salem, OR 97301; (503) 588-5455, fax: (503) 588-5495.]

Maryland Department of Housing and Community Development. 1994. "Partnership Rental Housing Programs." Semifinalist Application to Innovations in

State and Local Government Awards Program. [Nancy S. Rase, Director, Housing Development Programs, Department of Housing and Community Development, 100 Community Place, Crownsvillle, MD 21032; (410) 514-7446, fax: (410) 987-4097.]

Maryland Department of Human Resources. 1994. "CARE/Project HOME/AIDS Program." Semifinalist Application to Innovations in State and Local Government Awards Program. [Linda Ellard, Director, Community Services Administration, Maryland Department of Human Resources, 311 West Saratoga Street, 2nd Floor, Baltimore, MD 21201-3521; (410) 767-7350, fax: (410) 333-0392.]

Massachusetts Attorney General's Office. 1994. "Student Conflict Resolution Experts (SCORE)." Semifinalist Application to Innovations in State and Local Government Awards Program. [Kathleen Grant, Coordinator of Mediation Services, Consumer Protection/Antitrust Division, Massachusetts Attorney General's Office, One Ashburton Place, Boston, MA 02108; (617) 727-2200, fax: (617) 727-5765.]

Massachusetts Department of Environmental Protection. 1991. "The Blackstone Project." Semifinalist Application to Innovations in State and Local Government Awards Program. [The Honorable Trudy Coxe, Commissioner, Department of Environmental Protection, Environmental Affairs Executive Office, Commonwealth of Massachusetts, 100 Cambridge Street, Room 2000, Boston, MA 02202; (617) 727-9800, fax: (617) 727-2754.]

Massachusetts Department of Revenue. 1993. "Automated Child Support Enforcement System." Semifinalist Application to Innovations in State and Local Government Awards Program. [Robert Melia, Director of Strategic Planning, Massachusetts Department of Revenue, 100 Cambridge Street, Room 800, Boston, MA 02204; (617) 727-4201, fax: (617) 727-0379.]

Massachusetts Department of Social Services. 1994. "Parenting Partner Program." Semifinalist Application to Innovations in State and Local Government Awards Program. [Rachel Berman, Director, Office of Management Planning and Analysis, Massachusetts Department of Social Services, 24 Farnsworth Street, 5th Floor, Boston, MA 02210; (617) 727-0900 x505, fax: (617) 439-4482.]

Massachusetts Housing Finance Agency. 1994. "Building Community Campaign." Semifinalist Application to Innovations in State and Local Government Awards Program. [Arne Abramson, Development Officer, Massachusetts Housing Finance Agency, One Beacon Street, Boston, MA 02108; (617) 854-1000, fax: (617) 854-1029.]

Metropolitan Community College. 1994. "Omaha Job Clearinghouse." Semifinalist Application to Innovations in State and Local Government Awards Program. [Randy Schmailzl, OJC Project Director, Omaha Job Clearinghouse, Metropolitan Community College, 30th and Fort Sts., Omaha, NE 68111; (402) 449-8418, fax: (402) 449-8334.]

Metropolitan Transportation Authority. 1993. "The Station Manager Program." Semifinalist Application to Innovations in State and Local Government Awards Program. [Carol E. Meltzer, Chief Station Officer, Division of

Stations, New York City Transit Authority, 370 Jay Street, Room 427, Brooklyn, NY 11201; (718) 330-4637, fax: (718) 330-3341.]

Metropolitan Transportation Commission. 1993. "Joint Urban Mobility Project (JUMP Start)." Semifinalist Application to Innovations in State and Local Government Awards Program. [Brenda Kahn, Senior Public Information Officer, Metropolitan Transportation Commission, Joseph P. Bort Metro-Center, 101 Eighth Street, Oakland, CA 94607; (507) 464-7773, fax: (510) 464-6848.]

Michigan Partnership for New Education. 1994. Semifinalist Application to Innovations in State and Local Government Awards Program. [Judith E. Lanier, President, Michigan Partnership for New Education, 201 Erickson Hall, East Lansing, MI 48824; (517) 353-4996, fax: (517) 336-2634.]

Minnesota Department of Human Services. 1993. "Consolidated Chemical Dependency Treatment Fund." Semifinalist Application to Innovations in State and Local Government Awards Program. [Dr. Cynthia Turnure, Director, Chemical Dependency Division, Minnesota Department of Human Services, 444 Lafayette Road, Street Paul, MN 55155-3823; (612) 296-4610, fax: (612) 296-6244.]

Minnesota Pollution Control Agency. 1994."Voluntary Investigation and Cleanup." Semifinalist Application to Innovations in State and Local Government Awards Program. [Kenneth M. Haberman, Supervisor, Site Response Section, Ground Water and Solid Waste Division, Minnesota Pollution Control Agency (MPCA), 520 Lafayette Road North, St. Paul, MN 55155-4194; (612) 296-0892, fax: (612) 296-9707.]

Municipality of Anchorage, Alaska, Sexually Transmitted Disease Clinic. 1994. "Mobile HIV Testing Program." Semifinalist Application to Innovations in State and Local Government Awards Program. [Bonnie Long, Program Manager, STD Program, Department of Health and Human Services/Community Heath, STD Clinic, 825 "L" Street, Room 101, Anchorage, AK 99501; (907) 343-4612, (907) 343-6564.]

New York City Board of Education. 1993. "Central Park East Secondary School." Semifinalist Application to Innovations in State and Local Government Awards Program. [Paul Schwarz, Principal, Central Park East Secondary School, New York City High School Division, 1573 Madison Avenue, New York, NY 10029; (212) 427-6230, fax: (212) 876-3494.]

———. 1994. "Peer Intervention Program." Semifinalist Application to Innovations in State and Local Government Awards Program. [Clare Cohen, Coordinator, Peer Intervention Program, New York City Board of Education, 260 Park Street, South, 6th Floor, New York, NY 10010; (212) 598-9210, fax: (212) 260-3048.]

New York City Bureau of Child Health. 1994. "Child Health Clinics." Semifinalist Application to Innovations in State and Local Government Awards Program. [Dr. Katherine S. Lobach M.D., Assistant Commissioner, Child Health Services, Bureau of Child Health, New York City Department of Health, 125 Worth Street, Box 23, New York, NY 10013; (212) 788-4964, fax: (212) 788-2171.]

New York City Bureau of Motor Equipment. 1992. "In-house Research and Development Network." Semifinalist Application to Innovations in State and Local Government Awards Program. [Maurice Hogan, Director of Administration, New York City Department of Sanitation, 52-35 58th Street, Room 601, Woodside, NY 11377; (718) 334-9292, fax: (718) 334-9303.]

New York City Child Welfare Administration. 1993. "Early Permanency Planning Project." Semifinalist Application to Innovations in State and Local Government Awards Program. [Robert L. Little, Executive Deputy Commissioner, Child Welfare Administration, 80 Lafayette Street, New York, NY 10013; (212) 266-2222, fax: (212) 266-2493.]

New York City Department of Cultural Affairs. 1993. "Materials for the Arts." Semifinalist Application to Innovations in State and Local Government Awards Program. [Susan Glass, Director, Materials for the Arts, New York City Department of Cultural Affairs, 410 West 16th Street, New York, NY 10011; (212) 255-5924, (212) 924-1925.]

New York City Human Resources Administration. 1990. "Electronic Payment File Transfer System." Semifinalist Application to Innovations in State and Local Government Awards Program. [Ruth Reinecke, Director, Grants Office, New York City Human Resources Administration, 250 Church Street, Room 1233, New York, NY 10013; (212) 553-6797.]

―――. 1993. "HRA InfoLine." Semifinalist Application to Innovations in State and Local Government Awards Program. [Carol Viani, Director, Office of External Affairs, New York City Human Resources Administration, 92-31 Union Hall Street, Jamaica, NY 11433; (718) 262-3159, fax: (718) 262-3100.]

New York State Commission on Quality of Care for the Mentally Disabled. 1993. "Surrogate Decision-Making Committee Program." Semifinalist Application to Innovations in State and Local Government Awards Program. [Clarence Sundram, Chairman, New York State Commission on Quality of Care for the Mentally Disabled, 99 Washington Avenue, Suite 1002, Albany, NY 12210-2895; (518) 473-4057, fax: (518) 473-6296.]

New York State Department of State. 1994. "Self-Help Support System." Semifinalist Application to Innovations in State and Local Government Awards Program. [David Pilliod, Director, Office of Local Government Services, New York State Department of State, 162 Washington Avenue, Albany, NY 12231; (518) 473-3355, fax: (518) 474-6572.]

New York State Department of Social Services. 1992. "The Child Assistance Program." Semifinalist Application to Innovations in State and Local Government Awards Program. [Michael Warner, Team Leader, Region 3, Division of Temporary Assistance, New York State Department of Social Services, 40 North Pearl Street, 7th Floor, Albany, NY 12243; (518) 473-0691, fax: (518) 474-9347.]

―――. 1994. "Partnership for Long Term Care." Semifinalist Application to Innovations in State and Local Government Awards Program. [Gail Holubinka, Director, Health and Long Term Care Division, New York State Department of Social Services, 40 North Pearl Street, Albany, NY 12243-0001; (518) 473-7705, fax: (518) 473-4232.]

New York State Medical Care Facilities Finance Agency. 1993. "AIDS Facilities Financing Program." Semifinalist Application to Innovations in State and Local Government Awards Program. [Matthew P. Scanlon, Deputy Director, Health and State Programs, Medical Care Facilities Finance Agency, 3 Park Avenue, 33rd Floor, New York, NY 10016; (212) 686-9700, fax: (212) 696-5817.]

New York State Office of Alcoholism and Substance Abuse Services. 1994. "Health Care Intervention Services." Semifinalist Application to Innovations in State and Local Government Awards Program. [James Heckler, Coordinator, Health Care Intervention Services, New York State Office of Alcohol and Substance Abuse Services, 1450 Western Avenue, Albany, NY, 12203; (518) 485-2131, fax: (518) 485-2142.]

North Dakota Consensus Council. 1994. Semifinalist Application to Innovations in State and Local Government Awards Program. [Larry Spears, Executive Director, North Dakota Consensus Council, 1003 Interstate Avenue, Suite 7, Bismarck, ND 58501-0500; (701) 224-0588, fax: (701) 224-0787.]

O'Hare, Michael. 1991. "Site Visit Report on Massachusetts/Harwich Solar Aquatic Treatment." (June 11). Berkeley, CA. Unpublished.

————. 1992. "Site Visit Report on Humanitas." (June 7). Berkeley, CA. Unpublished.

Ohio Department of Alcohol and Drug Addiction Services. 1994. "Miracle Village." Semifinalist Application to Innovations in State and Local Government Awards Program. [Michael J. Stringer, Chief, Special Programming, Ohio Department of Alcohol and Drug Addiction Services, 280 North High Street, Columbus, OH 43215-2537; (614) 466-3445, fax: (614) 752-8645.]

Oklahoma Turnpike Authority. 1992. "PIKEPASS." Semifinalist Application to Innovations in State and Local Government Awards Program. [Richard L. Ridings, Chief Executive Officer, Oklahoma Turnpike Authority, P.O. Box, 11357, 3500 Martin Luther King Avenue, Oklahoma City, OK 73116; (405) 425-3634, fax: (405) 427-8246.]

Onondaga County, New York Sheriff's Department. 1993. "S.H.A.P.E. (Sheriff's Handicapped/Ambulatory Parking Enforcement Program.) Semifinalist Application to Innovations in State and Local Government Awards Program. [David Marcy, Lieutenant, Research and Development, Onondaga County Sheriff's Department, Headquarters Building, P.O. Box 5020, 407 South State Street, Syracuse, NY 13250; (315) 453-3056, fax: (315) 453-3943.]

Orange County, California, District Attorney. 1993. "Child Abuse Service Team (CAST)." Semifinalist Application to Innovations in State and Local Government Awards Program. [Michael R. Capizzi, District Attorney, District Attorney's Office, Orange County, P.O. Box 808, Santa Ana, CA 92702; (714) 834-3636, fax: (714) 834-4366.]

Oregon Department of Administrative Services. 1993. "Vendor Information Program." Semifinalist Application to Innovations in State and Local Government Awards Program. [Marscy Stone, Manager, Outreach Unit, Purchasing Section, Oregon Department of Administrative Services, DAS-TPPS-Outreach, 1225 Ferry Street Southeast, Salem, OR 97310; (503) 378-4651, fax: (503) 373-1626.]

Oregon Progress Board. 1994. "Oregon Benchmarks." Semifinalist Application to Innovations in State and Local Government Awards Program. [Duncan Wyse, President, Oregon Business Council, 1100 Southwest Sixth Avenue, Suite 1608, Portland, OR 97204; (503) 220-0691, fax: (503) 228-9767.]

Pennsylvania Department of Administration and Public Affairs. 1991. "Governor's Recycled Material Market Development Task Force." Semifinalist Application to Innovations in State and Local Government Awards Program. [Brian T. Castelli, Executive Director, Energy Office, Commonwealth of Pennsylvania, 116 Pine Street, Harrisburg, PA 17101-1227; (717) 783-9981.]

Pennsylvania Department of Labor and Industry. 1992. "Pennsylvania Job Centers." Semifinalist Application to Innovations in State and Local Government Awards Program. [William J. Lalley, Director, Office of Job Center Field Operations, Pennsylvania Department of Labor and Industry, 7th and Forster Streets, Room 419, Harrisburg, PA 17121; (717) 787-9874.]

Ramsey County, Minnesota, Community Human Services. 1990. "Electronic Benefit System." Semifinalist Application to Innovations in State and Local Government Awards Program. [Margaret Philben, EBS Project Manager, Community Human Services Department, Ramsey County, 160 East Kellog Boulevard, St. Paul, MN 55101-1494; (612) 298-5149.]

Regional Alliance for Small Contractors. 1994. Semifinalist Application to Innovations in State and Local Government Awards Program. [Mark L. Quinn, Executive Director, The Regional Alliance for Small Contractors, One World Trade Center, 44S, New York, NY 10048; (212) 435-6533 and 435-6506, fax: (212) 435-6187.]

Rindge School of Technical Arts. 1992. "CityWorks." Semifinalist Application to Innovations in State and Local Government Awards Program. [Lawrence Rosenstock, Executive Director, Rindge School of Technical Arts, 459 Broadway, Cambridge, MA 02138; (617) 349-6630 and 347-6753, fax: (617) 349-6770.]

Safe Streets Now! 1993. Semifinalist Application to Innovations in State and Local Government Awards Program. [Michael Bridges, Deputy City Manager, City Manager's Office, 475 14th Street, 9th Floor, Oakland, CA 94612; (510) 238-3390, fax: (510) 238-2223.]

Santa Ana Tribe Agricultural Enterprises. 1992. "Revival of Traditional Tribal Economy." Semifinalist Application to Innovations in State and Local Government Awards Program. [Jerry Kinsman, Program Manager, Agricultural Enterprises, 2 Dove Road, Bernalillo, NM 87004; (505) 867-3301, fax: (505) 867-3395.]

Santa Barbara County, California, Department of Social Services. 1993. "Business Advisory Team." Semifinalist Application to Innovations in State and Local Government Awards Program. [Charlene Chase, Director, Santa Barbara County Department of Social Services, 234 Camino Del Remedio, Santa Barbara, CA 93110-1369; (805) 681-4451, fax: (805) 681-4402.]

Seattle Workers' Center. 1993. "Community Voice Mail for Phoneless/Homeless Persons." Semifinalist Application to Innovations in State and Local Government Awards Program. [Patricia Barry, Project Director, Community Voice

Mail Project, Community Technology Institute, P.O. Box 61385, Seattle, WA 98121; (201) 441-7872 x150.]

Seminole County, Florida Circuit Court. 1992. "Automated Open Court Minutes Processing." Semifinalist Application to Innovations in State and Local Government Awards Program. [Maryanne Morse, Clerk of Circuit Court, Seminole County Circuit Court, 301 North Park Avenue, Sanford, FL 32771; (407) 323-4330.]

Southern Seven Health Department. 1993. "Non-Emergency Medical Transportation." Semifinalist Application to Innovations in State and Local Government Awards Program. [Sharon E. Mumford, R.N., M.S.N., Associate Administrator, Administrative Office, Southern Seven Health Department, R.R. 1, Box 53A, Shawnee College Road, Ullin, IL 62992; (618) 634-2297, fax: (618) 634-9394.]

State University of New York at Albany, Rockefeller Institute of Government. 1990. "Decision Techtronics Group—Decision Conferencing." Semifinalist Application to Innovations in State and Local Government Awards Program. [Sandor P. Schuman, Executive Director, Decision Techtronics Group-Decision, Conferencing, Rockefeller Institute of Government, 411 State. Street, Albany, NY 12203; (518) 465-8872.]

Texas Comptroller of Public Accounts. 1994. "Window on State Government." Semifinalist Application to Innovations in State and Local Government Awards Program. [Drew Scherz, Programmer/Analyst, Research Division, Comptroller of Public Accounts, LBJ State Office Building, Room 809, 111 East 17th Street, Austin, TX 78774; (512) 463-3920, fax: (512) 463-4294.]

Texas Department of Human Services. 1993. "Child Care Management Services." Semifinalist Application to Innovations in State and Local Government Awards Program. [The Honorable Burton F. Raiford, Commissioner, Texas Department of Human Services, P.O. Box 149030, Austin, TX 79714-9030; (512) 450-3030, fax: (512) 450-4220.]

Texas Water Commission. 1992. "Ground Water Protection Program." Semifinalist Application to Innovations in State and Local Government Awards Program. [Phyllis T. Romano, Manager, Community Support Programs Section, Texas Water Commission, 1700 North Congress Avenue, P.O. Box 13087, Austin, TX 78711-2087; (512) 371-6470.]

Thayer, New Hampshire, High School. 1994. "Here, Thayer, and Everywhere." Semifinalist Application to Innovations in State and Local Government Awards Program. [Jed Butterfield, Principal, Thayer School, 85 Parker Street, Winchester, NH 03470; (603) 239-4381, fax: (603) 239-4968.]

Town of Harwich, Massachusetts, Board of Health. 1991. "Massachusetts/Harwich Solar Aquatic Wastewater Treatment Project." Semifinalist Application to Innovations in State and Local Government Awards Program. [Paula J. Champagne, Health Director, Town of Harwich, 732 Main Street, Harwich, MA 02645; (508) 430-7509 and Megan Jones, Director, Massachusetts Centers of Excellence Corporation, 9 Park Street, Boston, MA 02108-4807; (617) 727-7430.]

Town of Paradise Valley, Arizona, Police Department. 1990. "Photo Radar." Semifinalist Application to Innovations in State and Local Government Awards Program. [Donald D. Lozier, Police Chief, Paradise Valley Police Department, 6401 East Lincoln Drive, Paradise Valley, AZ 85253; (602) 948-7418.]

Ventura County, California, Department of Parks and Recreation. 1991. "Ventura Senior Home Share Computer Match." Semifinalist Application to Innovations in State and Local Government Awards Program. [Lynda Hershey Frey, Recreation Supervisor, 501 Poli Street, P.O. Box 99, Ventura, CA 93002; (805) 658-4728.]

Washington State Department of Ecology. 1992. "Urban Bay Action Teams." Semifinalist Application to Innovations in State and Local Government Awards Program. [Carol Fleskes, Program Manager, Hazardous Waste Investigations and Cleanup, Waste Management Division, Washington Department of Ecology, MS PV-11, P.O. Box 47600, Olympia, WA 98505; (206) 438-3007.]

Washington State Workers' Compensation System. 1992. Semifinalist Application to Innovations in State and Local Government Awards Program. [Theresa Whitmarsh, Insurance Services, Washington Labor and Industries Department, P.O. Box 44000, Olympia, WA 98504-4000; (206) 956-4209, fax: (206) 956-4202.]

West Virginia Housing Development Fund. 1993. "Low-Income Assisted Mortgage Program." Semifinalist Application to Innovations in State and Local Government Awards Program. [Stephen P. Bailey, Manager, Housing and Community Improvement, Loan Origination and Development Division, 814 Virginia Street East, Charleston, WV 25301; (304) 345-6475, fax: (304) 345-8953.]

Wisconsin Department of Administration. 1993. "Multi-State Procurement of Recycled Xerographic Paper." Semifinalist Application to Innovations in State and Local Government Awards Program. [Leo C. Talsky, Deputy Director, Division of State Agency Services, Wisconsin Department of Administration, P.O. Box 7867, Madison, WI 53707-7867, (608) 266-3243, fax: (608) 267-0700.]

Wisconsin Department of Social Services. 1993. "The Children First Program." Semifinalist Application to Innovations in State and Local Government Awards Program. [John A. Wagner, Project Coordinator, Division of Economic Support, Department of Health and Social Services, One West Wilson Street, Room 358, Madison, WI 53702; (608) 266-2721, fax: (608) 267-3240.]

Wishard Memorial Hospital. 1993. "Wishard Patient Record System." Semifinalist Application to Innovations in State and Local Government Awards Program. [Dr. Clement J. McDonald, Associate Director, Department of Medicine, Wishard Memorial Hospital, 1001 West Tenth Street, Indianapolis, IN 46202; (317) 630-7070, fax: (317) 630-6962.]

Wong, Pat. 1994. "Site Visit Report on Living in a Family Environment." (June 6). Austin, TX. Unpublished.

Wyoming Department of Health. 1992. "Wyoming Smartcard." Semifinalist Application to Innovations in State and Local Government Awards Program. [James Moran, Manager, Women, Infants, and Children, Public Health

Division, Wyoming Health Department, Hathaway Building, 4th Floor, 2300 Capitol Avenue, Cheyenne, WY 82002-0480; (307) 777-6186, fax: (307) 777-5402.]

OTHER MATERIALS

Abt Associates. 1993. "Overview of the Impacts of State-Initiated EBT Demonstrations on the Food Stamp Program." Cambridge, MA. Unpublished.

Altshuler, Alan. 1996. "Ten Lessons from Innovation." Pp. 8–11 in Jonathan Walters, *Innovations in American Government: 1986–1996*. New York: Ford Foundation.

Altshuler, Alan and Marc Zegans. 1990. "Innovation and Creativity: Comparisons Between Public Management and Private Enterprise." *Cities* (February): 16–24.

Anderson, David. 1997. "Crime Stoppers." *The New York Times Magazine*, 9 February, pp. 47–52.

Arrandale, Tom. 1992. "John Hall: Agent of Transformation." *Governing* 6 (October): 20.

———. 1995a. "A Guide to Clean Water." *Governing* 9 (December): 57–62.

———. 1995b. "A Guide to Trash Management: The Changing Mix." *Governing* 8 (August): 67–76.

———. 1996. "Reinventing the Pollution Police." *Governing* 9 (January): 32–35.

Associated Press. 1997. "Clinton Hails Internet Use on Line and on Air." *The New York Times*, 20 April, p. 30.

Barzelay, Michael. 1992. *Breaking Through Bureaucracy: A new Vision for Managing in Government*. Berkeley: University of California.

Behn, Robert. 1988. "Management by Groping Along." *Journal of Policy Analysis and Management* 7:643–663.

———. 1991. *Leadership Counts: Lessons for Public Managers from the Massachusetts Welfare, Training, and Employment Program*. Cambridge, MA: Harvard.

———. 1993. "The Myth of Managerial Luck" Success from an Unlikely Place." *Governing* 7 (November): 68.

———. 1995. "The Benefits of the Private Sector." *Governing* 8 (June): 103.

———. 1996a. "Banking on Productivity." *Governing* 10 (September): 78.

———. 1996b. "Don't Do Pilot Projects." *Governing* 9 (January): 57.

———. 1996c. "The New Public Management Paradigm and the Search for Democratic Accountability." Paper presented to the APPAM Research Conference, Pittsburgh, PA. October 1996. Unpublished.

Belluck, Pam. 1996. "In Era of Shrinking Budgets, Community Groups Blossom." *The New York Times*. 25 February, pp. 1, 16.

Bibeault, Donald. 1982. *Corporate Turnaround: How Managers Turn Losers into Winners*. New York: McGraw-Hill.

Borins, Sandford. 1991. "The encouragement and study of improved public management: The Institute of Public Administration of Canada innovative management award." *International Review of Administrative Sciences* 57 (June): 179–194.

———. 1994a. "Public Sector Innovation: its Contribution to Canadian Competitiveness." Ottawa: Queen's University School of Policy Studies Government and Competitiveness Project, Discussion Paper 94–109.

———. 1994b. "Turnaround Management in the Public Sector." Paper presented to the APPAM Research Conference, Chicago, IL. October 1994. Unpublished.

———. 1995a. "Public management innovation awards in the US and Canada." Pp. 213–240 in Hermann Hill and Helmut Klages, eds. *Trends in Public Service Renewal*. Frankfurt: Peter Lang.

———. 1995b. "Public Sector Innovation: The Implications of New Forms of Organization and Work." Pp. 260–287 in Guy Peters and Donald Savoie, eds. *Governance in a Changing Environment*. Montreal: McGill-Queens.

———. 1995c. "Summary: Government in Transition—A New Paradigm in Public Administration." Pp. 3–23 in *Government in Transition*, ed. Commonwealth Association for Public Administration and Management. Toronto: Commonwealth Secretariat.

———. 1995d. "The New Public Management is Here to Stay." *Canadian Public Administration* 38 (Spring): 122–133.

———. 1995e. "Using Public Management Innovation Competition Data to Study 'Reinventing Government' and 'Groping Along'." Paper presented to the APPAM Research Conference, Washington, DC, November 1995. Unpublished.

Boston, Jonathan, John Martin, June Pallot, and Pat Walsh. 1996. *Public Management: The New Zealand Model*. Auckland: Oxford.

California Telecommunications Projects Web Site. 1996. <http://www.benton. Org/State/california.html>.

Carnes, Larry. 1995. "Current and Future EBT Plans." Paper presented to the APPAM Research Conference, Washington, DC, November 1995. Unpublished.

Chandler, Alfred A. 1962. *Strategy and Structure: Chapters in the History of the Industrial Enterprise*. Cambridge, MA: MIT Press.

Cohodas, Marilyn. 1996a. "Picture This." *Governing* 10 (March): 55–56.

———. 1996b. "The Tantalizing Promise of GIS." *Governing* 10 (October): 96.

Cohodas, Nadine. 1993. "Child Support: No More Pretty Please." *Governing* 7 (October): 20–21.

———. 1994. "Workers' Comp Reform: Who's Getting Squeezed?" *Governing* 7 (January): 22–23.

Conte, Christopher. 1995. "Teledemocracy For Better or Worse." *Governing* 8 (June): 33–41.

Contino, Ronald and Robert Lorusso. 1982. "The theory Z Turnaround of a Public Agency." *Public Administration Review* 42:66–72.

Creech, Bill. 1994. *The Five Pillars of TQM*. New York: Dutton.

Cuciti, Peggy et al. 1994. "Can This Superfund be Saved?" *Governing* 7 (April): 57–60.

Cushman, John. 1996. "States Neglecting Pollution Rules, White House Says." *The New York Times*, 15 December, pp. 1, 24.

Cyert, Richard and James March. 1963. *A Behavioral Theory of the Firm*. Englewood Cliffs, NJ: Prentice-Hall.

Daniels, Alex. 1995. "Waterway Watchdogs are Getting Their Feet Wet." *Governing* 9 (November): 74.

———. 1996. "Private Bucks to Build Neighborhood Police Bases." *Governing* 9 (March): 53–54.

Darman, Richard. 1996. "Riverboat Gambling with Government." *The New York Times Magazine*, 1 December, pp. 116–117.

Davenport, Thomas and Nitin Nohria. 1994. "Case Management and the Integration of Labor." *Sloan Management Review* 35 (Winter): 11–23.

Ehrenhalt, Alan. 1995. "Good Government, Bad Government." *Governing* 8 (April): 18–24.

Enos, Gary. 1997. "A Guide to Technology Mega-Deals." *Governing* 10 (January): 51–56.

Fallows, James. 1992. "A Case for Reform." *The Atlantic* (June): 119–123.

Finegan, Jay. 1987. "Four-Star Management." *INC* (January/February): 42–51.

Finkel, Ed. 1995a. "Ace of Database." *The Public Innovator* 23 (February): 1–2.

———. 1995b. "Towns STEP Toward Compliance." *The Public Innovator* 24 (March 16): 5–6.

Fountain, Jane et al. 1993. *Customer Service Excellence: Using Information Technology to Improve Service Delivery in Government*. Cambridge, MA: Program on Strategic Computing and Telecommunications in the Public Sector.

Frye, Northrop. 1982. *The Great Code: The Bible and Literature*. Toronto: Academic Press.

Fulton, William. 1996. "The Big Green Bazaar." *Governing* 9 (June): 38–42.

Golden, Olivia. 1990. "Innovation in Public Sector Human Services Programs: The Implications of Innovation by 'Groping Along'." *Journal of Policy Analysis and Management* 9: 219–248.

Goodsell, Charles. 1993. "Reinvent Government or Rediscover It?" *Public Administration Review* 53 (January/February): 85–87.

Gore, Al. 1993. *Creating a Government that Works Better and Costs Less: Report of the National Performance Review*. New York: Times Books.

———. 1995. *Common Sense Government Works Better and Costs Less*. New York: Random House.

———. 1996a. "Address at the Presentation of the 1996 Innovations in American Government Awards Ceremony." Washington, DC. 3 December.

———. 1996b. *The Best Kept Secrets in Government*. Washington: U.S. Government Printing Office.

Gurwitt, Rob. 1992. "Earl Phillips: Turnaround Artist." *Governing* 6 (October): 17.

———. 1994a. "Cities Enlist Landlords in the Fight Against Crime." *Governing* 7 (February): 15–16.

———. 1994b. "Indianapolis and the Republican Future." *Governing* 7 (February): 24–28.

———. 1995a. "Cops and Community." *Governing* 8 (May): 16–24.

———. 1995b. "Overload." *Governing* 9 (October): 17–22.

———. 1996. "The New Data Czars." *Governing* 10 (December): 52–56.

Heifetz, Ronald. 1994. *Leadership Without Easy Answers.* Cambridge, MA: Harvard.

Hirsch, E. D. 1996. *The Schools We Need and Why We Don't Have Them.* New York: Doubleday.

Hoffman, Richard. 1989. "Strategies for Corporate Turnarounds: What Do We Know about Them?" *Journal of General Management* 14 (Spring): 46–66.

Holmes, Malcolm and David Shand. 1995. "Management Reform: Some Practitioner Perspectives on the Past Ten Years." *Governance* 8 (October): 551–578.

Husock, Howard. 1991. "Solving Seattle's Solid Waste Crisis." Kennedy School of Government Case Program, case number C16-91-1047.0.

———. 1992a. "Community Voice Mail for the 'Phoneless': Starting Up in Seattle and Minnesota." Kennedy School of Government Case Program, case number C16-93-1228.0.

———. 1995. "Organizing Competition in Indianapolis: Mayor Stephen Goldsmith and the Quest for Lower Costs." Kennedy School of Government Case Program, cases numbers C18-95-1269, C18-95-1270.

Innovations in State and Local Government. 1992. *Updates 1992.* Cambridge, MA: Harvard.

John, DeWitt. 1994. *Civic Environmentalism: Alternatives to Regulation in States and Communities.* Washington: Congressional Quarterly Press.

Johnson, Curtis. 1995. "Renewing Community." *Governing* 8 (July): 51–58.

Kanter, Rosabeth. 1988. "When a Thousand Flowers Bloom: Structural, Collective, and Social Conditions for Innovation in Organizations." *Research in Organizational Behaviour* 10:169–211.

Kelling, George and Catherine Coles. 1996. *Fixing Broken Windows: Restoring Order and Reducing Crime in our Communities.* New York: Free Press.

Kelman, Steve. 1993. "Managing Student Aid in Sweden." Kennedy School of Government Case Program, case number C16-93-1161.3.

Kennedy, David. 1992. "Meeting for a Need: Jerry Abramson and CityWorks in Louisville, Kentucky." Kennedy School of Government Case Program, case number C16-92-1155.0.

Kettl, Donald and John DiIulio, ed. 1995. *Inside the Reinvention Machine: Appraising Government Reform.* Washington: Brookings.

Kirlin, John. 1995. "Findings from the EBT Demonstrations." Paper presented to the APPAM Research Conference, Washington, DC. Unpublished.

Kittower, Diane. 1997. "Serving the Public with Private Partners." *Governing* 10 (May): 65–75.

Kouzmin, Alexander and Nada Korac-Boisvert. 1995. "Soft-core Disasters: A Multiple Realities Crisis Perspective on IT Failures." Pp. 89–132 in Hermann Hill and Helmut Klages, eds. *Trends in Public Service Renewal.* Frankfurt: Peter Lang.

Kusserow, Richard. 1991. *Services Integration: A Twenty-Year Retrospective.* Washington: Department of Health and Human Services, Office of the Inspector General.

Lacey, Robert. 1997. "Internal Markets in the Public Sector: The Case of the British National Health Service." *Public Administration and Development* 17 (February): 141–159.

Lemov, Doug. 1997. "Bringing Order to the Courts." *Governing* 10 (February): 58–59.

Lemov, Penelope. 1993. "The Power of High-Tech Fun." *Governing* 7 (November): 46.

———. 1994. "Tough Times for TIF." *Governing* 7 (February): 19–20.

———. 1996. "Borrowing the Bucks for Gee-Whiz Technology." *Governing* 10 (August): 51–52.

Lewington, Jennifer. 1996. "Computer Gap Hurts Poor, Report Says: Skills and Access are Concentrated in the Hands of Rich Canadians, Statscan Study Finds." *The Globe and Mail*, 1 November, p. A5.

Levin, Martin and Mary Bryna Sanger. 1992. "Using Old Stuff in New Ways: Innovation as a Case of Evolutionary Tinkering." *Journal of Policy Analysis and Management* 11:88–115.

———. 1994. *Making Government Work: How Entrepreneurial Executives Turn Bright Ideas into Real Results.* San Francisco: Jossey-Bass.

Light, Paul. 1996. Review of Levin and Sanger, *Making Government Work. Journal of Policy Analysis and Management* 15 (Winter): 121–124.

Lindblom, Charles. 1959. "The Science of 'Muddling Through'." *Public Administration Review* 19 (Spring): 79–88.

———. 1965. *The Intelligence of Democracy.* New York: Free Press.

Linden, Russell. 1995. "A Guide to Reengineering Government: Advice from the Experts." *Governing* 8 (May): 63–74.

Little, Bruce. 1996. "Poor Left Behind in Computer Revolution: Richest Canadians More Than 4 Times as Likely to Own a PC Than Lower-income Households." *The Globe and Mail*, 15 January, p. B11.

Locke, Edwin and Gary Latham. 1984. *Goal Setting for Individuals, Groups, and Organizations.* Chicago: Science Research Associates.

Lynch, Roberta and Ann Markusen. 1994. "Can Markets Govern?" *The American Prospect* 16 (Winter): 125–134.

Lynn, Laurence. 1996. *Public Management as Art, Science, and Profession.* Chatham, NJ: Chatham House.

Martin, John. 1997. "Is the Web Explosion Fizzling?" *Governing* 10 (May): 54.

Mahtesian, Charles. 1994a. "Taking Chicago Private." *Governing* 7 (April): 26–32.

———. 1994b. "The Human Services Nightmare." *Governing* 7 (December): 44–49.

———. 1994c. "The Man Who Runs the Best-Run City." *Governing* 7 (December): 39.

———. 1995. "Showdown on E-Z Street." *Governing* 9 (October): 36–41.

Mechling, Jerry. 1994. "Reengineering: Part of your Game Plan?" *Governing* 7 (February): 41–52.

———. 1995a. "Reaching Across Organizational Lines." *Governing* 8 (June): 106.

———. 1995b. "Leadership and the Knowledge Gap." *Governing* 9 (December): 68.

Meyers, Marcia. 1993. "Organizational Factors in the Integration of Services for Children." *Social Service Review* (December): 548–575.

Mintzberg, Henry. 1994. *The Rise and Fall of Strategic Planning: Reconceiving Roles for Planning, Plans, and Planners.* New York: Free Press.

Moe, Ronald. 1994. "The Reinventing Government Exercise: Misinterpreting the Problem, Misjudging the Consequences." *Public Administration Review* 54 (March-April): 111–122.

Moore, Mark. 1995. *Creating Public Value: Strategic Management in Government.* Cambridge, MA: Harvard.

Mosle, Sara. 1996a. "Scores Count." *The New York Times Magazine,* 8 September, pp. 41–45.

———. 1996b. "The Answer is National Standards." *The New York Times Magazine,* 27 October, pp. 45–7, 56, 68.

National Association of State Budget Officers. 1995. "Top Techniques for Managing Change." *Governing* 9 (October): 46.

National Civic League. 1996. "Connecting Government and Neighborhoods." *Governing* 10 (October): 47–54.

National Conference of State Legislatures. 1996. "Byte Oversight." *Governing* 9 (February): 42.

Neustadt, Richard and Harvey Fineberg. 1983. *The Epidemic That Never Was: Policymaking and the Swine Flu Affair.* New York: Random House.

New York Times Magazine. 1996. "Letters on National Education Standards." *New York Times Magazine,* November 17, pp. 16, 18, 20.

Newman, Nathan. 1996. "Virtual Sunshine May Rain on Local Economic Development." *Enode* 1 (June 5). Electronic newsletter.

Niskanen, William. 1971. *Bureaucracy and Representative Government.* Chicago: Aldine Atherton.

Organization for Economic Cooperation and Development. 1995. *Governance in Transition: Public Management Reforms in OECD Countries.* Paris: OECD.

Osborne, David and Ted Gaebler. 1992. *Reinventing Government: How the Entrepreneurial Spirit is Transforming the Public Sector.* Reading, MA: Addison-Wesley.

Osborne, David and Peter Plastrik. 1997. *Banishing Bureaucracy: The Five Strategies for Reinventing Government.* Reading, MA: Addison-Wesley.

Perlman, Ellen. 1995. "Stephen Goldsmith: Busting the Government Monopoly." *Governing* 9 (December): 27.

Peters, B. Guy and Donald Savoie. 1994. "Reinventing Osborne and Gaebler: Lessons from the Gore Commission." *Canadian Public Administration* 37 (Summer): 302–322.

Peters, Thomas and Robert Waterman. 1982. *In Search of Excellence: Lessons from America's Best-Run Companies.* New York: Harper and Row.

Petersen, John. 1994. "Here's a City That's Really Being Reinvented." *Governing* 7:62.

Pindyck, Robert and Daniel Rubinfeld. 1991. *Econometric Models and Economic Forecasts,* Third edition. New York: McGraw-Hill.

Pressman, Jeffrey and Aaron Wildavsky. 1979. *Implementation.* 2nd edition. Berkeley: University of California Press.

Purdum, Todd. 1996. "President Helps Schools Go On-Line." *The New York Times,* 10 March, p. 13.

Putnam, Robert. 1995. "Bowling Alone: America's Declining Social Capital." *Journal of Democracy* 6 (January): 65–78.

Quinn, James. 1980. *Strategies for Change. Logical Incrementalism*. Homewood, IL: Irwin.

Reich, Robert. 1997. *Locked in the Cabinet*. New York: Knopf.

Reschenthaler, G. B. and Fred Thompson. 1996. "The Information Revolution and the New Public Management." *Journal of Public Administration Research and Theory* 6 (January): 125–143.

Roberts, Barbara. 1994. Interview in *The Public Innovator* 18 (15 December): 3–4.

Rosegrant, Susan. 1992. "Wichita Confronts Contamination: Seeking Alternatives to Superfund." Kennedy School of Government Case Program, case number C16-92-1157.0 and C16-92-1158.0.

Savoie, Donald. 1995. "What's Wrong with the New Public Management." *Canadian Public Administration* 38 (Spring): 112–21.

Schall, Ellen and Kathleen Feely. 1992. "Guidelines to Grope By: Reflections from the Field." *Innovating* 2 (Spring): 3–11.

Schall, Ellen. 1996. "Innovations from the Inside: A Practitioner's Perspective." Pp. 12–14 in Jonathan Walters, *Innovations in American Government: 1986–1996*. New York: Ford Foundation.

Schorr, Lisbeth. 1988. *Within our Reach: Breaking the Cycle of Disadvantage*. New York: Anchor Doubleday.

———. 1993. "What works: Applying What We Already Know About Successful Social Policy." *The American Prospect* 13 (Spring): 43–54.

Schwartz, Herman. 1994. "Small States in Big Trouble: State Reorganization in Australia, Denmark, New Zealand, and Sweden in the 1980s." *World Politics* 46 (July): 527–55.

Scott, Esther. 1993. "Preventing Pollution in Massachusetts: The Blackstone Project." Kennedy School of Government Case Number C16-93-1197.0.

Seglin, Jeff. 1995. E-mail message regarding Community Voice Mail, June 28.

Simon, Harvey. 1992. "Profit Sharing for the Public Sector: The Shared Savings Program in Pittsburg, California." Kennedy School of Government Case Program, case number C16-92-1153.0.

———. 1994. "Info/California: Using Computers to Deliver Service With a Smile." Kennedy School of Government Case Program, case number C16-94-1256.0.

Sizer, Theodore. 1984. *Horace's Compromise: The Dilemma of the American High School*. Boston: Houghton Mifflin.

———. 1996. *Horace's Hope: What Works for the American High School*. Boston: Houghton Mifflin.

Sparrow, Malcolm. 1994. *Imposing Duties: Government's Changing Approach to Compliance*. Westport, CT: Praeger.

Spicer, David. 1995. "Managing the Underground City: The New York City Transit Authority Reclaims its Subway Stations." Kennedy School of Government Case Program, case number C18-95-1275.

Stevens, Larry. 1995. "Bringing Government to the People: A Guide to Interactive Government." *Governing* 9 (October): 67–76.

Sweeney, Paul. 1994. "Corporate Giving Goes Creative." *The New York Times*, 15 May, p. F6.

Swope, Christopher. 1995. "A Hang-Up for Online Government." *Governing* 9 (December): 49–50.

Sylvester, Kathleen. 1992. "Beyond Shop Class." *Governing* 6 (October): 37–38.

Teltsch, Kathleen. 1993. "Paying Tribute to Six in Public Jobs Well Done." *The New York Times*, 7 December, p. B2.

Thatcher, Margaret. 1993. *The Downing Street Years*. New York: Harper Collins.

Thompson, Fred. 1997. Review of Organization for Economic Cooperation and Development, *Budgeting for Results*; Pollitt, *Managerialism and the Public Services*, 2nd edition; Schedler, *Ansatze einer wirkungsorientierten Verwaltungsfurung*; Trebilcock, *The Prospects for Reinventing Government*; World Bank, *Bureaucrats in Business*. *Journal of Policy Analysis and Management* 16 (Winter): 165–175.

U.S. General Accounting Agency. 1992. *Integrating Human Services: Linking At-Risk Families With Services More Successful Than System Reform Efforts*. Washington: General Accounting Agency.

Vantour, Jim, ed. 1991. *Our Story: Organizational Renewal in Federal Corrections*. Ottawa: Canadian Centre for Management Development.

Varley, Pamela. 1987. "Ellen Schall and the Department of Juvenile Justice." Kennedy School of Government Case C16-87-793.0.

Walters, Jonathan. 1994. "The Benchmarking Craze." *Governing*. 7 (April): 33–37.

———. 1995. "The Gainsharing Gambit." *Governing* 8 (July): 63–64.

———. 1996a. "Fad Mad." *Governing* 9 (September): 48–52.

———. 1996b. "Flattening Bureaucracy." *Governing* 9 (March): 21–24.

———. 1996c. *Innovations in American Government: 1986–1996*. New York: Ford Foundation.

———. 1997. "Performance and Pain." *Governing* 10 (July): 26–31.

Weber, Max. 1959. *From Max Weber: Essays in Sociology*. eds. H.H. Gerth and C. W. Mills. New York: Oxford.

Weick, Karl. 1984. "Small Wins: Redefining the Scale of Social Problems." *American Psychologist* 39 (January): 40–49.

Wilson, James and George Kelling. 1982. "Broken Windows: The Police and Neighborhood Safety." *The Atlantic Monthly* (March): 29–38.

Wilson, James. 1989. *Bureaucracy: What Government Agencies Do and Why They Do It*. New York: Basic Books.

Wilson, William. 1987. *The Truly Disadvantaged*. Chicago: University of Chicago.

Winnick, Louis. 1993. "Is Reinventing Government Enough?" *The City Journal* 3 (Summer): 18–29.

Wright, Robert. 1995. "Hyperdemocracy." *TIME*. 23 January.

Yin, Robert. 1984. *Case Study Research: Design and Methods*. Beverly Hills: Sage.

Zegans, Marc. 1990. "Strategy: Innovation and Inertia: Unbundling Some Old Assumptions." Paper presented to the APPAM Research Conference, San Francisco, CA. October 1990. Unpublished.

———. 1992. "Innovation in the Well-Functioning Public Agency." *Public Productivity and Management Review* 16 (Winter): 141–156.

Index

Note: Page numbers followed by "t" denote a table.